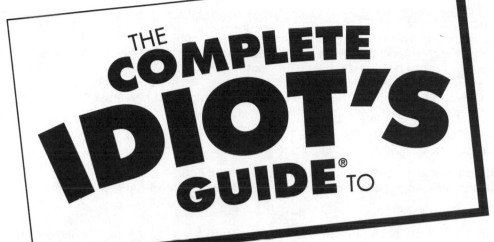

Decorating Your Home

Second Edition

by Mary Ann Young and David Nussbaum

**alpha
books**

Macmillan USA, Inc.
201 West 103rd Street
Indianapolis, IN 46290

A Pearson Education Company

Ten Questions to Ask Yourself Before You Start Decorating

1. What do you wear when you are alone at home?
2. Do you put your feet up on the furniture?
3. Does clutter drive you crazy?
4. In which room of your house do you spend the most time?
5. Do you collect interesting items that you can put on display?
6. Where is your favorite chair?
7. Which piece of furniture has the most meaning for you?
8. Do you like bold patterns or small-scale prints?
9. What movie setting would you like to have for your home?
10. How long do you plan to stay in your home?

Five Places to Start Your Redecorating

1. The room in which you spend most of your time
2. The room that holds your most treasured possessions
3. The room where you engage in your favorite hobby
4. A room that can be converted to meet an urgent need
5. A room that needs basic repair or structural upgrading

Decorator's Tool-Kit Basics

➤ Twenty-five-foot retractable tape measure
➤ Sixty-inch cloth measuring tape
➤ Yardstick and triangular scale ruler
➤ Calculator
➤ Muslin cloth to model draperies
➤ Sewing kit and scissors
➤ Picture hooks, wire, and nails for hanging art
➤ Hammer

tear here

alpha
books

Four Ways to Change a Space with Color

1. Paint a large and uninviting room a warm yellow to "draw in" the walls and ceiling.

2. Lower a high ceiling by painting it a slightly darker tone than the walls.

3. Paint a small room in a cool pastel blue to make it appear bright and spacious.

4. Shorten a lengthy hallway by painting the end walls a warm orange or red.

Name-Dropping: Fabrics a Decorator Must Know

See Chapter 12, "It's a Material World," for more information.

Brocade	Damask	Silk
Burlap	Faille	Tapestry
Canvas	Gingham	Ticking
Chambray	Lace	Toiles de Jouy
Chenille	Matelasse	Velvet
Chintz	Muslin	

Publisher
Marie Butler-Knight

Product Manager
Phil Kitchel

Managing Editor
Cari Luna

Acquisitions Editor
Amy Zavatto

Development Editor
Doris Cross

Production Editor
Christy Wagner

Illustrator
Jody P. Schaeffer

Cover Designers
Mike Freeland
Kevin Spear

Book Designers
Scott Cook and Amy Adams of DesignLab

Indexer
Angie Bess

Layout/Proofreading
Fran Blauw
Svetlana Dominguez
Jeannette McKay

Contents at a Glance

Contents

Part 3: Getting the Goods   **79**

Part 4: Tackling the House Room by Room   145

Introduction

Be passionate about your style. Let your style loose! Indulge in the tastes that tempt you and experiment with the decorating techniques that delight you. Build your home around beauty: Showcase the lovely and beloved things you already have, and splurge on the one gorgeous thing that perfectly captures what you love.

Be practical and realistic about your style. Your style should be completely compatible with how you and everyone in your home use your living space every day. And it should richly express your personality, without necessitating that you be a rich person!

Be flexible about your style. Your style will change as your needs, your family's needs, and your resources change. Don't be afraid to get rid of things that no longer work in your life or appeal to you. Change is glorious!

Let your style break the rules. Most of us have gained a lot of conventional wisdom that dictates a conventional look in most homes. Forget the rules and the ironclad design ideas that you think you need to follow: Give your imagination and your intuition free rein! Put a dark color on your walls; put a sofa in the kitchen; combine checks and stripes; mix Victorian furniture and post-modern art. Remember, you make up the rules for your personal style!

How to Use This Book

Let's be honest: Even though successful decorating can be full of creativity, self-expression, artistry, and fun, it doesn't always feel that way. Designing and implementing decorating plans in the midst of busy lives can be a demanding and time-consuming task. Certain projects entail significant expense, sometimes more than you can afford. You may need to learn new design concepts and physical skills; you may need to assess your lifestyle and your needs in a new way; you may need to face limitations on what you can do with the space and resources you have. You may have to do some plain old dirty work. And you most definitely have to make decisions! Decorating is always a process of discovery and decision-making.

We have designed this book to help you make the many decisions you will face, so that you learn just what you need to know. You can't just jump into a decorating project. If you have never done home decorating before—or even if you have—you will want to do some creative thinking about yourself, the lifestyle you lead, and the design approach that suits you. Then you'll be ready to figure out where in your home you want to start, what it is you want to achieve, the options for that project, and how much they will cost. For each of these steps, we lay out the questions you need to ask and the choices you need to evaluate, and ultimately help you choose the answer that's best for you.

Here's how we have organized the book.

Part 1, "Making Your House a Home," is for all decorators, novice or expert. We suggest that everyone start here. We present the foundation for all decorating efforts: how to discover your personal style and how to plan, prioritize, and budget for every decorating project. We also present the basic tools that every home decorator needs. You will come back to the planning chapters again and again as you consider specific room-by-room projects.

Part 2, "You Were Not Born a Decorator ... but You Can Learn," is where you'll gain a sense of confidence in your own design decisions by studying the principles of color, texture, form, balance, and proportion. You'll also become familiar with period styles and other fundamentals of interior decoration.

Part 3, "Getting the Goods," points out that the smart decorator knows everything about all the stuff in the home. Get a grasp on your choices of furnishings, fabrics, floors, walls, windows, lights, and more.

Part 4, "Tackling the House Room by Room," shows you how each room presents a host of intriguing possibilities for redecorating. Each chapter has a Master Planning List of possible projects and materials that you can use in the budgeting and prioritizing process. You may want to go right to the chapter on the room you know you are going to work on, or you may want to browse through this part first to check out your options.

Part 5, "Quick (and Easy-on-the-Budget) Makeovers," will get your creative juices going quickly and help you make some satisfying changes in your kitchen, bathroom, and bedroom without spending a lot of time or money.

Extras

We highlight some of the best, simplest, and most important ideas throughout the book in the following types of special elements. Some of these are necessary for every decorator to know, whereas some are specific solutions for particular situations. They might not fit your circumstances exactly, but they may inspire you to come up with a brilliant design solution in your unique style.

Decorator's Diary

These notes feature my own unique solutions to a number of decorating problems I've encountered over the years. Hopefully, you'll find these inspirational.

Designer's Dictionary

These sidebars define decorating terms that will help you speak the decorating lingo while you're shopping for supplies or dealing with contractors.

Interiors 101

These boxes offer a glimpse at some historical decorating tidbits and contain a few well-kept secrets.

Expert Advice

Here you'll find valuable decorating advice.

Acknowledgments

We would like to thank all of the people who made this book possible: Larry Lauck at the American Lighting Association; Marci Kenneda at Gear Holdings; Eliza Hindmarch at Laura Ashley; Michelle Marino at Susan Becher Public Relations for Smallbone, Waterworks, and Cassina; Lina Morrow at Lee Industries; Margie Ford at F. Schumacher; and Connie Carrol at The Paint Spot.

Most of all, we would like to thank Meagan and Kathleen for pushing us along the road to authorship.

Trademarks

All terms mentioned in this book that are known to be or are suspected of being trademarks or service marks have been appropriately capitalized. Alpha Books and Macmillan USA, Inc. cannot attest to the accuracy of this information. Use of a term in this book should not be regarded as affecting the validity of any trademark or service mark.

Part 1

Making Your House a Home

First steps are the hardest ones in any venture, and home decorating is no exception. "I just don't know where to begin" is something that we interior decorators hear from our clients all the time. In Part 1 of this book, you begin the same process of discovery that we start our clients on: the discovery of your personal style.

You'll find it an enjoyable challenge to get to know yourself and your everyday needs better—from an interior designer's viewpoint. And as you do, you will gain confidence in your choices and find new ways to express your individuality. These are the foundation stones of all your successful decorating projects.

In this part you will gain another fundamental skill: turning decorating dreams into affordable reality through planning and budgeting. And to get you outfitted for the fun (and, on occasion, work) that lies ahead, we will introduce you to the basic tools of the designer's trade to keep you going forward in a straight line—or to help you zig and zag in just the right places.

Chapter 1

You've Got Style: Flaunt It!

In This Chapter

➤ Whose home do you live in?

➤ Learn to strengthen and believe in your style

➤ The importance of education, observation, and evaluation

➤ Style assessments: Focus in on who you are, how you live, and what you like

➤ Bring total awareness to the decorating process

Whether you are aware of it or not—whether you like it or not!—your home has style right now. It's you! Just like the clothes you chose to wear today, or the flip of your current hairstyle, your home is an intimate expression of your personality. Somber or vivacious, carefree or fastidious, humorous or serious, your character traits create a style that is evident throughout every detail in each room in which you live.

You put a distinctive mark on your home—you "decorate" it automatically—just by being you, surrounding yourself with things you love, things that are appropriate for the way you live, and things that are full of beauty to you.

But for many of us, that natural process might seem downright intimidating or impossible. We've been taught that "beautiful" home style is something that just a few experts have—and based on spaces and possessions that most people can't afford. And the multi-billion-dollar home-furnishings industry is eager to convince us to try someone else's style, to be contemporary like Calvin, Martha, Ralph, or Laura. Or to be classic like some long-departed characters named Louis, George, Victoria, or Art Deco.

Don't buy it! You can learn from the styles of others and from the beauty of the past, but a home decorated to satisfy you has to be founded upon your unique sense of beauty and taste, and the manner and time in which you live. You may think this is impossible: You may think you are colorblind or geometrically impaired; you may not know damask from doilies, or armoires from afghans; and you may insist that you have no style at all. With this book, you will discover that design principles can be learned, that technical information you need to know is readily available, and that wonderful spaces are affordable. Most of all, you will learn that you already have within you the foundation of personal style—and that's your best decorating guide of all.

Born with Good Taste: What Is Personal Style? Where Does It Come From?

Personal style is that unique blend of tastes and preferences that you have acquired and shaped over your lifetime. It is inspired by the home that you grew up in, the places you have visited, the people you've met (and admired or detested), and just about everything else that you have experienced: music and museums, literature and movies, gardens and garage sales.

Think back. Discovering and asserting your likes and dislikes started very early in your life. As a baby, you may have preferred a fuzzy blanket to a smooth one; you might have adored squash but hated bananas. That's the start of personal style. Think of your own kids. Have you tried to dress a three-year-old in a color that she didn't want to wear that day? Or tried to tell a 13-year-old boy how to decorate his room?

Personal style occurs naturally. Like every other fashion, it is never set. It can grow and deepen, shift and develop. As your life changes, your needs change, and your tastes change with them. And your evolving style will guide the new choices you make each day.

Personal Style at Home: Creating Spaces to Match Your Personality

Decisions, decisions, decisions. In every area of your life, day in and day out, you purposely add and discard elements that define your personal style. Time to send that backless dress to Goodwill? Maybe that previously owned station wagon is a better fit than the Stingray you thought expressed your essential wild nature!

In your home you are always making choices about your environment to create a mood that feels comfortable and expressive. You automatically weed out items you don't care for and give your focus to possessions that give you pleasure ... things you value and love. You are happy if your paint colors are harmonious with your personality. You love that antique chest you inherited and so you highlight it by giving it the best spot in the dining room. You smile at the sight of family pictures artfully arranged on the round, skirted table.

On the other hand, a space that is out of sync with your personal style will leave you discontented. If you love order, a disorganized and messy room will leave you feeling confused, and you'll be lonely in a room devoid of anything you value.

In your home you are in control: Assess each part of it and see if it is uplifting or dragging you down. Focus on the items that give you pleasure and get rid of ones that are dated and not useful. This is the editing process that underlies home decorating. As you read this book, you will learn to make choices among more demanding design elements— like paint colors, patterns of fabric, sizes and shapes of furnishings, and the arrangement of personal objects. With every decision, you will deepen your knowledge of your personal style and enhance the distinctive mood of your home.

Expert Advice

Think of your rooms as children. Dress them casually for play with suitable materials and dressier for festive occasions with special accessories.

This dining room arrangement defies convention and exudes marvelous personal style by the placement of upholstered wing chairs around the table.

(Photo by Gear Design)

5

You Gotta Believe: Confidence in Yourself and Your Decisions

Remember your absolute conviction that your dolls needed to be arranged in a certain order on your shelf? Or that a neatly made bed would destroy the image that you wanted to project in junior high? What can be frustrating about the choices of youngsters is also worth noting: Children have no trouble knowing what works for them. It is only as we get older that we begin to doubt our personal style.

One of the basic principles of this book is to have faith in your selections for your home. Be confident in yourself and your decisions. Trust your instincts. Your initial reaction to a particular color, design, or piece of furniture is usually the right one. An attitude of "I think I can live with it" about a possible purchase just doesn't cut it if you want your true personal style to be your decorating guide.

Confidence, of course, rests on knowledge: knowing yourself, knowing your choices, knowing how things work and what works for you. With all the messages, images, promotions, and possibilities of modern life, careful consideration is essential in developing a strong sense of personal style. There are a number of ways you can know more about what is out there to choose from and what you want to bring into your home.

Expert Advice

If you're in the mood for a movie, consider renting a home-improvement video. If you attend a theater and find yourself loving a room plan, an idea, or a stage set, jot down the reasons why on a small notepad. Help yourself to remember special settings and details by sketching the furniture arrangement or drapery detail. The same applies to a visit to a museum or a house tour. Always have your notepad handy; you never know where your next source of inspiration will come from.

A useful list of magazines, books, videos, house tours, and other resources for learning about home decor and furnishings is in Chapter 8, "Beyond the Basics: Resources for Novice Decorators."

Cultivate Your Personal Style Through Exposure, Reading, and Critiquing

Gain confidence in your personal style through reading and critiquing, exposure and observation. Start perusing home magazines and books on interiors: Begin by noting rooms and designs that seem logical and doable for your lifestyle. Expose yourself to as many different decorating styles as possible by visiting your local furniture and home stores. Gather any brochures and swatches of fabrics and samples of wall covering, paint chips, and flooring. Be on the lookout for inspiration in unusual places: Perhaps a silk scarf or a bouquet of flowers has all of the right color combinations for a dining room wall covering; there might be pictures of interesting interiors or furnishings in mail-order clothing catalogs.

Start a filing system for these new ideas. Label folders with all the names of rooms and spaces you might want to decorate someday, for example, master bedroom, children's bath, entry and hallway, and so on. (Use a sturdy cardboard file box or a decorative wicker file basket to hold them all.) Read, evaluate, cut, and file. These folders will form the master resource for your decorating projects.

You will gradually fine-focus your vision. If you see a sofa detail that you like but the entire room isn't your style, circle the detail and file it in your Living Room folder. If a wrought-iron lighting fixture catches your eye, file it in the folder for the room where you would hang the light. The accumulated pictures and brochures will become pieces of a puzzle that you are putting together to reveal a style suited to yourself and your home.

Know Thyself: Discovering Your Personal Style in Home Decorating

Just as you need to know what is out there to choose from, you have to know what's inside. By taking the following series of personal inventories, or quizzes, you will gain knowledge about your personality, your life, your home, and your possessions. You will start to gather the thoughts about yourself and your home that have always been scattered—or that may never have occurred to you. These numerous factors about yourself—the activities you enjoy, the specific home requirements you have or want, and your feelings about what you own—all have a critical impact on your decorating style.

Take your time with the following questionnaires. Write down your answers; discuss them with others in your home and keep them available for reference.

Style Inventory/Assessment One: Who Are You?

Dig deep and be honest. You want the real you.

➤ What is your favorite movie? Would you like to live in the same style as the characters in that movie? Why?

➤ What do you wear when you are alone at home?

➤ Is comfort your mantra in life?

➤ Are aesthetics more important to you than function?

➤ Does clutter drive you crazy?

➤ Are you messy?

➤ Do you put your feet up on the furniture?

➤ Do you want to be energized or calmed by your home?

➤ Do you like to snuggle? Are you a romantic type?

➤ Do you put cartoons on the refrigerator? Are you funny, and do you like to show it?

Style Inventory/Assessment Two: How Do You Live?

Knowing how you use the rooms in your house and the activities of your life are the basis of many decorating decisions. Concentrate on your daily schedule, and see which rooms you use the most and for what purpose.

➤ How long do you plan to stay in your home?

➤ What point are you at in life now? Are you just starting out, or is retirement not far off? Will you need room for expansion, or is it time for downsizing?

➤ Where do you spend most of your time? The kitchen? The living room? In front of the TV? Your bedroom?

➤ Where do you do most of your entertaining? Do you entertain large or small groups? How often?

➤ Where do you eat? Do you eat different meals in different areas?

➤ Do you like to cook?

➤ Do you have children? Do you plan to? How many? Is there room for a playroom? Are there enough bedrooms?

➤ Do you own pets? Are they allowed throughout your home?

➤ Are you a collector? What types of things do you collect? Big or small?

➤ Are you a reader? Do you own a lot of books? Do you need bookshelves? Do you read in one room or in all rooms? Is the lighting good for reading?

➤ Do you work out of your home? Full-time or part-time? Can you get by with just a desk in the kitchen or family room, or do you need a separate space?

➤ Do you do large-scale projects? Do you need a special room? Does it bother you to do projects in the living room?

➤ What are your hobbies? Do you like to garden? Do you need a woodworker's shop?

➤ Do you enjoy plants and fresh-cut flowers throughout your house?

➤ Are you able to do any improvements to your home yourself, or are you willing to learn?

Style Inventory/Assessment Three: What Do You Have to Work With?

By taking inventory of your possessions you can begin the process of getting rid of things that are not current with your lifestyle now, rearranging items that you want to keep, and making a list of items that you would like to acquire.

➤ What are your most valued possessions?

➤ Name five items in your home that you walk by each day. Assess the pleasure they give you. What is your favorite?

➤ Do you enjoy artwork? Do you have any artwork? What type?

➤ Do you have a favorite sitting area? Where is your favorite chair?

➤ Which piece of furniture has the most meaning for you?

➤ Where is the lighting in each room? Is it sufficient?

➤ Are there items that you wish to highlight? A prized collection? An antique rug? Intricately carved woodwork?

➤ How do you heat your house? Is there a fireplace, wood stove, open hearth? How often do you use them?

➤ Do you have enough storage areas? Could you use more? For what items?

Style Inventory/Assessment Four: What Decor Works for You?

Now you need to look at some of the specific home style decisions that everyone has to make. You may already know more than you think. You may not have answers to every question, but it will help you to see what areas you will have to consider (and read about in coming chapters!).

➤ What colors are you comfortable with? What are your favorites? Which could you live with day in and day out?

➤ Do you like bold patterns or small-scale prints?

➤ Do you prefer carpet or wood floors and area rugs? Other floor coverings?

➤ Do you prefer paint to wall covering? Stained or painted woodwork? Heavy draperies or low-maintenance blinds?

➤ Do you have a favorite decorating style that you would like to incorporate into your home?

Coming into Focus: A Picture of Your Personal Style

Congratulations! You have gotten every answer right! The awareness that comes from systematically evaluating your likes and dislikes and your living habits will be an enhancement to your personal style. You might find that just by asking yourself these questions you have gained a new idea about how to change your home—or why you should keep some things as they are. And you will be using this knowledge throughout the decorating process, beginning with the planning steps introduced in the next chapter.

But of course, your personal style and those of your family members will never be exactly the same. You should discuss your answers with everyone in your home. If your personal preferences do not mesh exactly with those of your partner, children, or other relatives, you may need to make some practical compromises to adjust for differing tastes. Teamwork creates happy households.

The Least You Need to Know

➤ Personal style is the foundation of home decorating.

➤ Confidence is key to developing personal style.

➤ Enhance your personal style through observation, critiquing, reading, and exposure.

➤ A thorough inventory of who you are, how you live, and what you love will help you focus in on your personal style.

Chapter 2

From Castles in the Air to Down-to-Earth Decorating

In This Chapter

➤ Long-term improvements or short-term decor?

➤ Repair and renovate or ready to decorate?

➤ Where to start—zeroing in on the first room

➤ Necessities to dream items—prioritizing projects and needs

➤ Budgeting your room plans

➤ Allocating your resources for a grand plan

Are you full of grand decorating ideas, just waiting, hammer in hand, to start knocking down walls this very minute? Or are you paralyzed in the foyer, not knowing which direction to turn to start perking up your surroundings? Whatever your situation, this important chapter will get you going toward the house of your dreams, step by step—and room by room—at a safe rate of speed.

Successful home decoration begins with a realistic assessment of what needs to be done first and how much you can afford. Based on how you live and what you need—referring to the personal lifestyle information you gathered in the first chapter—you can decide which room to start with. Then, with specific room guidelines found in this book, you can effectively prioritize the essential tasks and purchases for every living space in the house. Researching prices and money-saving possibilities will yield a realistic budget for each room—and ultimately a grand plan for your whole home. Room by room, you can create your dream house on a logical and affordable schedule.

Speed Bumps—Commonsense Cautions Before Beginning

There are a few basic questions that you must answer even before you begin your decorating plan.

Do You Rent Your Home, or Do You Own It?

The caution here is obvious but too often overlooked. Don't put money into permanent or custom-made items if you rent your home. Gear your planning toward movable possessions such as new furniture, free-standing bookshelves, and area rugs. Avoid questionable items such as custom draperies (they most likely will not fit in another home), built-in cabinets (not removable), or nontransportable projects like special paint effects on the walls. On the other hand, as a renter, you will be free of making fundamental repairs. A homeowner has to consider that question next.

Decorator's Diary

Don't be penny-wise and dollar-foolish. My client disregarded a "little" leak in the ceiling of her living room. She opted to spend her money on a gorgeous wool sofa. The little leak gave way to a big leak, and she was aghast to come home to her soaking-wet and stained sofa. Not only did she have to pay for cleaning, she had a hefty plumbing bill.

Need to Repair or Ready to Decorate?

Not the most fun, but basic home repair must precede big decorating projects. Problem plumbing, outdated electrical work, sagging floors, or chipping paint needs to be your budget priority. This doesn't mean that style and personality are left out of these projects altogether. Consider repair work as the first step in redecorating, and approach it as a designer would. Your windows may leak and need to be replaced. That's a perfect opportunity for you to add more attractive windows or larger ones for more light. If your electrical system needs upgrading, assess the lighting in each room: Could you use more outlets? Would you like ceiling lighting added? Since your electrician is coming, get a price on all of your design ideas and see if you can make a mundane repair job into a room-enhancing decorating job.

How Long Will You Live in Your House? What Can You Sell It For?

Homeowners must ask themselves these questions before undertaking major improvements. If you will be remaining in your home less than five years, consider making only cosmetic changes such as wall-covering and repainting or necessary repairs like plumbing and electrical work for safety reasons. As a simple rule, major redecorating and renovations like kitchens or bathrooms are worth it only if you stay in your home for five years or more. Such an investment can upgrade your housing for resale as well as make it more functional and livable. However, you must do some comparison-pricing of the homes in your neighborhood. Be sure that the range of local market prices will allow you to recover the money you have put into permanent improvements. If you paid $90,000 for your home and plan to put $30,000 into renovations, don't do it if the most expensive homes in your neighborhood sell for $100,000.

One Room at a Time Ensures Steady Progress

Unless you live in an undivided artist's loft space, your home comes naturally partitioned into distinctive living areas perfect for project planning. Whatever space you choose, the experience of carefully planning for one room—following this chapter's steps of prioritizing, pricing, and revising your plan and budget—will give you invaluable experience with the many possibilities (and pitfalls) that every decorating project entails and will make every subsequent step easier.

Where to Begin: The Scary First Step

Whether you are absolutely certain or completely confused about which room you want to change first, this is a good time to review or complete the Style Assessments in the previous chapter. They contain a number of criteria you can follow to select your first room such as:

➤ The room in which you spend most of your time (be sure to consider all household members).

➤ The room that has—or could best show off—your most treasured possessions.

➤ The room where you engage in your favorite hobby.

➤ A room that can be converted to meet an urgent need, such as changing a den into a home office.

➤ A room that needs basic repair or structural upgrading.

In fact, this first step need not be scary at all; there are no wrong choices at this stage. The important step is to pick one room as a focus for planning and budgeting. The next steps of prioritizing projects and price review (see the following section) may lead you to another, more appropriate, room in which to actually begin work.

Essentials to Options—Prioritizing the Projects in Each Room

This is the step that will really open up the world of decorating to you—and get you to open this book to many different sections. For whatever room you have chosen, your job is now to critique and prioritize the needs and possibilities for that space: You must list the absolute essentials first and continue through all of the optional accessories that can enhance the room.

How do you know what a room needs or what is possible? That's what this book is for. In Part 5, "Quick (and Easy-on-the-Budget) Makeovers," you'll find that each room chapter contains a planning list. This list can serve as a master outline of all the jobs, furnishings, and enhancements suitable for that kind of living space. You will not need to do everything, of course, but the master list will help you evaluate the state of your room—and then you can decide what you want to do to establish a customized plan in your personal style.

For example, if you have decided to make the dining room your first decorating job, read Chapter 17, "Dining Rooms That Whet Your Appetite," and photocopy the Master Planning List at the end of the chapter. Use this as a guide while you are critiquing that room.

First you have to assess the need for repairs—this is the top priority in every room's Master Planning List. Check your walls, ceiling, and flooring. Are they in good shape, or does the ceiling need patching? Is the heat source working? Are there enough lights and outlets? Do you have wiring for a ceiling fixture? Go through the master list and write down your answers next to each item.

As you go through the master list and the categories of typical furnishings, lighting, flooring, window, and accessory choices, you will constantly be evaluating what you have and noting your particular needs. Refer to the personal inventory assessment that you made in Chapter 1, "You've Got Style: Flaunt It!" to fill in the appropriate places, checking off the possessions you have and ones that you need and want. Remember to build your list around items that you love, for example, you already have a fabulous oriental rug and a classic set of Windsor chairs. Plan your dining room around those items. The rug looks great on the wood floors. The chairs are your most prized possessions. What size dining table can accommodate your chairs and fit the room? Which wall would best suit a buffet? Where would you hang a mirror? (You will learn measuring and be able to familiarize yourself with room arranging in Chapter 3, "Tools of the Trade.")

This is also the time to open your Dining Room file—if you have started one—which should be filled with clippings of furnishings and accessories that you like. Is there a similarity among your choices of room arrangements, colors, and furniture styles? You may also want to read Chapter 9, "Furniture to Last a Lifetime," keeping in mind your personality profile. As a romantic, you may want to choose a nonelectrified chandelier with candlelight illuminating a round table for intimate gatherings. The casual person will choose a simple hammered metal ceiling fixture hung over a rough pine table. A formal person may choose a crystal chandelier brilliantly lighting a period Queen Anne table. The not-so-formal person might gravitate toward slick recessed lighting over a neat Parsons table for an orderly look.

Whatever your choices, you will need to refer to the Master Planning Lists again and again to help guide your planning. Notice the categories and how they are listed by importance from Contractors to Accessories ... critical repairs first before blowing your money on that soup tureen. The most important and challenging part of this process is prioritizing. The master list is arranged in a general order of priorities, but you can adjust this according to your style and situation. For instance, in our dining room example, you may need a china cabinet and ceiling light, too. If your budget will allow for only the electrical work and chandelier and you decide to buy the china cabinet instead, how will you see the cabinet in the dark? Thus, a customized priority list for a dining room— from essentials to room options—might start with performing electrical work, purchasing a ceiling fixture, selecting a dining table, performing nonessential carpentry work (two built-in cabinets), and adding some accessories. In other words: repairs first, lighting second, furniture third, and decorative elements last. This is what the customized master list will look like:

Designer's Dictionary

Queen Anne style is a decorating style that originated during the reign of Britain's Queen Anne (1702–1714) but gained popularity in the late 1800s, especially in America. Queen Anne furniture is often recognized by its simple lines, curved legs, and "ball" or "claw" feet.

Interiors 101

Most decorators will caution: Don't buy anything unless you LOVE it. Thinking something may grow on you is not realistic ... and it's a waste of money.

Dining Room Master Planning List

Priority	Project/Purchase	Comment	Estimated Price
Contractors			
____	Electrician: All electrical	Rewire room; add outlets and dimmer switch	_____
____	Plumber/heat: Check heating	Not necessary	_____
____	Flooring person: Sand, repair floor; retile	Not necessary	_____
____	Painter: Paint walls, ceilings, casings	Walls and ceiling need repainting	_____
____	Carpenter	Two built-in china cabinets	_____
Lighting			
____	Ceiling fixture	Need to buy	_____
____	Wall lights	Would like some	_____
____	Candelabra, candlesticks	Would like some	_____
Furniture			
____	Dining table	Buy	_____
____	Chairs	Already have	_____
____	Sideboard/buffet	Would like one	_____
____	China cabinets	Get price on two	_____
Floor			
____	Carpet	Not necessary	_____
____	Wood	In good shape	_____
____	Tile	Not necessary	_____
____	Area rugs	Already have	_____
Windows			
____	Draperies	Would like someday	_____
____	Shutters/blinds	Not necessary	_____
____	Window seat cushions	Not necessary	_____

Priority	Project/Purchase	Comment	Estimated Price
Accessories			
____	Artwork	Have some, need more	_____
____	Mirrors	Would like	_____
____	Misc. (spoon rack, decanters, tea service, impulse items)		_____

Reality Check: Pricing Your Priorities

With a roomful of projects and furnishing plans selected, the next necessity is putting a price in that big, empty column on the right. Extensive—but easy—research will give you the most accurate (and affordable) estimated price tag for your room plan. By consulting with contractors for renovations and repairs, making visits to home stores, reviewing mail-order catalogs and other publications, and perhaps calling in a design professional, you will give yourself the invaluable advantage of having costs firmly in hand—well before you begin decorating.

Contractors

At the top of the list are the costs of necessary repairs and renovations. Get at least three estimates from reputable contractors. Use the average of these estimates in your customized planning list. Contractors will be able to quote pricing on repairs, renovation materials, and labor. For designer elements, they will probably refer you to showrooms with which they are associated, such as a kitchen and bath showroom or a lighting store. You will learn more about selecting the best contractor for your job, and then working with that contractor, in Chapter 8, "Beyond the Basics: Resources for Novice Decorators."

Expert Advice

Remember: The highest price doesn't always mean the best quality.

Stores

The most easily obtained pricing can be found at local or regional furniture stores and your local home improvement stores such as Home Depot. Tour the stores to review their complete inventory. Bring your room files to help guide you. Sales personnel at retail stores should be able to provide estimates for many items on your planning lists. Consider delivery charges and taxes, too.

Home and furniture stores frequently offer decorating services. Ask if there is a fee for services and whether it can be applied toward purchases. Often, the decorator will come to your house, take measurements, and give estimates on most of the projects and purchases you have planned (see Chapter 8).

Catalogs

Mail-order catalogs are an excellent, convenient source of price information. Mail-order suppliers such as Crate & Barrel, Pottery Barn, Ballard Design, and Spiegel sell home furnishings from carpets to sofas to draperies to lighting, often at the most reasonable prices. Be sure to note shipping charges and return policies since you can't inspect the quality of goods just by looking at the catalog. For more resources, including Web sites, see Chapter 8 and the Appendix, "Bibliography and Resources."

Design Professionals

At this stage, you might also choose to call a private design firm and get a consultation with a designer for a flat rate. You can get a professional review of your plans, or have the designer prepare a plan from the beginning. Designers have access to professional suppliers and a different range of goods that you can't find in retail stores, and you may find it useful to include this in your price research. (You'll read more about design professionals in Chapter 12, "It's a Material World.")

Bottom Line: Hard Facts for Easy Decorating

When you have completed researching prices, you can total up the estimated cost for your first-priority room. Our sample Dining Room plan, with costs for all priority projects filled in, might look like the one that follows.

Dining Room Master Planning List

Priority	Project/Purchase	Comment	Estimated Price
Contractors			
1	Electrician: All electrical	Rewire room; add outlets and dimmer switch	$750
2	Painter: Paint walls, ceiling, casings	Materials—do myself	$100

Priority	Project/Purchase	Comment	Estimated Price
Contractors, continued			
5	Carpenter	Two built-in china cabinets	$1,400
Lighting			
3	Ceiling fixture	Buy from Ballard Design	$157
Furniture			
4	Dining table	Buy from Pottery Barn	$1,100
Accessories			
6	Mirrors	Would like— antique shop	$300
Total			$3,707

As you can see, electrical, painting, and lighting are high on the priority list with a new dining table, whereas accessories are less important.

Forward or Refocus: Matching Your Plans with Your Financial Resources

Now you are in a position to judge whether and where this room cost fits into your financial picture. If your resources can cover the costs quoted, you are to be congratulated! You are in a good position to proceed with your general plans—after you have read this book and learned all the great possibilities home decorators enjoy!

However, don't be shocked, surprised, or disappointed if the real world of repair, furnishing, and decorating prices is higher than what you were anticipating. If your total planning list price falls 20 to 30 percent over your budget, you can eliminate the lower-priority items and meet those needs when you have the money—or, with good fortune, take care of them with finds from flea markets and yard sales. In our sample, for instance, you would have to get the electrical system fixed for safety reasons, as well as the fact that you need overhead

Expert Advice

Take your time—a buying plan can be figured as slowly or quickly as your pocketbook allows.

lighting. As the budget eases, you can think about that buffet, but it would be silly not to have the electricity working, have no lighting, and not be able to serve from the buffet in the dark!

A revised plan list with prices would look like this:

Dining Room Master Planning List Revision #1

Priority	Project/Purchase	Comment	Estimated Price
Contractors			
1	Electrician: All electrical	Rewire room, add outlets and dimmer switch	$750
2	Painter: Paint walls, ceiling, casings	All surfaces to be painted materials—do myself	$100
5	Carpenter	One built-in china cabinet	$700
Lighting			
3	Ceiling fixture	Buy from Ballard Design	$157
Furniture			
4	Dining table	Buy from Pottery Barn	$1,100
Total			$2,807

By eliminating one built-in cabinet and totally removing the accessory budget, you can still make the repairs, add some basics, and have one china cabinet made—all with a 25 percent reduction in planning costs.

If you are more than 30 percent over your budget, it is wise to review your planning approach thoroughly. Don't be discouraged. This is not a mistake on your part; it's just a standard part of the decorating process. You might consider an entirely different, low-cost, and short-term approach to fixing up your chosen room. Many worthwhile ideas for this are presented in Part 5.

You could also consider a radically reduced priority plan, as shown in the following table.

Dining Room Master Planning List Revision #2

Priority	Project/Purchase	Comment	Estimated Price
Contractors			
1	Electrician: All electrical	Rewire room; add outlets and dimmer switch	$750
2	Painter: Paint walls, ceiling, casings	All surfaces to be painted—do myself	$100
Lighting			
3	Ceiling fixture	Buy	$157
Total			$1,007

Repairs and lighting are your first priority. Since you can paint the room yourself and the materials are relatively inexpensive, you should keep that in the plan but forgo the new dining table. You will need to use a makeshift table, and if it's not exactly what you had in mind, cover it with a pretty cloth until you can afford the one of your dreams. Browse yard sales for rock-bottom prices.

Another option—and a common one—is to choose another room, with lower-cost priority items, to begin your decorating. Now that you have planned and budgeted for one room, you will find each room easier to accurately assess, prioritize, and price.

Making a Grand Plan and Budget You Can Trust

Just as you did with the sample dining room, you can critique, prioritize, and prepare a budget for every room in your home. You can customize the Master Planning List in each room chapter in Part 4, "Tackling the House Room by Room," adjusting the list to your needs and possessions, and prioritizing according to your style and physical situation. Room by room, you can create a reliable and informed grand plan for your home and an overall estimated budget as well. With this information, you will be able to plan the anticipated outlay in coordination with your resources. Whether you try to do everything all at once, do a project every year, or spread the projects over 10 years, you will always have a firm grasp on what you can choose to do and how much it will cost.

Reading this book, evaluating your rooms, researching prices—these are the steps to follow to get the big picture. And you won't have to worry that you are going to miss any possibilities. As you learn more about decorating and your style, your room priorities will constantly be changing and becoming clearer. You will learn where to put your money for the most impact on your lifestyle and the least drain on your finances. Step by step and room by room, your dream house can turn out to be more beautiful—and more affordable—than you can now imagine it.

The Least You Need to Know

➤ As a renter or homeowner, determine how much decorating is appropriate.

➤ Evaluate your lifestyle to determine a place to start your plan.

➤ Use Master Planning Lists to prioritize projects and purchases.

➤ There are several ways to research prices for your home plan. Be familiar with all of them so that you can be the best shopper.

➤ Budgeting consists of constantly matching your plans with your resources and going ahead if possible or making revisions if necessary.

Tools of the Trade

With room plans that please and a budget that lets you breathe, you are ready to get to work. But before you start, you will need the right tools. A designer's workspace and toolbox ensure accurate measurement and ideas that translate from the planning page to real, three-dimensional space.

The Design Space—a Suitable Site for Planning

It's a must to have a comfortable and accessible place to work on your home plans. When a bright idea hits, you want to have paper and pencils handy. An angled drawing table will help you work like a professional, but a kitchen table or desk will do, especially if you are working on one room at a time. Along with paper, hard lead pencils (to prevent smudging), and good erasers, your desktop will need rulers and furniture templates.

The Decorator's Portable Kit

Like a doctor armed with his bag for house calls, you'll want to have a carrying basket handy and complete. In fact, you might want to have two portable kits:

1. **A mini one to take while traveling.** This kit should contain a steel and cloth tape measure, pencils, erasers, and a sketch notebook. When you are doing research in stores and showrooms, these will help you measure furnishings and sketch good ideas that you will want to try out in your house.

2. **A complete tool kit.** This should be kept together in a transportable, handled basket and should contain all rulers and tape measures discussed in the following section, as well as a calculator. To make your decorating efficient, also have scissors, needles, thread, and common pins for any quick fixes; a length of muslin or other plain cotton fabric to imitate a possible drapery; and picture hooks of various weights, along with wire, nails and a hammer for hanging or rearranging wall decor. Like any good craftsman, return all of your tools to this basket and you will never waste time trying to remember where you left the hammer or your favorite tape measure.

Measure for Measure—the Essential Tools

Accurate measurement of space and furnishings is essential at every stage of decorating. Rest assured, you will find a good use for all of these different measuring tools!

➤ **Tape measure.** Invest in one like the pros use, a 25-foot metal tape measure (these cost about $14 and are available at any home or hardware store). These tapes are good for use by one person because of their rigid extension and are easily retractable. Twenty-five feet is sufficient for most rooms.

➤ **Cloth measuring tape.** This is available at any department or fabric store and is great for measuring soft goods such as pillows, sofa cushions and arms, and hems of table skirts. It is pliable and can bend around goods to take correct measurements that a metal tape could not. Get one that is at least 60 inches long.

➤ **Yardstick.** A yardstick is useful to take furniture dimensions from the floor up, such as seat heights and slipcover skirt hems. Simple but irreplaceable!

➤ **Scale ruler.** A three-sided ruler calibrated in 12 different scales. They are triangular rulers and cost between $10 and $25, depending on whether they are made of plastic or metal. They are available in art stores.

➤ **Straightedge.** A standard straightedge of heavy-duty plastic is available in any department or art store for a couple of dollars. These come in handy for drawing any straight lines.

➤ **Furniture template.** A nifty outlining pattern that allows you to draw various common furniture pieces onto small-scale plans. They are available from any home or art supply store. Preferred is the translucent plastic type (such as Pickett Home Furnishings Indicator #111PI), which allows you to see underneath the template while you are working. This eliminates an overstuffed chair from being drawn on top of the fireplace!

Another form of template is made up of cutout furniture shapes. These shapes often are sold in a kit with graph paper and can be found at home stores such as Home Depot.

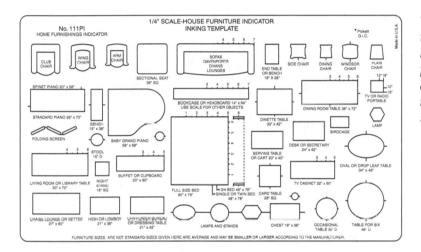

The template allows you to draw sofas, chairs, tables, bedding, and other furnishings to scale. It also helps you become familiar with their dimensions.

Experiment on Paper: Measure Your Rooms to Scale

Drawing rooms to scale is an easy way to visualize a total room—and to try out different furnishing arrangements on a piece of paper. The first step is to take very accurate room measurements that you can translate to a smaller scale. You can draw on graph paper with a straightedge or on plain paper using a scale ruler.

Graph paper is lined to form boxes from left to right and top to bottom, with the boxes in different dimensions. You should work on paper with ¹/₄-inch boxes, so that each box (or each ¹/₄-inch) represents one foot of your room's dimensions. This ¹/₄-inch scale (the one most designers and architects use) allows you to draw even a large floor plan on a single piece of paper. To work on plain paper, you will need to use your scale ruler—making sure you are working on the edge with ¹/₄-inch markings.

Either method is easy. If your room length measures 20 feet, then you would draw a line to scale on the graph paper (with your straightedge), counting off 20 boxes. On plain paper, you would use the scale ruler to draw a line from point zero to the number 20 on your ¼ scale edge. You would do the same with a measure width of 15 feet, giving you a scale drawing of your room that looks like the following figure.

Working with ¼ scale, each box represents a foot.

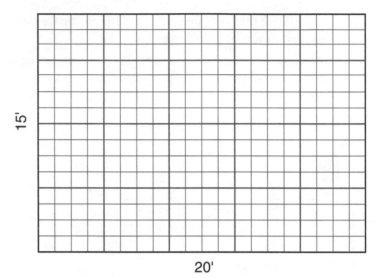

15'

20'

Drawing Your Own Room to Scale

Now practice with a real room in your home. First measure and record the length and width (and note the wall height for later use). Transfer your dimensions to the graph paper or plain paper and make several copies for changing plans. Be sure to measure and transfer the dimensions of any jogs, windows, doors, fireplaces, and built-in furniture. Also note the placement of the TV cable, electrical outlets, phone jacks, and heating elements. All of these will have a great effect on furniture placement. As you are using your tape measure, it is good practice to record the width and height of your doors so that you can determine whether certain pieces of furniture can pass through.

After completing your floor plans, you may want to measure your walls and draw them complete with windows drawn to scale. Use these "elevations" of your walls to sketch possible drapery choices (see Chapter 13, "Opening Up the World of Windows").

Interiors 101

The floor is sometimes considered the fifth wall. While drawing elevations, reverse the theory and treat the walls as four more floors and the thought of drawing elevations won't be intimidating.

What Furniture Fits? Using Templates

Now you are ready to use your furniture templates (or cutouts). If your plan is in $1/4$ scale, be sure your template is the same scale! You wouldn't want to be drawing $1/8$-scale furnishings on a $1/4$-scale floor plan. You will be arranging more furniture on your paper plan than would fit in real life!

Practice tracing a couple of chairs in front of the fireplace. Add some end tables and a sofa. Note that the dimensions of the tables, sofas, beds, and miscellaneous furniture are standard industry sizes. You may have to draw odd-shaped pieces freehand with your scale ruler or the edge of your template, which is calibrated in $1/4$ scale as well.

The more you practice, the better your designs will be. Measure and lay out on graph paper the room you intend to decorate as your first project—first with the furniture arranged just as it is now. Next, make different arrangements of the furnishings that you have put into your planning list. This step will tell you a lot about your plans: Does the room function for its intended uses? Is the traffic flow practical? Do you need more space? Look at the following plans and see how one floor plan can be arranged to suit the personal styles of three different families. Where would you place the furniture?

The floor plan is versatile to accommodate many different families and lifestyles.

The Future of Floor Planning: Computer Drawing Programs

Once you master the traditional method of room planning using scale drawing, you may want to try out the latest home design software for personal computers. This cutting-edge computer technology is not just for the technical elite. Many programs are available for the home computer user that give you tremendous design power. With these programs, you can draw up plans quickly, make changes in an instant, add various textures with the stroke of a finger, and make a 2D plan into 3D in a flash!

Some of the various kinds of programs (or applications, as computer buffs call them) available now include general CAD programs. CAD means *computer-aided design,* and these programs enable the user to do a variety of engineering and design projects, including home decorating plans. You can program your recorded measurements for a custom floor plan that you can easily redraw if you want to rearrange your furniture or decide to knock out a wall. To use a CAD program, you must have an idea of furniture measurements and spatial relationships and be at ease using a computer.

Other technical programs have the capability to instantly change a floor plan into a three-dimensional figure. Patterns and textures can be imitated, and colors can be changed in a second's time.

Are Computers Necessary for the Home Decorator?

Although a computer can give you a whole new way to plan your home, it is only part of the process. You still need to go through the more basic exercise of getting to know your personal style, and to plan a room and a budget that meet your style and resources. It is also useful to know the concepts of scale drawing before starting to do your room arrangements on your computer.

While it obviously isn't necessary to do your planning on a personal computer, it can bring a new kind of fun and a rich source of information to your projects. If you are computer-literate and have an interest in computer technology (and have access to a personal computer), this is a growing field you will want to explore. For more information about decorating programs, try computer stores, magazines, adult computer courses, and even home design sites on the Internet.

The Least You Need to Know

➤ A workspace and basic tool kit make home decorating projects and planning efficient and easy. Keeping a kit handy while traveling can help you save inspiring ideas and measure possible purchases.

➤ Learning the concepts of measuring, scale, and room planning allows you to be able to see the many possibilities for your room.

➤ Although computers are not necessary for successful home decorating, there are software programs and Web sites that can help you plan your projects and provide you with important information.

Part 2

You Were Not Born a Decorator ... but You Can Learn

Face to face for the first time with a room desperately in need of redecorating? It's understandable if you are struck with momentary panic. "Help!" you might suddenly worry. Suppose you make some terrible mistake in your very first project! Suppose the IDP (Interior Design Police) get word of your crimes against good taste!

Relax, and read on. There are no absolute rules to decorating—let alone laws to break—but there are general principles of design that you can easily learn. In the following chapters, you'll get a grasp on how color and texture work, and how they can work for you. You'll see how easy it is to put physical space into basic balance and pleasing proportion.

You'll also take a quick tour of design history: The distinct look of a bygone era might be just the right one for your future. And these chapters are just the beginning: We'll tell you about a host of ways to increase your fund of knowledge—and your confidence.

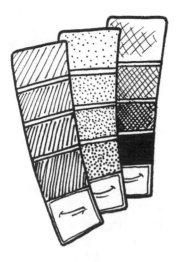

Color: The Decorator's Most Powerful Tool

There is no other design element that has the quick impact or dramatic effect of color. With just a gallon of yellow paint and a couple of yards of cobalt blue fabric, you can transform a room from dull-as-a-dungeon into a vibrant, energizing living space. For the experienced pro or first-time home improver alike, color is the most powerful design resource there is.

Now, you might think that choosing a color for your home would be easy. After all, you have preferred certain colors all of your life, and you make color selections every day with relative ease—for example, your clothing, flowers, and hair color. Yet, it is precisely the lasting power of home color that makes people nervous. Even normally assured do-it-yourself home decorators get in a dither about a color for one room, not to mention a color scheme for an entire house.

Like the squirming of some bachelors I know, I call this reluctance "fear of commitment." When you are going to live with a color for a long time, you have to know what you are really getting into. The key to choosing correct and pleasing colors for your home—colors you can commit to—is understanding just what color is, how it behaves, and how you behave around it. You can learn to narrow down your preferences from the vast selection available by testing color combinations and mastering the fascinating art of combining colors successfully.

Interiors 101

Businesses use the mood-enhancing qualities of color in many ways. Fast-food restaurants use bright and warm colors such as red, yellow, and orange to stimulate appetites and thus sell more food. Manufacturers use red in packaging to draw attention to their products on store shelves because of its "advancing" quality. Hospitals use restful colors like lavenders and blue-greens to help soothe their patients.

The Power of Colorful Thinking

One power of color is its effect on your mood. Sunny colors such as red, yellow, and orange can enliven your soul—or even stir your fiery passions! On the other hand, blues, greens, and purples turn down the visual heat and the emotional intensity. Use these effects in your living areas: You can select warmer colors to make a chilly room feel cozier to those inside. Similarly, if you have a very bright area, you could use cooler colors to create a more relaxed atmosphere.

Color also has the power to alter your perception and trick your mind. Warm and dark colors make elements of a room advance and appear closer to you. Cool colors cause elements to recede. These "advancing" and "receding" qualities can be used to alter the perception of room size and proportions. With a few simple tricks, you can use these optical illusions to make small rooms appear larger and make an oversized area cozier. Even the height of your room can be transformed with color.

Color Tricks

Here are a few tips that can help you change your room size without picking up a hammer!

➤ Both dark colors (such as "eggplant") and warm colors (such as brilliant yellow) can be used to make a room seem smaller. If you have a large room with a cold and uninviting atmosphere, paint the ceiling and walls a warm tone (any color between yellow and red on the color wheel), which will draw in the walls and bring down the ceiling.

➤ Use cool and pastel colors to make a small room grow larger. Pastels, which contain a lot of white, reflect light, and cool colors recede. For example, a small room with ceiling, walls, and floor painted in tones of pastel blues, greens, or purples will appear bright and spacious.

➤ Raise the ceiling by painting it a lighter color than the walls. Or, lower a high ceiling by painting it a tone slightly darker than the walls. If the ceiling still feels too high, you can bring it "down" further by painting a band of the dark tone around the top of the wall (where it meets the ceiling).

➤ Shorten a lengthy room or hallway by painting the end walls a warm and dark color (such as deep reds, oranges, yellows) so that they "advance" into the room.

➤ Apply color tricks to furnishings and elements: A sofa chosen in a hot color will be accented and appear larger, while a pale-colored sofa will remain subtle and inconspicuous.

➤ Highlight strengths. "Outlining" such elements as door and window casings, baseboards, and moldings in a darker or lighter color than the walls will draw the eye to desired details.

➤ Mask weaknesses. Ugly radiators, unattractive woodwork, and other poor room details can be "painted out." Make them the same color as the walls, blending them away from the viewer's attention.

The Power of Association

The associations we make with different colors—based on our everyday experiences, our past, and the world we live in—can often have a profound effect on our response to interior space. Pleasant or unpleasant, these often unconscious feelings can affect the way you feel about any room in your house.

Many color associations are based on common social conventions. Holidays, flags, common objects, and certain color combinations—red and green, orange and black, black and white—all create distinctive feelings. You also might be affected by certain gender associations. For instance, colors such as

Expert Advice

Use color association to make magic in your home. Love the ocean but stuck in a city apartment? Paint your room a soothing sea green; imitate the sand with a jute rug and the colors of the sky and clouds with the upholstery. Tie it all together with accessories in shades that combine all of the colors, or choose an accent color like purple or pink.

Warm up a home in a northern climate with rooms painted in sunny yellow. And if the summer's heat gets to you, paint the ceiling of your sun porch a cool blue. You can lower your temperature just by staring at it!

navy, deep red, and dark green are usually perceived as masculine colors, while pinks, yellows, and pastels are considered feminine.

The point here is that the way you perceive certain colors affects the way you feel in your home. Yellow may remind you of warmth or sunflowers, and red may remind you of joyful Christmas holidays. You'll want to incorporate those feelings into your home. On the other hand, unpleasant associations can make you feel averse to other colors. Try to figure out why you dislike them.

Decorator's Diary

Red, red, red! As far back as I can remember, red was a significant color in my childhood. Each summer my eight brothers and sisters donned their red bathing suits for the beach with their requisite red gingham towels. We exchanged them for nine red ski parkas and hats in the winter. My family's home had a red library, red and navy carpets, and a Christmas tree in the early 1960s with all white lights and red balls. Our black Labrador had a red bow.

When my daughter was five years old she said to her younger brother, "Mommy's favorite color is red." How did she know that? As I looked around, both children were outfitted in red corduroy pants and red-and-white reindeer-patterned sweaters and were sitting on their denim and red-trimmed playroom sofa!

The Simple Science of Color

Color is actually light energy broken down into vibrations. Differences in the wavelength of the vibrations cause us to see it as different colors. As light strikes an object, certain light wavelengths are absorbed and some are reflected. We perceive these reflected vibrations as colors: The longest wavelength is perceived as red, and the shortest wavelength is registered as violet. For instance, the blue walls of a room appear blue because the wall reflects "blue" wavelengths and absorbs the rest. White is the reflection of all the wavelengths from an object. Black, on the other hand, is the absence of color: The object essentially absorbs all of the light-energy wavelengths.

VIOLET	
BLUE	
GREEN	
YELLOW	
ORANGE	
RED	

A ray of white light projected through a prism separates into the colors of the rainbow.

Welcome to the Color Wheel—the Circular Rainbow

We can see the component wavelengths of light—what we think of as a rainbow—when a beam of sunlight passes through a prism and breaks up into the visible *spectrum* of light hues. This progression of colors through the wavelengths (see the color insert later in this book) is often presented as a circle—a "rainbow in the round." The *color wheel* is an essential tool used by designers to create successful color schemes.

The color wheel is broken down into 12 basic colors, with three primaries, three secondaries, and six tertiaries. By graphically showing how colors are related to each other, a color wheel can help you make sense of the endless possibilities of color combinations. Studying the color wheel and learning the language of color will help you gain confidence as you enter the realm of the rainbow.

➤ **Primary colors.** Red, blue, and yellow are the pure hues that all other colors are derived from. They are not mixed from any other colors. They are spaced equidistant from one another on the color wheel.

➤ **Secondary colors.** Orange, green, and violet are the three colors mixed from equal amounts of two primary colors (red + yellow = orange; yellow + blue = green; red + blue = violet).

➤ **Tertiary colors.** These are the six colors produced by mixing a primary with its adjacent secondary. For example, red + orange = orange-red; red + purple = red-purple … and so on.

➤ **Complementaries.** Colors directly opposite each other on the color wheel. For example, red and green, blue and orange, and yellow and violet.

➤ **Harmonies.** Closely related colors that lie between two primaries on the color wheel, such as blue, blue-violet, and violet.

➤ **Hue.** An identifying name for a specific color, such as sea green, apple green, or hunter green.

➤ **Tone.** Defines the lightness or darkness of a color.

➤ **Tint.** A color's range from a pure hue to white (for example, red to pink to white). These are considered light tones.

➤ **Shades.** A color's range from a pure hue to black (for example, yellow to deep gold to black). These are considered dark tones.

Color Changes with Other Colors

In the real world, colors never exist in isolation. Colors always come in some combination, whether we plan them or not, and they always affect each other. Take a red pillow. Put it on a white sofa and it shows up with a dramatic intensity. The same red pillow on a black sofa will be lightened up, but the effect will be different. This red pillow on an orange sofa (two harmonious colors) will look darker and not as pure as it would on a green sofa (two contrasting colors), where the red pillow would appear very bright.

Expert Advice

Putting red and orange together is not illegal! An all red-and-orange room may be a little difficult to live with, but a room with pale-yellow walls and lively red and burnt-orange slipcovered furniture could be a delightful use of those colors. The walls counteract the hot sofa.

Although we all talk about colors that clash, the truth is that there are *no* colors that don't go together. The success or failure of combinations is due to the amounts of color and their relationship to the whole design. For instance, many people think that red and orange clash: Obviously they have never seen a room done well in those colors! Look back at the color wheel. Red and orange are harmonious colors, closely positioned on the wheel and with a natural affinity for each other. It's the amount of each color used that creates the good or bad design of the room.

Observing the Color Schemes You Already Like

The basic step in learning how to combine colors is observing. Noting great combinations—whether in travel, nature, or in inspiring photographs—is a sure way of adding to your bank of color knowledge. Refer to the personal quizzes that you took in Chapter 1, "You've Got Style: Flaunt It!" and clippings from your files from Chapter 3, "Tools of the Trade," and notice what colors you lean toward and for what reasons.

For more ideas of what works for you, go through your wardrobe to see if there is a particular piece of clothing with a color combination that you can translate to your home decor—possibly a scarf or tie. Flowers in a garden may draw your attention with their harmonious arrangement, or dress patterns in fashion magazines just might get your creative juices flowing. As always, start with something you love in a room: perhaps a piece of fabric, a set of draperies, or a treasured heirloom such as a rug, needlepoint, or painting. It may contain the color combination that will guide you to a scheme for the whole room.

Use the Color Wheel to Inspire Combinations

The color wheel provides reliable and fascinating ways to explore color schemes. You can either link color families or take advantage of their contrasting qualities. A simple approach is a monochromatic color scheme that uses one hue in various tints and shades but provides enough contrast so as not to appear dull. Using harmonious colors—colors that are next to each other on the color wheel—is another method, either combining various tones or different ones. A combination of blue, blue-violet, and violet illustrates a harmony of colors.

Interiors 101

Many brilliant decorating schemes use colors we think don't go together. Yet often the most interesting color combinations are those that exploit differences. There are many ways to find the color schemes that work for you. Follow each of these paths to create successful rooms.

You can even use the primary colors on the wheel for wonderful possibilities. While the intensity of the pure hues may be too strong for you, you could subdue the yellow to gold, the red to claret, and the blue to navy; the primaries take on a whole new feeling. Another triangle of colors—the secondaries of violet, orange, and green—might work for you as well.

Complementary colors are pairings of colors that are opposite each other on the color wheel, such as red/green, orange/blue, or yellow-green/red-violet. Sometimes the more receding color (the cooler color) is given dominance and the more advancing color is used as an accent. Think of a drapery in sage green and trimmed in a muted red. The colors are modified to lessen the visual contrast.

Finally, there are color schemes that provide the maximum visual contrast. These are contrasts of tones such as black and white, black and yellow, or white and dark blue. This approach stresses the dark-to-light tones.

Color-Coordinated by the Experts

For a look at what other eyes have chosen, there are many predone color schemes sold through large retailers (from designers such as Laura Ashley). These are schemes for the entire house with everything coordinated: paint, wall covering, fabrics, upholstery, and accessories. Ralph Lauren and Martha Stewart prepackage paint colors available through home improvement and paint stores. Often these are marketed as "theme" palettes—with names like Thoroughbred, Country, and Santa Fe—that specify colors that can work together.

Expert Advice

If you decide to use a commercial designer's off-the-shelf color plans, you won't make big mistakes. But you could easily "overcoordinate"! There is nothing less interesting than a perfect-looking interior, one that looks prepackaged. Impart your distinctive style to your color schemes by adding heirloom pieces or flea-market items, pillows, or carpets that have colors that are somewhat related but not exact matches to the package design.

Interiors 101

A total home scheme is just a larger version of room color scheming. Consider the position of the rooms and the flow from one room to another. Approach coordinating the colors based on the same principles you used in one room, choosing combinations that relate to each other in color or to a quilt or treasured piece that inspires you.

Putting Color in Its Best Light

Whatever color scheme you decide on, remember that the light in an interior space has a tremendous effect on its colors. An eastern-facing room receives early morning sun, and its color will change at night under artificial light. Daylight creates shadows and highlights the objects it falls on. A western-facing window will make colors glow with the setting sun but may cause them to look a little flat in the morning. Natural evening light's bluish cast changes colors like red to maroon and yellow to yellow-green. Artificial light warms colors that have a certain softness with a yellowish cast.

Choose your colors to work with these effects of light. With a cool northern-facing room, you may decide to paint the room red or yellow to warm up the chilly atmosphere. A southern exposure receives the sun's hottest rays, so cool or neutral colors can cool off a bit of the heat. Observation and testing are essential: Be sure to check out your fabrics, wall coverings, paint, and carpeting in both daylight and artificial light in each room to see how they are affected by the changing light.

A Trial Marriage: Testing Your Color Combinations

Don't commit yourself to a color scheme until you have lived with samples for a few days in the room where they will be used. Be sure to get the largest samples available when choosing paint, fabrics, and carpets. Stores use color-corrected fluorescent lighting to resemble daylight, which alters colors' appearance, so the samples might not look the same in your home's artificial lighting.

Hang drapery fabric samples by the window, lay carpet on the floor, and lean paint samples (paint a three-foot-by-three-foot piece of sheetrock for your "swatch") against the wall so that the samples receive lighting from the direction that they would if they were in place. Walk by your colors at different times of the day and decide whether you like the colors in natural and artificial light. Do your color choices go together as planned? Does the carpet still have the deep color it did at the store? Is the paint color the right strength in artificial light? Study your "mini set" for a couple of days in various lights, and see if you still feel delighted with your selections.

The Least You Need to Know

➤ Color is the most powerful element in room design.

➤ Color has almost magical effects on our emotions and mental perceptions.

➤ The color wheel is a helpful tool in understanding color relationships.

➤ Know how colors affect each other before trying to combine them.

➤ Find color combinations you like from your clothes, your own decorating files, nature, and commercial color schemes.

Chapter 5

Getting a Feel for Texture

In This Chapter

➤ The doubly sensual nature of texture

➤ Texture's impact on interior elements

➤ An age of opposites: unexpected textural pairings that work

---

Without texture, a room would be devoid of sensual pleasure. Every material in it—whether it's a stainless-steel range in a kitchen or an overstuffed chair in a family room—has a unique textural appeal to your senses. The stove feels cool and smooth; the chair beckons, soft and warm. Texture, like color, stimulates emotions, and to create a feeling of well-being, the interior of your home must use variations in textures that are warm and inviting. Windows, walls, floors, furnishings, and fabrics are tactile as well as visual experiences for the occupants of the home. You can choose from among an endless combination of textures to make these elements an exciting and harmonious whole.

Texture's Dual Personality

In decorating your home, texture provides two kinds of powerful impact: visual and tactile.

Visual texture can be produced through various media. Paint is the most versatile, used to create various finishes and visual textures on everything from walls and furniture to floors and accessories. Glazes on pottery and walls make flat finishes shiny for

Expert Advice

Designers use colors to evoke the "feel" of a certain substance. For instance, using the color terra cotta evokes the feel of clay: You think of a rough tile floor or a pot of flowers, tinged with aged moss. Some "jewel" colors, such as deep red, purple, and gold, evoke more luxurious textures, while mustard yellow, wheats, and moss greens recall earthy and natural textures. Think about the association of color and texture in every room.

a distinct visual texture. Designs printed on fabrics or certain weaves of textiles can create visual appeal, such as raw silk or rough burlap. Wood furniture and wood floors, sanded to the same degree of smoothness, will create different visual textures due to the differences in the wood grains, such as oak or cherry.

Tactile textures, ones that directly stimulate your sense of touch, create their impact by the materials used. Whether it's a rough and bumpy sisal rug for your floor, nubby raw silk for draperies, uneven old plaster walls, or velvet upholstered sofas, the varied surfaces give pleasure as we run our hands over them. Combining several textures in a room can be tricky, but the incorporation of different elements in one space is a hallmark of contemporary decor.

Texture and Color

Texture affects the perception of color in your home. As light reflects off rough and smooth surfaces, the differentiation can change the colors dramatically. A rough plaster wall and a smooth sheetrocked wall will look different even when painted with the same-color paint. The rough surface will absorb the light, creating surface shadows and highlights. The smooth-surface wall uniformly reflects the light, causing it to appear lighter in color than the heavy, textured one. Look around your own home and compare two red or blue objects with different textures. The medium-blue bedspread looks so different than the medium-blue lamp; one is matte woven fabric and one is shiny-smooth porcelain.

Different textures create different effects in a room. Slick and shiny objects like brass and glass lighten up a small room. Rougher, natural textures like wood, stone, and nubby fabrics can add a sense of warmth and coziness to a large room. Professional designers use this trait of texture to their fullest advantage in creating rooms to set moods.

Texture Throughout Your Home

You probably aren't that aware of the impact of texture on your home, but it affects you in every room. You will enjoy understanding and controlling its subtle power.

Windows

From copper Venetian blinds to ornately draped and swagged curtains, window dressings are a rich source of texture in a room. Metal blinds give a cool and stiff appearance to a room and at the same time reflect light, intensifying the textured effect. On the other hand, fabric blinds soften the hard edge of reflected light and still remain cool-looking with their neat and trim design. Rich draperies made from velvet or tapestry assume a luxurious and warm texture just by the weight of the fabric and the accent of light on the heavy, hanging folds. Sheer curtains made of lightweight fabrics are a soft dressing for window areas, creating an airy texture, heightened when light shines through to reveal the porous weave of cloth.

Walls

Wall texture is one of the defining factors in establishing the "feel" of a room. A meal enjoyed in a dark wood-paneled dining room will be a completely different experience than one taken in a pale salmon-painted room. A rough brick wall adds warmth to an eat-in kitchen that a plain piece of sheetrock just can't match. Different types of paint and paint techniques can create harmony among textures in a room and can fool your eye by creative illusion—using three-dimensional *trompe l'oeil*. Paint finishes, such as matte, eggshell, and gloss, also create different moods.

Wall coverings other than paint can be important textural elements. Printed, embossed, or woven, these can range from vinyl imitations of fabrics to paper that is printed or embossed with patterns to natural fabrics such as wool, linen, or silk. Even natural stone can be used for an emphatic texture on walls, with sheer weight giving a feeling of permanence. The possibilities are virtually unlimited.

Interiors 101

Windows can support several textures at one time. Consider a roll-up matchstick blind, a very natural and roughly textured window dressing. You could add a layer of cotton panels hung on a wooden rod and pulled to the sides of the window. These two varying treatments double the textural impact of the window space.

Designer's Dictionary

Trompe l'oeil means fooling the eye. In decorating, as in art, a surface design can fool the eye in a sense of "visual texture." Examples are a wood floor with an "oriental rug" painted on it, a table with a faux marble top, a fabric with a geometric design that looks 3D, or a wall with a set of false bookshelves complete with textured wood grain and aged leather book covers.

Furnishings

Furnishings introduce distinct shapes, styles, and interesting textures into a space. A slick polished cherry table, a peeling painted Windsor chair, a worn wicker rocker, or a rusted iron table—all gain much of their appeal from their surface finish. Brass, chrome, or glass tables can be cool and smooth to the touch, while handmade wooden pieces have a rich patina that is warm and natural. Paint the wooden pieces and they take on a whole new look with a worn, crackled, or lacquered finish.

Fabric texture is introduced primarily by the upholstery or slipcoverings of sofas and chairs. As you will learn in Chapter 12, "It's a Material World," fabric/texture options are endless, using the vast number of cloth weaves now available. In general, rough and loosely woven fabrics tend to make for casual atmospheres, and smooth and satiny fabrics usually are found in more formal decor. Used together, they can create delightfully stimulating rooms. Using patterned cloth draws on the power of visual texture. A floral-patterned fabric on a sofa or pillows can bring textured life to a dull room.

Flooring

Flooring is a large area that can be made more interesting with texture. With a tremendous number of flooring options, it is necessary first to decide what textures are consistent with the purpose of the room. Kitchens and bathrooms, which get a different kind of use and need certain kinds of maintenance, require different flooring than living or bedroom areas. Carpeted areas can be the most texturally interesting, as the smooth, bumpy, sculpted, or patterned surfaces create both visual and tactile textures. Area rugs can add a splash of pattern and texture to define a cozy space for a conversation area.

Other materials make clear statements: Marble, stone, or tile flooring that is hard and cool brings an atmosphere of permanence. Wood floors show off their natural beauty with flowing, grainy textures. They can also be stained, painted, bleached, and highly polished—or left to wear—for varying patinas. New technology in printing, embossing, and coloring has increased the variety and quality of vinyl flooring. Vinyl can be used effectively to simulate stone, brick, or marble textures. The "Possibilities Underfoot" are more closely detailed in Chapter 10.

Varied textures of exposed beams, pine cabinets, tiled floor, and walls of old brick combine naturally to give this kitchen a warm atmosphere.

(Photo by Smallbone)

The Taste of the Times—Combining Textures

Compared to past times, when protocol demanded rigid adherence to textural styles, we are living in an era when unusual combinations are accepted; in fact, they are essential to the most sophisticated interiors. Artistic pairings of rough and refined fabrics, such as denim and velvet or burlap and silk, often make for the most interesting decorating today.

With so many elements and so many textures available, how do you put them together? One method is to review your fabrics and wall textures before choosing furniture to ensure the different textures complement each other nicely. Or you can use a piece as a starting point and move to the texture of surrounding surfaces. For instance, if the sofa is a rich, soft, sage green velvet, you may want to counteract that plush look with curtains fashioned from a nubby, rugged, natural burlap. Each texture plays off the other, contributing to a personalized statement.

Experimentation with textures is wonderful fun. Create test boards with different materials and visual effects, and live with them as you do color boards. The feeling of your world will be more varied than you can imagine.

The soft bed dressings are a nice contrast to the iron bed.

(Photo by Smallbone)

Decorator's Diary

I once had to do a neutral room using only elements of ivory, cream, and stone textures. I combined a soft washed cotton slipcover for the sofa, sheer billowy curtains, a chair in a heavy woven upholstery, and sponged walls. The effect was very dynamic.

Here is an example of a room with imaginative textural combinations:

A living room with mottled green-painted walls and a dark stained wood floor. An antique map of Paris in a gilt frame is hung over an oversize down-filled sofa covered in a rich damask fabric. You can change the sofa's texture with a wrinkled, floral linen slipcover, lending ease to the room's stiffer elements. A brass floor lamp adds light and a classic touch.

The Least You Need to Know

➤ The sensuality of texture is an important element in creating the feel of a room.

➤ Texture has an impact on interiors through the qualities of visual texture and tactile texture.

➤ Different textures will show color off in different ways.

➤ Every element of a room can bring a number of textures, including windows, walls, floors, and furnishings.

➤ Don't be afraid to combine textures in unusual ways. Experiment with material combinations.

Chapter 6

It's All a Matter of Balance and Proportion

In This Chapter

➤ The nature of balance and proportion

➤ The heavyweight of balance

➤ Room arranging—how to achieve a delicate balance

If color and texture in the previous chapters can be thought of as some of the raw ingredients of design, then balance and proportion may be considered the binding agents that complete the recipe for successful decorating. Proportion is an ingredient of balance and involves the relationship of the size and shape of a part to its whole—for example, the size of a lampshade in relation to its base, or an end table appropriately sized for a sofa. Balance appeals to our sense of equilibrium, a rather visual "weight" as opposed to an actual weight of an object. Both balance and proportion tell us how and why certain combinations and relationships of elements please us or perhaps seem slightly off kilter. Balancing patterns, textures, colors, and emotions throughout the elements in your home creates harmony of design.

Balance and Proportion

You already have an inherent sense of good proportion. You automatically place the sofa against the long wall in the family room, don't you? If you are short, you probably avoid wearing clothes that will overpower you, like large hats and big jewelry. Each day you are using the principles of proportion and balance without realizing it. You're constantly sizing up and comparing shapes. At home, you apply your sense of proportion when you select and arrange objects in a room; you place a rug on a floor, a sofa against a wall, a table and a lamp next to a chair. When the objects are of the right proportions and placed according to their visual weights, the room is balanced.

There are three forms of balance that apply to room design: symmetrical, asymmetrical, and radial balance.

Symmetrical Balance

Symmetrical balance is achieved by arranging furniture or objects on each side of a center or dominant point. This formal balance is easily imagined with two wing chairs on either side of a fireplace or the proverbial candlesticks placed on either side of a bowl of fruit. Sometimes this formal balance can be expected. Little imagination is required and we easily understand the concept.

The symmetrical placement of seating on either side of the fireplace is tempered by the varied accessories of artwork, fireplace tools, and flowers.

A good way to enliven symmetrically arranged seating in a living area is to use different-textured pillows and end tables and lamps of varying textures and heights.

Asymmetrical Balance

Asymmetrical balance is achieved by arranging equal visual weights that are not identical, such as a vase of flowers and a bowl of fruit placed on either side of a chest. Although their actual weight may not be the same, their visual weights are balanced.

There are two ways to achieve asymmetrical balance. One is to arrange different furniture or accessories with similar visual weights equidistant from a center of a focal point: a sofa, a fireplace, a painting, or a mirror. You can also place unlike pieces at unequal distances from the focal point, usually placing the "heavier" object closer to the center. For instance, place a large wing chair immediately to the right of a fireplace (focal point) and balance it with a dainty side chair and a small end table positioned 1½ feet to the left side of the fireplace. They will balance.

Expert Advice

To help visualize asymmetrical balance, think of a child's teeter-totter. Two children of equal weights placed equidistant from the center of the board are balanced. Place children of unequal weights, and the balance is disturbed. If you place the heavier child closer to the center, the difference in weight is offset. Use this concept when arranging furnishings or accessories.

Asymmetry in a room seems natural for today's casual lifestyles.

Radial Balance

Radial balance is a circular balancing of parts or objects around a center, often found in small, round items such as plates, bowls, or pillows. Radial balance can also be asymmetrical, like the circular flow of a spiral staircase, or symmetrical, like a dining table with chairs.

Decorator's Diary

Not only does a round dining table with chairs establish a radial balance of design, it makes for great dinner conversation!

The chandelier, glass-top dining table, and traditional chairs mix nicely in a radial balanced design.

The Weight of Balance Throughout Your Home

The proportions and "weights" of varying elements in a room play a significant part in establishing their impact on the total design. In Chapter 4, "Color: The Decorator's Most Powerful Tool," you learned that strong, warm colors advance and can be used to call attention to an object.

Textures that reflect light or patterned areas also tend to increase the importance of an area. Contrasting colors and textures will emphasize desirable details, and negative areas can be minimized by manipulating their properties and proportions. Rectangular or square furniture carries less weight than freeform furniture. This applies to art, accessories, and patterns. You will notice swirling shapes more than plain shapes. In Chapter 14, "Lighting Up Your Life," you will learn that brightly lit areas of a room are "heavier" than dim areas. Reviewing the weights of balance will help you become better at judging the equilibrium of objects and whole rooms:

➤ Rough and busy textures and patterns seem "heavier" than smooth or plain ones. Burlap is heavier than taffeta. Busy floral chintz is heavier than a solid peach chintz.

➤ Large sizes have greater visual weight to your eye than small sizes. A rocking chair appears heavier than a smaller wooden chest.

➤ Freeform shapes have greater weight than geometric shapes. A freeform coffee table is heavier than a rectangular table of approximately the same size.

➤ Warm and bright colors have greater visual weight than cool, dull colors. A red sofa would weigh more than a pale blue one of the same size.

➤ Diagonal lines call your attention more so than straight lines. A wallcovering with a diagonal pattern has more visual weight than a vertically striped one.

➤ Brightly lit areas in a room have greater visual weight than dim ones.

Expert Advice

Emphasize a sofa's marvelous lines using contrasting cording around the cushions and arms, such as green upholstery with red trim.

Balance and Harmony

Room arranging takes some careful consideration, although there are no real rules. For every decorative decision made, there needs to be an equal counterreaction. The harmony of a room depends on the relationship of the elements. A romantically dressed bed can be balanced by a heavily distressed armoire; this creates a delicate look "weighted" by a solid, textural piece. A hot-pink sofa may be anchored by a chair and ottoman with "basic" gray walls and carpeting. Colorful curtains of blues, greens, and yellows may be echoed in a painting or by splashes of colorful pillows on a sofa on the other side of the room. An area rug can hold the key to colors that you could choose to repeat with the fabrics of the room. Think of tall bookcases along a long wall. To counteract their height, fill the bookcases with books and smaller objects. To counteract their weight, place a piece of furniture of mass such as an armoire at the other end of the room.

All elements are considered when adjusting the balance. You might balance a small, brightly colored area with a larger, neutral one or a small, rough-textured one with a larger, smooth one.

Choose a focal point in each room. This is a good place to start. In a living area, a fireplace is an obvious choice. A sofa and two chairs arranged on either side of the fireplace is a tried-and-true arrangement. A tea table used as a coffee table will contrast with the seating heights with an eye-pleasing balance. If there is no focal point, make one with a patterned rug, a painting, or a wall of bookshelves. Constantly address each decision you make with a weight reaction.

It doesn't matter if your furnishings are antiques or yard-sale finds; the way the pieces react together is the secret of a successful room arrangement. Function and comfort, of course, always have to be in check, but the emotions you feel need to be balanced as well. Just as with texture and color, the room's feeling needs to be a combination of wit and seriousness, of simple and ornate, of solid and delicate. That is the art of combining and arranging elements in a room that represents you!

The Least You Need to Know

➤ Proportion is an ingredient of balance concerning the relationship of a part to a whole.

➤ Balance is the visual equilibrium caused by the handling of correct proportions.

➤ The visual weight of balance can bring an equilibrium to objects and rooms.

➤ Begin to balance a room by starting with a focal point or a cherished piece of furniture or art.

➤ Don't forget that a room needs emotional balancing as well. You want to feel good about your choices and arrangement.

From Classic to Contemporary ... and Country, Too

By developing an eye for color, a feel for texture, and a way with balance, your sense of style is heightened. But what actually is style? There are really two types. A personal style, which you read about in Chapter 1, "You've Got Style: Flaunt It!" emphasized what you love and how you live. Another style establishes identities of a period of historical decoration or that of a particular region or country. For example, traditional decorating schemes suggest time-honored furniture styles and colors, while a country scheme emphasizes a sense of place and natural materials. And a modern approach strips itself down to the basic elements free of decoration. You may like to experiment with items from many different styles for a very personal decor.

Familiarize yourself with the different decorating styles discussed in this chapter so that you can translate them to the best feeling for your home.

Selecting a Style That Works for You

Although choosing a color scheme for your home can make the most confident wince, there are some ways to make choosing a style easier—one that will fit your sense of beauty, your budget, and your lifestyle. The first place to start is to address your living space. Take your cue from the architecture and geographical location. Is it

a studio apartment in the city, a rambling farmhouse in the country, or a modern oceanside retreat? Does the inside have "good bones" with fine architectural details? A fireplace? Carved moldings? Vintage light fixtures? If not, you may have to start with an item you already own, such as a hooked rug or a wonderful sofa. If you live in a Colonial home, beautiful wood floors can dictate your choice for furniture style and arrangement. A modern home with many large windows allows tremendous light, creating airy spaces. You may want to stick to a sparsely furnished room and revel in the ample breathing space. A country retreat may contain natural elements on which to focus—from stone floors to old wood ceiling beams.

But don't worry about decorating with only a single period or regional style. Those types of rooms tend to look like a museum or a cliché of the latest fad. Develop your own style through education. Scour the bookstores for decorating books that appeal to you. Read or subscribe to magazines that picture appropriate room settings to match your lifestyle. Critique the pictures in depth. Figure out why you love an idea or, more important, why you loathe it. Go over your files again and again. Your style is surfacing. As your taste in styles develops through awareness and research, let your rooms benefit by allowing them to evolve as well. The best style for you is one that is in harmony with the way you live—a constant balance of form and function.

Style: Beauties with a Past

Period styles often suggest rigid decorating schemes with certain colors, fabrics, and styles of furniture. While not too many people decorate their homes to re-create period interiors in the purist forms, many aspects of some are appealing and may be adapted for today's home. Professional decorators use the most beautiful aspects of period seating arrangements, fabric selections, wall treatments, and window dressings and merge the past with the present to form a style with a sense of tradition.

Neoclassical

Neoclassicism is a style with ancient beginnings in Egypt, Greece, and Rome, and the classic rules of scale, balance, and proportion dictate every furniture line and decorative motif. The style has reemerged in several countries since the eighteenth century, each interpreting the style in its own way. The Federal period style of the United States was popular in the late eighteenth and early nineteenth centuries. France had its Empire style, England had its Regency style, and Austria and Germany had a Neoclassical style called Biedermeier.

The common denominator of these Neoclassic movements is simple furniture lines in light woods, and Egyptian and military motifs on wall coverings and upholstery. Sheer, light, and airy fabrics hang asymmetrically on windows, and the naturals—muted terra cottas and cream colors—are revived (this is very popular today). From country to country, the colors may change to brilliant colors of greens, yellows, and reds.

Colonial

The Colonial period is probably the most familiar because it is one style that has endured since the 1600s. The middle eighteenth-century Colonial period evokes a time of simple elegance that is widely reproduced today. Rooms are simple but rich in classically designed furniture. Only the best-quality materials of fine woods, silk and needlework fabrics, and silver metals are used. Dining chairs are splat-backed—with a thin wood slat in the back—and surround space-saving drop-leaf tables, side tables stand on pedestals, desks open up for writing, and high chests stand tall on dainty, curved legs.

Window coverings are kept simple, and upholstery is covered in figured patterns of muted shades.

At the same time, Americans were influenced by the Georgian period occurring in England. S-shaped legs and carved shell motifs decorated chairs, tables, and chests. Japanning, the art of painting Oriental scenes and figures on furniture, was practiced, and the imitation of anything Oriental—chinoiserie—became the rage. The late Georgian period, influenced by the English Neoclassical architect Robert Adam, retired the curves and ornateness. People responded to Adams's reinterpretations of the Neoclassical style of light and airy colors and effects. The fashion soon entered the mainstream of American decorating, giving way to the Federal period.

Victorian

Queen Victoria reigned from 1837 to 1901. During this time there was enormous growth in her empire, and private fortunes were amassed in England and America. Neoclassical styles were still appreciated and were mixed in with the new age. Excess was best, using the most ornate carved furnishings in dark woods; marble-topped tables; large, round, pedestal dining tables; overstuffed leather chairs; and heavy, mirrored hat stands. Industrialization offered factory-produced furniture and fabrics in mass quantities. Fabrics made of needlepoint, velvet, silk, and *damask* in rich, deep colors covered everything from mantels to chaises to shelves. Windows were stained glass or elaborately dressed in layers of lace and heavy fabrics trimmed with fringe

and cording. Patterned rugs were scattered throughout the room and walls were covered in fabric-like textures similar to damask. Accessories of botanical prints, animal trophies, Grecian busts, needlepoint pillows, and knickknacks were used extravagantly.

Used with restraint, Victorian details can be adapted to a 1990s' interior mixed with new and old pieces, collections, and framed pictures.

Arts and Crafts/Art Nouveau

The Arts and Crafts movement was born around the turn of the century. The cheapening of the quality of furnishings mass-produced by machines and the extravagance of decorating during the Victorian period gave way to a new philosophy of simple style and pure function. William Morris of England and Gustav Stickley of the United States produced the Arts and Crafts styles of plain oak furniture that was upright, rectilinear, solid, and handcrafted. Morris used fabrics and wall coverings inspired by the Middle Ages for his interiors, while Stickley borrowed themes and colors from nature. These sparsely adorned interiors were to bring about the advent of the modern age.

Art Nouveau (new art) originated just before the turn of the century and was popular in many European countries. Its spare but elegant style is characterized by lavish floral motifs, curvaceous lines, and light colors of lavender, pinks, pale greens, and white. Handprinted wall coverings, stenciled borders, silk fabrics, and Japanese art are common among the various interiors associated with Art Nouveau. The most famous Art Nouveau designer, Scotsman Charles MacIntosh, is recognized for his elongated furniture lines reminiscent of the Arts and Crafts style, and color combinations hinting at the debut of the Art Deco and modern era.

Modern

The positive acceptance of a new industrial age opened the way for new artists to create designs with new machines and materials. A variety of modern styles occurred after World War I. Art Deco and Modernism shared the decades of the 1920s and 1930s. Art Deco still engaged the past with touches of Neoclassicism and Orientalism but embraced the new use of plastics, chrome, and glass with a fervor. The speed of trains, planes, and autos influenced the designers to streamline chairs and sofas, removing hard edges in favor of rounded corners. Chrome was combined with glass to form tables and with leather to create chairs. Early on, unusual color schemes were derived from modern ballet sets incorporating exotic greens and oranges, with touches of black or gold. Muted colors of mauve, gray, cream, and yellow with black as an

Designer's Dictionary

Damask is a durable, sturdy, and lustrous fabric with rich, figured patterns produced by a combination of weaves. It takes its name from Damascus, where it is thought to have originated.

accent were also popular. The style was characterized by round mirrors, lacquered furniture, and walls with geometric designs with stylized female, jazz-age, and Egyptian figures.

Many modern furnishings portray clean lines and monochromatic color schemes.

(Photo by Cassina USA)

Modernism, on the other hand, celebrated the paring down of interior elements. "Only useful furnishings" was the mantra of Modernism. Walls were painted white, windows dressed in simple blinds or plain drapes, floors in wall-to-wall commercial carpet or bare wood, and tables were freeform or geometrically designed of light woods, glass and chrome, or plastic laminate. Highly contrasting white upholstered sofas with black accents typified many modern interiors, while leather, animal skin, and earth tones contrasted nicely with cool steel and plastic.

European designers of the 1920s and 1930s were Miës van der Rohe, Marcel Breuer, and Le Corbusier. The most famous American master of Modernism was Charles Eames.

Postmodernism

Postmodernism developed in response to complaints from people about industrial materials used in homes and the sterile environments in which they lived. Italian and American designers were at the forefront of change in the 1980s, using colors in outrageous ways to inject humor into everyday objects. As people accepted the movement, serious designs were being produced for fabrics and furniture. Designers of the postmodern approach are known as The Memphis Group. They emphasized a mix of styles from different periods combined with new finishes and a magical vision, all in one piece!

Designer's Dictionary

The **Shakers** are a religious sect that flourished in the nineteenth century. Their communities produce beautiful, spare furniture that reflects their belief that creativity is a form of worship to God.

Country

A Country interior is a less-formal and warm, eclectic, traditional style. Country style is comfortable. All of the many regional country styles include stripped pine, painted chests, and large cupboards. Windows are curtained with lace or simple cotton shutters, or use roll-up natural blinds. Walls sport a rough texture with beams exposed. Floors are wide pine, ceramic tile, or stone. Accessories are the personality of Country style, and they include ceramic ware, decorated tile, exposed collections, old signs, pillows of weathered fabrics, and natural materials.

The best thing about the Country style is that it is inexpensive to achieve. Simplicity and a rustic look are the keys to its charm.

American Country

American Country is all about furnishings and objects made by our ancestors. These include quilts and homespun fabrics of rusty reds and pale blues, hooked rugs, duck decoys, crocks with stenciled borders, and painted floor cloths. Other American country furnishings include clean and spare-lined furniture of the *Shakers,* Windsor-style chairs and settees, and four-poster beds and rocking chairs.

Comfortable and casually arranged seating, pillows, throws, and quilts add a relaxed air to this American Country style living area.

(Photo by Gear Design)

The Southwest region of America's Country style adheres to the same relaxed, unpretentious, comfortable, decorative style but uses materials indigenous to the American and Spanish cultures—for example, adobe walls that showcase Navajo hangings and local pottery. Furniture is large and rough-hewn. Colors are bright, and accessories are cast with Native American designs.

English Country

English Country style represents cluttered spaces—for instance, rooms filled with upholstery with worn flowered slipcovers in faded colors of greens, pinks, yellows, and blues. Floors are wood or stone with sisal matting or are covered with well-worn oriental rugs. Plaster walls are decorated with pictures from the country life of field sports, dogs, and horses.

Old pine furniture, casual flower arrangements, and old throw blankets are also part of this relaxed style.

French Country

French Country is closer to the styles of the Mediterranean countries. It embodies the use of provincial prints in deep reds, yellows, greens, blues, and terra cotta. Fabrics are of blue or red checks and faded *toile de Jouy*.

Furniture may be made of walnut or chestnut, plain or painted with a floral motif. Chairs have rush seats and curved legs, and armoires are fabric-lined. Floors are terra-cotta tile, brick, or bare wood with *sisal* matting.

Eclectic Style

Although inspiring, pure period-decorated homes can be expensive and stiff and highly unlikely to fit your current lifestyle. By taking the best lessons from the various historical and regional styles, combining your treasured pieces, and arranging them with your own personality and lifestyle, the eclectic approach can be the most fascinating and interesting way to decorate. It's not as easy as just throwing everything together. There is an adherence to the basic elements of design, particularly color, texture, form, and scale. Many professionals identify themselves with eclectic design and not one type of style.

Designer's Dictionary

Toile de Jouy is a fabric of French origin with country scenes and figures historically printed on a light background cloth.

Sisal is a strong fiber produced from the leaves of the desert plant **agave**, which is also the source of tequila! Sisal matting is a durable floor covering woven from these fibers.

Decorator's Diary

My favorite blending of East meets West was in a home where I placed a beautiful old oriental trunk for a coffee table between two loveseats. I covered them with my favorite ticking—a blue-and-white striped sturdy cotton fabric.

Matching coffee and end tables are dull—be inventive. Why not try a 36 × 36 square piece of glass resting on four antique crocks?

Thinking of different styles together can be made easier by choosing a unifying background. A monochromatic color scheme for walls and upholstery creates a dramatic display of varied styles. A neutral *sisal* matting grounds different patterns, textures, and shapes, while a heavily patterned area rug creates harmony among plain and simple furniture. The most important thing is to use your imagination, your treasures, and your knowledge. Don't be afraid to experiment!

Traditional seating pairs nicely with a modern coffee table for an elegant, eclectic-styled living room.

(Photo by Lee Industries)

The Least You Need to Know

➤ The architecture or time that your living space was built may reveal some clues of a style that works for you.

➤ A crash course in the history of period styles increases your awareness of the art of decoration.

➤ Regional styles are scrapbooks of the way people live and decorate their homes in their native locations. Many styles are adaptable to today's casual living.

➤ The eclectic style is really the most natural way to decorate. Bits and pieces of historically and regionally important ideas can be approached with design for today and combined with your great personal style!

Chapter 8

Beyond the Basics: Resources for Novice Decorators

In This Chapter

➤ Looking, learning, and leafing through catalogs and magazines

➤ Browsing, buying, and chatting online

➤ Hitting the road: real room designs in stores and home tours

➤ Going to the pros: tips for consulting with or hiring an interior decorator

If you need guidance to help you further your quest of learning more about decorating, this chapter is for you! From free catalogs to charge-by-the-hour professionals, education beyond the basics is as easy as leafing through, reading from, watching, walking through, or calling up! Most are closer and more easily accessible than you think.

And then there's the whole new world of Web sites, where you can explore endless possibilities and do all your shopping—without even getting out of your chair!

Mail-Order Catalogs: A Range of Goods ... and Great Ideas

You would be surprised at the plethora of merchandise for your home that you can buy through mail-order catalogs. From drawer pulls to draperies, forks to fabrics, and paints to pillows, catalogs are packed with treasures to round out every style of decor—and at very reasonable prices! Most catalogs are free, but some companies charge a few dollars to get you on their list. Many mail-order catalogs arrive in your mailbox seasonally with a couple of small-sale catalogs interspersed.

When ordering from a catalog, be sure to note the catalog company's shipping charges. Pricing is based on size, weight, and destination. Sometimes that cute "little" chair at a bargain price may not be so affordable after you tack on the freight charges.

Aside from the merchandise, most mail-order companies have the following helpful services and policies:

➤ Gift boxing

➤ Express or air delivery

➤ Customer service hotlines

➤ Liberal refund policies

The best looks carry your personal signature. Buy furnishings and accessories from catalogs with discretion. Don't duplicate a room setting detail for detail or buy all of your furnishings from one style of catalog. A "cookie-cutter" look doesn't exude originality or imagination. Combine new items with older pieces you might have, and arrange them in your style!

Most catalogs are artfully presented and can actually help you see how their goods are incorporated into a well-done interior. To help you find a catalog to suit your needs and tastes, consider some of my favorites for kitchens, linens, furniture, rugs, and curtains:

➤ **Chambers.** Tasteful bed linens, garden furniture, bath towels, accessories, and furniture; 1-800-334-9790.

➤ **Crate & Barrel.** Great selection of furniture, rugs, kitchenware, and accessories; 1-800-323-5461 (for a catalog and store locations).

➤ **Ballard Designs.** Stylish furnishings, accessories, decorative wall paints, and accents for the garden; 404-352-1355.

➤ **Garnet Hill.** Creative bed linens, throws, rugs, and a small amount of adult and children's bedroom furniture stressing natural elements; 1-800-622-6216.

➤ **Gardner's Eden.** Decorative accessories for home and garden, furniture for indoor/outdoor, and gardening supplies; 1-800-822-9600.

➤ **Laura Ashley.** Tasteful and well-coordinated fabrics, custom and premade draperies, furniture, and accessories; 1-800-429-7678.

➤ **Pottery Barn.** Great selection of furniture, ready-made window treatments, and accessories; 1-800-922-5507.

➤ **Smith & Hawken.** Quality indoor/outdoor furniture, garden accents; 415-389-8300.

➤ **Williams Sonoma.** A cook's catalog with kitchen accessories, utensils, linens, dishes, and bonus recipes; 1-800-541-1262.

➤ **Country Curtains.** Ready-made curtains of lace or print geared toward traditional or country homes; 1-800-456-0321.

➤ **Edgar B.** Discount brand-name furniture retailer; 1-800-255-6589.

➤ **Rue de France.** A variety of lace curtains and shades; 1-800-777-0998.

➤ **Spiegel.** A large assortment of ready-made draperies and decorative accessories; 1-800-345-4500.

Expert Advice

Catalogs and magazines are great for pictures of styles and room arrangements that you like. Cut them out and add them to the files you've started. But when you order from a catalog or magazine, try to order goods that you truly intend to keep. With most mail-order companies, you have to prepay the shipping charges on returned goods.

An eclectic mix of furnishings and bed linens available through Laura Ashley catalogs.

(Photo by Laura Ashley)

Decorator's Diary

It's best to analyze room settings done by a designer and not one done for a company advertisement. A designer will specify furniture and accessories from a variety of sources; therefore, the room will be an eclectic mix of styles and resources and a much more interesting design. A company is trying to sell its products. The photo may coordinate too many matching items not appropriate for good design. For example, a wall-covering/fabric company may advertise with a picture of a room with a floral wall covering, matching border, bedspread, draperies, and hatboxes wrapped in the same paper! No imagination is required.

Magazines: Inexpensive Sessions with Top Professionals

Most home magazines offer total room settings that are professionally executed. They also feature articles on interiors done by talented owners that are worthy of praise. The room furnishings, colors, textures, and shapes are shown with attitude. Furniture arrangements are clever, and details are brought to an artistic level. The best way to increase your decorating skills is to analyze rooms that you love. Each room is credited with a designer name and information on where to purchase some of the furnishings that are shown. This information is usually located in the resource guide at the back of each magazine.

Some magazines you may want to subscribe to or pick up at your local newsstand include ...

➤ *Architectural Digest.* High-end designs by top-notch designers.

➤ *Classic Home.* Traditional, timeless interiors.

➤ *Country Living.* Real-life, comfortable, and creative country interiors.

➤ *Elle Decor.* Inspirational and adaptable European design.

➤ *Metropolitan Home.* Contemporary design.

➤ *House Beautiful.* As the name implies, beautiful homes with beautiful interiors featuring a variety of styles.

➤ *Martha Stewart Living.* Includes a little bit of everything: cooking, entertaining, projects, and decorating.

➤ *Traditional Home.* Tasteful, traditional designs.

➤ *Victoria.* For the homeowner with a romantic touch.

It is always fun to buy an issue that features national design, like a French *Vogue* or British *Homes & Gardens*. Some of the decorating may not fit your lifestyle, but it could inspire you. Remember these two words you should live by: modify and adapt.

For the Advanced Amateur: Bookstores, Libraries, and Night School

Books catering to the home abound at your local bookstore or at book-selling giants like Barnes & Noble or Borders. They inventory a wide variety of books on decorating your home, regional styles, and do-it-yourself projects. It makes sense to buy a book that seems to cater to your taste, budget, and lifestyle (not to mention the fact that some of the grand picture books are good coffee-table material). If you do not live near a bookstore with a large inventory a small local bookstore can order any book you may desire. Also, book clubs advertised in magazines that cater to the home decorator offer books at discounted retail prices.

Public libraries are the best sources for free books, magazines, and videos (some are free or as little as $1 to rent) on every subject about the home. The only drawback is that there is a time limit on how long you can hold on to library material—usually one week for new books and magazines and a month for older books. Videos are usually lent for a three-day period. If you would like to add a publication or video to your own library, copy the author's name, title, and publishing or manufacturing firm. If it's a book, also note the ISBN (International Standard Book Number) on the back. You can order a copy through a bookstore. Magazine publishers are happy to send you back issues as well.

If you still feel you need a bit more formal education, try taking a night course at your local adult-education center. These courses usually cater to working adults and are offered at times convenient to your schedule. A class in basic art, elements of design, oil painting, and even perennial gardening can heighten your awareness of color, texture, balance, and proportion—the elements that make a room sing.

Expert Advice

The old adage "don't judge a book by its cover" holds true especially at the bookstore. If a beautiful cover catches your eye, flip the pages, making sure a style or project you are looking for is included and is well presented.

The New Media: TV Shows and Home Videos

Don't change the channel if you see a show on cooking or travel. Some cooking shows may be shot on location in various regions and different nations. Customs, foods, and entertaining may be discussed and photographed with native interiors. Travel shows often point out national museums, interior shots of places to eat, and homes of interest. Both types of shows can provide a study in regional tastes and decor.

Lifestyle and learning channels are full of how-tos and tips on making your home a prettier place to live. Many feature how-tos on wall coverings, painting techniques, sewing, and making decorative accessories. Check your local public broadcasting channel or *TV Guide* to see when home shows will be featured. They usually are shown on a weekly basis. If you've missed shows on TV, videos can be a great source for an extra education; you can view them when you have the time. Check out your local library or bookstore. They will have current informational shows that you can buy or rent that detail your interests. *Martha Stewart Living* TV shows and videos are particularly good, as well as some home shows produced by PBS (Public Broadcasting System).

The New Age of Doing It All Online

If you haven't heard by now, the *Internet* is a worldwide computer network called "the Information Superhighway." With a computer, modem, and online software program (America Online, for example), you can get connected and start browsing for furnishings, decorating items, antique collectibles—even sign up for an online chat. But before you can start "surfing the Net," you'll need a computer.

Computer + Modem + Phone Line = Internet

If you have a computer you can gain access to the Internet by adding a modem and signing up with an *Internet service provider* (*ISP*), which will give you access to the *World Wide Web* (the *Web*), e-mail, and other Internet services. If you aren't plugged in and want to be, you'll need a computer, monitor, keyboard (or a laptop or small computer that includes all three), modem, CD-ROM drive, basic printer, and software. The three main outlets for computers are large discount houses, mail/Internet ordering, and small retail stores. Large discount houses have computers to try out and usually a knowledgeable staff. Sometimes their prices are higher than with mail/Internet ordering. If you order by mail, you'll probably get the lowest price. Be sure to know the exact make and model you need. Your small retail store will offer the best technological support and best service, but the prices will be higher.

It is a good idea to familiarize yourself with the technological terminology:

➤ **CPU.** Central processing unit, the brain of the computer.

➤ **Modem.** The device that connects your computer to your phone line, a must-have for accessing the Internet.

➤ **RAM.** Random-access memory, the computer's temporary storage for programs in use.

➤ **Hard drive.** The computer's main storage—its memory.

➤ **CD-ROM.** Compact Disk-Read Only Memory, another storage piece that holds a tremendous amount of information—like an encyclopedia.

➤ **E-mail.** Electronic mail; enables you to communicate with others while on the Internet.

Designer's Dictionary

The **Internet** is an electronic communications network that connects computer networks around the world for information storing, sharing, and routing. An **Internet service provider (ISP)** gives you access to all the services of the Internet and the **World Wide Web** (the **Web**), which helps you navigate the network through the use of graphical user interfaces and hypertext links.

The Search Is On

After you become adept at using your computer, you can install an online program that will allow you to gain access to the Internet. When you're online, you can plug in an Internet address (some examples follow). Maybe you want to buy some furniture? Plug in www.furniture.com (an online furniture store). With a specific address, the company's Web site (a page for the company's online info and goods) comes up on your screen to allow you to view its merchandise. Some companies have online staff to help answer questions. Retailers have forms to fill out for placing orders—all online! It's not even necessary to leave your home.

If you don't know the Internet address, you can type in "furniture." This is called searching. A host of subjects and stores will come up on your screen, each with an explanation of what the site or page is about. You'll probably need to weed through the search results and find what you're looking for. If it's wallpaper, paint, lighting, fabric, draperies, flooring—you name it—you can find it on the Internet.

Going, Going, Gone—Online Auctions

If you are an antiques collector or a collector of any kind, a good site to look up is eBay online auctions at www.ebay.com.

eBay is by far one of the busiest and largest online auction houses. First you register, then look around the site for that certain piece you must have. When you find it, you enter your top bid you're willing to pay for it. The bidding process may last a couple of days, and the highest bidder wins the auction and takes the prize. eBay's community is user friendly and welcomes new customers. There are message boards, a glossary for auction terms, and bidding tips. Be careful, though, because a bid is legally binding, so be sure you really want what you're bidding on.

Find It on the Web

The Internet is an exceptionally convenient way to shop. Check out some of the following sites:

➤ **www.marthastewart.com.** Goods for the home, paint, garden supplies, kitchenware, decorating books, and videos.

➤ **www.furniture.com.** A retail furniture store.

➤ **www.baranzelli.com.** Exclusive collections of fabrics, furniture, and trimmings, manufactured by the finest mills in the world.

➤ **www.anthropologie.com.** A store with unusual pieces.

➤ **www.ebay.com.** A busy auction site that has an endless amount of antiques and collectibles.

➤ **www.pier1.com.** A store with affordable home products from candles to sofas.

Expert Advice

Although large chain stores have huge selections, sometimes small boutiques can offer more personal service and can order goods for you. Almost every large city has a street known for its fancy boutiques with elegant furnishings and one-of-a-kind creations—like Madison Avenue in New York City. Next time you're in a large metropolitan area, check out its small boutiques.

Real Rooms to View: Chain Stores and House Tours

Browsing through model rooms in large department stores can be a real treat. Big chain stores like Marshall Field, Bloomingdale's, Lord & Taylor, Bullock's, Macy's, and Neiman-Marcus offer well-appointed furnishings set up for purchase. Critique the rooms. If one catches your eye, find the name of the decorator. He or she will be glad to help you make some selections. Ask if there is an extra charge for decorator consultation or a fee-toward-purchase arrangement. Also check out your local furniture stores; you may find a talented decorator in your own town.

Some stores devote themselves to a particular look and clientele. Ralph Lauren's Home Store in New York City boasts floors of luxurious furnishings, wall coverings, fabrics, and decorative accessories—all with a well-bred air and high-ticket prices! His rooms are arranged in themes or eras and are intriguing and thought-provoking. Even if these goods are not in your budget, the trip through is worth it.

Many catalogs and department stores offer one-stop shopping for drapery, upholstery, wall covering, lighting, paint, and accessories.

(Photo by Laura Ashley)

The Laura Ashley Company owns chains of home shops worldwide. It specializes in collections of furnishings with simplicity and style, using skillful mixing of color and pattern. A home book is available that details its ideas and products for a small charge that is refundable on purchase. For a catalog, call 1-800-429-7678.

ABC Carpet and Home in New York City is also a visual delight. Fantastically classic and offbeat items mesh to make some of the most artistic displays around. Its inventory includes table linens, rugs, lighting, and indoor and outdoor furniture. It also operates a restaurant decorated with furniture for purchase. You can analyze, shop, and eat at the same time. Call 212-677-6970 for more information.

Another great source worth noting is local house tours. They are usually held during holidays or festive seasons. One local group, say, the garden club, may choose a home to dress up for holiday viewing. Not only do you get to see garlands, wreaths, and boughs, but you also get to see the interior of an attractively decorated house. A minimal charge usually benefits charitable causes. Call your local Chamber of Commerce to find out when and where the next house tour might be.

Professional tours are usually held in major metropolitan areas. They consist of polished interiors, orchestrated by highly skilled professional designers who combine unusual colors, fabrics, and furniture. The best approach to getting the most out of a professional viewing is ...

1. Get out your notepad and start taking notes or sketch what you love.

2. Check the before and after pictures so you can learn the art of disguise, a designer's best asset. Every room has its negatives: exposed pipes, ugly radiators, too small, and so on.

3. Know what you love and what you loathe.

4. Imitate the simple ideas or modify the flamboyant ones.

5. Check out the resource list filed at each showroom and copy the names of manufacturers. Some may be available "to the trade" only but can be purchased through professional designers.

6. If you like the overall effect of the room, ask for a consultation with the designer. He or she may charge $100 and up per hour, but that's worth every penny if you love the style and need guidance.

These professional showcases are worth the customary admission price (often in the $15 range). All proceeds benefit charitable organizations. The showcases are usually held at the end of April into the beginning of May. It is best to call and confirm showings. Here are a few:

➤ **The Kips Bay Boys and Girls Club Decorator Show House**, New York, New York; 718-893-8600

➤ **The Atlanta Symphony Decorator Showhouse**, Atlanta, Georgia; 404-733-4935

➤ **The Kansas City Junior Women's Symphony Alliance Designers Showcase**, Kansas City, Missouri; 913-345-0920

➤ **The San Francisco Decorator Showcase**, San Francisco, California; 415-749-6864

Calling on the Pros and Still Being the Boss

Taking on a decorating project can sometimes be daunting, even if you understand the basic concepts, know your favorite colors, and have a general idea of what you are looking for. Sometimes an opinion or a total partnership with a professional decorator is a good way to help you complete a small-scale or total home project. Professionals range in skill and price. Some at large housewares stores like Home Depot may specialize in kitchen and bath design. Their help may be included with purchase or charged per plan or by the hour—usually at reasonable prices. A local decorator may charge anywhere from $50 and up per hour or charge a percentage of total purchases.

Whichever you choose, good professional help is worth its weight in gold. Their knowledge can save you time (they know all of the resources) and money (they can keep you from making costly mistakes). Each designer has his or her own fee structure, so be sure to ask.

Remember that a good designer will make your decorating project successful by expressing your tastes and interests on your budget, with style.

Handy Advice on Hiring an Interior Decorator

1. Word of mouth is always reliable. Was your friend satisfied? Do you like her rooms?

2. If your project is detailed and quite extensive, it's best to hire a knowledgeable and reliable designer affiliated with professional organizations such as ASID (American Society of Interior Designers).

3. Interview as many designers as you can. Don't be afraid to ask to see some of their work and to hear about their education and experience.

4. Ask for references.

5. Are you comfortable around the designer? Do your personalities work together? Long projects involve long hours spent together.

6. Does the designer listen when you express your needs?

7. Is he or she passionate and positive about your project?

8. Can he or she work within your budget?

Interiors 101

A high-end, prominent decorator from a prestigious firm will charge anywhere from $100 and up per hour or work on a cost plus basis. "Cost plus" is common when a designer helps you purchase furnishings, fabrics, or decorative services such as hanging draperies or custom slipcovering. You are billed for the *cost* of the goods *plus* a fixed percent, which is the designer's fee.

The Least You Need to Know

➤ Catalogs and magazines are super resources for ideas and merchandise for your home.

➤ Bookstores, libraries, and night courses hold the keys to opening the door to further your decorating education.

➤ Home shows on TV and videos offer easy viewing of how-tos and tips to make your home attractive.

➤ With a computer, modem, and Internet service provider, you can do all your browsing, chatting, and buying right from your chair.

➤ Trips through a large chain store and professional show houses are visual treats.

➤ Hiring an interior designer is money well spent, whether it's for a consultation or for an entire project. A designer can save you time, money, and a lot of worry.

Part 3

Getting the Goods

Cave dwellers had it easy, at least when it came to decorating: rock below, rock above, rock on all sides—and a selection of furnishings and fabrics pretty much limited to what they could hunt or gather.

Today, more products and materials are available for decorating your home than at any time in history. If you have trouble making decisions, you might find yourself wishing for fewer choices—maybe even a cave to hide in—when facing the multitude of possibilities for every room.

Just the surrounding surfaces—floor, ceiling, walls, and windows—bring dozens of decisions. And when you turn to filling the interior space with necessary furniture and optional accessories, your mind might be boggled by the range of selections. What to do? Get the basic info on all your choices in the following chapters before you head out to do your hunting and gathering. It will make it all easier, more economical, and more fun.

Chapter 9

Furniture to Last a Lifetime

In This Chapter

➤ The basics of buying "soft goods" and "case goods"

➤ Getting—and staying—comfortable

➤ Mattresses and box springs for years of good sleep

➤ Wood, plastic, metal, and more

➤ The buyer's checklist

When you plan to buy new furniture, you naturally try to purchase pieces that will appeal to your sense of beauty and individuality. The design, color, and texture must harmonize with the mood of the room and with other pieces you may own. In other words, the *style* must be appropriate for your *lifestyle*.

Another factor you must also consider when purchasing new furniture is cost. Does the price of the furniture fit within your budget plan from Chapter 2, "From Castles in the Air to Down-to-Earth Decorating"? New furniture should be purchased with the idea that it will be used for a long period of time. Does the quality match the price? With the variety of furniture available today, quality ranges from poor to excellent. Many features that determine quality are based on the manufacturer's reputation, the construction employed, and the materials used. Be a better consumer by taking the time to read this chapter and learn about furniture quality. You'll find that your money will be spent much more wisely.

Furniture: The Original "Soft"ware and "Hard"ware

In the home-furnishings world, furniture is classified as soft or hard goods. Soft goods include upholstered sofas and chairs and bedding. Hard goods are called "case" goods. Case goods generally include tables, desks, chests, chairs, and benches. A little background knowledge of these goods may help you to make the right selections.

The Goldilocks Touch—Choosing Soft Goods That Are "Just Right"

Aesthetics and design are usually the first things that attract you to a piece of soft goods, but it is equally important to consider comfort, construction, and fabric when purchasing any upholstered chair or sofa.

The comfort of an upholstered sofa or chair is dependent on its size, fabric, and construction. Be sure the piece will fit your body and fit the room. Is it deep enough to relax in and shallow enough to be able to support you? Is the size proportional to the room? Is the fabric made of fibers that feel good to your skin? Will its cushiness last? Knowing how a sofa or chair is made and what materials were used may help answer these questions.

The construction of a typical moderately priced sofa. The use of more-expensive materials and handwork creates a higher-priced or "custom" sofa. The use of softer, inferior woods, weak joints, and low-grade fabrics reflects cheaper sofas.

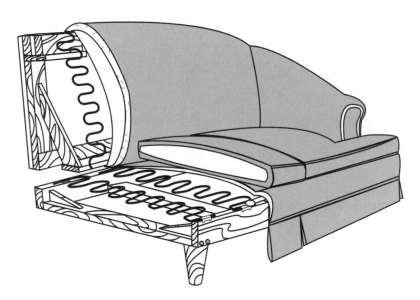

The framework of an upholstered sofa or chair should be made of hardwood, such as ash, birch, oak, or maple, that has been kiln dried (moisture content reduced by the manufacturer for greater stability). Acceptable joints on sofa frames are double-dowel construction reinforced with glue and corner blocks. The blocks should also be fastened with glue and screws.

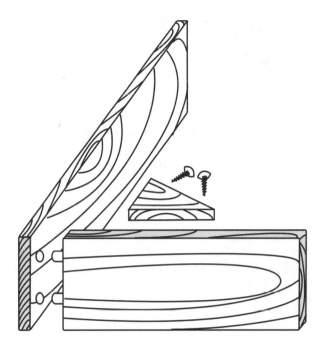

Double dowels are insert-ed into grooves on inter-secting pieces to create a strong joint, reinforced with glue and screwed corner blocks.

The spring construction should be at least eight-gauge S-shaped wires that attach to the frame to provide proper back cushion and sufficient seating support. The higher-quality construction coil springs are placed close together and tied in place with good-grade twine. An "eight-way," hand-tied spring system (each coil is hand-tied eight times), properly done, provides excellent resiliency.

Filling ranges from down (duck feathers) to Polyfill. Cushions filled with down are the most expensive and softest. A foam-core cushion wrapped in down is perfect for softness and firmness. Less expensive but very acceptable are foam-core cushions wrapped in polyester batting. Depending on the foam core, cushions can be soft or firm and are pri-marily used in moderately priced sofas of good quality.

All sofa manufacturers offer fabric selections classi-fied in different grades. The grades refer to the price of the basic sofa with a particular "grade" of fabric ranging from "A" to "Z," with "A" being the least expensive. Price depends on what type of fab-ric it is and how much it costs to manufacture. Durable fabrics and stain-resistant finishes are usu-ally available in all grades. Check for the cleaning codes to be sure the fabric that you choose is ap-propriate for its use.

Interiors 101

Most companies offer "custom" ordering. With this, you can choose the spring system and cushion filling, all for an upgrade in price from the basic model on the floor.

Expert Advice

Make sure you get a mattress with a good warranty. An inner-spring mattress should have at least a 20-year warranty. And a good latex mattress should come with a lifetime warranty. Be sure to turn your mattress regularly to equalize the wear and increase its longevity.

Interiors 101

What differentiates "good" bedding from "less-desirable" bedding?

1. Less-desirable bedding lacks support in the mattress (too soft) and does not properly support the back and hips.

2. Less-desirable bedding lacks proper padding and results in a board-like feeling.

3. Less-desirable bedding may be sold by nonreputable dealers who actually take used bedding and recover it. So buy from a reputable dealer!

Bedding: The Furniture You Use the Most

Steer clear of "bargain" bedding! It is likely to be of poor construction and low-quality materials. Although you might not have thought of including bedding in your decorating budget, it is one of those essentials like electrical repair or plumbing that you need to have to form the foundation of further decorating plans.

Inner-spring mattresses are the most popular and widely used mattresses today. Their inner-coil construction and padding of comfort layers affect their firmness, which ranges from soft to extra-extra firm. Statistics show that 15 percent of consumers like a soft mattress, 60 percent want firm, and 25 percent prefer extra-extra firm.

Coils are made from different gauge wire, and the thicker the wire, the firmer the mattress. Each size of mattress also has a different standard number of coils—a decent-quality "full-size" bed, for instance, should have at least 385 coils. A mattress with less than the standard number is usually a cheaper product. Always check with a reliable retailer on the number of coils in a mattress.

Check out padding layers, too. Top-quality mattresses have the padding layers sewn together and will use such materials as Polyfill, cotton, wool, and down. Some expensive mattresses even use silk and cashmere as padding. The firmness will vary, but the surest way to check out the firmness is to lie down on the bed!

Another popular bedding choice is natural rubber latex mattresses. The advantages to this type of mattress are that it will not sag, it is hypoallergenic, extremely durable, non-toxic, and provides superior body comfort. One disadvantage to latex mattresses is their weight: They are heavy to move! And they are more expensive than inner-spring mattresses.

One thing you should remember is that box springs are an essential foundation to a good mattress. The box spring cradles and absorbs the shock of the mattress. Better-quality box springs are heavy-gauge coil springs that are supported by a simple hardwood frame and covered with a sturdy fabric. We suggest you buy "matched" sets of mattresses and box springs because they are designed to work together for a comfortable sleep and have longer lifespans.

It's Not Hard to Find Quality in Wood Furniture

Wood is still the most popular choice for furniture today. It's timeless, durable, and beautiful for all styles of decorating. There are many types of wood—and different descriptive terms—that you should be familiar with when choosing wood furniture:

➤ *Hardwoods* include oak, birch, cherry, mahogany, and maple, to name a few.

➤ *Softwoods* include pine, cedar, and fir.

➤ *Wood products* is a term that refers to wood-based substitutes for solid wood, such as particle board. This common product is manufactured from small wood fragments that are bonded with synthetic resins.

Learning the Local Joints

The types of joints used in joining furniture parts are crucial to the furniture's quality, durability, longevity, and appearance. Take a look at the following kinds of joints:

Designer's Dictionary

Be sure you check out the sales tag on wood furnishings and know what the terms mean:

Solid hardwood. The exposed parts on furniture are made of a hard wood such as mahogany, oak, maple, birch, or cherry, but this doesn't mean the entire piece is hardwood.

Veneers. Thin slices of wood adhered to a core of solid wood, plywood, or particle board that allow for inlaid pattern surfaces and matched wood surfaces.

Hardwood veneers and **all wood** furniture include a veneer of hardwood bonded to a wood product.

Solids and veneers can be some solid wood parts and wood veneers or laminates bonded to particle board.

Finishes. "Fruitwood," "cherry," or "oak" finish is the color stains used, not the type of wood.

Distressed wood. A process used to give an old look to new woods; the surface is beaten with light chains and rubbed to develop a patina.

The way wood is joined affects the durability of a piece of furniture.

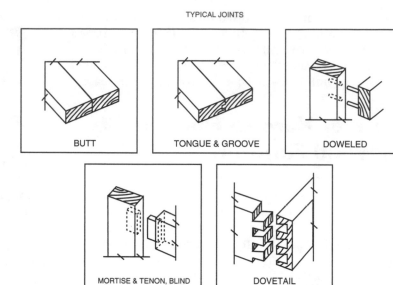

TYPICAL JOINTS

BUTT

TONGUE & GROOVE

DOWELED

MORTISE & TENON, BLIND

DOVETAIL

➤ **Butt.** A simple joint made by nailing or gluing two ends together. It is the weakest of joints.

➤ **Tongue and groove.** A projection of one edge that fits into a matching groove. This is a strong joint that is used on drawers and wood flooring.

➤ **Dowel.** One or more small pegs used to join two edges. This is a strong joint that's used on upholstery frames and chairs.

➤ **Dovetail.** A series of fan-shaped projections that fit into a series of grooves. Fine craftsmen use these to secure joints on drawers.

➤ **Mortise and tenon.** One of the strongest joints, a groove (mortise) on one edge is cut to fit a projection (tenon) on the other edge. Glue and screws may be added for extra strength. This type of joint can be used to join frames of chairs and tables.

Other Materials for Case Goods

Wood has for centuries been the primary material used in constructing hard goods, but in recent times, new manufacturing and design processes have given us furniture made in a host of solid materials. Who knows what the next century will bring?

➤ Plastics provide sturdy, durable, lightweight, and easily maintained pieces that are impervious to moisture. Outdoor use of plastics makes great sense, but high-tech *laminates* are still popular for indoor use because of their slick look and moderate price range.

➤ Glass is used to protect the tops of wood furniture or to make coffee table and dining table tops combined with metal or wood. The size, thickness, and shape of the glass determine its price. Marble is used in similar applications.

➤ Metals such as brass, steel, wrought iron, copper, and aluminum are used to make furniture for inside and outside use. The increased appeal of artificially aged metals has made for a wider range of choices, with imitations of verdigris, pewter, and bronze. Even a rusted-metal look is popular today.

➤ Wicker is actually a weaving process, but its use as a material for furniture for indoors or outdoors is popular today. Fibers of willow or rattan are woven around a frame. Quality wicker that will last is sturdy and tightly woven. Styles vary from simple and natural to quite ornate and lacquered.

Designer's Dictionary

Laminate is a solid-color or "photo" finish (reproduced photograph) surface of plastic that is bonded to particle board.

A set of pretty wicker "porch furniture" could easily be moved to a sunroom for indoor use.

(Photo by Brunswig & Fils)

Your Handy Buyer's Checklist

Now that you've learned everything from the different types of woods and soft goods available to the importance of knowing the quality of joints used, here is a rundown of the kinds of questions you should be asking yourself before buying any piece of furniture:

❏ Does the furniture wobble?

❏ Does the furniture grain match?

❏ Is the finish applied evenly and is it of the same color? Are the corners and carving free of drips and runs?

❏ Is the distressing too fake-looking?

❏ How is the piece joined together?

   If the furniture is wood, is a strong joint used?

   If plastic, is it smoothly molded?

   If metal, are the joints solid and secure?

   If glass, are the edges smooth?

❏ Do the drawers slide easily? Are the insides of drawers snag-free and free of excess glue?

❏ If it has cabinets, do the doors swing correctly?

❏ Is the hardware securely fastened? Are the pulls on the drawers attached with screws?

The Least You Need to Know

➤ When choosing any piece of furniture, remember that comfort, construction, and materials are as important as aesthetic design.

➤ The comfort of upholstered furnishings depends on their size, fabric choice, and construction. Make sure the furniture is made of hardwood framing and has solid construction.

➤ There are many customizing options for upholstered goods. Check them out.

➤ Bedding must be bought for durability and comfort; proper body support is essential.

➤ Case goods or "hard" furnishings are made in many grades of woods, plastics, and metals. Construction quality varies: Be a wise buyer!

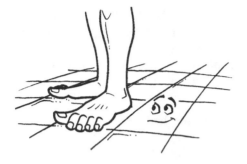

Chapter 10

Possibilities Underfoot

In This Chapter

➤ Floor space: not just something to cover

➤ An introduction to wood, vinyl, and tile uses and options

➤ Carpeting styles for different spaces, styles, and budgets

➤ Effective use of area rugs

Floors are the foundation of any room. Because of this, they need to be chosen for decorative and practical purposes; you want a handsome floor in the right material and shade that is also affordable, durable, and requires little maintenance. From hardwood to tile, carpet to sheet vinyl, many flooring options are available to fit your personal style and your budget. Be sure to explore the many possibilities of floor patterns, colors, and textures.

The Natural Choice: Wood

Wood floors are natural beauties that add warmth to any style or decor. A traditional hardwood floor made of oak is the most popular, but it could also be made of birch or maple. Softwood floors are made of pine, cedar, fir, or spruce. Hardwood boards are available in various widths, but the standard is a $2^1/_2$-inch strip floor with a tongue-and-groove edge. Softwoods come in random widths in a square edge. In addition, very wide pine boards are available through specialty manufacturers.

Wood floors should be sealed and finished with a clear, hard urethane in either a gloss or matte finish and waxed and buffed occasionally. Wood floors are relatively easy to clean if they are maintained properly. It's a good idea to give them a fresh coat of

Interiors 101

"Hard" and "soft" woods refer to a botanical difference rather than a degree of hardness. Softwood trees have needles that keep year-round, like evergreens. Hardwood trees, on the other hand, have broad, flat leaves that fall off seasonally.

Parquet patterns are simple enough to create a visual texture underfoot or intricate enough to be a focal point as floor art.

polyurethane once a year—do the same if they have been coated with oil—but be prepared to sand them first.

Another kind of flooring, parquet, is composed of thin strips of wood arranged in various patterns. Light and dark woods may be joined to emphasize a pattern. Twelve-inch tile squares are also available with ready-made patterns for easy installation.

Consider the style of your furnishings before you choose a wood floor. A dark-stained strip floor that is highly polished offers the perfect foil to a modern interior that is light and airy with sleek surfaces. A casual interior in a country setting might be enhanced by lightly stained wide pine boards complete with knots and imperfections. An oriental rug on parquet flooring adds a classic touch to any traditional or eclectic interior.

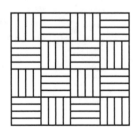
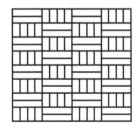

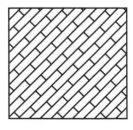

Wood floors may also be stained, bleached, or painted. Painted floors have risen to an art form with the many paint techniques available in kits from art stores, craft shops, home catalogs, and museums. From faux marbling complete with imitation veining to painted-on area rugs with fringe askew, the options are endless. "Spattering" and a checkerboard pattern are the easier do-it-yourself techniques. Stencil kits also aid the novice with a variety of precut patterns and instructions. You can even hire a professional to do intricate detail work. Read Chapter 11, "Walls That Work," for more information about different paint techniques.

Vinyls

Vinyl flooring is known for its durable and low-maintenance qualities and is a good choice for heavy-traffic areas and rooms, like the kitchen and bathroom, where spills may occur.

Sheet vinyl is available in wide rolls, which allows installation without seams. The newer patterns that imitate brick, stone, marble, wood, and tile textures are more realistic than ever.

Vinyl is also available in 12-inch-by-12-inch tiles. You can customize your floor by designing your own patterns and textures with a wide variety of colors. Both types are available in many grades and price ranges.

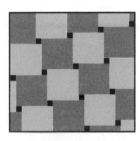
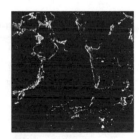

Some patterns that you can artistically arrange with vinyl tiles.

| Inlaid border | Checkerboard design | Marbled pattern |

Tile: A Style for All Time

Natural tile is available in quite an array of materials. From ceramic to marble, nothing can compare to its natural beauty and durability.

➤ **Ceramic** tile is fired clay that is glazed or unglazed and is available in a bounty of colors, patterns, and sizes.

➤ **Quarry** tile is also a fired clay but is a little less refined than its ceramic cousin. It is sometimes irregular in shape and earth-colored like terra cotta. It makes for a most handsome, informal floor reminiscent of old European country homes.

Expert Advice

Be sure your tile is recommended for floors. Some tiles are only decorative (for fireplace surrounds, kitchen backsplashes, or wall surfaces). They cannot withstand heavy traffic and will crack and crumble.

Interiors 101

Grouts that secure tile are available in a variety of colors. Use contrasting-colored grout to emphasize your tile pattern and the same color grout as the tile to achieve a continuous look.

➤ **Mosaic** tiles are made of glazed or unglazed clay or glass tiles. They are small squares that are attached to a backing for ease of installation. They range from soft to very vibrant colors.

Some disadvantages and advantages of tile that you should be aware of are …

Possible Disadvantages of Tile:

1. Cold underfoot.
2. Costly (there is a range of tile prices, but tile is almost always more expensive than vinyl).
3. Noisy.
4. Slippery.
5. Items can break if dropped on it.
6. Floors must be secure to hold the tile's weight.
7. Standing on tile for long periods can cause leg and back strain.

Advantages:

1. Extremely durable.
2. Minimal upkeep.
3. Beautiful to the eye.
4. Excellent pattern availability.

New and old brick is another solid flooring. Its rectangular shape and rugged texture can form some very exciting patterns that exude a rustic, informal feeling. Although it is "used," old brick is more sought after and expensive today. Typically, it is common red block, recycled from old houses and chimneys. New brick is available in different finishes and colors.

Marble tiles add a geometric pattern underfoot in this rustic cottage kitchen.

(Photo by Smallbone)

Marble, slate, and stone are quarried. Although all three are expensive and more difficult to install, marble and slate are available in tile form in different colors to make beautiful patterned floors from foyers to bathrooms. Stone is easier to install and is especially unique. Granite or flagstone can add a timeless quality to any kitchen.

The Comfort of Carpet: Soft, Warm, and Quiet

Wall-to-wall carpeting is the perfect choice for adding a splash of color, pattern, or texture to a room. It is soft on your feet, adds warmth to a cold room, absorbs sounds (good if you live in a condominium or townhouse), and is relatively inexpensive. A carpet's real talent is camouflaging floors that are damaged, stained, or of low quality.

Carpet is made of a variety of fibers and methods. Tufted carpet is made from short lengths of fiber, which are pinched to form "tufts" and set into a backing with a latex adhesive. Woven carpets are fibers that are directly woven together with a backing to make a solid piece. Most carpets are installed over a cushion to increase the carpet's longevity and add further comfort and noise absorption. A carpet's construction, fiber, and finish generally reflect the price per yard.

Expert Advice

Order a bit more tile than your floor requires in case you need some replacements. Some tiles may even be broken on arrival.

Some common carpet terms you may find useful to know are the following:

Carpet Finishes

➤ **Saxony.** Tufted carpet that is looped and sheared for a dense, soft pile. Today's saxonies have stain-resistant finishes and wear well.

➤ **Level loop.** Tufted loops that are even and have good durability. A two-level loop is formed of tufted loops that are uneven, forming a textured look.

➤ **Twist.** A twisted fiber that is heat-set and not sheared creates a nubby, textured effect. If two-tone yarns are used, a heathered effect is achieved.

Carpet Types

➤ **Berber.** A popular tufted carpet today that is a "multi"-level loop, durable, and specified in all styles of decor. Usually is made of "tweedy"-looking yarns.

➤ **Broadloom.** Any carpet made on a wide loom. Most wall-to-wall carpets today are made 12 feet wide or more.

➤ **Axminster.** A patterned, woven carpet that adopted its name from a European factory that specialized in its manufacture.

Carpet Fibers

➤ **Wool.** A natural but expensive fiber. It has a warm, luxurious feel and excellent durability but is harder to clean than some synthetics.

➤ **Nylon.** A very strong synthetic; continuous-filament fibers reduce pilling (small balls formed by fuzz). If treated with stain-resistant finishes, nylon cleans easily.

➤ **Acrylic.** A synthetic that most resembles wool, cleans well, but may pill.

➤ **Polyester.** Durable and resilient synthetic fiber that cleans well with stain-resistant finishes but will pill.

➤ **Olefin.** Moisture-resistant synthetic that can be used indoors or outdoors. Very durable but fades in direct sun. Cleans easily with stain-resistant treatments.

Interiors 101

Carpet is magic! To make a room seem ...

Larger. Use solid, light-color carpet.

Wider. Run a linear pattern the width of the room.

Longer. Run a linear pattern the length of the room.

Smaller. Use a darker-color carpet that is highly patterned.

Cohesive. Use one small patterned carpet without area rugs.

Sisal Carpet

Sisal carpet is a natural carpet woven from plant fibers in many textural patterns and is a great alternative to traditional carpeting. From beach cottage to stately mansion, sisal, seagrass, or coir (all different plant fibers) fits in naturally with every style of decorating. Mostly used in its natural color, sisal can be dyed or handpainted with fun colors and patterns. It is truly a classic choice.

Art Underfoot: Using Area Rugs

Area rugs are hard to beat for adding pizazz to any room of the house. Aside from being soft and warm, their colors, patterns, and textures can inspire total room schemes. From expensive orientals to affordable dhurries, antique to reproduction, area rugs are available at every price, and their attributes are limitless. Area rugs can

1. Define seating and conversation areas.
2. Unify a mishmash of furniture.
3. Protect wood flooring.
4. Be easily transported from room to room and house to house.
5. Provide warmth underfoot.
6. Create a focal point for any style of decor.
7. Be made in styles for every budget.

Some area rugs to be familiar with are ...

➤ **Aubusson.** A French classic that is usually handwoven in muted colors and a center medallion design.

➤ **Bessarabian.** Flat-weave rugs depicting geometrics and florals, usually of Russian or Turkish origin.

➤ **Braided.** Strips of cloth braided and stitched together to form rugs with casual, rustic charm.

➤ **Dhurrie.** Flat-weave rug handwoven in India, usually of muted colors and numerous designs in wool or cotton.

➤ **Kilim.** Similar to a dhurrie but colors are usually richer.

➤ **Hooked.** A nubby pile rug made with yarn or fabric pulled through a backing. Colors and textures vary with the maker, whether by hand or machine.

Expert Advice

Always use a nonskid cushion underneath all area rugs to prevent the rugs from moving. Cushions will increase the longevity of the rugs as well as prevent people from slipping on them.

➤ **Needlepoint.** A rug stitched on canvas with woolen yarns that form many floral, geometric, or scenic patterns.

➤ **Oriental.** Truly the king of carpets, handknotted orientals are prized possessions. Their patterns are usually named after their place of origin. Their rich colors, beautiful patterns, and durability make the most traditional eclectic schemes come to life!

➤ **Rag.** Flat-weave rugs that are made with cotton or wool strips on a loom and create a charming, handcrafted look.

➤ **Sisal.** A natural-fiber rug woven into different textural patterns that can be decoratively bordered, handpainted, or dyed.

To make carpets and bare floors more interesting, use area rugs in different textures and patterns. Link them through color or similar overall effect.

Wood floors and an oriental rug are a classic choice for this informal library. The traditional patterned fabric on the armchair and ottoman complements the geometric pattern of the rug.

(Photo by Brunswig & Fils)

The Least You Need to Know

➤ Decorative aesthetics and practical considerations—such as maintenance and durability—are essential factors in choosing flooring.

➤ Different types of wood, wood finishes, and floor patterns make wood a very versatile and beautiful flooring option.

➤ High-use areas in the home are well-served by choosing from different vinyl flooring options.

➤ If your budget allows, natural materials like ceramic tile, brick, stone, and marble can provide dramatic floors in select spaces.

➤ Carpeting choices should be made with careful consideration of room use, carpet type, and fiber.

➤ Area rugs can be used with all kinds of flooring materials to create special effects within any room.

Walls That Work

Walls are the largest surface areas of your home and always play an important role in decorating schemes. It may be a supporting role—a plain backdrop for pictures and furniture—or a dominating one, with visually commanding paint, finishes, and coverings. In any case, you need to explore all of the options so you can choose what will work for your rooms.

The possibilities are endless! Paint is the most versatile and common treatment for walls. Cheap and durable, it provides an instant face-lift to any tired room. Wall covering comes in a wide range of colors, patterns, and price ranges. Often imitating painted textures, landscapes, or luxurious fabrics, it can provide needed visual texture to an otherwise bland decor.

Fabric applied directly to walls has a special beauty: Its textures not only provide a visual excitement, but a tactile one as well. As you will learn, its uses can be simple or ornate. Similarly, wood applied to walls can be modest, like moldings and wainscoting to better define a small space. Or, wood can be elegant, with completely paneled walls setting a dramatic mood. In either case, wood on walls adds an element of natural beauty to a room.

And there are more possibilities: Earthy materials like tile, brick, or stone bring texture and a sense of permanence to walls and are practical, too. As you learn more about your options, you will find the right ones to bring a personal flair to all the walls in your home.

Paint: A Perfect Complexion for Your Rooms

Paint is the most popular and practical wall treatment. Why? Because it is quick, easy, and generally the least-expensive way to give a room an instant "makeover." Like cosmetics, paint can call attention to fine details or mask less-than-perfect ones.

There are two basic kinds of paints, and their different composition affects their color and use.

1. Latex paint is water-based, washable, and quick to dry.
2. Oil-based paints take longer to dry and need solvents for cleanup, but have rich colors and are durable.

Both are available in finishes that range from high gloss to flat. Gloss paints intensify their colors and cover more area per gallon of paint (approximately 600 feet). Flat colors are more subdued and cover approximately 400 square feet per gallon. Both types are washable. Check with your local paint dealer for advice on which type of paint is best for your project.

Expert Advice

To quickly calculate your wall area, multiply the height of your walls by the perimeter of the room. This will help you, or a paint salesperson, estimate how much paint or wall treatment you need.

As we suggested in Chapter 4, "Color: The Decorator's Most Powerful Tool," paint color choices should be tested. Use large samples of paint, along with the fabrics and textures that you plan to use in a room, and observe them in natural light and evening light. If you don't like what you see, keep experimenting until you are ready to commit.

If it's easier, you can use some of the "pretested" colors, such as Benjamin Moore's historical palette or Ralph Lauren's new line of designer paints available through Sherwin Williams. These are affordable paints in well-appointed colors, widely available at home and paint stores. Benjamin Moore's colors reflect classic historic decor, and Lauren's "go-together" palette presents colors of regional decor and sporting lifestyles. If you are uncertain of your color-combining sense, using pretested paints is a good way to avoid costly mistakes.

Paint Effects

There's more to decorating with paint than just brushing or rolling. Consider the range of unusual paint techniques—from easy-to-do to those that require a high skill level—that give ordinary walls great impact. There are many how-to books and videos available to help you learn these methods (check your library, home improvement stores, and bookstores, and see the Appendix, "Bibliography and Resources"), and many home improvement stores are offering classes and free literature supplied by paint companies.

Here are some of the popular techniques:

➤ **Sponging.** Applying small amounts of paint to a wall with a sponge. Textures will vary with the pattern of the application: A subtle effect is achieved with sponging done close together, whereas greater visual texture is achieved with widely spaced sponging.

➤ **Combing.** Dragging a tool with "teeth" through a wet topcoat to create various "combed" patterns.

➤ **Rag rolling.** Applying or removing color with a bunched-up rag. Wet or dry cloths may be used, but a wet cloth will produce softer patterns. Also, the weave of the rag will affect the pattern. A bit of practice is required to execute this procedure.

➤ **Spattering.** Spotting an area with flecks of different-colored paints by running your fingers over the bristles of a wet brush or flicking the brush to "spatter" paint.

➤ **Stenciling.** Paint dabbed on a wall, ceiling, or floor through a plastic stencil that is cut in various shapes and motifs. Home stores offer precut kits, or you can make your own pattern. This is a quick-and-easy method.

➤ **Trompe l'oeil.** The "fooling your eye" paint technique that creates the impression of marble, stone, or other surfaces, as well as painted-on architectural details. Use this technique for landscape murals that bring the outdoors indoors—or even place painted books or other rare objects on your trompe l'oeil shelves!

Interiors 101

The "fifth wall" is the ceiling. Ceilings can be painted a color, painted with special effects, or wallpapered. A visual display overhead is surely an unexpected touch.

Floors can also be painted using all of these techniques. Be sure to ask your home store dealer for paints and finishes to use in high-traffic areas.

Decorative paint effects.

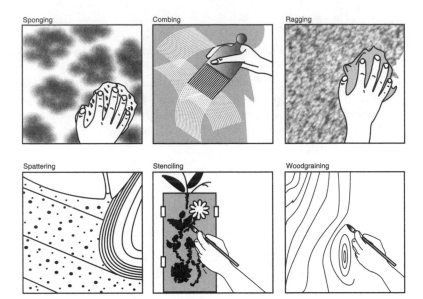

Wall Coverings: Patterns for Every Room and Its Furnishings

Wall coverings are available in every pattern, color, and texture imaginable—and at every price. The most common types of wall covering are prepasted vinyls and vinyl-coated paper. In general, they are all washable, easy to hang, affordable, and widely available. The least expensive are vinyls, which are extremely durable. Machine-printed paper with vinyl-coated surfaces is often clearer in pattern and richer in color than most other vinyls.

More expensive choices include handprinted papers with one-of-a-kind patterns or reproductions of antique patterns. Also, natural-looking coverings such as burlap, linen, or *grass cloth* are paper-backed and can be used to add texture and dimension to walls. They are much more expensive than vinyls.

You can explore the world of wall-covering patterns in specialty books that cater to all styles of decor. Many books carry borders and coordinated prints in different scales for easy combinations (see the Appendix). "Designer" wall coverings are available in coordinated patterns and colors, shown in photographs of well-appointed rooms. These name-brand wall coverings can be expensive, but the patterns and colors are often some of the most beautiful.

Designer's Dictionary

Grass cloth is loosely woven grasses and reeds adhered to a paper back that is applied like a wall covering. It is available in smooth and rough textures, and in many colors as well as natural. Its textured appearance can be accentuated with a glazed top-coat.

A kitchen wall is given dimension with a triple row of wall-covering borders that simulate a set of shelves with jugs, pitchers, plates, and bowls.

(Photo by Gear)

Why and When to Use Wall Covering:

➤ To camouflage stains and defects in walls.

➤ To add visual excitement, texture, and color to an ordinary room.

➤ To create a look of dimension in a sparsely furnished room or a room without architectural details.

➤ To transform a room quickly, easily, and affordably.

➤ To enliven hallways, foyers, and stairwells that might go unnoticed.

➤ To make rooms "grow" or make them appear cozier.

➤ To unify eclectic furniture and a mix of artwork.

Interiors 101

Larger patterned wall coverings take more rolls per room than small patterns. Why? Because there is a lot more wall covering wasted when matching adjoining strips of large-scale patterns.

Decorator's Diary

My client Jean wanted fabric walls in her family room. She lived in a Colonial Revival home with large windows. I specified a red-and-black buffalo check fabric of wool, and painted the woodwork black. It became an incredibly warm and inviting room.

Expert Advice

Your wall-covering store can order a three-yard sample piece for free from most wall-covering companies. The sizable sample helps you see and test the pattern more easily.

Designer's Dictionary

Wainscoting is an added wall material—usually wood panels or boards—that covers the lower part of the wall (typically about three feet up from the floor) and sets it apart from the finish of the upper wall. This is a traditional decorating technique that is many centuries old.

Fabric Walls: Easily Applied Elegance

Fabric applied to walls creates rooms with unmatched character. You can actually feel the softness or roughness of the material. And fabric is the perfect cover-up for walls in poor condition. A fabric's pattern, colors, texture, and application technique develop the mood of a room. Fabrics can be flat and tailored or shirred to create luxurious folds for a soft, sensual effect. Both add wonderful ambiance and hide wall imperfections.

Stapling is the easiest and fastest way to apply fabric to the walls. Panels are cut to fit walls. They are stapled at the length and the width with edges turned under. Shirring is a method of gathering fabric at least two to three times the width of a wall and attaching it with rods or dowels at the top and bottom of the panels. Since a larger amount of fabric is used, shirring can be costly, but with inexpensive muslins or lightweight cottons, it can still be a wonderfully effective technique.

Woodwork for Natural Warmth

Whether in panel form covering an entire wall, or simple strip moldings, wood is a natural choice to add warmth and beauty to any room. *Wainscoting* adds structure and division to walls, and moldings immediately give a room a craftsman-like character. Wood walls can be rustic, polished, natural, stained, or distressed. Many restoration projects recycle old boards that can be used to lend an instant sense of history to a new room. You can find these in renovators' catalogs and shops that carry hard-to-find architectural pieces, often salvaged from old houses.

Walls covered in dark stained wood lend a cozy atmosphere to a casual living room.

(Photo by Lee Industries)

Tile, Stone, and Brick for Durability and Drama

As they do for floors, ceramic tile, stone, and brick can bring warmth to a wall that only natural materials can. In addition to being highly decorative, these materials are easy to maintain. As wall materials, these are all relatively expensive choices—and stone is usually the most expensive of the three. They come in a wide variety of finishes and colors and can be applied in many different patterns. Of course, they can be used to dramatize select areas in a room, such as a fireplace or a cookstove alcove, or to give a "wainscoting" effect. The best way to explore the multiple possibilities is to visit specialty tile and masonry product stores. Make sure you see large sample areas of the materials that interest you.

Tile is ideal for bathrooms or kitchens, where spills can be wiped with no fuss. Using patterned tiles or patterned tiles interspersed with plain ones is a great way to bring striking or subtle visual impact to certain areas. Solid-tile walls can be bordered with a contrasting color or pattern for added pizazz. Though not as widely used, mosaic tiles, with their small size and vibrant colors, make some of the most interesting patterned walls.

Stone and wood walls are natural combinations for everlasting beauty.

(Photo by Lee Industries)

Interiors 101

Mirrored walls can visually expand a small room and double the visual interest by reflecting the furniture and accessories.

Brick is often used in new kitchens or family rooms to give a sense of permanence and to vary the monotonous texture of sheetrock walls. In older homes or renovation projects, old brick is exposed to show off its natural earthy texture and to emphasize its aged character. Stone facing can be used for similar effects.

Don't paint yourself into a boring corner. The options for wall treatments are so many—and often so easy—that you owe it to yourself to try something new. Start with a small area: You can experiment with a wall covering or a paint effect on one exposed panel of a bathroom wall or in a study. This should give you the confidence to bring a bold look to a larger area next time!

The Least You Need to Know

➤ Besides paint and common wallpaper, there are many new materials and techniques that are easy, affordable wall treatments. Take time to learn about them.

➤ Use pretested color palettes to combine colors without worry.

➤ Paint is the easiest and often the most affordable way to decorate walls. Check out different kinds and colors of paints as well as special application techniques.

➤ Wall coverings include durable vinyl, vinyl-coated paper, handprinted papers, and many natural-looking materials such as grass cloth.

➤ Designer books offer coordinated wall-covering patterns and borders for easy combinations.

➤ Using fabric or wood on wall surfaces adds elegance and special warmth.

➤ Tile, brick, and stone are durable, practical, and add a sense of permanence to new rooms.

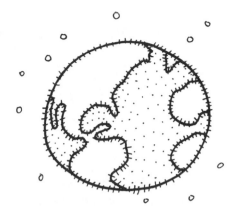

It's a Material World

Fabric makes a house a home. It brings texture, pattern, color, and warmth (or coolness) to living spaces. It softens the angular lines of furniture and architecture, making a room look and feel comfortable. With unlimited colors and patterns, fabrics can set varied moods for all the rooms you live in.

Knowing a bit about the wide range of fabrics used in decorating, and about their construction, will help you select the best fabrics for your design and functional needs. Take this information with you to a good fabric store. Remember to look and feel—get to know the many different fabric personalities. It will inspire you to select materials that will create a warm, personal ambiance for your home.

A World of Woven Fibers

Fabrics are made of natural or manufactured fibers. Natural fibers, such as cotton, linen, wool, and silk, are derived from plants or animals. Some manmade fibers are derived from materials found in nature, such as cellulose. Rayon is regenerated cellulose from materials like wood chips, whereas acetate is chemically changed cellulose.

Most manufactured fibers, called synthetics, are created from chemicals that are formed into strands or filaments by machines. Familiar synthetic fibers include nylon, polyester, and acrylic.

The properties of different fibers determine their strength, draping quality, how they feel, and how durable they are. The type and weight of fibers used and the way they are woven affect their appearance and performance. For example, a tightly woven fabric with highly twisted yarns will have the strength to upholster heavily used furniture. A loosely woven fabric, on the other hand, will be best for drapery, bedding, or light decorative uses.

Expert Advice

Many fabrics are treated with a topcoating that resists stains—some resist only water-based stains, and some resist both water- and oil-based stains. With new furniture purchases, check to see how the fabric is finished. Don't be duped into paying the store for treatments on furnishings or fabrics that have already been finished by the manufacturer.

Most fabrics are variations of three basic weaves:

1. A **plain** weave is the simplest. One fiber is carried over another in a regular pattern, usually at right angles, similar to the weaving of a potholder made by a child. Changing the weight or texture of the fibers creates a unique material.

2. **Twill** weaves form a diagonal line. Twills are sturdy fabrics that have better draping quality than plain weaves of the same fiber. Many jeans are made with this weave.

3. **Satin** weaves are very smooth by construction and allow light to reflect from their surface.

The Nuts and Bolts of Different Fabrics

There are fabrics for style, budget, and use. This review of some commonly used decorating fabrics will help you make the right decisions:

➤ **Brocade.** A heavier-weight fabric, richly decorated with raised patterns that resemble embroidery. Brocade was historically made of silk but now is made of synthetics and cottons.

➤ **Burlap.** A loosely woven, coarse fabric of jute that is simple but very textural, used for shades, drapes, dust ruffles, and table skirts. Burlap is popular in today's interiors and is very inexpensive.

➤ **Canvas.** A heavy, tightly woven cloth of cotton or linen that is perfect for shades and outdoor cushions. Sailcloth is similar but lighter in weight and great for draperies, cushions, slipcovers, and shower curtains.

➤ **Chintz.** A fine cotton in a glazed finish in solids and popular florals. Used primarily for light slipcovers, pillows, and draperies.

➤ **Chambray.** A lightweight cotton in a close weave that has a "frosted" appearance. Popular today is a blue denim chambray that resembles lightweight denim. Good for light slipcovers, pillows, and draperies.

➤ **Chenille.** A fuzzy-surfaced cloth that is produced by clipped, twisted yarns. It is popular today for soft upholstery, throws, trims, and accessories.

➤ **Damask.** A reversible, flat fabric richly patterned by combination of weaves. It is a sturdy and lustrous fabric. Once made of silk, it now is available in various fibers. Once considered formal, it is now combined with homespun fabrics for eclectic combinations. Damask is used primarily for upholstery and decorative accessories.

➤ **Faille.** A plain, woven fabric that has fine ribs with good draping qualities and a luster. Good for draperies, table skirts, and pillows.

➤ **Gingham.** A lightweight cotton cloth with a checked pattern, usually of two colors, typically red and white or blue and white. Great in informal interiors for curtains, cushions, and lightweight slipcovers.

➤ **Lace.** Delicate, open-weave cloth made by hand or machine of cotton, linen, silk, or synthetics. Often used for draperies, table covers, and pillows to add an informal, romantic atmosphere.

Interiors 101

Chintz really isn't "chintzy." Suzanne Slesin is quoted in an article in *The New York Times:* "Chintz, it could rightly be said, is the basic black dress of the English-style interior."

➤ **Matelasse.** A double-woven fabric with puckered surface effects. Used for draperies, upholstery, and slipcovers. Especially popular today in natural cotton.

➤ **Muslin.** A plain cotton that varies in weight. Unbleached muslin is natural with brown flecks, and bleached muslin is much whiter. It is inexpensive. Muslin makes good slipcovers and plain draperies for a relaxed interior.

➤ **Tapestry.** A heavy cloth (even heavier than brocade or damask), woven by hand or machine, that shows pictorial scenes or floral patterns. Tapestry is typically used for wall hangings or as upholstery fabric and made from cotton, wool, or cotton blends.

➤ **Ticking.** Heavy, closely woven fabric of cotton. Usually in a stripe such as blue and white, black and white, and many other colors. Great for upholstery, slipcovers, and decorative accessories. Fits into many styles of decor.

➤ **Toile de Jouy.** Traditionally, an ivory cotton with scenic designs of pastoral life in red or navy. Originally made in Jouy, a town in France. Today toiles are made in vibrant background colors with varying contrasting colors. Perfect for slipcovers, draperies, bedding, and fabric walls.

This toile de Jouy fabric features eighteenth-century fantasies of the Far East with chinoiserie sailboats, pagodas, birds, and Oriental figures.

(Photo by Schumacher)

➤ **Silk.** A lustrous natural fiber that varies in appearance. Some silks are woven with their natural slubs, which enhance their appearance. Dyed silks are usually of bright, beautiful colors that are stunning for draperies and upholstery slipcovers.

➤ **Velvet.** A heavy-weight fabric with a soft pile made of silk, cotton, or rayon. Used for upholstery, slipcovers, and draperies. Velvets that look aged and faded are popular today.

Fabric on Furnishings

The two most common fabric uses in decorating are to dress windows (see Chapter 13, "Opening Up the World of Windows") and to cover new or old furnishings. Sofas and chairs can be coordinated into any design through reupholstery or slipcovers. Reupholstery requires a fabric selection appropriate for your piece. The material is stretched and tacked on the frame, providing a neat and tailored look. In general, re-upholstery is more costly than slipcovers.

Slipcovers are custom covers sewn to go over existing upholstery and can miraculous-ly hide unsightly or outdated fabric and increase the longevity of a prized piece. If seasonal slipcovers are made—one for summer, one for winter—you get double the wear of your covers. Slipcovers can easily vary with your personal style: Wrinkled and loose, or neat and tailored, they adapt to all lifestyles. You can customize a cover by choosing contrasting trims and braids, mixing patterns, or adding buttons, ruffles, or bows.

You can find professionals who make slipcovers or do upholstery in the Yellow Pages. Be sure to ask to see some of their work. If you are considering new furniture, manu-facturing firms usually offer a basic muslin-covered sofa with your choice of slipcover. Mail-order catalogs like Ballard Designs and Pottery Barn offer attractive selections (catalogs and Web sites are listed in Chapter 8, "Beyond the Basics: Resources for Novice Decorators"). Some manufacturers will also accept your fabric to upholster on their frame. A price is calculated on a "customer's own material" (COM) grade.

Pillows can also be covered to add comfort to any room setting. They require mini-mal yardage and are easy to make. Pillows in a variety of patterns and textures give a room a casual, inviting appearance, whereas matching pillows placed "just so" reflect a somewhat stiffer atmosphere.

Decorator's Diary

How to get a regal look on a modest budget? I often advise my clients to splurge on ex-pensive, luxurious fabrics for pillows. The minimal yardage needed for pillows is a perfect example of "affordable" elegance.

Fabrics can also add softness to bedrooms. Using a skirted round table for a night table and draping vanities with delicate fabrics are two simple techniques that add to a sensual atmosphere. (Be sure to read Chapter 26, "Adding a Touch of Romance to Your Bedroom.")

The Art of Combining Fabric Patterns and Colors

Just as you can mix colors and textures, you can learn how to mix fabric patterns and colors by following these simple ideas:

1. Get the largest samples of fabrics and observe them together with your carpets or rugs and paint colors.

2. Study photos in wall-covering books from top designers. See how the pros coordinate their fabrics.

3. Study existing color combinations in rugs, antique textiles, and historical decor.

4. Try patterns that are the same but with different colors (for example, blue-and-white gingham check and red-and-white gingham check).

5. Reverse colors often work, too. Try blue floral on white ground with white floral on blue ground.

6. Mix opposite textures—coarse and soft, flat and nubby, plain and luxurious. (For example, a blue-and-white cotton toile with a blue damask combines simple textures with more ornate textures.)

7. The most important thing to do is *experiment* until you are happy.

The dark solid and checked pillows are a nice contrast to the neutral sofa.

(Photo by Lee Industries)

Decorator's Diary

For a client who loved fabrics and flowers, I assembled a bouquet of different patterns, colors, and textures. I covered a sofa in a large-scale floral chintz and coordinated this with a similar floral pattern on the drapes—but in a smaller scale and reverse colors. For accents, I covered a table with a skirt in coarse linen with a geometric print and then scattered pillows all around—some in the geometric print and some in a solid crimson to match the peonies on the draperies.

The Least You Need to Know

➤ Fabrics add an essential element of comfort to every room, and their many colors, patterns, and textures can set different moods.

➤ Fabrics come in different weaves and fibers that affect their look and their use.

➤ Get to know the whole range of available decorator fabrics before making your choices.

➤ Furniture can be revitalized with fabric, through reupholstery or custom slip-covers.

➤ Fabric combinations can be varied but should be tested through samples and observation.

Chapter 13

Opening Up the World of Windows

In This Chapter

➤ Look *at* your windows—not just through them

➤ The Glass Gallery: types of windows used today

➤ Draperies and curtains

➤ Shades, shutters, and blinds

➤ Tops, trims, ties, and other dressings on the side

Our eyes naturally turn toward light, but that's not the only reason why windows are an important focal point in any room. Windows and their treatments play a big decorative and practical role in your home. Well-dressed windows emphasize the distinct architectural style of the windows and the room. If necessary, the dressings can also disguise a window that has been oddly placed or a window that is unappealing. Window dressings also introduce dramatic design elements that can transform a space, whether you're using long and flowing curtains or simple, trim shutters. There are window treatments that complement every decor; therefore, you can coordinate surrounding furnishings and wall coverings. Finally, window treatments serve many practical purposes, such as control of light, added privacy, and important thermal insulation. Learning the many options in windows and window dressings—including the right terms for the many different elements—is the first step in choosing the right window treatments for your home and lifestyle.

A Gallery of Glass: Basic Window Styles

The way a window is shaped and how it functions are the first factors to consider when you're deciding on your decorating options. Some standard window styles include ...

➤ **Double-hung.** The most common window, with sashes that slide up and down.

➤ **Casement.** Windows that are hinged at the side and swing in or out.

➤ **Picture.** A large, fixed pane of glass with possible moveable sections at the sides.

➤ **Awning.** Horizontal panels of glass that open outward from the bottom.

➤ **Bay.** A group of three or more windows set at angles that project to the outside. Windowseats are often built in.

➤ **Bow.** A curved window that projects to the outside with a possible windowseat built in.

➤ **Palladian.** A curved arch at the top of a window.

➤ **Jalousie.** Narrow strips of glass that open out to the desired angle.

➤ **French doors and sliding glass doors.** Functional room elements that often require, or are improved by, window dressings.

Assorted window styles.

Double-hung   Casement   Picture

Awning   Bay   Bow

Palladian   Jalousie   French doors

Dressings Are a Window's Wardrobe

Draperies are window dressings that open and close on a rod that is threaded with a pulley cord system. They frame a window when they are open and completely cover the window when closed. Drapes are usually at least the height of the window, and often are longer.

Curtains are a simpler window treatment. They are opened and closed by hand and attach to a rod with pockets, ties, or rings. Curtains can vary from café, window, or floor lengths. Café curtains cover the lower half of windows. They are hung from rings on a café rod. A great choice in casual settings is tier curtains—two sets of café curtains hung one above the other, covering the entire window.

Tier curtains are functional as well as decorative.

119

Expert Advice

Attractive, ready-made curtains, draperies, and blinds are available through many of the mail-order catalogs and Web sites listed in the Appendix, "Bibliography and Resources," at the end of this book.

Headings

Draperies and curtains are often gathered or pleated at the top with various headings. Some are fashioned by sewing heading tapes at the top of the drape. Each tape is a fabric containing strings that form a particular pleat when pulled.

Pencil, pinch, or box pleats are tailored, neat headings. Smocked headings resemble a handworked pattern on the front of a little girl's dress. These attach to rods with pins. Scalloped headings attach to rings and a rod. Tab headings tie directly to the rod or form loops that are attached to the drape to allow a rod to run through. A rod run is a pocket casing that easily slips over a rod to form gathered panels in the drape. It is the simplest and most commonly used heading.

Headings.

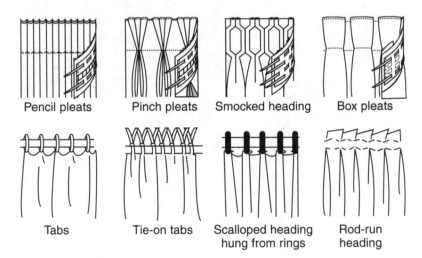

| Pencil pleats | Pinch pleats | Smocked heading | Box pleats |

| Tabs | Tie-on tabs | Scalloped heading hung from rings | Rod-run heading |

Top Treatments

Decorative window dressings that cover the top portion of a window or a drapery heading can be soft or stiff. Soft fabric headings are typically called *valances*. They can be pleated or gathered with the same headings as those of curtains or draperies. Valances can stand alone as simple dressings or combine with full drapes to finish a look or disguise rods or hardware.

Plain valances are easy to sew, but more elaborate valances, such as swags and jabots, are a decorator's delight. Swags are made from fabric draped in an arch at the top of the window. Jabots are tails that hang at each side. These are a bit tricky to sew, requiring precise measurement for correct proportion and a perfect fit.

Festoons are luxurious valances, with voluminous material and a grand appearance. They are fashioned from stationary panels of fabric that are tied up with strings and hooks. End strings can be eliminated for festoons with tails.

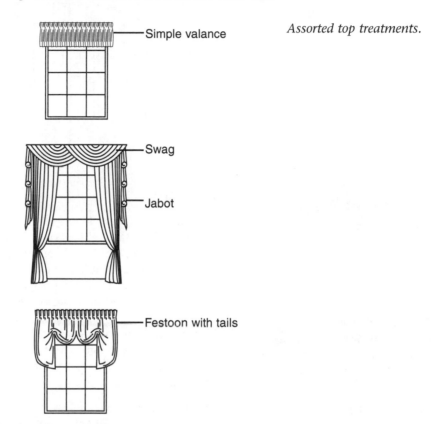

Assorted top treatments.

Hardtop treatments are called *cornices*. These pieces box the top of windows to add definition or hide hardware and headings of the drapery underneath. Usually made of painted or upholstered wood or sculptured metal, cornices can match fancy architectural motifs or be simply styled with added trims or braids. Elaborately shaped cornices are expensive and usually are a permanent installation.

Pelmets are stiffer than valances and softer than cornices. They are made from fabrics backed with a very stiff material (buckram) that can be shaped along the bottom edge and trimmed just as a cornice. Like the other top treatments, pelmets can hide hardware and add a decorative finish to a shade or curtain.

A simple cornice.

Linings

Curtain and drapery linings protect your fabric from the sun, block the light, give body to fabrics, and provide insulation. The most commonly used lining is a cotton sateen, available in basic white or cream. It usually has a stain-resistant finish. Blackout lining is a heavier, rubberized fabric for completely blocking out light. It is available in white to pale colors. Remember, however, that it changes the appearance of your drapery fabric, because light cannot shine through it. Be sure to test a sample with your fabric so that you understand the effect.

Interlinings are used to give extra body to a drape and provide extra insulation. A layer of soft, loosely woven fabric is sewn between the decorative fabric and lining. Interlining adds exceptional softness to draperies, creating a luxurious appearance. Interlining also adds weight to draperies, making them very heavy. Be sure your walls and rods can support them.

Consider that not all window dressings need linings. Curtains or draperies that are stationary and purely decorative often do not. And very sheer fabrics may also look and drape beautifully without linings.

Cutting the Glare: Shades, Blinds, and Shutters

A shade is any window treatment that closes from top to bottom and that covers from casing to casing. Fabric shades vary from plain roller types to opulent festoons operated with a cord system. Blinds are slats made of metal, plastic, or wood that also raise and lower with a cord system. Shutters are mounted panels that can be opened and closed.

Shades

Roller shades are a simple, neat treatment. A piece of cloth the size of the window is wound and attached to a roller, to be raised and lowered with a simple pull. When raised, roller shades take up minimum space. Today, roller shades are available in ready-made, handsome, linen-like fabrics or can be customized with your own fabrics and decorative edges.

Roman shades are sewn with horizontal tucks that stack neatly when drawn with a system of cords and drawstrings. Roman shades offer a softer look than roller shades but are still neat and tailored.

Festoon shades are made in a variety of ways, but all are raised by a series of cords and drawstrings into generous and billowy folds. Trims, fringes, and ruffles will add to the extravagant style.

Pleated shades are made of permanently pleated paper or stiffened polyester fabric. They are operated by cords and drawstrings as well. Generally quite inexpensive, they are either used alone as a minimal dressing or under full curtains and valances for privacy and light control.

Blinds

Venetian blinds are made of two-inch slats—usually plastic, metal, or wood—that can be raised or lowered with cords and tapes, and tilted to desired angles. *Mini-* and *micro-blinds* are similar, but their slats are an inch or less in width.

Matchstick blinds are made from split bamboo, woven together with a series of strings to roll or pleat up when raised.

All blinds can be used alone for minimal dressing or under curtains or draperies for a layered, textured look.

Interiors 101

We call slatted window shades "Venetian blinds" after the early Venetian traders who brought them to Europe centuries ago. But they were really invented by the Persians—in Italy, they call them "Persiani blinds."

Shutters

Wood shutters add a dimension to any window. Shutters are mounted inside a window frame or on window casings. They can be full window height or attached at half height, and the panels can be solid or louvered. Louvered shutters enable you to control light by raising the slats or and down. Solid-paneled shutters control light by being opened or closed.

Trims and Tiebacks

Trims are used to accentuate the lines of a particular window covering and act as an integral part of the overall design. Braids, ribbon, and piping can border the leading edges or hems of a shade, drape, or blind. Ruffles, fringe, and tassels add soft dimension.

Some of the many different trims and tiebacks available.

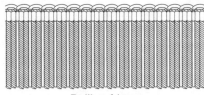

Bullion fringe

Six-inch tassel

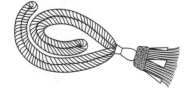

Swag tassel tie back

5¹/₂-inch tassel with 2¹/₂-inch rosette for upholstery

Tiebacks hold curtains on either side of a window. They can be straight or contoured pieces of fabric of the same material as the drape, or they can be made of contrasting fabric. They can be trimmed with various piping or ruffles. Solid or multicolored tasseled cords or braids can hold a curtain back with a decorative effect. Metal hooks usually made of brass act as stationary tiebacks. They are attached to the sides of the windows to hold each panel of the curtains. Rosette tiebacks resemble carved doorknobs that attach to the sides of the windows and protrude from the wall to hold the curtain fabric. Tiebacks can also be "built-in" curtain panels with strings that are pulled tightly to form a tied-back look.

A tieback's placement affects the overall look of the curtain: Placed high on a window, a curtain will be tighter looking at the top; placed low, a curtain will drape fuller at the top.

A curtain without conventional tiebacks is "tied back" with invisible cords sewn into the back panels.

Hardware

Successful window coverings require the right hardware. Each style of drapery you choose requires particular rods, hooks, or some sort of wood for mounting. Utilitarian rods that are basic white metal should be hidden under a top treatment or by the heading of a drape. Curtains attach to the rods with casings or hooks. Decorative rods that can be wrought iron, brass, pewter, or wood are specified for their form as well as function. Curtains attach to them with a casing or by hooks and rings. Many catalogs, furniture stores, and curtain stores carry an amazing assortment of decorative hardware. (Check the drapery sources in the Appendix.)

How to Measure a Window

To make shopping for draperies easier, it is smart to have several measurements on hand so that you can ask salespeople for estimates on custom-made draperies, or so that you'll know whether ready-made draperies (usually in standard sizes) would fit your windows. Always use a metal tape for accurate measurements. You will need to know a number of dimensions to see which window treatments can work for you.

Important window dimensions.

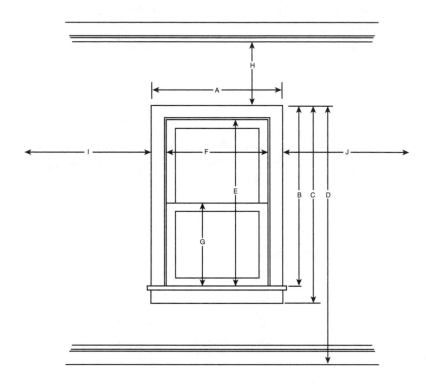

To measure lengths, do the following:

A. Measure the width of the window from casing to casing.

B. Measure the length of the window from the top of the casing to the top of the sill.

C. Measure from the top of the window to the bottom of the sill.

D. Measure from the top of the window to the floor.

E. Measure the inside of the window from the sash to the top of the sill.

F. Measure the inside of the window from jamb to jamb.

G. Measure the lower portion of the window from the top of the lower sash (if there is one) to the top of the sill.

H. Measure from the top of the window to the ceiling or ceiling molding.

I. Measure the wall area from outside of the left casing to any obstruction, such as a radiator, corner of the walls, or another window. (If there are any light switches, draw them on your illustration.)

J. Measure the wall area from the outside of the right casing to any obstruction, such as a radiator, corner of the walls, or another window. (If there are any light switches, draw them on your illustration.)

Note that if a rod is present, you will need to measure the width of the rod and how far it projects (returns). All lengths are measured from the top of the rod to the desired length, unless it is a rod with rings. In that case, measure from the bottom of the rings.

The Least You Need to Know

➤ Windows and their decorative treatment can be a design focus in any room, lending drama or coordinating other furnishings and surfaces.

➤ Window dressings include many styles of drapes and curtains, and such dressings "extras" as trims and tiebacks, valances and cornices, and linings.

➤ Simpler window elements that provide light control, privacy, and decorative effect include shades, blinds, and shutters—all of which come in a wide range of styles and materials.

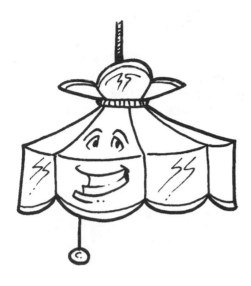

Chapter 14

Lighting Up Your Life

In This Chapter

➤ Flipping a switch for activities and atmosphere

➤ The three purposes of lighting in every living space

➤ Fixtures fit the purpose—and your individual fashion

➤ Brightness, color, and cost: choosing different light bulbs

In our high-tech age, lighting your home when the sun goes down has never been easier—in fact, it's as easy as flipping a switch (in "smart" houses, that can happen automatically when you walk into a room!). And there are certainly more kinds of lights and switches to choose from than ever before.

But lighting isn't only for illuminating dark rooms; it is the stage lighting for the daily drama of our lives. Interior lighting creates moods and atmosphere, emphasizes room areas of importance, and highlights prized possessions. And selecting the best interior lighting for both practical illumination and as a powerful decorating tool isn't automatic.

You need to develop a lighting plan for each room that serves your lifestyle and complements your personal decorating style. The first step is to note the activities that are performed there, the ambiance you want to create, and the activity "zones" or decorative elements you want to spotlight. You need to define the type of lighting you need, and then select the style of lighting fixture and bulb that fits the lighting purpose and enhances the character of the room.

What Do You Want to See? The Three Types of Lighting

With all the practical and decorative roles that lighting plays, you can organize your lighting plan into the three types described by the American Lighting Association: *general, task,* and *accent lighting.* Most spaces will incorporate all three types, working together to optimally light your home.

General Lighting

This is a home's basic replacement for sunlight: It's the overall illumination for regular activity at nighttime. General, or ambient, lighting provides a comfortable level of brightness, allowing adequate vision to safely function in a room. It is usually produced by ceiling- or wall-mounted fixtures, in the specific form of chandeliers, recessed lighting, or track lights. General lighting is fundamental to a lighting plan.

Task Lighting

This is the illumination assigned to help you conduct specific tasks such as reading, cooking, performing hobbies, or playing games. More focused than general lighting, this should be bright enough to prevent eyestrain and should be free of distracting glare and shadows. Varying with the kind of task or activity it serves, this lighting can be provided by recessed and track lighting, pendant (hanging) lighting, and portable lamps.

Expert Advice

With imagination and a little know-how, lamps can be made from a variety of bottles, vases, or jugs. An adapter kit with instructions is available at most lighting supply stores.

Task lighting can often be adjustable lighting that can be positioned directly on the work at hand. And the brightness levels can vary with different tasks. For instance, the area and amount of light you need to read alone is different than the amount you need to play a card game with four or more people around a table.

Accent Lighting

This is an important type of lighting for decorating, because it focuses on elements of visual interest, emphasizing the aesthetics of a room. Accent lighting can spotlight paintings, houseplants, sculpture, and other prized possessions, or it can emphasize the stylish texture of a wall, drapery, or outdoor landscaping. These focal points add to the drama of a room.

To be effective, accent lighting requires at least three times as much light on the focal point as the room's ambient lighting provides. It usually comes from track or recessed fixtures on a ceiling, or wall-mounted fixtures. Traditional picture lights and spot-lights are common accent lighting fixtures.

Fixtures: The Many Sources and Shapes of Lighting

When you know the types of illumination you need in a room, you can begin to choose fixtures. Your lighting plan will probably combine at least two or all three lighting types. Now you must consider the quality of light a fixture gives off and its aesthetic appearance. This will be fun! Lighting fixtures come in all forms, materials, sizes, and textures to suit your personal taste. Following are the general categories of fixtures.

Interiors 101

Opaque shades direct light in one direction. Translucent materials diffuse light in several directions.

Portable Free-Standing Lamps

These are fixtures such as table lamps and floor lamps used for generalized task lighting. They give you the flexibility to move light wherever you need it and do not require any effort to install beyond just plugging in. Some require conventional shades that are integral to the function and beauty of the lamp. From reproduction to modern, rustic to chrome, portable lamps come in all styles to suit any decor.

A lamp's beauty can be sabotaged by an improperly scaled shade. Take your lamp base with you to a lighting store to try the shade with the lamp.

Some classic portable lamps for beauty and function.

Chinese vase table lamp

Classic three-candle branched lamp

Floor lamp

Desk lamp

131

Ceiling Fixtures

Pendant—or hanging from the ceiling—lighting provides task and general illumination. Covered with shades or globes to prevent glare, they are suspended from the ceiling over small kitchen tables or counters, game tables, and work areas. Small pendants can be used in groups of two or three for sufficient light and a decorative effect.

Chandeliers are the most decorative pendant fixtures and also the most decorative kind of light. Suspended from the ceiling, usually in entryways or over dining tables, chandeliers provide ambient lighting. The quality of light will vary with the number of bulbs used and whether the bulbs are shaded. Care should be taken when choosing a chandelier, as it is a room's dramatic focal point. The use of a dimmer control allows you to vary the light to suit the occasion and create different moods.

A truly decorative and functional chandelier.

Basic ceiling fixtures that are a single globe or several small globes that attach close to the ceiling provide general lighting and are practical in busy areas such as hallways, bedrooms, kitchens, baths, and laundry rooms.

Decorator's Diary

My client Jill and I chose a beautiful chandelier for her dining room. Since she used the room only at night for entertaining, we decided to hire an electrician to "de-electrify" the fixture so that she could use candles for ambient lighting instead of bulbs.

Downlights are fixtures that are inconspicuously mounted into ceilings and cast light directly "down" on a surface. They can provide all three types of lighting, especially task lighting, and so are often placed over kitchen counters or work surfaces. As accent illumination, downlights can add punctuation by emphasizing a particular section of a room. They are ideal for low ceiling areas where pendant lighting would be inappropriate.

Spotlights can be recessed into ceilings, mounted on tracks, wall-mounted, or used individually with clips. For accent lighting, spotlights are usually adjustable, so they can focus on specific areas. Some have a cover to disguise the bulb, and others have exposed bulbs. Bulbs should be chosen not only for aesthetic reasons but to cast light appropriately for your needs, in a narrow beam or over a wide area.

Track lighting provides a flexible arrangement of spotlights and downlights attached to a track mounted on a ceiling. General, task, and accent lighting can all be incorporated into one unit. You can swivel, rotate, or aim the individual fixtures in any direction. Tracks can be open or enclosed: Open tracks allow the fixtures to be moved but are more difficult to clean. Installation of track lighting is inexpensive compared to installing fixtures that require extensive electrical work.

Wall-Mounted Fixtures

Wall-mounted lights are generally used to provide ambient lighting in hallways, entries, and stairways or to supplement other room lighting. They are available in traditional candle-like shapes or modern half-sphere or cone shapes called *sconces*.

Uplights direct light at the ceiling or wall and "bathe" a surface with soft illumination. Many uplights attach directly to the wall, but some are placed directly on the floor (in a can-like fixture) to create shadows among groups of plants, light up a dark corner, or shine on glass shelving.

Lighting fixtures.

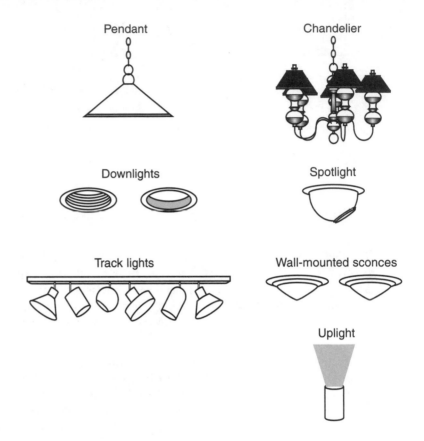

Pendant

Chandelier

Downlights

Spotlight

Track lights

Wall-mounted sconces

Uplight

Selecting the Source: Types of Bulbs

The ultimate impact of any light fixture depends very much on the essential light source—the bulb. The brightness of the light and its quality—its color and "warmth" or "coolness"—will vary with the bulb choice you make.

> ➤ **Incandescent bulbs.** These are the most common light bulbs and are available in two types: general-service and reflectorized. General-service bulbs are inexpensive and come in a variety of wattages and shapes. They produce a yellowish-white light that is emitted in all directions, suitable for general lighting in table, floor, and pendant fixtures. They are available in clear or frosted bulbs, which give a more diffused light. In general, incandescent bulbs are inexpensive but need frequent changing. They also emit heat and are not as energy-efficient as halogen bulbs.

> ➤ **Reflectorized bulbs.** Incandescent bulbs that use a reflective coating inside the bulb. The coating directs light forward, giving you better beam control than general-service bulbs. Floodlights spread light and spotlights concentrate light.

Reflectorized bulbs can put approximately double the amount of light (measured in foot-candles) on a subject as can a general-service bulb of the same wattage.

➤ **Tungsten-halogen bulbs.** These bulbs produce a bright, white light. They have a longer life and provide more light (lumens) per watt than incandescent bulbs, but are more expensive.

➤ **Fluorescent bulbs.** This is a common type of bulb that often casts a bluish light, which changes the appearance of colors in a room. "Warm white" fluorescent bulbs are available that emit light similar to incandescent bulbs. The initial purchase of fluorescent bulbs is expensive, but these bulbs use one third to one fifth as much electricity as incandescents and last up to 20 times longer. Compact fluorescent bulbs, which can be used in conventional fixtures, are great for energy-efficient residential use. All fluorescent bulbs are cool to the touch.

Designer's Dictionary

Wattage is the amount of electricity consumed by a bulb. **Lumens** are the amount of light that a bulb produces. **Foot-candles** are the amount of light reaching a subject.

Where to Place Your Lighting Fixtures

Getting the most out of your chosen lighting fixtures means placing them in the optimal position for their lighting purpose. Use the following guidelines when situating your fixtures:

➤ **Table and floor lamps used for reading.** The bottom of the shade should be placed slightly below eye level when you are seated: approximately 40 to 42 inches above the floor. If the lighting is above your eye level, the lamp should be placed about 10 inches behind your shoulder, at a minimum of 47 inches from the floor to the bottom of the shade.

➤ **Pendant fixtures for task lighting.** The height of the fixtures can vary. Place them about 30 inches above a dining table top and 36 inches above a game table top.

Interiors 101

According to the American Lighting Association, using dimmer switches has many advantages. You can ...

➤ Lower light levels to conserve energy and increase bulb life.

➤ Vary the mood of a room.

➤ Alter the intensity of the light to suit the activity.

➤ Create and save a number of different lighting schemes in each room.

➤ **Wall-mounted fixtures.** These are usually placed above eye level and do not protrude more than 4 inches, unless they are more than 80 inches above the floor.

➤ **Down lights.** These should be placed approximately 24 to 36 inches apart.

➤ **Track lighting for accent lighting of wall objects.** It is most effective to aim fixtures at a 30-degree angle. Refer to the following distance chart to figure out where to mount the track:

A to B Distance	B to C Distance
13 inches	2 feet
20 inches	3 feet
27 inches	4 feet
34 inches	5 feet
41 inches	6 feet

For example, the distance from the ceiling to the center of the painting is 4 feet. Mount the track on the ceiling 27 inches away from the wall.

The angle for mounting track lighting.

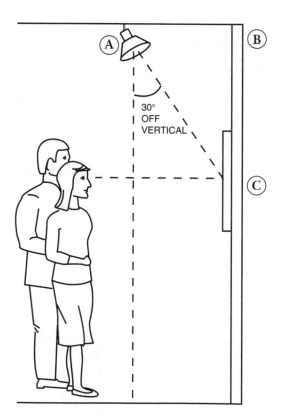

There are literally thousands of lighting options, and it's fun to explore them. Check out lighting showrooms as well as home stores and mail-order sources for new ideas and lamp styles. A final word on lighting: We live in an electric era, but the most pleasing light for certain occasions still comes from ancient sources, like candles and lanterns. Light your dinnertimes and intimate moments with these. You will have more fun and save on your energy bills, too!

The Least You Need to Know

➤ Adequate lighting is both a critical resource for functional rooms and a powerful element of decorating.

➤ A lighting plan for each room determines the type of lighting needed and the fixtures that will enhance the room's decorative style.

➤ The three types of lighting are general, task, and accent lighting. Most spaces need light for a combination of purposes.

➤ Lighting fixtures come in several forms—portable and free-standing, ceiling-mounted and wall-mounted—and within each form, there are fixtures for every style of decor.

➤ The choice of bulbs must be made to produce the amount and quality of light needed to serve the lighting purpose.

➤ Follow some simple placement guidelines to achieve the optimal lighting effect from different fixtures.

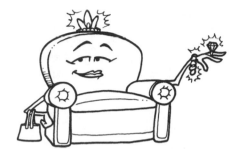

Chapter 15

The All-Important Accessories

> **In This Chapter**
>
> ➤ Accessories are the "jewelry" of a well-dressed room
>
> ➤ The design principles that guide accessory display
>
> ➤ Collections that catch the eye
>
> ➤ Plants and flowers: natural choices for every room
>
> ➤ Pictures and wall hangings: art at the heart of your home

You have to make many big decisions as you design your home: paint color, flooring material, fabric for the sofa, window dressings, lighting fixtures. And with each decision, you are establishing a decorating plan that's comfortable and well coordinated. But in the end, it is with the addition of accessories—small objects, chosen thoughtfully and artfully displayed—that you finish a room with your personal touch. It is much like the small, elegant brooch that visually completes a gorgeous evening ensemble: It draws all the compliments.

Brass tools that frame a fireplace, a pillow with a ball fringe, a spray of fresh flowers—these are the accessories that make the room. You can go for a clean, minimal look with just a few choice pieces, carefully selected and judiciously placed. Or you might go all out for a cozy atmosphere, offering many objects and collections in a warm, generous, and visually interesting display.

Be sophisticated in a lasting way: Accessories shouldn't be trendy items that go out of style and date your decor. And instant collections are not nearly as interesting as treasure troves that evolve mixes of old and new, valuable and priceless memorabilia. Accessories are your most intimate statement in the room: Make it passionate!

The Art of Display: Avoiding Clutter and Distraction

Coordinating, grouping, and displaying accessories throughout your home is an art in itself. All of the elements of design that you learned in the previous chapters come into play. Whether you go for a modern or traditional look, successful display considers color, texture, balance, and proportion. There's an added element, too, as theme can be an important coordinator of accessories.

Color, of course, can be a common visual connection if you are arranging unrelated and otherwise dissimilar accessory items. For instance, red quilts and a red area rug make a powerful punctuation to a bedroom. Texture can do the same: Similarly textured porcelain jars, even in different sizes and patterns, make a unified and interesting display.

Expert Advice

You don't need to show off Fabergé eggs! Even items that are not high in value can make a fun and unexpected display. For instance, small vintage pocketbooks arranged around a bedroom vanity will make an eye-catching display. Or balls of colored yarn arranged in a basket, wreaths placed three in a row on a wall, or jars filled with beach sand—all make a statement, without much cost.

Remember balance and proportion, too. The "visual weights" of your objects must balance within the display. The shapes and sizes of objects must be in proportion to each other and the whole display must be in proportion to the space or surface it occupies. Also, although symmetrical displays are easier to arrange, consider that asymmetrical displays are often more interesting and exciting. There's a lot to think about!

Use thematic displays to arrange objects of the same type, color, or shape. Small objects (stones, butterflies, bottles, toy soldiers) should be displayed together, perhaps in a case with a glass front or on wall-mounted shelves. When scattered throughout a room, they lose their impact as a collection and as a decorative element.

Large pieces of sculpture or pottery can stand alone on a floor or be mounted on bases of stone or wood. But theme works with large objects, too. If large pieces are related in subject or texture, grouping them together makes a particularly strong statement.

The symmetrical arrangement of china on the upper shelves is balanced by the asymmetrical display of accessories on the lower shelves.

(Photo by Smallbone)

A horse enthusiast prominently displays a collection of prized ribbons and statues over the fireplace mantel.

(Photo by Gear)

Flowers and Plants: Borrowing from Mother Nature's Jewelry Box

Bring the garden into your home with plants and freshly cut flowers, accessories that are appropriate for any style of decor. Living plants and fresh flowers soften hard lines in a room and add wonderful focal points. And they fill empty spaces with unbeatable color and liveliness.

141

For the best effect with plant displays, group small ones together and balance tall and thin plants with short and bushy ones. Consider containers as well, balancing color and texture. Plants can grace many interior spots: Use a pair to flank the bottom of a staircase, or place a plant in an entryway or on a console table. You can hang a plant from a hook at the top of a window to add color. With a large and tall plant, set it on a plant stand and use it to fill a corner of a room with height and color.

To display fresh-cut flowers, consider the area where your arrangement will be placed, the colors you need, and whether it should be casual or formal. Keep everything in scale: The space will help you determine the container's size and shape. And the container will determine the scale of the arrangement. Tall, geometric vases call for arrangements with height; low, shallow bowls allow flowers to spread out.

The style of your home will dictate the way you put the flowers together. Formal interiors may call for formal arrangements that require particular materials, time, and a bit of finesse. But remember that casual arrangements can balance the stiffness of a formal room with unexpected natural charm. Casually bunched flowers naturally match relaxed interiors. They are easy to arrange and usually are lower in cost. For maximum versatility to bring flowers into your rooms, it's a good idea to have many shapes and sizes of vases in varying textures. Also, some of the most stunning arrangements are flowers of one type in generous bunches. Choosing two colors of the same type also works well, such as green and yellow, pink and purple, red and orange, or yellow and orange. If you refer back to Chapter 4, "Color: The Decorator's Most Powerful Tool," you can apply all the same rules of color and decoration to flowers!

Expert Advice

Fresh flowers can be an important color element in a room. You might contrast your flowers with the room colors—for instance, with green walls, you'll use pink or red flowers. Or go for an all-white arrangement with lovely greenery. Consider taking a class to learn the true art of flower arranging. For more information, contact your local garden club.

Wall Hangings Bring Large Surfaces to Life

Old textiles, rugs, quilts, or unique materials hung on walls offer fabulous decorative visuals for large areas. A wall hanging adds a soft texture to a room and can be a great coverup for blemished walls. If antique rugs or quilts are not in your budget, you can use several yards of contemporary fabrics (refer to Chapter 12, "It's a Material World"). Hang your fabric from clip-on curtain hardware, and attach the hardware to nails on a wall. It'll make a perfect wall accessory, especially if you do not own art or pictures.

If you want to pin up memorabilia like cards and pictures, free-standing fabric-covered panel screens are perfect.

A bold and colorful patterned fabric wraps this chair in a lively personality.

(Photo by Lee Industries)

The delicate wall mural of birds and trees brings a realistic outdoor image inside this pretty bedroom.

(Photo by Laura Ashley)

A colorful chintz, bold tapestry, and luxurious damask.

(Photo by Schumacher)

Accessories of porcelain vases, flowers, a picture frame, and fruit form a still-life scene on this living room end table.

(Photo by Brunswig & Fils)

This exquisite handmade "pot board" dresser conceals household paraphernalia behind paneled doors and drawers and has open shelves for displaying cups and plates, baskets, and books.

(Photo by Smallbone)

Loose denim slipcovers match this rustic living room setting.

(Photo by Lee Industries)

Light painted cabinets contrast beautifully with the natural wood floors, table, and countertop edges.

(Photo by Smallbone)

A bathroom window dressed with a floral festoon valance and lace panel softens the lines of the detailed woodwork and tile floor and walls.

(Photo by Smallbone)

An elaborately dressed four-poster bed and custom wall units add traditional luxury to a bedroom.

Primary colors, a parrot motif, and a "tent" canopy enliven this child's bedroom.

(Photo by Laura Ashley)

A little girl's pink-and-white room decorated with her favorite ballet motif.

A young girl's vision of dress-up: A dressing area wall-covered in hats with feathers and big bows, stylish handbags, and hatboxes, all surrounded with beautiful ribbons.

A young boy's room wall-covered in a light-hearted design of a "mariner's map."

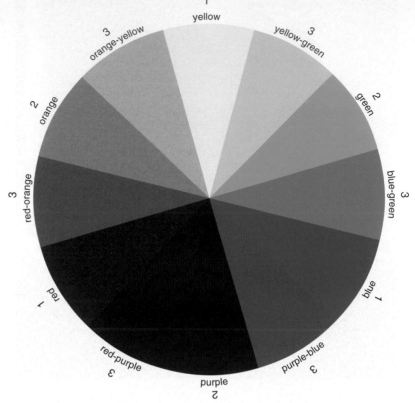

A color wheel showing primary (1), secondary (2), and tertiary (3) hues.

Displaying Pictures: Your Personal Art Gallery

Hanging pictures on walls can be daunting, especially when you have many pictures of different sizes, and with different mats and frames. Consider the following guidelines the next time you take out your hammer and nails. You'll get the most attention for the pictures and the best effect for your room.

➤ Unify a mismatched collection of prints with the same mat and frame.

➤ Group pictures together instead of scattering them around a room.

➤ Hang several small, identical frames close together to make one large "picture" over a sofa.

➤ For symmetrical arrangements, hang similar sizes and frames in rows, either vertically or horizontally (for example, a group of eight frames hung in two rows of four; a group of six frames hung in three rows of two; or a group of three, with two smaller pictures flanking one large picture).

➤ Asymmetrical arrangements often place the largest picture to one side, and smaller ones are arranged together on the other side to balance out the display.

➤ Just because you're tall doesn't mean you should hang pictures high. Conversely, if you are short, do not hang them too low. Consider the proportions of the picture and the wall surface area as well as the surrounding furnishings. From the bottom of the picture frame, measure six to eight inches above a mantel, sofa back, or table. This is only a guideline. You also have to consider other accessories, the size of your frames, and the size of the piece over which the picture is being hung.

➤ Horizontally arranged pictures make walls look longer. Vertically arranged pictures make walls look higher.

Interiors 101

Oil paintings often look just fine without frames, and some pictures, with or without frames, don't need to be hung on a wall. You can casually rest them, singly or in groups, atop a table or mantel and lean them against a wall.

Expert Advice

A framed mirror, properly placed, can add the illusion of space to a room. For the most dramatic effect, hang the mirror opposite a window or other outside view.

Decorator's Diary

Remember to put **accent lighting** on your displays (see Chapter 14, "Lighting Up Your Life," for more information about lighting). Spotlights can highlight special wall art, and **uplights** can add atmosphere as they shine through a grouping of plants or emphasize the texture of a wall. My client Sam had a wonderful collection of black-and-white photos of his grandfather's fishing expeditions. I had him mat and frame them in identical simple frames and hang them in rows in his long hallway, gallery style. We mounted spotlights on the opposite wall to emphasize them at night. Although the pictures were valuable only to Sam, the gallery was priceless and a constant source of conversation at all of his gatherings.

Accessories by their very nature are among the easiest decorative elements to change. You can quickly revive interest in a room by giving it fresh accents. Put new artwork into the wall spaces that you have spotlighted; display photographs and memorabilia of your most recent trips; find some jazzy slipcovers for your sofa pillows; find a new plant that will thrive near a sunny window. All of these small transformations will add a spark to the life of a room.

The Least You Need to Know

➤ Like clothing accessories, decorative accessories are the finishing touches to a room with style. They should be carefully selected and displayed. DON'T CLUTTER!

➤ Accessory displays should be guided by the design principles of color, texture, balance, proportion, and theme.

➤ Collections can be eclectic and inexpensive, as long as they are artfully displayed.

➤ Plants and fresh flowers are suitable accessories for any room.

➤ Follow design principles when accessorizing walls. Fabric wall hangings can enliven large walls.

➤ Hanging your pictures in different groupings can heighten the impact of your art collection.

Part 4

Tackling the House Room by Room

Pretty comfortable with your personal style? Confident with color, texture, and other principles of design? Certain about where you want to put your decorating talent to work—and how much money you have to work with? If you answered yes to these questions, you are ready to tackle a room for real.

In the following chapters, we discuss in detail all the elements that you, as a decorator, will need to consider in each room in your home. The general challenges are the same: Which furnishings are necessary and what arrangements maximize their utility, what the lighting needs of the room are, and how you can enliven the space with accessories. But each room also presents special possibilities, problems, and opportunities to make it a personal statement.

These chapters are where you will find the Master Planning Lists that we introduced in Chapter 2. Each list is a comprehensive guide to the typical projects and furnishings you'll want to consider for each room. We encourage you to use these lists to plan and prioritize a successful and affordable project.

Chapter 16

Living Rooms to Actually Live In

In This Chapter

➤ Today's living room—a multipurpose activity center

➤ Furniture placement begins with a focal point

➤ Smart seating

➤ Lighting the living room

➤ Storage strategies for all those artifacts

As the place where families "withdrew" after dinner, a living room used to be the best-dressed room in the house, with formal decor and atmosphere. Today, your living room probably serves as a family and activity room as well as a place to entertain guests—it's the daily site where you read, listen to music, watch TV, play games, and celebrate special occasions.

Today's living room, then, has to be decorated and arranged for both aesthetics and practical use. Furniture must be comfortable and fabrics must be durable. Room arrangements must be set up for easy conversation and good traffic flow, and to accommodate a variety of activities. Appropriate lighting must add to the comfort and mood of the room. Furniture chosen with storage in mind can help to efficiently organize books, games, hobbies, and even hide toys and media equipment. And wall storage units can have built-in display shelves for collections and other accessories that add a personal touch. In this chapter you'll learn how to create a living room that you can actually live in and enjoy every day—not just on special occasions.

Finding the Focus: Furniture Placement in the Living Room

How do you arrange a living room that you can actually live in? The best place to start is with an attractive visual focal point. It could be a naturally beautiful piece such as a fireplace, a piano, or a tall, antique *armoire*—or even a spectacular window view. You might need to create your own focal point from an object that's less obvious. Maybe you have a great rug, a beautiful mirror, an extensive collection, or a large coffee table.

Designer's Dictionary

Armoire is the French term for a large, free-standing wooden wardrobe used as storage for clothing and linen. Today, armoires can be a wonderful antique hiding place for high-tech multimedia equipment!

Interiors 101

Mario Buatta, a prominent interior designer, is quoted as saying, "I like all the chairs to talk to one another and to the sofas and not those parlor-car arrangements that create two Siberias."

Group different types of furniture of various shapes and sizes around the focal point. Balance large sofas with a couple of smaller chairs, or flank a fireplace or a large armoire with two small loveseats. Have enough seating for six to eight people. For larger gatherings, supplement seating with small moveable chairs placed about the house (entryway, hallways, dining area). Comfortable sofas and armchairs arranged around a focal point are the beginnings of a working living room.

Another principle of seating arrangements is to place your furniture so there's ample room to pass through openings. This makes it easy and inviting for people to reach seating areas and promotes a free flow of conversation. This also gives the room an appearance that is "comfortable" to your eye—that is, an open and inviting look, without barriers or narrow passages.

While it facilitates movement, seating, and conversation, your arrangement must also allow several activities to be enjoyed at the same time. Chairs and sofas must be placed to accommodate a group that wants to converse and permit an individual to read, do needlework, write, and so on. For instance, a chair and ottoman placed in a corner is a great place to put up your feet and relax with a book. Add a small table for a drink, a floor lamp, and—voilà—a private niche away from the main activity area is created. As you can see, your preferred activities will dictate some of your furniture selections and their placement.

All seating should have occasional tables close by for drinks or books. End tables can be chests or bureaus to display accessories and hold table lamps. Coffee tables can be small or overscaled, low, or tea-table height. Large, low coffee tables are useful for displaying large books or subbing as a dining table for an impromptu dinner. A tea table is higher than seating level and can be a nice contrast when the rest of the pieces are the same height. And yes, tea or drinks can be served easily from a higher table. Sofa tables or desks can be arranged behind the length of a sofa to hold lamps, books, and accessories. A desk or sofa table can also be placed against a wall with artwork or mirrors.

If you have a fireplace, think of it as a perfect focal point and a great decorative element in itself. Decorative tiles or Vermont verde antique marble used to frame the opening adds color and texture. The mantel provides an area for creative displays of art, candles, flowers, clocks, or small collections.

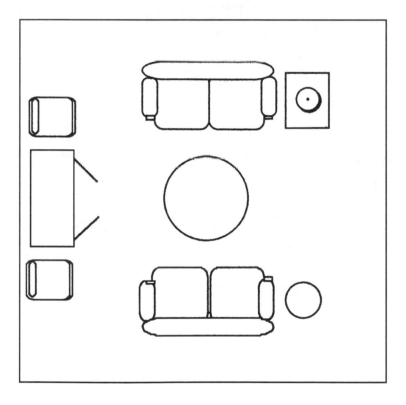

Two low loveseats balance the height of an armoire. TV is easily viewed when the armoire doors are opened.

The table placed behind the sofa doubles as a desk and holds two small lamps that provide light and decoration.

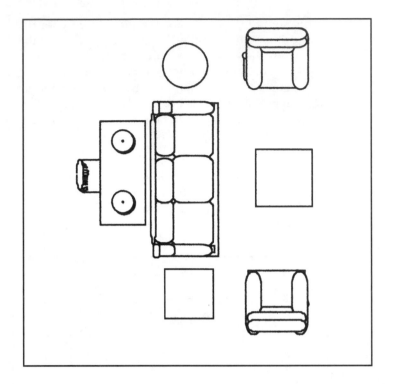

A small living room might benefit from seating placed in a circular arrangement that offers a big fashion statement.

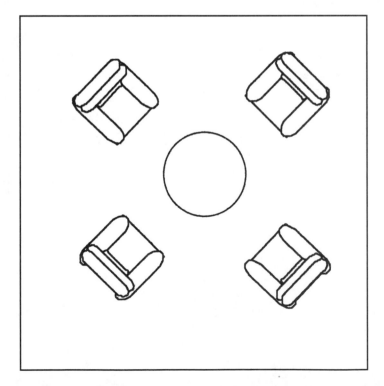

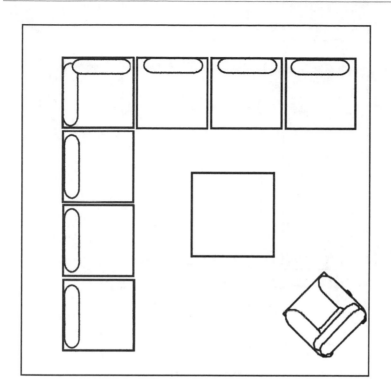

A large, square coffee table is useful to all the modular seating as well as the armchair.

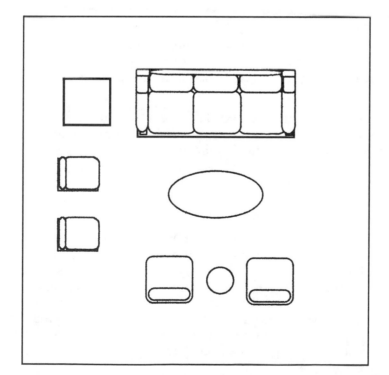

This formal arrangement allows plenty of seating and tables for drinks or books.

More than one size and shape of coffee tables adds visual interest and can serve separate functions. The large chair and ottoman provide a space to put up your feet and relax.

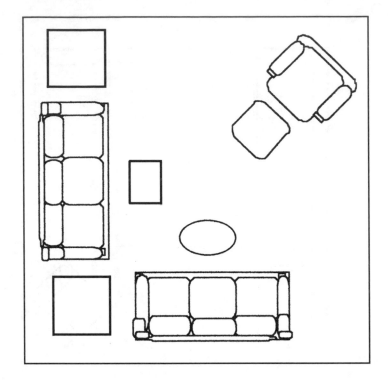

Lighting for Living

Loads of natural light make a living room a pleasure during the day, but living rooms that do not have good daylight or are used in the evening need proper lighting. All three types of lighting—general, task, and accent—should be incorporated into your living room plan.

General lighting will provide background lighting and may be a combination of lights. A single overhead fixture should be supplemented with wall or mounted lights or up-lights that are hidden by plants and accessories. A choice of several downlights and sconces provides eye-pleasing background lighting. The sconces can add a decorative effect as well. Track lighting can be angled to light walls to add visual space to your living room or spotlight favorite accessories. It is best to place all of your background lighting on dimmer switches to vary the mood to suit the occasion.

Task lighting can be provided by table, floor, and desk lamps. These types of lamps also provide decoration with their particular shapes, textures, and styles. No other lighting can quite replace the aesthetic beauty of a table lamp and shade or the light that it casts. If you think of your table lamps as art accessories, you will take time and care to coordinate them into your lighting plan and your decor. For added style, use fabric-covered shades and be sure your lamps have three-way switches for varying the degrees of light and changing the mood. You can also vary the light with glass shades for a floor lamp and use a colored or frosted shade on a desk lamp.

Accent lighting highlights prized artwork, collections, or wall hangings. Ceiling-mounted spotlights, track lights, or picture lights work well. Review Chapter 14, "Lighting Up Your Life," to rethink all your options.

Behind Closed Doors: Storage Strategies for Uncluttered Living Rooms

Since many living areas double as family rooms, storage is of critical importance to maintain neatness and order. Cabinetry that can hold and hide TVs, VCRs, and CDs is a godsend. Many are available in sleek, unornamented styles with bookshelves attached, forming a single wall unit. Reproduction or rustic cupboards fitted for TV and stereo cords are quite attractive for decorative as well as functional purposes.

Expert Advice

For a plain table lamp that needs detail, attach a small tasseled fringe to the bottom of the shade with a glue gun.

Games, needlework, magazines, and toys can be hidden in built-in storage units like windowseats that lift up or behind doors that are fitted to the bottom of shelves. Bookshelves that surround a doorway offer architectural structure as well as organizers for books and showcases for china, candlesticks, clocks, pictures, or pottery. Glass shelves placed in windows can hold colored-glass collections that sparkle when sunlight shines through.

There are some stylish *ottomans* (large footstools) that lift open for blanket storage. And trunks serve a dual purpose when used for coffee tables or end tables. An idea for more storage is to cover a 36-inch round table with a skirt for both storage and display.

This living room plan allows for playing music, reading or relaxing by the fire, and having an easy conversation because of its comfortable and decorative arrangement.

(Photo by Lee Industries)

The central coffee table can be accessed from each seat in this contemporary living room plan.

(Photo by Cassina)

Decorator's Diary

Old footstools can easily be renovated with minimal material and labor. I once covered an old tiny stool with exposed legs in a leopard print and trimmed it with long, antique fringe. It was my favorite accent piece in my client Francie's living room.

Striped wall covering, floral draperies, and checked pillows add interesting patterns and textures to this comfortably arranged living room.

(Photo by Laura Ashley)

This large ottoman triples as seating, a coffee table, and an extra bed, as shown here.

(Photos by Lee Industries)

Using the Master Planning List: Prioritizing and Pricing Your Living Room Projects

As you learned in Chapter 2, "From Castles in the Air to Down-to-Earth Decorating," the key to successful and affordable room decoration is prioritizing the many decorating possibilities in each room, using the following master list. If you forgot the points discussed in Chapter 2 (or have never even read the chapter!), this is a good time to go back and review it. Then you'll be able to make a realistic plan for your living room without losing your sanity or your kid's college tuition.

Here's a brief review of how to use the master list, which is an outline of all the jobs, furnishings, and enhancements suitable for most living rooms:

➤ Evaluate the state of your living room, using the master list as a guide. Repairs are always the top priority. Go through the master list and write down your answers next to each item that pertains to your situation.

➤ Refer to the personal inventory that you made in Chapter 1, "You've Got Style: Flaunt It!" to fill in the appropriate places, checking off the possessions you have and the ones that you need and want. Remember to build your list around items that you love.

➤ Prioritize: The master list is arranged in a general order of priorities, but you can adjust items according to your situation.

➤ Price your priorities: Get accurate price estimates for every item on your proposed list by consulting contractors, department and home stores, mail-order catalogs, and other resources. Total up the estimated cost for all your living room projects.

➤ Match your plans with your resources: If your total cost falls 20 to 30 percent over your budget, eliminate the lower-priority items. If you are more than 30 percent over your budget, review your planning approach thoroughly. You may need to consider an entirely different—low-cost and short-term—approach to fixing up the room.

Living Room Master Planning List

Priority	Project/Purchase	Comment	Estimated Price
Contractors			
___	Electrician	_____	____
___	Plumber/heat	_____	____
___	Flooring person	_____	____

Priority	Project/Purchase	Comment	Estimated Price
Contractors, continued			
___	Painter	_____	___
___	Carpenter	_____	___
Lighting			
___	Ceiling fixtures	_____	___
___	Table/floor lamps	_____	___
___	Wall lights	_____	___
___	Uplights	_____	___
Furniture			
___ ___ ___	Sofas (slipcovers, upholstery)	_____	___
___ ___ ___	Loveseats (slipcovers, upholstery)	_____	___
___ ___ ___	Armchairs (slipcovers, upholstery)	_____	___
___ ___ ___	Chaise (slipcovers, upholstery)	_____	___
___ ___ ___	Ottomans (slipcovers, upholstery)	_____	___
___	Side chairs	_____	___
___	Armoire	_____	___
___	Wall/shelving units	_____	___
___	Desk/secretary	_____	___
___	Highboys	_____	___
___	Chests	_____	___
___	Sofa/library table	_____	___
___	Coffee tables	_____	___
___	End tables	_____	___
___	Game table	_____	___
___	Piano	_____	___
___	Misc.	_____	___

continues

Living Room Master Planning List   (continued)

Priority	Project/Purchase	Comment	Estimated Price
Floor			
___	Wood	_____	____
___	Stone/tile	_____	____
___	Carpet	_____	____
___	Area rugs	_____	____
Windows			
___	Draperies	_____	____
___	Shutters/blinds	_____	____
___	Shades	_____	____
Accessories			
___	Small footstools	_____	____
___	Pillows/trims	_____	____
___	Decorative lampshades	_____	____
___	Art/pictures	_____	____
___	Mirrors	_____	____
___	Clocks	_____	____
___	Decorative sconces	_____	____
___	Folding screens	_____	____
___	Wall hangings	_____	____
___	Plants/flowers	_____	____
___	Collections	_____	____

The Least You Need to Know

➤ Most living rooms today serve many functions, and the room furnishings and arrangements must allow a free flow of activity.

➤ Finding an aesthetic or thematic focal point in the room is the first step in determining living room furniture placement.

➤ Seating arrangements in the living room should allow conversation among a large group of people as well as more private areas.

➤ Lighting in a living room should be multifaceted and adjustable, with dimmers, permitting a variety of uses and moods.

➤ Accommodate activity material, audio and video entertainment equipment, and the display of accessories.

Chapter 17

Dining Rooms That Whet Your Appetite

In This Chapter

➤ Formal or casual: dining rooms for festivities

➤ Tables and chairs with style and comfort

➤ Enough room for furniture—and guests, too!

➤ Lighting to set the mood for meals

➤ Display and storage for all your finery

➤ Accenting your dining room with accessories

➤ Your Master Planning List

Whether it's a lazy Sunday morning around a table spread with newspapers or an Easter afternoon crowded with cousins, a dining room is the natural place for family gatherings and traditional celebrations as well as for everyday eating.

As it is the special-occasion space in your home, you will want to grace your dining room with your finest accessories: your best china, silverware, linens, and furnishings. The formal stiffness of dining rooms in earlier eras, however, has given way to the more relaxed style of contemporary eating and entertaining. In many homes today, the dining area might be part of the "great room"—a living room–dining room combination—or it might be part of a kitchen or other dual-purpose space.

Whatever space is devoted to the dining area, you will want to decorate it with a focus on comfort and festivity. Well-chosen tables and chairs are the basics, with enough space to sit and move around comfortably. Proper lighting will enhance the ambiance for day and evening dining. Pieces that store linens, silverware, and china will organize the room and display the cherished items that make a meal memorable. And most of all, a truly successful dining room is decorated with your personal style, conducive to memorable conversations and feasts with family and friends.

Dining Room Furnishings: Comfort Is More Important Than Matching

Of course, the literal center of your dining room will be taken up with a table and chairs. Whether they are made to match or come from different styles and materials, the table and chairs must work together, both aesthetically and to allow comfortable seating and eating. You will learn more about proper spacing in the following section. Here's a guide to some common dining room table and chair types.

Expert Advice

To add seating to a small table, have a circular piece of plywood cut to the circumference needed. Place the wood on top of the existing table, and cover it with cloth. When it's not in use, you can store the plywood, along with extra folding chairs.

Tables

Most dining tables are round, oval, rectangular, or square. The size and shape of table best for you is determined by the number of people you want to seat and the size of your room.

Tables can be made of many types of softwood or hardwood and can be finished with paint, stain, or clear varnish. Wood tables are classic choices for most dining areas. Glass tabletops are usually mounted on metal or wood bases. Unusual bases and decorative rugs show through the glass for visual interest. Laminate or ceramic tile-topped tables are often combined with wood trim and bases.

Tables that expand with leaves are very handy to accommodate more people. Drop-leaf tables also work well in small dining areas that occasionally hold a large group. Circular tables are excellent for small rooms, because they take up less space than conventional rectangular or square ones. Circular tables can be fitted with 12-inch to 18-inch leaves to make different oval lengths. If space is truly at a premium, use folding tables that can be put away after use. For large gatherings, use several tables together. Square or rectangular tables work well abutted together for dinner or a buffet. Sometimes two or three small separate tables are perfect for relaxed get-togethers.

You need to make sure your table fits into your available space. The following section contains a table of recommended minimum room sizes for approximate seating needs. When choosing your table, review these minimum table- and room-size requirements to ensure good furniture clearances.

Chairs

Many dining chairs are armless and straight-backed, with wooden, upholstered, or rushed (caned) seats, and are placed at the sides of the table (or, in the case of round tables, placed around the table). Chairs with arms are wider than side chairs and are often placed at the head of the table. Wood chairs, like tables, can be painted, stained, or varnished. Some chairs that are made of wood have upholstered seats or are fully upholstered or slipcovered. Metal-framed chairs often combine wood seats and backs of wood and cane.

Expert Advice

Add extra comfort and style to chairs with a thin cushion that you can cover with fabric, place on the seat, and secure with ties.

A fully upholstered chair for comfortable dining.

(Photo by Lee Industries)

Dining Room Arrangements: No Cramped Knees or Elbows!

As a place for enjoyment and eating, dining rooms need to be functional as well as attractive. Whether you choose a beautifully matched dining room set or a delightfully eclectic mix of furnishings, the room must have ample space for chairs to move back and forth, tables with enough space to hold a place setting and accommodate your guests' knees, and enough space for people to move around the room.

163

Decorator's Diary

I am definitely the type of person who likes to mix dining chairs and tables that are not matched. Blending different styles and woods or materials has led me to some original choices: My dining room has a 72-inch sofa that is placed on one side of the table for seating. Use your imagination, and you can defy convention, too!

Make sure you have enough space for each guest at the table. How much room does one person need at a dining table? A place setting is approximately 14 inches deep by 25 to 27 inches wide. This allows for elbowroom and enough space to accommodate plates, glassware, and silverware.

How many people can sit comfortably at a dining room table? Here are some guidelines:

➤ If you want your dining table to regularly accommodate four people, you will need to have a circular table of at least 39 inches to 42 inches in diameter; a square table of at least 36 inches to 42 inches in diameter; or a rectangular table of 30 × 60 inches.

➤ For six people, you will need a circular table of at least 48 to 52 inches in diameter; a square table of at least 48 inches to 54 inches in diameter; or a rectangular table of at least 30 × 60 inches.

➤ For eight people, you will need a circular table of at least 60 to 72 inches in diameter; a square table of at least 48 to 60 inches in diameter; or a rectangular table of at least 36 × 72 inches.

In addition, you have to make sure your chairs work with your table and with the room space.

➤ Chairs are usually 18 inches from floor to seat height or 12 inches below the table height. The table height should be about 29 to 31 inches. This should place most average-sized people in a comfortable eating position. If many tall people will be seated at the table, be sure the wood panel under the top of the table (apron) isn't so low that your guests cannot cross their legs.

➤ When a person is seated, a chair may project back from the table about 20 inches. For people to be able to stand up and sit down, they need a minimum of 32 to 36 inches from the edge of the table to be able to pull the chair in and out.

➤ For a person to "edge" past a seated person, a minimum of 38 to 40 inches is needed.

➤ Walking past or serving from a tray behind a seated person requires 46 to 48 inches of clear space. Be aware that all side chairs and chairs with arms differ in depth and width measurements, so clearances need to be adjusted after final selection.

➤ Stop kicking me! Tables should be wide enough to allow 20 inches of foot-extension space underneath for all seated persons.

Although all of these measurements may sound confusing, don't get overwhelmed. You can use the following table of measurements to help you meet these table- and room-size requirements.

Some Recommended Minimum Room Sizes for Approximate Seating

Shape	Diameter	Circumference	Approximate Seating	Minimum Room Size
Round	3'6"	11'0"	4–5	10'6" × 10'6"
	4'4"	12'6"	5–6	11'6" × 11'6"
	5'0"	15'9"	7–8	13'0" × 13'0"

Shape	Width	Length	Approximate Seating	Minimum Room Size
Square	3'0"	3'0"	4	9'0" × 9'0"
	3'6"	3'6"	4	10'6" × 10'6"
	4'0"	4'0"	4–8	12'0" × 12'0"
	4'6"	4'6"	4–8	12'0" × 12'0"
	5'0"	5'0"	8–12	13'0" × 13'0"

Shape	Width	Length	Approximate Seating	Minimum Room Size
Rectangular	2'6"	5'0"	4–6	9'0" × 12'0"
	3'0"	6'0"	6–8	10'0" × 13'0"
	3'6"	7'0"	6–8	10'6" × 14'0"
	4'0"	9'6"	8–10	12'0" × 16'0"
	4'0"	11'0"	10–12	12'0" × 19'0"

A dining room for 12.

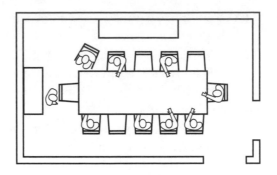

Seating for four with the table against a wall.

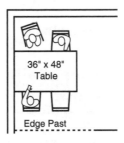

Dining space with benches for four.

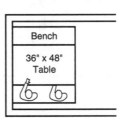

Use a corner bench to get the most out of a tight dining arrangement.

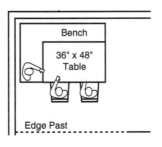

A round dining table is not just a space saver; it allows for easy conversation.

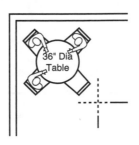

Chandeliers and Candles for Delicious Dining Illumination

Good lighting is particularly important in a dining area. An overhead fixture or pendant on a dimmer switch will allow plenty of ambient lighting to create various moods.

Chandeliers can add drama and sparkle as well as be the focal point of the room. Recessed or track lighting can provide general lighting and can be used to highlight prized possessions. A ring of four recessed downlights set above the dining table supplements light from a chandelier while providing accent lighting for your tableware.

A buffet or sideboard can be flanked with wall sconces. Displayed objects can be accented with recessed downlights installed in the ceiling above.

For intimate dinners and festive occasions, candlelight is the most flattering light. It is best to place candlelight above or below eye level. Small table lamps on serving pieces, wall lights, or uplights in addition to candlelight will add suitable illumination. China cabinets or hutches can be fitted with miniature spotlights to highlight prized possessions and give off a subtle glow.

Expert Advice

So, you don't have a dining room at all? You can create dining areas in other rooms such as the kitchen, library, or living area by using dividers. Half walls with display tops, free-standing bookshelves, folding screens, or even the back of a sofa are all excellent dividers. Also, use area rugs and a change of lighting to help define the space.

Decorator's Diary

Be careful with candles! Once during a holiday dinner party, I lit small votive candles and placed them on the shelves of my corner cabinet. To my horror, the shelf above one set of candles began to burn!

If your dining area is part of a "great room" or a multipurpose space, place several types of lighting on separate switches and dimmers to illuminate the area you are using and darken the areas you don't need.

*Recessed downlights
accent tableware.*

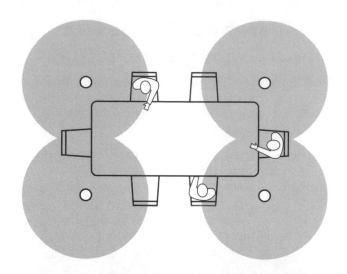

*A lace tablecloth, lots of
candlelight, and a chaise
at the head of the table
make a very romantic
dining room.*

(Photo by Gear)

For All Your Fine China: Storage and Display Pieces

Storage units in a dining room serve multiple purposes. Attractive in themselves, they can properly store china, linens, and silverware, and provide surfaces that can be used for serving or display. A *sideboard* or buffet piece is especially hardworking. Its drawers or doors can hold trays, china, extra glassware, and linens, and during a meal, drinks or food can be served from it. When you're not dining, the sideboard can display special trays, dishes, crystal, candlesticks, or decanters. A serving cart can do much the same but is smaller and has legs with wheels to allow it to be moved around for easy serving. (For serving from behind a chair, position your cart or buffet at least 48 inches from the table.)

A *breakfront, china cabinet, hutch,* or corner cupboard can hold extra china, glassware, and vases on its lower half and display bowls, dishes, and plates on the upper shelves. A *curio cabinet* may hold delicate collections behind glass doors. Refer to Chapter 15, "The All-Important Accessories," to learn more about the art of display. Again, the cupboard does not have to match your dining table or chairs. Blending traditional with modern or old with new adds your personal signature.

A great way to add flair and storage to your dining room is to attach a wide shelf at picture-rail height around the room (approximately one foot below the ceiling). This can store and display large plates, pitchers, or collections of china or pewter. Spoon racks can hold special silver spoons or baby cups.

Designer's Dictionary

Sideboard. Long, low cabinet usually placed against a wall. May have drawers and compartments or a combination of both.

Highboy. Tall chest that appears to be in two sections.

Breakfront. Tall unit that usually has glass-enclosed shelves on top of a drawer cabinet, with a projecting center section.

Hutch. A tall cupboard or sideboard that usually has open shelves on the top section and cabinets below.

China cabinet. A cabinet designed for display of china or glasses. Usually has a glass front or sides.

Curio cabinet. A cabinet with glass doors and sides to display various types of collections.

Expert Advice

If your dining area is separated from the kitchen by a door, be sure it swings in both directions for easy serving.

Accessories for a Festive Atmosphere

Small accessories, as everywhere in your house, make the difference in a dining room. A buffet piece, a polished tea service, crystal decanters, and candlesticks are classic accessories. A punch bowl is fun for special occasions, and other tabletop pieces can include fresh fruit in wooden or ceramic bowls or plates. A soup tureen doubles as a serving bowl and makes a beautiful centerpiece. And of course, fresh flowers are always a wonderful addition to any dining experience.

Walls are key in a dining room. They can be hung with an arrangement of china plates with plate hangers (available at any hardware store) or prints or paintings of culinary objects. Botanical prints and sporting artwork bring nature indoors.

Other objects can adorn walls: Small brackets spaced on one wall can give special attention to a collection of teapots or vases. Hang a mirror above the buffet, and the accessories are reflected with double the impact. Light the candles, and the reflected flickering light illuminates the polished surfaces and sparkles in the crystalware. Enchanting!

Using the Master Planning List: Prioritizing and Pricing Your Dining Room Projects

Once again, here's a brief review of how to use the master list, which is an outline of all the jobs, furnishings, and enhancements suitable for most dining rooms:

➤ Evaluate the state of your dining room, using the master list as a guide. Repairs are always the top priority. Go through the master list and write down your answers next to each item that pertains to your situation.

➤ Refer to the personal inventory that you made in Chapter 1, "You've Got Style: Flaunt It!" to fill in the appropriate places, checking off the possessions you have and the ones that you need and want. Remember to build your list around items that you love.

➤ Prioritize: The master list is arranged in a general order of priorities, but you can adjust items according to your situation.

➤ Price your priorities: Get accurate price estimates for every item on your proposed list by consulting contractors, department and home improvement stores, mail-order catalogs, and other publications. Total up the estimated cost for all your dining room projects.

➤ Match your plans with your resources: If your total cost falls 20 to 30 percent over your budget, eliminate the lower-priority items. If you are more than 30 percent over your budget, review your planning approach thoroughly. You may need to consider an entirely different—low-cost and short-term—approach to fixing up the room.

Dining Room Master Planning List

Priority	Project/Purchase	Comment	Estimated Price
Contractors			
____	Electrician	_____	_____
____	Plumber/heat	_____	_____
____	Flooring person	_____	_____
____	Painter	_____	_____
____	Carpenter	_____	_____
Lighting			
____	Ceiling fixture	_____	_____
____	Wall lights	_____	_____
____	Candelabra/ candlesticks	_____	_____
Furniture			
____	Dining table	_____	_____
____	Chairs	_____	_____
____	Sideboard/buffet	_____	_____
____	China cabinets	_____	_____
Floor			
____	Carpet	_____	_____
____	Wood	_____	_____
____	Tile	_____	_____
____	Area rugs	_____	_____

continues

Dining Room Master Planning List   (continued)

Priority	Project/Purchase	Comment	Estimated Price
Windows			
____	Draperies	_____	_____
____	Shutters/blinds	_____	_____
____	Seat cushions	_____	_____
____	Windowseat cushion	_____	_____
Accessories			
____	Artwork	_____	_____
____	Mirrors	_____	_____
____	Misc. (spoon rack, decanters, tea service, impulse items)	_____	_____

The Least You Need to Know

➤ A contemporary dining room should be designed for comfort as well as for an elegant celebration.

➤ Dining room furnishings do not have to be matched, as long as they work well together and in the available space.

➤ Table and chair arrangements must allow for comfortable dining and movement throughout the room.

➤ Lighting should be flexible and multifaceted to allow for different moods and illumination.

➤ Storage and display pieces are essential elements of a functioning dining room.

➤ Accessories enhance the atmosphere of the room and the enjoyment of occasions.

Chapter 18

Kitchens to Cook in—Even If You Can't

In This Chapter

➤ Efficiency and organization: keys in planning a kitchen

➤ Kitchen layouts that minimize steps and maximize space

➤ Storage units that fit the space and hold everything

➤ Surfaces that are safe and look good

➤ Lighting the kitchen for all its purposes

➤ Display ideas for decorative effects and practical cooking

➤ Your Master Planning List

Because your kitchen is probably the busiest place in your house, it's important that it reflect the atmosphere you like and the way you want to live. You may want a traditional country kitchen with down-home comfort, or a sleek, high-tech, modern culinary center. Whatever style of kitchen you prefer, all successful kitchens have some common elements. They are laid out with efficient and organized cooking areas. Storage is practical, while surfaces are designed so that they are attractive, easily cleaned, and durable. Lighting is adequate for all kitchen uses, whether you're cooking, eating, gathering, or just helping the kids with homework.

There are many resources for information and professional help available for kitchen design, planning, and actual renovation (see Chapter 8, "Beyond the Basics: Resources for Novice Decorators"). If you are starting a kitchen from scratch, you will certainly want to consult with professionals about appliances, electrical work, plumbing, and cabinet installation. And even if you are just refreshing your kitchen, you will want to consider updating certain appliances, installing more efficient storage, or perhaps replacing your countertops. Here too, professional consultation will be useful. With all the use your kitchen gets, you want to make sure you do things right!

A Multitude of Kitchen Plans for Every Cook's Style

There are many ways to arrange kitchens efficiently, and you will learn some of them here. A good first step is to practice making floor plans (see Chapter 3, "Tools of the Trade"), measuring your own space to scale, and experimenting with various arrangements and sizes of appliances and cabinets to see what will fit in your home. Try some of the following styles of kitchen layouts.

The Work Triangle

A standard formula for placement of appliances and efficient traffic patterns in the kitchen is based on the relation of the sink, stove, and refrigerator, known as the *work triangle*. Some experts assert that the stove, refrigerator, and sink should be placed to enable a cook to use these elements without walking clear across the room for each one. The work triangle dictates that the sink should be four to seven feet from the stove and four to seven feet from the refrigerator, thus creating the triangle. The three measurements added together should be anywhere from 12 to 21 feet.

There are various ways to lay out the work triangle. Following are some distinctive kitchen floor plans, showing the positioning of appliances and work-area surfaces.

The U plan.

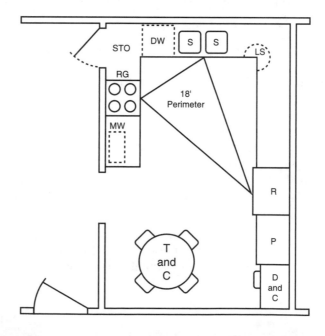

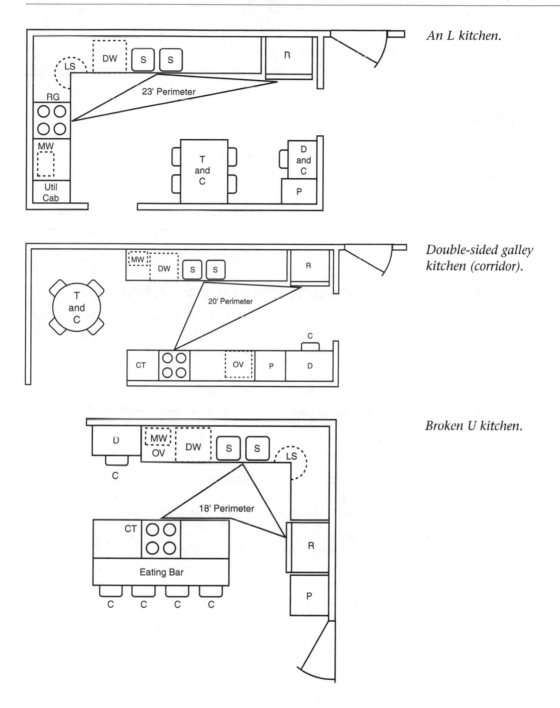

An L kitchen.

Double-sided galley kitchen (corridor).

Broken U kitchen.

Galley kitchen.

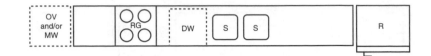

Zone Planning

The work triangle is one approach to organizing a kitchen. Some kitchen designers prefer to lay out kitchens according to how the room will function, the type and quantity of cooking that will be done, how many will cook, or who will serve.

Deborah Krasner, author of *Kitchens for Cooks,* suggests that readers organize their kitchens by zones and create different working areas for "wet," "dry," "hot," and "cold" cooking tasks. You can find exact specifications for setting these zones in her excellent book.

Cabinets Are the Modern Home's Pantry

The storage of food, as well as cooking and eating utensils, is one of a kitchen's most important functions. With the disappearance of separate pantry rooms, kitchen cabinets perform this essential role. (Pantries are coming back in some new homes, but for most of us, cabinets still do the job.)

Cabinet style is a matter of personal taste, and fortunately, cabinets come in every shape, material, and finish under the sun. Visit kitchen showrooms for plenty of choices, including slick and smooth laminates to distressed pine and other beautiful woods, such as spruce, maple, oak, beech, birch, or cherry. Of course, you will also want to consider cabinet shape, detail, finish, and hardware.

Cabinets are often factory-made in predetermined sizes and create a "built-in" style of kitchen. Built-in kitchens save space and look less cluttered. Consider this option if your kitchen is on the small side and you need to maximize your storage units.

A growing recent trend is toward the "unfitted kitchen"—one with free-standing pieces of furniture that may not match other cabinets but provide storage and decoration. Many companies are building these free-standing pieces, which can be combined with open shelving and mismatched hutches or cupboards of various finishes. An unfitted kitchen style works particularly well in large country kitchens that have open wall space.

Whatever the style, cabinets need to provide adequate storage for all your kitchen needs. Base cabinets can have single or double doors that hide fixed or slide-out shelves. They can also house drawers of various depths to hold different sizes of kitchen equipment. If the units have open bases, baskets can be fitted to hold vegetables and fruits. Upper cabinets may have shelves with glass doors that store and display glasses, plates, or food items. You can attach shirred panels of fabric inside the door or order frosted glass if you don't want to show the goods.

Built-in cookbook shelves, a hanging pot rack, and a large island with doors and drawers provide this kitchen with plenty of storage space.

(Photo by Smallbone)

To provide better organization in your cabinets, purchase plastic-wrapped wire drawers, baskets, or shelves from home stores. These come with proper hardware for installation. Some drawers already have built-in fittings for silverware and sharp-knife storage. Corner cabinets can be fitted with *lazy Susans*—rotating circular shelves—for efficient use of space and easy access. If you do your ironing in the kitchen, cabinets with built-in ironing boards that pull down might work for you.

Here are some other storage ideas for your kitchen:

➤ Open shelving can take the place of some upper cabinets. Dishes, cups, and glassware are stacked visibly for easy access and a charming display. Plate drying racks do the same for everyday dishes. You can place hooks at the bottom edge of upper shelves or cabinets for storage of cups and mugs.

Interiors 101

Many kitchens are incorporating features to make recycling and composting easier. For instance, many factory-built kitchen cabinets are fitted with separate covered containers for recyclables. Those interested in composting can find various kits and plans for countertop and under-counter collection of organic kitchen scraps. (Check "green" sources such as catalogs and retailers.)

Expert Advice

Make your own kitchen racks. Be inventive and use an old ladder, wagon wheel, or window frame fitted with hooks to hold pots, herbs, braids of garlic, teacups, and other kitchen accessories.

➤ Hanging pot racks and rails are a stylish and efficient way to store pots and kitchen tools. Pot racks come in several shapes and finishes to fit any style kitchen. (Enclume Designs makes especially good-looking racks, which are available at Williams Sonoma.)

➤ Some racks are fitted with grids for maximum storage capacity; others have a shelf for cookbooks or plants. Grids can also be placed on empty wall space or at the end panel of a cabinet to hold small items like potholders, lids, and so on.

➤ Shelving can be installed inside a door or at the end of a cabinet panel to hold spices. Other efficient placements for rails are behind stoves or under cabinets.

➤ Islands are work areas that often stand in the middle of the work triangle. They range from simple tables to full cabinets with various tops used for food preparation. Full cabinets provide the most storage, with open shelves, doors, or drawers, or a combination of these. While a two-foot by six-foot island is a very useful size for a large kitchen, even a small two-foot-square butcher-block table works in small kitchens.

An island with a lowered granite surface for rolling pastry and a raised butcher block for chopping makes this unfitted kitchen a cook's dream.

(Photo by Smallbone)

Open shelving.

(Photo by Gear)

Cabinets with doors and open shelving.

(Photo by Smallbone)

Cabinets with glass fronts and open shelving.

(Photo by Smallbone)

Solid Sanitary Surfaces for Your Kitchen

Your kitchen can have durable, washable surfaces that don't need to look sterile or compromise your style.

Your kitchen countertops are really worktables, so choose materials appropriate for the type of cooking that you do. Marble and granite are great for pastry making. While a kitchen with marble on all countertops is extremely expensive, you can probably place a slab of marble on one set of the cabinets or on the top surface of the island.

The most affordable countertop material is a stock laminate counter with square or rounded edges, which is basically a sheet of laminate on a wood base. Corian is a resin-based product that is molded and shaped to fit your cabinets. Both laminates and Corian are easily washed, but whereas laminates often have seams that catch dirt, Corian is seamless.

Ceramic tiles make attractive countertops but are somewhat more difficult to clean than smooth surfaces. Maple butcher-block countertops are solid and can be scrubbed clean easily.

Kitchen floors get the biggest workout of the home. Handling spills and traffic are the main concerns in choosing a practical flooring. Ceramic tiles are durable, attractive, and easy to clean if their grouting is sealed—but many items that are dropped will shatter. Wood flooring needs extra maintenance with coats of varnish, and cracks in the wood planks can trap food sweepings. Often, the best solution is vinyl, which is inexpensive, can be easily maintained, and is available in a number of creative patterns. Read more about floor surfaces in Chapter 10, "Possibilities Underfoot."

Interiors 101

Sometimes just replacing or rejuvenating old countertops is all a tired kitchen needs. New laminates or tiles can be placed over old ones.

Lots of Lighting for the Busy Home Kitchen

A single fixture centered on the ceiling is insufficient lighting for the full range of kitchen activities. This fixture is essential for general lighting but must be supplemented by task lighting placed over the stove, oven, sink, island, or other work surfaces.

Track lighting or recessed downlights over the sink or stove can provide sufficient light to wash dishes or cook. Islands or dining tables can be lit with decorative pendants. When connected to dimmer switches, these will provide both adequate task lighting and general lighting for dining or entertaining.

Light countertops with fixtures placed at the bottom of overhead cabinets. Position them close to the front edge of the upper cabinets for best light and least glare. Be sure they are slim in size and not too noticeable.

Cabinets with glass fronts can be fitted with miniature lighting to highlight pretty china and glassware. Also for accent, spotlights can illuminate a beautifully displayed open cupboard.

Expert Advice

You can never have enough electrical outlets in a kitchen! If your kitchen is old, you can have an electrician add two- and four-socket outlets. If you are planning a new kitchen, double the amount you think you may need. An island fitted with electrical outlets is very handy!

Kitchenware Makes a Great Display

Many kitchen storage pieces double as display units. Plate racks, cup hooks, glass-door cabinets, open shelves, and cupboards can all show off pretty plates and glassware. The very tops of cupboards can hold oversized baskets, bowls, and trays. Nothing in a

181

kitchen is more appealing or appropriate than bowls or plates arranged with fresh vegetables or fruits. Pot racks can show off a great set of copper pots.

Walls and windows are useful, too: As in the dining area, china plates can be hung on spring plate hooks, preferably in groups. Window shelves can hold a group of fresh green tomatoes waiting to ripen or herbs in pots.

Decorative containers such as olive-oil cans or ceramic jugs can organize and display kitchen tools. If you are lucky enough to have bookshelves and are an avid cook, you could fill the shelves with cookbooks arranged vertically and in stacks—with spaces left to fill with pretty pottery or casserole dishes.

Expert Advice

Use your imagination when choosing accessories for your kitchen. For example, place a child's chalkboard prominently in the kitchen to write daily messages or the menu of a special dinner. Place a birdcage—no canary necessary—over the dinner table for a focal point (if you have other sufficient lighting). Read more about adding accessories and quick kitchen makeovers in Chapter 24, "Give Your Kitchen a Fresh Look—Fast!"

Endless Accessories for the Kitchen

Accessories personalize a kitchen. Trims made of cutout paper, lace, or wallpaper borders can add interest and soften the hard edges of shelves. Fabric panels placed inside glass doors add texture, color, or pattern to the room while hiding clutter. Lace panels add a romantic touch and allow items to remain partially hidden. The space between the counter and the cabinets (the backsplash) can be decorated with vintage or new ceramic tiles.

Vintage linens can be brought to new life as simple cafe curtains over the sink window. Baker's racks of stainless steel can hold a collection of bowls. Old wooden shoe racks make great areas to display fresh breads, picnic baskets, and baskets of fruits and vegetables. Use different sizes of metal or wood stands for cultivating a variety of herbs.

A comfortable chair may not be an accessory, but if you have the room, it is a wonderful way to make a kitchen into a retreat. And of course, the ambiance of an open fireplace (admittedly a big-ticket accessory) or a small open grill can turn a kitchen into a sensational entertaining area. Similarly, an old cookstove is a distinctive way to add warmth and charm in the winter.

Using the Master Planning List: Prioritizing and Pricing Your Kitchen Projects

As you review the master list, remember the following points:

➤ Evaluate the state of your kitchen, using the master list as a guide. Repairs are always the top priority. Go through the master list and write down your answers next to each item that pertains to your situation.

➤ Refer to the personal inventory that you made in Chapter 1, "You've Got Style: Flaunt It!" to fill in the appropriate places, checking off the possessions you have and the ones that you need and want. Remember to build your list around items that you love.

➤ Prioritize: The master list is arranged in a general order of priorities, but you can adjust items according to your situation.

➤ Price your priorities: Get accurate price estimates for every item on your proposed list by consulting contractors, department and home improvement stores, mail-order catalogs, and other publications. Total up the estimated cost for all your kitchen projects.

➤ Match your plans with your resources: If your total cost falls 20 to 30 percent over your budget, eliminate the lower-priority items. If you are more than 30 percent over your budget, review your planning approach thoroughly. You may need to consider an entirely different—low-cost and short-term—approach to fixing up the room.

Kitchen Master Planning List

Priority	Project/Purchase	Comment	Estimated Price
Contractors			
_____	Electrician	_____	_____
_____	Plumber/heat	_____	_____
_____	Flooring person	_____	_____
_____	Painter	_____	_____
_____	Carpenter	_____	_____

continues

183

Kitchen Master Planning List   (continued)

Priority	Project/Purchase	Comment	Estimated Price
Lighting			
_____	Ceiling fixtures	_____	_____
_____	Table/floor lamps	_____	_____
_____	Wall lights	_____	_____
Furniture			
_____	Chairs/bench	_____	_____
_____	Table	_____	_____
_____	Chairs	_____	_____
_____	Worktable/island	_____	_____
_____	Comfortable seating	_____	_____
_____	Cookstove	_____	_____
_____	Free-standing cupboards	_____	_____
Floor			
_____	Tile/stone	_____	_____
_____	Brick	_____	_____
_____	Wood	_____	_____
_____	Area rugs	_____	_____
Windows			
_____	Curtains	_____	_____
_____	Blinds	_____	_____
_____	Shutters	_____	_____
_____	Shades	_____	_____
Accessories			
_____	Hanging pot racks/rails	_____	_____
_____	Herb racks	_____	_____
_____	Plants/flowers	_____	_____
_____	Paper/lace shelf edging	_____	_____

Priority	Project/Purchase	Comment	Price
Accessories, continued			
____	Chalkboard	_____	_____
____	Plates hung on spring racks	_____	_____
____	Bowls, trays	_____	_____

The Least You Need to Know

➤ Careful consideration and professional consultation are necessary to make plans for kitchen remodeling or renovation.

➤ A kitchen layout should be explored extensively with efficiency and organization as the goal. Placement of the sink, refrigerator, stove, and countertops can follow several different models.

➤ Cabinets and other storage units are key elements in the functioning of the kitchen and can complement the decorative style as well. Space considerations play a big role in the choice of storage.

➤ Surface materials—both floors and countertops—should be chosen for durability, maintenance, cost, and aesthetics. Countertop materials should also be appropriate for the uses of the kitchen and the cook.

➤ Overhead lighting in the kitchen must be complemented by task lighting on work areas and accent lighting for decorative displays.

➤ Display of accessories in a kitchen melds with function, as storage units and containers can display equipment and food items with decorative impact.

Chapter 19

Bathrooms with Practicality and Personality

In This Chapter

➤ Bathrooms can be beautiful but demand careful planning

➤ Assess your lifestyle to design your dream bath

➤ Floor plans for bathrooms are an exercise in efficient use of space

➤ Lighting options for bathrooms—you need a lot

➤ Shelves, cabinets, racks, and hooks are essential to bathroom design and function

➤ Bathroom accessories add softness and sensuality

Like the kitchen, the bathroom is a complex workhorse of a room; it must be efficient, functional and durable, but still be comfortable and decorated to your taste. Fortunately, as with kitchens, there are many books, catalogs, Web sites, and professionals available to help you with your design decisions. And there's a rich range of choices, from bathtubs to soap dishes, that can strike the right notes in your design.

Whether you are planning a new bathroom and selecting all new materials or doing a little renovating with existing elements, you can consider decorating possibilities as you investigate your options for necessary fixtures, plumbing and electrical work, storage, and lighting. Begin as always with an assessment of how you live, what you like, and what you have. You're on the road to creating a bathroom that works ... and works and works.

Arranging the Bathroom: A Few Fixtures but Many Possibilities

How much space do you have? What would you like the bathroom to serve as? Do you want a dual-purpose bath/dressing area, or a bath/workout-exercise room? Or, do you have just enough space for a tub, toilet, and sink and want it to look better?

Before you plan your bathroom, review your Personal Style Assessments from Chapter 1, "You've Got Style: Flaunt It!" Your lifestyle will dictate the fixtures and features you want your bathroom to have. Then refer to Chapter 3, "Tools of the Trade," for drawing floor plans to scale, and figure out the space you have and what fixtures will fit. This is an excellent room to draw floor plans for, because there are just a few essential furnishing elements and the floor space is relatively small.

You will be consulting with professionals about matters of plumbing, electricity, flooring and tiles, and perhaps cabinets and other storage units as well. But as you plan your bathroom, keep some of these pointers in mind:

➤ Plumbing changes can be costly; try to place fixtures so that the space is effectively used and plumbing work is minimized.

➤ You need room to move and relax: At least 24 to 28 inches of clearance is needed to carry out activities like stepping out of the tub and washing in the sink, and for foot room in front of the toilet.

➤ Space-saver: Consider a corner-shaped shower stall to fit into a crowded bathroom.

➤ A corner-shaped toilet is a good space-saving idea for a closet turned into a bathroom or one built under a stairwell.

➤ A standard tub-and-shower combination will eliminate the need for two separate fixtures.

➤ Two sinks mounted in a countertop vanity cabinet will allow two to use the bathroom at the same time and also provide good storage space.

➤ Pocket doors (ones that slide into the wall) eliminate the need for door-swinging space.

➤ Dark green, burgundy, or navy fixtures are hard to keep looking clean. Plain white or pastel colors are easier to clean.

➤ If you have the room, consider projecting the tub into the room instead of against a long wall.

➤ Try to place the toilet where it is not the first thing that you see.

➤ Placing a tub underneath a window provides a view for a relaxing bath.

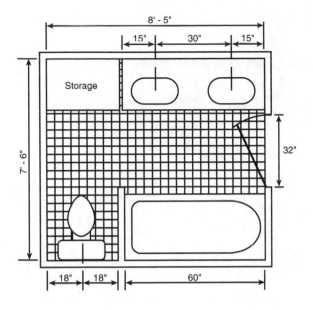

A double-sink vanity allows plenty of storage in addition to the floor-to-ceiling shelving. This layout allows adequate room at the toilet and sink areas.

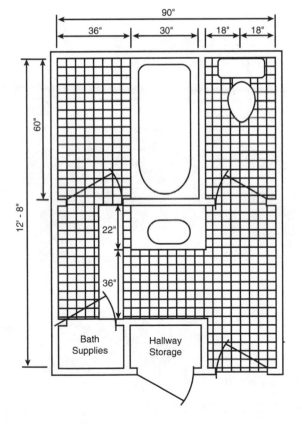

With the three fixtures in separate compartments, this large bath plan can replace a second bath, allowing more than one person to use it (and saving you the cost and plumbing of a second set of fixtures!).

189

Old-fashioned brass fix-tures and a traditional-style sink add a sense of timelessness to a bath-room.

(Photos by Waterworks)

A large marble-topped table substitutes as a vanity, providing an area for display and storage.

(Photo by Schumacher)

Safe Surfaces and Attractive Materials for Floors

Bathroom floors take a bath, too: It is crucial that they are washable and water-resistant, and *not* slippery when wet. Ceramic tile for flooring should be grouted with epoxy grout and be functionally slip-resistant. (Be cautious: Even slip-resistant tiles are often not slip-proof, especially for children and elderly people.) Tiles do make beautiful floors but are hard, unyielding surfaces—falling items tend to shatter. Marble tiles make a luxurious surface for a bathroom floor but are slippery when wet, especially when highly polished.

Vinyl and vinyl tiles are often the perfect choices because of their waterproof and resilient surfaces. And with vinyl tiles, you can create lovely patterns, too.

Wood floors shouldn't be your first choice for bathrooms, but if you are restoring an older home, you might find usable wood. If you find good boards under old flooring, be sure to coat them with several coats of varnish to seal them to water. Wood floors are beautiful but demand work to be maintained. (See Chapter 10, "Possibilities Underfoot," for more on flooring.)

Decorator's Diary

Painting or wall covering the ceiling adds visual delight while soaking in the tub. For a bit of extra relaxation during our Vermont winters, I have painted on the walls and ceiling above the bathtub a mural of my favorite beach scene from the Bahamas.

Add cotton rugs or mats with nonskid backing to all types of bath flooring to absorb water and cushion your feet. If you use several small mats instead of one large rug, it is easier to wash them more often.

Bathroom walls can be tiled with ceramic or marble, covering the entire walls, part of the walls, around the bathtub, or even for as limited an area as a backsplash behind the sink. As with floor tiles, wall tile grout needs to be sealed to resist moisture and mildew. (No sealing is necessary with state-of-the-art epoxy-based grout.)

Vinyl is excellent as a bathroom wall covering, too. It is washable, durable, and adds a nice decorative effect. Using a proper paint is an economical way to spruce up bathroom walls. A washable paint finish is easy to clean. Be sure to look for paints with mildew-resistant finishes.

Designer's Dictionary

Bead board is a type of thin wood paneling with a decorative "bead" feature running the length of the strips. The panels are locked together with tongue–and–groove joints.

Another attractive choice is *bead-board paneling*—narrow strips of wood joined by tongue-and-groove joints. Attached to bathroom walls, these can be painted or stained-painted for a lovely aesthetic.

Bathroom Lighting: Seeing Yourself in the Best Light

For safety, comfort, and convenience in daily grooming, sufficient bathroom lighting is a must. For most situations, a ceiling fixture and lights on either side of your mirror (or mirrors, in case you have double sinks) will provide enough general and task lighting. Often a light placed directly over the toilet and/or the bath is a good addition for those who may want to linger and read.

A large, round mirror, clover-shaped pedestal sink, and tiled walls add up to a contemporary styled bathroom.

(Photo by Flos USA)

For the most flattering light when applying cosmetics, use incandescent bulbs in fixtures with glass shades that diffuse the light, or opt for energy-efficient warm white fluorescent bulbs that can come close to the color of incandescent bulbs. (See Chapter 14, "Lighting Up Your Life," for more on lighting.)

For specific areas, you can use downlights or spotlights. And of course, small night-lights are a comfort for trips to the bathroom in the middle of the night.

Storing All the Stuff: More Than Medicine Cabinets

There are many stylish ways to store and display bathroom supplies and accessories. Overhead cabinets above the toilet can be fitted with doors to hide lotions, makeup, and showering supplies. Depending on placement, a towel bar can be added or built into an overhead cabinet bottom. The top of the cabinet could hold a collection of colored bottles, oversized seashells, or baskets for small items.

Interiors 101

You should have at least the same number of towel bars as there are people living in the house.

Of course, a handsome medicine cabinet serves double duty, both as a place to store prescription medicines and as a fixture for bathroom mirrors. If your bathroom is large enough to accommodate a vanity table and chair, it can display perfume bottles, powders, and a pretty mirror-and-comb set, while other grooming supplies are hidden away in drawers.

Built-in or free-standing shelving can hold towels, and if you have enough shelves, assign one to each person who is using the bathroom. Children may use lower shelves for storing bathtub toys. Pegged racks or towel racks can be topped with shelves for extra storage or attractive displays.

If your bathroom serves as a catchall for dirty laundry, install an attractive chrome or wicker hamper with a pullout, washable liner for easy transport to the laundry. Of course, if you have lots of space, more shelves, tables, or cupboards are always useful. Magazine holders are handy near the tub or toilet. A small shelf placed above the sink or sinks can hold favorite perfumes or colognes.

Custom cabinets, architectural moldings, and large mirrors give this bathroom an elegant look.

(Photo by Smallbone)

Accessories for the Bath Are Always Attractive

Accessories are a sure way to decorate a bathroom without making any large structural changes. Plants are natural beauties for window ledges or on the backs of toilets. They will thrive in a steam-filled bath. Aromatic bath gels in pretty bottles, perfumes, or scented soaps and candles can be placed on open shelves or tables to please the eye as well as the nose. Plush bath rugs with nonskid backing are soft on your feet. Terrycloth seating feels good to bare skin and lends visual texture, too. Plush towels— all white or combinations of colors and patterns—also add visual softness and simple luxury.

Small accessories that are decorative and functional consist of the following:

➤ Toothbrush and soap holders in metal, ceramic, or wood.

➤ Towel or bathrobe hooks or knobs, and metal shower curtain rings in interesting motifs of shells, arrows, or stars.

➤ Coordinated wastebasket and tissue holders in chrome, silver, wicker, or painted wood.

➤ Luxurious products such as heated towel bars and candlelit bathtub valets. These can turn an everyday bathroom into a private spa! (See Chapter 25, "Brighten Your Bathroom Without Breaking the Bank," for more ideas for your bathroom.)

Using the Master Planning List: Prioritizing and Pricing Your Bathroom Projects

Here's a brief review of how to use the master list, which is an outline of all the jobs, furnishings, and enhancements suitable for most bathrooms:

➤ Evaluate the state of your bathroom, using the master list as a guide. Repairs are always the top priority. Go through the master list and write down your answers next to each item that pertains to your situation.

➤ Refer to the personal inventory that you made in Chapter 1 to fill in the appropriate places, checking off the possessions you have and the ones that you need and want. Remember to build your list around items that you love.

➤ Prioritize: The master list is arranged in a general order of priorities, but you can adjust items according to your situation.

➤ Price your priorities: Get accurate price estimates for every item on your proposed list by consulting contractors, department and home improvement stores, mail-order catalogs, and other publications. Total up the estimated cost for all your bathroom projects.

➤ Match your plans with your resources: If your total cost falls 20 to 30 percent over your budget, eliminate the lower-priority items. If you are more than 30 percent over your budget, review your planning approach thoroughly. You may need to consider an entirely different—low-cost and short-term—approach to fixing up the room.

Bathroom Master Planning List

Priority	Project/Purchase	Comment	Estimated Price
Contractors			
____	Electrician	_____	_____
____	Plumber/heat	_____	_____
____	Flooring person	_____	_____
____	Painter	_____	_____
____	Carpenter	_____	_____
Lighting			
____	Ceiling fixtures	_____	_____
____	Wall lights	_____	_____
____	Small table lamps	_____	_____
____	Night-lights	_____	_____
Furniture			
____	Chaise	_____	_____
____	Chair	_____	_____
____	Vanity	_____	_____
____	Vanity chair	_____	_____
____	Small table	_____	_____
____	Exercise equipment	_____	_____
Floor			
____	Ceramic tile	_____	_____
____	Brick/stone	_____	_____
____	Vinyl	_____	_____
____	Vinyl tiles	_____	_____

Priority	Project/Purchase	Comment	Estimated Price
Windows			
____	Curtains	_____	_____
____	Blinds	_____	_____
____	Shutters	_____	_____
____	Shades	_____	_____
Accessories			
____	Wastebasket	_____	_____
____	Mirrors	_____	_____
____	Display shelves	_____	_____
____	Plants	_____	_____
____	Mats	_____	_____
____	Towel bars	_____	_____
____	Clothes hooks	_____	_____

The Least You Need to Know

➤ Bathroom floor plans should consider aesthetics, plumbing requirements, space-saving fixtures, and sufficient room for comfortable washing, bathing, and relaxing.

➤ Safety and sanitation are key considerations for bathroom floors. Nonslip and water-resistant surfaces are essential.

➤ Wall surfaces have many decorative and practical options, including tile, vinyl, paint, and wood.

➤ Overhead bathroom lighting must be supplemented with mirror lights and downlights for specific areas.

➤ Storage and accessory options for bathrooms are nearly unlimited but must combine functionality with decorative considerations.

Chapter 20

Bedrooms Big and Small

In This Chapter

➤ The most personal room in your home

➤ More than just a bed: bedroom furniture arrangements

➤ Storage for the most personal stuff

➤ Bedroom lighting for many moods and purposes

➤ Accessories that beautify the bedroom

➤ From nursery to teen's pad: changing your child's room naturally

---

Bedrooms are our private sanctuaries. They are the personal spaces where we keep our most precious treasures, enjoy our most relaxed and intimate moments, and drift on to our hidden dreams.

You may ask, "If no one goes into my bedroom besides me and other family members, why should I go to the trouble of decorating it?" The answer is that no other room so clearly reflects your personal passions and style. And if you express them well in your bedroom, you will deepen your relaxation, add pleasure to your private moments, and sweeten your dreams.

For adults and children of all ages, the bedroom should be a place to call one's own. It is a place to fill with favorite colors, patterns, textures, and styles. You may want this to be your palace of luxury, beautifully furnished and with elaborate and sumptuous accessories from window dressings to bed linens. Or you may choose a refuge of refreshing simplicity, with a spare but comfortable atmosphere of simple furniture and clean lines.

Children's rooms will change as quickly as they do, so they must be designed with flexibility in mind. Durable furniture—adaptable to the needs and activities of different ages—makes kids' bedrooms manageable and affordable. Accessories and artwork reflect the individual choices of each child. (And washable fabrics and materials on walls and floors will help, too!)

Comfort is the key for bedrooms big and small. And you can achieve this through inviting arrangements, carefully designed lighting, lots of storage with easy access, and accessories that soothe and inspire you.

Bedrooms for More Than Just Sleeping

Bedrooms are great places for many activities other than sleeping. With proper design, you can make your bedroom a practical and private place for such varied activities as reading, writing, workouts, and enjoying hobbies. It can be a good dual-purpose site for a study or office, a dressing room or vanity area, a crib space or childcare space, or an exercise or workout area. Here are some important questions to ask yourself as you plan a bedroom for privacy, relaxation, and varied uses:

➤ What activities or purposes does your bedroom serve now? What activities would you like to find a place for in your bedroom?

➤ Is there room for seating? Room for a desk?

➤ Does the room provide adequate privacy and quiet? Do you need to add draperies, carpets, or other soundproofing?

➤ Does your room provide adequate natural light (or too much)? Do you want to enlarge windows, add a skylight, or put up blackout shades?

➤ Where are the light sockets and switches? What are your electrical requirements? What about television or telephone jacks?

Assess the room and start your planning with the essentials. One of your first questions should be where to place the bed—the most dominant (and most used) piece of furniture. Here are two requirements for a bedroom that works:

➤ Leave plenty of space around the bed for changing sheets and cleaning (at least 15 inches).

➤ Leave ample space between doorways, dressers, and the bed (at least 36 inches).

The most common and often the most practical bed placement is in the middle of the longest wall. This is especially advisable if there's a window adjacent to or across from the bed to provide light and possibly a view. (If you like to wake with the sun, place the head of the bed to face an east-facing window for morning light.) If lack of space demands, or if you choose to place the bed in front of a window, use the sill of the window for plants, and use window dressings to frame the bed dramatically.

Decorator's Diary

Long ago, I learned that a bed set on a diagonal, protruding from a corner of the room, gives the room an especially airy and spacious feeling. A folding screen can fill in the triangular area between the head of the bed and the corner of the walls—and it makes a fun headboard.

Placing Other Bedroom Pieces

A conventional bedroom plan usually allows for two night tables, one on either side of the bed. A good variation on this is to place a skirted round table on one side and a chest of drawers on the other (both good storage pieces!). If there is enough space at the foot of the bed, you can set a trunk there—again, gaining valuable storage space. In addition, a large ottoman or a small loveseat placed at the foot of a bed allows for central seating (and is a good place to sit to tie your shoes).

Another piece adjacent to the bed could be a long table, triply useful as a desk, nightstand, and vanity, all of which make great use of limited space. If this table is set by a window, it's especially appropriate for writing or putting on cosmetics.

If there are built-in closets with sliding doors on one side of the bed, be sure there is at least 15 inches of clearance from the closet to the bed and 36 inches of clearance from the foot of the bed to the wall or dresser for easy movement and access.

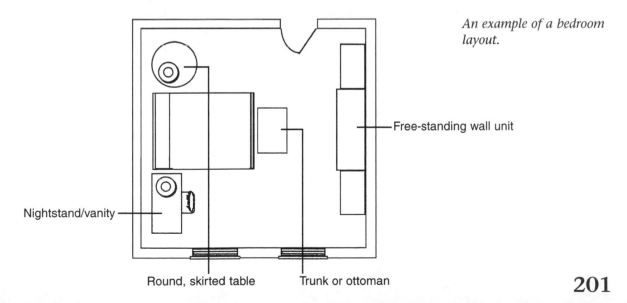

An example of a bedroom layout.

Free-standing wall unit

Nightstand/vanity

Round, skirted table

Trunk or ottoman

The floor plan illustrated here demonstrates an efficient use of space. A 36-inch, round, skirted table used as a nightstand provides storage underneath the tablecloth and a generous-sized top for display of books, picture frames, and accessories. A nightstand that doubles as a desk or vanity makes good use of limited space. Bookshelves or a mirror can be wall-mounted above the table. A trunk or ottoman that opens, placed at the foot of the bed, can add extra storage space and a place to sit while you put on your shoes. For maximum use of space, a freestanding unit is placed along the wall to conceal a TV/stereo and provide generous clothes storage.

With twin beds, it is common to place the headboards along the longest wall with a night table in between. However, try positioning them like an "L," and place a low table, holding a lamp, in the corner where the heads meet. Or place the beds with their sides along a wall, with a chest in between. These two arrangements can be great space-savers.

If space allows, a few additions to the usual furnishings will give the room a special appeal and usefulness. An intimate dinner or cozy Sunday brunch are memorable in a bedroom: Place two side chairs and a breakfast table in a corner of the room or at the foot of the bed. For reading or light resting, a chaise (an elongated sofa) is an elegant addition for any bedroom.

On the other hand, if space is at an absolute minimum (or if you live in a studio apartment), sleep sofas or beds that fold up into wall storage (a Murphy bed) might be the perfect choice. If your bedroom has to serve dual or triple purposes, use folding screens, back-to-back dressers, or bookshelves to divide up the space into office, exercise, or private dressing areas.

The Best Bed for Your Room

You may feel like you never get to be there, but in fact, you spend about a third of your life in bed. So it is essential that your bed be comfortable and fit you and your room. Consider that most people are comfortable in a bed that is at least six inches longer than they are tall. And keep in mind the clearances mentioned earlier when you think of what size bed is best for you. (Refer back to Chapter 9, "Furniture to Last a Lifetime," for information on buying a well-built mattress.) Standard adult bed sizes are as follows:

➤ King—76-inch width × 80–84-inch length

➤ Queen—60 × 80 inches

➤ Full—54 × 75 inches

➤ Twin—39 × 75 inches

➤ Twin/X-Long—39 × 80 inches

Expert Advice

If you have a headboard or foot-board, it will add to the size of your bed. Be sure to consider this when measuring and laying out floor plans.

Bedroom Storage and Display

With the variety of personal items that we keep in our bedrooms—clothing, linens, and living accessories of all kinds—finding the right storage is almost as important as finding the right bed. Consider the general choice of built-in or freestanding units. Built-ins maximize storage space using every possible nook and cranny and can make a room streamlined and cohesive. Built-in storage units can be expensive custom-made pieces that cover an entire wall, combining drawers, doors, and shelving for clothing and entertainment. They can be built in to surround and frame a bed, with storage space and lighting units, too.

Free-standing pieces like bureaus, dressers, armoires, and trunks are the traditional approach to clothing storage. They serve perfectly, too, as the place for dressing mirrors and for displaying personal objects.

This free-standing wall unit not only provides dual closets and a writing desk for this bedroom, but architectural character as well.

(Photo by Smallbone)

Consider some of these other ways to add storage to your bedroom:

➤ Add storage drawers that maximize space and fit under a bed with a metal frame and pull out for easy access. Or use a platform base with drawers that the mattress and box spring rest on.

➤ Use nightstands with double drawers.

➤ Skirted tables used for display can also hide storage units under the fabric.

➤ Professional closet organizers are experts who design custom storage for your closets. Maximize closet space with custom storage (look in your Yellow Pages under *closet organizers*).

➤ Attractive quilt racks can hold extra quilts or bedding.

➤ Trunks or ottomans can be used to hold extra bed linens and pillows.

➤ Hang tie racks, shoe shelves, and mirrors on your closet doors.

➤ Vanities fitted with drawers are a great place to hold your personal clutter, and you can display other items on the vanity itself.

The Right Lighting for Many Moods and Uses

Lighting in a bedroom must be varied and flexible to fit with the many uses of the room. You will always need general overhead lighting for dressing, room chores, and getting objects from dressers and bureaus. You will want mood lighting to create an atmosphere of quiet relaxation and intimacy. And you need some bright-light capacity for activities like reading or performing hobbies.

Remember, dimmer controls give you the flexibility to vary the light to suit your different moods and activities.

A streamlined bed with built-in night tables and pendant lighting.

(Photo by Cassina)

Here are some tips for lighting a bedroom effectively:

➤ Swing-arm wall lamps on either side of the bed will provide adequate light for reading, while leaving night tables free for clock radios, books, or drinks.

➤ Table lamps placed on either side of double, queen-, or king-size beds must be tall enough to provide good light.

➤ Recessed lights placed directly over the head of the bed can be a very effective solution for reading. (If two people are sharing the bed, make sure lights have separate switches so that one person can read and one can sleep.)

➤ Closets can be equipped with recessed or surface-mounted lights and wired to turn on when the doors open.

Accessories That Beautify the Bedroom

Accessories play an essential role in a bedroom. Bedding, window dressings, and wall hangings have practical purposes and can bring a particular style to the room as well.

There are things you want to look at every day, and photos of loved ones and family portraits can be displayed on tops of dressers and vanities. Storage pieces can also hold mirrors on top surfaces, or on the front of built-in cabinets or armoires, dressers or vanities. Wherever placed, mirrors give the illusion of added space and reflect light.

With the natural focus of the room on your bed, bed linens and dressings are the place to make a personal statement of style. Lace bed skirts and loads of fluffy pillows add a romantic touch, while a mix of plaids and florals adds an English Country air. (For more tips on adding a touch of romance to your bedroom, see Chapter 26, "Adding a Touch of Romance to Your Bedroom.")

Along with warmth and coziness, bedding adds a lot of visual texture to the bedroom. Down comforters, feather beds, and pillows make a luxurious atmosphere. Colorful cotton sheets feel good to the skin and please the eye. Open-weave blankets used in warm weather and wool or acrylic blankets used in cold seasons have a visual effect, too.

The window treatments can be coordinated with the bedding to heighten the style in the room. Trims, fringes, and tiebacks take curtains out of the ordinary. The motifs can be continued or complemented with skirted tables, which also add softness and texture to the room.

Some other touches to consider are …

➤ Folding screens, which can add a private dressing place.

➤ Wall hangings and overscaled prints, which can add a focal point to the head wall of a bed.

➤ A radio or CD player, which can be an important mood enhancer (and serve as a wake-up call for you).

➤ Plants and flowers, which add an unequaled natural beauty.

Rooms for Kids to Grow Up In

The bedroom is a place for your child's creative self-expression and is also one of the rooms that you will have the most fun decorating. Colorful walls and bedding, washable paint surfaces, easy-care fabrics and flooring, safety features, and fun accessories all provide you with many great choices for practical and decorative improvements. But you must give a child's room a lot of thought so that it can affordably expand and change from a baby's nursery to a teenager's pad. Furnishings, storage, and wall accessories should be planned for each stage, and some can last a lifetime.

Infants—the Nursery

An infant's needs are simple. A crib for sleeping and a table for diaper changing will suffice for a year or two. A changing table with drawers or shelving can hold grooming aids. You'll need a diaper pail for used diapers and a bureau for small clothing—choose a bureau that a child can use for many years. One great piece to have is a comfortable rocking chair that you can use when feeding your baby and when singing lullabies.

For lighting, a plain lamp with a solid-color ceramic base can be used for several years. A night-light will produce a soft glow so that a youngster isn't in a completely darkened room—it also allows for nighttime feedings and changes.

In general, keep the colors light in your infant's room and use simple wall coverings, borders, and window curtains. A wall mural is a lovely but costly treatment, so choose a motif that will last for several years. Many accessories for the nursery are available. For example, musical mobiles hung over the cribs provide the baby with visual and audio stimulation and bring lovely color into the room.

This "Bunny Business" chintz fabric is a perfect choice for curtains and beddings for a nursery or toddler's room.

(Photo by Brunswig & Fils)

Toddler

Toddlers are mobile and need a lot of space for play. Added storage in the form of open chests should be low and easy for a toddler to reach. A bookcase or added shelving for books also organizes a toddler's room.

This is a time to make some changes to the infant's room. The rocking chair may be replaced with a comfortable upholstered chair for reading bedtime books. Bring in a junior bed or a regular-size twin bed with a guardrail attached. The table that was used for changing can be used as a craft and drawing center. A chalkboard hung low on a wall encourages a child to scribble. A round ottoman acts as a piece to practice walking around and climbing on. Here are some other ideas:

➤ Track lighting with lights positioned on the play area and reading areas can be repositioned for hobby and homework areas as the child grows.

➤ Wood flooring with small, washable area rugs (use nonskid mats underneath) or washable, textured carpet is the best floor option for easy maintenance and long wear.

➤ Accessories, such as large wall hangings depicting familiar storybook characters and motifs like dinosaurs, can enliven the room. A playhouse or mini-fort is always a fun place to hide and pretend. And a small tape player with tapes of songs will help make the toddler's room a happy place to be.

The School-Age Child

As children begin school, they will also become involved in hobbies and sporting events. Whether they are in dance classes, piano lessons, horseback riding, or soccer, accessories from these activities will affect their lives and their personal style.

Older children will need more storage to accommodate larger items and more clothes—and storage furnishings should help them learn to be neat and have an organized room. A pegged rack with a shelf hung at a child's level (low on the wall) will serve as a place for dolls and stuffed animals as well as for hanging clothes. A large table (the former nursery changing table) can be adapted to a play surface or a desk area. Bookcases and shelving need to be sufficient to hold plenty of reading materials, games, school supplies, and books.

If room allows, you may want to add another bed for a friend to sleep over. Or replace a twin bed with bunk beds to maximize sleeping space and free up the floor space for play.

Your child should be involved with choosing the colors or theme of his or her room. Discuss favorite colors and hobbies to encourage self-expression. If your child likes ballet, a simple stencil of ballerinas or ballet shoes may be painted around the perimeter of the room. Horses or sailboats could work as well. Your child's style will emerge!

Preteens

The older school child wants a place to entertain his or her friends. The latest computer game or hottest new music star may be the focus of his or her life!

This is the high-tech age, too. Make sure the room has enough electrical outlets to accommodate the latest technology. A wall unit that can hold a computer, stereo, or CD player; books; and a desk surface will help to keep a busy preteen's room in tiptop shape. Bulletin boards are great to hold sports posters, photos, and personal items in a neat way.

Folding chairs and tables are a good idea for accommodating visiting friends. Perhaps a small sofa or floor pillows can be added to give a feeling of independence, privacy, and comfort. Let your preteen decide on the decor (of course, with your approval).

Teenagers

The teen years are the most intense time of self-expression—and your teenager may want a complete change of scene! Teens often want to arrange their own rooms and choose all the materials. You may disagree with your teenager's choices, but remember: This is your teenager's place to feel independent and do as he or she wishes (within some limits, of course).

Your teen's room must be a combination of a sleep, study, and entertaining area. He or she may need to bring in a larger bed. Friends are very important at this time, so you may want to add a sleep sofa if there is room. Large floor cushions add casual seating quickly. The wall unit from the preteen age may be enlarged for more storage and more desk space, too.

Using the Master Planning Lists: Prioritizing and Pricing Your Bedroom Projects

Here's a brief review of how to use the master list, which is an outline of all the jobs, furnishings, and enhancements suitable for most bedrooms:

➤ Evaluate the state of your bedroom, using the master list as a guide. Repairs are always the top priority. Go through the master list and write down your answers next to each item that pertains to your situation.

➤ Refer to the personal inventory that you made in Chapter 1, "You've Got Style: Flaunt It!" to fill in the appropriate spaces, checking off the possessions you have and the ones that you need and want. Remember to build your list around items that you love.

➤ Prioritize: The master list is arranged in a general order of priorities, but you can adjust items according to your situation.

➤ Price your priorities: Get accurate price estimates for every item on your proposed list by consulting contractors, department and home improvement stores, mail-order catalogs, and other publications. Total up the estimated cost for all your bedroom projects.

➤ Match your plans with your resources: If your total cost falls 20 to 30 percent over your budget, eliminate the lower-priority items. If you are more than 30 percent over your budget, review your planning approach thoroughly. You may need to consider an entirely different—low-cost and short-term—approach to fixing up the room.

Adult Bedroom Master Planning List

Priority	Project/Purchase	Comment	Estimated Price
Contractors			
____	Electrician	_____	____
____	Plumber/heat	_____	____
____	Flooring person	_____	____
____	Painter	_____	____
____	Carpenter	_____	____
Lighting			
____	Ceiling fixtures	_____	____
____	Table/floor lights	_____	____
____	Swing-arm lamps	_____	____
____	Book lights	_____	____
Furniture			
____	Mattress	_____	____
____	Box spring	_____	____
____	Frame	_____	____
____	Headboard	_____	____
____	Footboard	_____	____
____	Night tables	_____	____
____	Dresser/bureau	_____	____
____	Armoire	_____	____
____	Highboy	_____	____
____	Wall units	_____	____

continues

Adult Bedroom Master Planning List   (continued)

Priority	Project/Purchase	Comment	Estimated Price
Furniture, continued			
____	Sofa	_____	____
____	Loveseat	_____	____
____	Chaise	_____	____
____	Chair	_____	____
____	Ottoman	_____	____
____	Blanket chests	_____	____
____	Breakfast table	_____	____
____	Desk	_____	____
____	Vanity	_____	____
____	Vanity chair	_____	____
Floor			
____	Wood	_____	____
____	Area rugs	_____	____
____	Carpet	_____	____
Windows			
____	Draperies	_____	____
____	Blinds	_____	____
____	Shutters	_____	____
____	Shades	_____	____
Accessories			
____	Mirrors	_____	____
____	Bed linens	_____	____
____	Decorative pillows	_____	____
____	Art/pictures	_____	____
____	Family pictures	_____	____
____	Folding screens	_____	____
____	Breakfast tray	_____	____
____	Alarm clock	_____	____
____	Quilt racks	_____	____
____	Candles	_____	____

Children's Bedroom Master Planning List: Repairs, Renovations, and Purchases for All Stages

Priority	Project/Purchase	Comment	Estimated Price
Contractors			
_____	Electrician	_____	_____
_____	Plumber/heat	_____	_____
_____	Flooring person	_____	_____
_____	Painter	_____	_____
_____	Carpenter	_____	_____
Floor			
_____	Wood	_____	_____
_____	Area rugs	_____	_____
_____	Carpet	_____	_____
_____	Vinyl	_____	_____
Windows			
_____	Curtains	_____	_____
_____	Valance	_____	_____
_____	Blinds	_____	_____
_____	Shutters	_____	_____
_____	Shades	_____	_____
Lighting—Nursery			
_____	Overhead fixtures	_____	_____
_____	Table/floor lights	_____	_____
_____	Night-light	_____	_____
Furniture—Nursery			
_____	Crib	_____	_____
_____	Changing table	_____	_____
_____	Small bureau	_____	_____
_____	Rocking chair	_____	_____
Accessories—Nursery			
_____	Small footstools	_____	_____
_____	Pillows/trims	_____	_____
_____	Diaper pail	_____	_____

continues

Children's Bedroom Master Planning List: Repairs, Renovations, and Purchases for All Stages (continued)

Priority	Project/Purchase	Comment	Estimated Price
Accessories—Nursery, continued			
____	Small shelves	_____	____
____	Mirrors	_____	____
____	Musical mobile	_____	____
Lighting—Toddler			
____	Overhead fixtures	_____	____
____	Table/floor lights	_____	____
____	Night-light	_____	____
Furniture—Toddler			
____	Junior/twin bed	_____	____
____	Bureau	_____	____
____	Toy/storage chests	_____	____
____	Table for crafts	_____	____
____	Small chair(s)	_____	____
Accessories—Toddler			
____	Colorful bed linens	_____	____
____	Floor pillows	_____	____
____	Mirror hung low	_____	____
____	Chalkboard hung low	_____	____
____	Mini-playhouse	_____	____
____	Wall hangings	_____	____
____	Music box	_____	____
____	Tape player	_____	____

The School-Age Child's Room—Master Planning List

Priority	Project/Purchase	Comment	Estimated Price
Lighting—School-Age Child			
____	Overhead fixtures	_____	____
____	Table/floor lights	_____	____

Priority	Project/Purchase	Comment	Estimated Price
Lighting—School-Age Child, continued			
____	Night-light	_____	____
____	Desk lamp	_____	____
____	Wall-hung reading lamp	_____	____
Furniture—School-Age Child			
____	Bed (twin, bunks)	_____	____
____	Dresser/bureau	_____	____
____	Armoire	_____	____
____	Built-in storage	_____	____
____	Desk	_____	____
____	Bookcases/shelving	_____	____
____	Chair	_____	____
____	Project table	_____	____
____	Table/chairs	_____	____
Accessories—School-Age Child			
____	Bed linens (child's pref.)	_____	____
____	Wall hangings	_____	____
____	Mirrors	_____	____
____	Plants	_____	____
____	Tape player	_____	____
____	Framed artwork from school	_____	____
Lighting—Preteen			
____	Overhead fixtures	_____	____
____	Table/floor lights	_____	____
____	Desk lamp	_____	____
____	Wall-hung reading lamp	_____	____
Furniture—Preteen			
____	Bed	_____	____
____	Dresser/bureau	_____	____
____	Armoire	_____	____

continues

The School-Age Child's Room—Master Planning List (continued)

Priority	Project/Purchase	Comment	Estimated Price
Furniture—Preteen, continued			
____	Wall units/built-in storage	_____	____
____	Desk	_____	____
____	Bookshelves	_____	____
____	Small sofa	_____	____
____	Table/chairs	_____	____
Accessories—Preteen			
____	Bed linens	_____	____
____	Music system	_____	____
____	Mirrors	_____	____
____	Plants	_____	____
____	Floor pillows	_____	____
____	Computer	_____	____
Lighting—Teenager			
____	Overhead fixtures	_____	____
____	Table/floor lamps	_____	____
____	Desk lamp	_____	____
____	Wall-hung reading lamp	_____	____
Furniture—Teenager			
____	Bed (twin, double)	_____	____
____	Dresser/bureau	_____	____
____	Armoire	_____	____
____	Wall units/built-in storage	_____	____
____	Desk	_____	____
____	Bookshelves	_____	____
____	Small sofa	_____	____
____	Table/chairs	_____	____

Priority	Project/Purchase	Comment	Estimated Price
Accessories—Teenager			
____	Music system	_____	____
____	Mirrors	_____	____
____	Plants	_____	____
____	Floor pillows	_____	____
____	Computer	_____	____

The Least You Need to Know

➤ As a quiet, private space, the bedroom has potential for many purposes besides sleeping. Think how you want to use it.

➤ Bedroom furniture arrangements can allow for different activity areas, using the bed and storage pieces to divide the space.

➤ Placement of the bed must allow for easy movement and cleaning, and access to utility furnishings. The placement in relation to windows and light is also important.

➤ Storage furnishings in the bedroom, whether built-in pieces or free-standing cabinets, help define room style and serve as display pieces as well.

➤ Lighting in the bedroom must be adequate for general activity and specific needs such as in-bed reading, and it should help set a relaxed atmosphere.

➤ Your child's bedroom must serve many purposes—and must have different furnishings and arrangements at each stage of the child's life.

Chapter 21

The Ultimate Home Office

In This Chapter

➤ Your work habits and home office planning

➤ The role of ergonomics

➤ Choosing the best space

➤ Furnishings and storage for the home office

➤ Accessories for comfort while you work

As we begin the twenty-first century, the world of technology and information is growing at a rapid rate—certainly faster than the space in our homes. More and more people are doing some or all of their work at home and have a room or space entirely devoted to it! Even if you make your living by going to a traditional workplace every day, you may need a home office for any number of reasons: to do work you bring home, work on activities or projects you're engaged in, or just keep track of household maintenance, repairs, and expenses.

Of course, you may not be able to devote an entire room to a home office. In that case, you may partition a section of the living room, kitchen, or bedroom into a separate space, using folding screens, bookshelves, or simply a change of floor coverings. Or you may find just enough room in a stair landing or nook under the stairs to set up a desk, some storage, a small chair, and lighting. Wherever you locate it, your home office will have to be a quiet, well-lit zone where you can concentrate on your work.

Homework for the Home Worker

To create a successful method of working at home and a suitable home office environment, the first thing you should do is consider your personality. Some questions you might ask yourself are …

➤ Will I be using my office alone, or will colleagues, clients, or members of the household be coming in and out to use the office?

➤ Am I a neat and organized worker?

➤ Can all office items be left out, or do they need to be hidden when the office is not in use?

➤ Does my work require my undivided attention?

➤ Will household calls or conversations distract me?

➤ Do I need total privacy?

➤ Am I disciplined enough to work at home?

➤ Are my hours flexible?

A well-designed office is the ultimate expression of personal choice, allowing you to create an atmosphere to meet your needs, tastes, and idiosyncrasies. A home office can have all of the advantages of a traditional workplace: furnishings, equipment, technology, communications equipment, and supplies, but the decor, colors, lighting options, and comfort level should be tailor-made to your specifications. Creating a very effective work environment will make you a very effective worker.

Designer's Dictionary

Ergonomics is the study of the relationship between a worker and his or her office surroundings and equipment.

Ergo What? Your Environment's Effect on Your Work

Your home office needs to be planned with practicality in mind. For you to be creative and productive, it should be designed ergonomically. *Ergonomics* is the study of the relationship between you (the worker) and your environment, particularly the equipment that you use. To be productive, you need to be in surroundings that are pleasing to you. Uplifting wall colors, an adequate heat and air-conditioning system, proper lighting, correctly designed chairs, desks that fit and function properly, and equipment that is efficient and up-to-date all play a role in your environment and the psychology of working.

Do you leave the house at different times of the day? How much time will you spend at your desk? How do you work? What will you need to equip your office? Can you adapt any existing furniture to office use? Once you've determined what your essential furnishing and equipment needs are, you'll be ready to consider the size and type of space you'll want for your office.

Where to Put Your Office

Of course, choosing the right space in your home is very important. If you spend most of your day in the office, choose a space that will be bright and attractive. Unless it suits the kind of work you do, a dark space will diminish your productivity and creativity. Ask yourself what you want from your office. Some priorities may be that it is ...

➤ **Simple.** A workspace with a table and a chair and outlets.

➤ **Warm and homey.** Part of the kitchen used as desk area.

➤ **Bright, with a view.** Windows necessary.

➤ **Mobile.** A cart used as a desk on wheels.

➤ **Concealable.** Workspace that is simply hidden away at day's end.

➤ **Eclectic.** An imaginative blend of vintage furnishings with modern technology.

➤ **Very private.** Positioned on the quietest side of the house in an area that can be closed off (in which case, a washroom nearby is a necessity).

You may wish for several of these features. All have their benefits. Decide which will work best for you. Depending on the options you have, take time to analyze your work habits and your lifestyle. If remodeling is called for, research the costs involved before you proceed. Once you've made your major decisions, choosing your furnishings and equipment will be a breeze.

Decorator's Diary

Space was so limited at Andy's home that I suggested using a closet for his home office. The back of the door held a bulletin board, and the computer desk and chair were on wheels. They could be pulled out for use and stored afterward. Clever!

Space Solutions: Corners, Nooks, and Closets

If you live in a small home, you may have to set up an office in an area of a room that is already used for other tasks—a multipurpose room. A den could be the relaxing room, the office for working, and the library for study. Multipurpose spaces need various kinds of furnishings. A comfortable loveseat or sofa is perfect for a room that promotes quiet relaxation. An ottoman placed in front of the chair or sofa says "put your feet up and relax." It also makes a comfortable and convenient place to meet with colleagues or clients. A table can double as a desk and hobby surface. Bookshelves can house your work papers and the family's books.

If you live in a one-room apartment, you may have to resort to a corner or nook and adapt a surface to hold your computer or other equipment. Add shelves above the table and be very neat! Why, even a closet can be fitted to hold a pullout office!

The Whole-Room Office

If you have a choice of rooms to convert to your office, locate it away from the family hubbub in a quiet area. If natural light is important, choose the room with the most windows. Air flow is important, and proper heat and air conditioning affect the way you work. Do they work sufficiently in the room you chose? Your choice may be the room that is most aesthetically pleasing, with paint color or wall covering you like. Is there a room that is already outfitted with bookshelves? Are there several outlets in one particular room?

Consider these options before you plunk down your desk.

Furniture and Storage for the Home Workspace

Ideally, a room that serves as a home workspace will have a desk; the right desk chair; filing cabinets; proper lighting; probably a computer, printer, and fax; and plenty of bookcases and/or shelving.

Sitting Pretty

Choosing the right desk and chair is the first step in applying ergonomics to your furnishings. Do your homework! By testing out different chairs and desks, you can save yourself discomfort and needless expense. Ask yourself how much time you'll spend at your desk each day. You'll need a desk that accommodates your body size and paperwork. Do you sit all the time when you're working? If so, your most basic need will be the right chair.

Ergonomically speaking, a comfortable desk chair is a must for good posture; it should also look attractive. Before you buy, make sure you test it. Sit in it, and check whether it has good back support and a padded seat. If an office-style chair is not an option, some dining chairs can be substituted if they have upholstered backs, seats, and arms (and preferably, if they have castors, or wheels, as well).

If your workspace is large, you can add various furnishings to make it more comfortable for yourself, visitors, and colleagues. Choose materials that are durable for casual use. And if there's room, you can consider a sleep sofa to accommodate guests. (Buy one with a good mattress!)

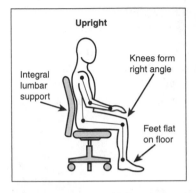
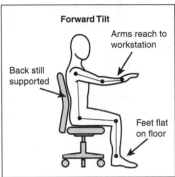
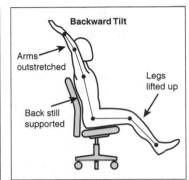

The correct chair. Upright: Sit upright so that your back is supported. Forward tilt: Be able to tilt forward and reach across your desk. Backward tilt: Be able to tilt backward and to stretch your limbs.

What's the Setup?

There are two approaches to arranging your work equipment. You can conceal each piece of equipment in a storage unit or leave it out on surfaces in open space.

Decorator's Diary

Kathleen used an old farm table for a desk. I suggested she cover the top with galvanized sheet metal for a smooth surface and a great look!

Consider what your storage needs may be. Do you have a fax machine, computer, and printer? A scanner? Do you own a photocopier or special music or media equipment?

Factor in your work style. Many mail-order catalogs offer factory-built desk and workstation units specifically designed to hold a computer, keyboard, printer, and fax—and sometimes much more. These range in style from rustic to modern to suit many decorating tastes.

Expert Advice

A plastic wire basket hooked under a desk can manage the cords from the various office equipment that tend to tangle. Tags on the cords will help identify them.

Of course, desk units, bookshelves, or wall units can be custom-made to house unconventional equipment and to fit into any available space. Such built-in units provide a clean, uncluttered look with equipment concealed behind doors. On the other hand, open shelving affords excellent storage, display of books and other items, and easy access to work materials.

Metal stacking units are versatile and affordable. If you rent your home, such portable storage is a good choice. For a more traditional style, a free-standing storage piece like an armoire or chest can lend an office area a more homey feel.

A wall-hung shelving grid supplies plenty of storage and fits perfectly in this bedroom alcove.

Whatever their style, units such as filing cabinets should be easily accessible. You can find files on wheels that you can move easily whenever and wherever you are doing your work. (Filing cabinets come in rattan, wood, or metal to fit attractively into almost any living space.) Use attractive and coordinated desktop organizers for papers, pencils, and mail to eliminate the messy-desk syndrome. Check the resources in the Appendix, "Bibliography and Resources," for suppliers of affordable and attractive furnishings and accessories.

Some Light on the Subject

Proper lighting is essential to defining the task areas in the home workplace, and it also prevents eye strain, of course. General lighting provided by an overhead fixture is fine for normal activities but must be supplemented by adequate task lighting.

Place a lamp at each area where you work. Adjustable architect's lamps are useful because of their capability to swing to any position, laterally and vertically, to illuminate your work. You may want to purchase a few inexpensive clip-on lights, which can attach to the side of a bookcase or shelf. Table or floor lamps that shine light downward are useful on either side of a seating area. (See Chapter 14, "Lighting Up Your Life," for more on lighting.)

Natural light is an enhancement to any office (unless it interferes with the kind of work you do). To illuminate your space with window light, try to orient the desk so that natural light enters over your shoulder. When working with a computer, however, a window behind the desk can cause glare on the computer monitor, and it may be necessary to draw shades or blinds.

Getting Plugged In

Communications technology has made it possible for more and more people to work from home by giving us a way to stay in constant touch with the people we work with, even though we may never meet them face-to-face. A typical home office may have a computer, modem, fax, and at least two phone lines. The number of phone lines you'll need will depend on how much communications equipment you have, and the amount of lighting and other electrically powered accessories will determine whether you need to upgrade your electrical system.

Expert Advice

If you are creating a new home office, always add more electrical outlets than you think you'll need. It's more economical to do it in the construction phase rather than after the room is completed.

Before setting up your office, call your local phone company to see how many lines are available to you. Know your options. You may need three lines: one for a home phone number, another for a business line, and a third for Internet service.

If you have access to cable programming through your TV, a cable modem instantly connects you to the Internet, which eliminates the need for a dedicated telephone line and always having to "dial in"—plus, it's a very fast service. Also, check out DSL (digital subscriber line), which does require a telephone line but allows you to gain access to the Internet without dialing in.

As far as home phones go, wireless is where it's at. Mobile phones allow home-workers to catch up on household duties while still engaging in business conversations. A headset (a phone that fits on your head like stereo headphones … no hands required) gives you the luxury of discussing the Asian currency crisis while doing the laundry and getting dinner ready! Be sure your phones are at least 900 MHz (megahertz), because this frequency provides the most clarity for the money. Most modern cordless phones require two cords: the telephone line connection and the household electricity. To keep working if there's an electrical outage, keep an old noncordless phone—one that operates with one telephone company connection and does not require an electrical source—in the closet so that it can be connected to the telephone jack and operate fully on the telephone company's power alone.

If you need more electrical outlets to operate extra office equipment, call an electrician for expert advice.

Quiet, Please

The home office can be made more soundproof with smart decorating choices. Here are a few:

➤ Use wall-to-wall carpeting for flooring treatment.

➤ Maximize fabric use on walls and window dressings to absorb sound.

➤ Use bookcases filled with books to act as a functional and decorative sound baffle.

➤ Use oversized cork bulletin boards or cork tiles on walls. These are super sound absorbers.

The Five-Star Office

If you have a room entirely dedicated to your home office, there are many small luxuries you can add as you go that will help you work, think, create, or even retreat from the outside world if you feel like it.

Accessories you can add include …

➤ A CD player loaded with your favorite music. CD racks can be hung behind closed doors or in a freestanding CD rack. A set of headphones can be used when you share your office.

➤ A small kitchen center in a corner of the workspace behind a folding screen. A tea or coffee maker is a nice addition that can fill the space with a wonderful aroma. A small, dorm-size refrigerator can keep cold water and drinks handy.

➤ Down-filled pillows covered in fabrics that can take a beating may be placed on the sofa for a truly comfortable head- or backrest. If you want to splurge, use down-filled cushions for your chair or sofa. You'll never want to get up!

If you've made your choices, it's time to make your plans. The following Master Planning List will help you set priorities and determine the costs of your new home office. Remember that repairs are always the top priority. Next, go through the list and write down your answers next to each item that pertains to your situation.

To fill in the appropriate places, refer to the personal inventory that you made in Chapter 1, "You've Got Style: Flaunt It!" checking off the possessions you have and the ones that you need and want. Remember to build your list around items that you love. Also keep in mind to …

➤ **Prioritize.** The master list is arranged in a general order of priorities, but you can adjust items according to your particular conditions.

➤ **Price your priorities.** Get accurate price estimates for every item on your proposed list by consulting contractors, department and home improvement stores, mail-order catalogs and other publications, and the Internet. Total the estimated cost for all your projects.

➤ **Match your plans with your resources.** If your total cost falls 20 to 30 percent over your budget, eliminate the lower-priority items. If you are more than 30 percent over your budget, review your planning approach thoroughly. You may need to consider an entirely different—low-cost and short-term—approach to fixing up the room or space.

Home Office Master Planning List

Priority	Project/Purchase	Comments	Estimated Price
Contractors			
_____	Electrician	_____	_____
_____	Plumber/Heat	_____	_____
_____	Flooring person	_____	_____
_____	Painter	_____	_____
_____	Carpenter	_____	_____
Lighting			
_____	Ceiling fixtures	_____	_____
_____	Table/floor lamps	_____	_____
_____	Wall lights	_____	_____
_____	Architect's light	_____	_____
_____	Clip-on light	_____	_____

continues

Home Office Master Planning List   (continued)

Priority	Project/Purchase	Comments	Estimated Price
Equipment			
____	Computer or laptop	_____	_____
____	Phones	_____	_____
____	Headset	_____	_____
____	Modem	_____	_____
____	Fax	_____	_____
____	Copier	_____	_____
____	Scanner	_____	_____
____	Audio/video	_____	_____
____	Cable modem	_____	_____
____	TV	_____	_____
Furniture			
____	Desk and chair	_____	_____
____	Sofa	_____	_____
____	Loveseat	_____	_____
____	Armchairs	_____	_____
____	Ottoman	_____	_____
____	Side chairs	_____	_____
____	Armoire	_____	_____
____	Wall/shelving units	_____	_____
____	Filing cabinets	_____	_____
____	Media storage	_____	_____
____	Sofa/library table	_____	_____
____	Coffee table	_____	_____
____	End tables	_____	_____
Floor			
____	Wood	_____	_____
____	Area rugs	_____	_____
____	Carpet	_____	_____
Windows			
____	Draperies	_____	_____
____	Blinds	_____	_____
____	Shutters	_____	_____
____	Shades	_____	_____

Priority	Project/Purchase	Comments	Estimated Price
Accessories			
____	Mirrors	_____	_____
____	Plants	_____	_____
____	Decorative pillows	_____	_____
____	Music system	_____	_____
____	Coffee maker	_____	_____
____	Small refrigerator	_____	_____

Whether you're working with a small nook and a very limited budget or the sky's the limit, the key to an efficient home office is proper and current equipment housed in a pleasing space with ample and creative storage.

The Least You Need to Know

➤ Home offices—even in the smallest space—should be created around your personal tastes, work habits, and lifestyle. Accessorize to make your workplace as inviting, comfortable, and efficient as possible.

➤ Ergonomically designed office spaces are those that consider the worker, the working environment, and the type of equipment used.

➤ Lighting for the home office must include general and adequate task lighting. Bring in natural light whenever possible.

➤ Furniture arrangements in a sizeable office should include work pieces like built-in wall units, desks and/or computer stations, file cabinets, and comfortable pieces like a small sofa or a chair and ottoman.

➤ Sound-absorbing elements like curtains, bookcases, and carpeting are useful in the office area.

Chapter 22

Entries, Stairways, and Halls

In This Chapter

➤ Furniture for the foyer

➤ Storage in the passageways

➤ Lighting the entryway and passageways

➤ Accessories on display

The entrance foyer is usually the first place you and your guests see when coming into your home. Make a good impression on others, and please yourself, with carefully chosen wall treatments, flooring, furniture, and accessories. Dare to be bold and dramatic, leaving your guests intrigued (and making you love to come home).

Furniture for the Foyer: Small Touches That Count

Even a small table and chair are great pieces in an entryway. A table serves as a natural resting place for your keys, pocketbook, or mail (and can do double duty as a small desk as well). It is always nice to have a quick rest on entering or leaving, too: A seat in the foyer is perfect for taking off shoes or boots and is a place for guests to rest a minute before leaving. A simple chair, bench, loveseat, or a traditional combined hatrack/hall seat will do.

If your entry is small, a wall-hung hatrack with a shelf—or even a plain shelf—helps the foyer to serve its practical purpose with a touch of style.

A small entry is made useful with seating and a coat rack.

(Photo by Gear)

A grand entryway is en-livened with wall-covering patterns of birds and flowers.

(Photo by Schumacher)

Hallways can be more than just a narrow corridor from the entry to other rooms. Make them useful by placing narrow console tables or chests against the wall, with large mirrors hung above. Wall-hung mirrors and tall pieces—such as a mirror-fronted armoire—will give the illusion of more space. Stairways can be enlivened with wall hangings, too. And if your landing has enough space, a large, low trunk can serve as a resting spot and a storage piece.

This hallway is opened up by a patterned wall covering with views of a country village-patterned wall covering.

(Photo by Gear)

Storage in the Passageways

An entryway should provide attractive storage for umbrellas, hats, gloves, and coats. An antique hall rack with a mirror, seat, drawers, and umbrella stand is a time-proven all-in-one storage solution for entryways—especially if it has a seat that lifts for extra storage space. If you can't find an old one, have a carpenter custom-fit one. A classic coat rack along with a circular porcelain umbrella stand take up little space and fit nicely in a corner.

For hallways, narrow tables or chests can hold many small items. Again, custom carpentry might be useful to fill unused space with narrow cupboards, chests of drawers, or a seat with a lift top and storage space for extra blankets and throws.

Lighting the Entryway and Passageways

Light in a foyer should be lovely and bright enough to provide a warm welcome for all. A dramatic choice for a large entryway is a chandelier that provides ambient lighting. Smaller entryways may have an overhead fixture with a decorative shade that diffuses the light for atmosphere and general illumination. Matching narrow candlestick lamps on a console table or sconces placed on either side of a mirror add enough light for greeting guests and general passage.

It is wonderful to bring natural light to the foyer through windows positioned on either side of or above the door. You can get a marvelous effect and ensure privacy with stained glass or frosted panes that diffuse light.

Expert Advice

Give everyone, including yourself, a warm welcome by placing your entryway table lamp on a timer set to illuminate the foyer before you arrive home. Plan to have lighting switches at the bottom and top of a stairwell so that they can be turned off easily after use.

Stairways and hallways often lack natural light, so general and accent lighting are necessary. Sconce fixtures placed at the bottom and the top of a stairwell provide background illumination as well as a decorative touch. They should be supplemented with adequate accent lighting so that stair treads are clearly visible.

Spotlights can be positioned to shine on the ceiling of the stairwell to visually enlarge it or to highlight artwork. Some stair landings have windows with natural light during the day but need lighting for evening. Place sconces on either side of the window or a small table lamp on a table to provide enough general lighting for safe movement.

Hallways also need general lighting from overhead lights or wall sconces. An additional table lamp placed on a chest or table (or several, if the hall is long) and accent lighting on wall-hung art, photos, or prints can make the hall seem more like a gallery than a passageway.

Accessories on Display in Passageways

Mirrors—even large ones, if the space permits—are perfect accessories for foyers and entryways. They reflect light, visually enlarge the space, and offer you (or your guests) a final glimpse at your appearance before the party starts.

Decorative shelves or small cubbyhole pieces can be wall-hung or rested on the back of the foyer table to showcase a small collection. Fabric cushions add softness to chairs or benches. In addition, door holders in the shape of fruit baskets or animals, and bricks covered in needlepoint, for example, personalize an entryway, too.

Stairways and hallways are natural sites for hanging artwork or framed pictures. An eclectic grouping of frames might be coordinated by similar matting. Small decorative shelving or cupboards add dimension and display space. Larger stair landings and hallways can display large plants, using natural light, if available, and highlighting them at night with uplights or spotlights.

The risers on your staircase—the vertical boards between each tread—are the perfect place to install decorative tiles. You can usually fit four or five eight-inch tiles on the face of the riser (affix them with tile adhesive and then grout, as on a kitchen backsplash). You will enjoy the color and pattern of your tiles every time you walk up the stairs!

Interiors 101

A collection of unusual boxes can be stacked under a table in a hallway for an eye-catching effect. Use your imagination and fill these transitional spaces with collections of interesting objects.

Using the Master Planning List: Prioritizing and Pricing Your Entryway, Stairway, and Hall Projects

Here's a brief review of how to use the master list, which is an outline of all the jobs, furnishings, and enhancements suitable for most entries and passageways:

➤ Evaluate the state of your area, using the master list as a guide. Repairs are always the top priority. Go through the master list and write down your answers next to each item that pertains to your situation.

➤ Refer to the personal inventory that you made in Chapter 1, "You've Got Style: Flaunt It!" to fill in the appropriate places, checking off the possessions you have and the ones that you need and want. Remember to build your list around items that you love.

➤ Prioritize: The master list is arranged in a general order of priorities, but you can adjust items according to your situation.

➤ Price your priorities: Get accurate price estimates for every item on your proposed list by consulting contractors, department and home improvement stores, mailorder catalogs, and other publications. Total up the estimated cost for all your projects.

➤ Match your plans with your resources: If your total cost falls 20 to 30 percent over your budget, eliminate the lower-priority items. If you are more than 30 percent over your budget, review your planning approach thoroughly. You may need to consider an entirely different—low-cost and short-term—approach to fixing up the area.

Stairways, Halls, and Entryways Master Planning List

Priority	Project/Purchase	Comment	Estimated Price
Contractors			
____	Electrician	_____	_____
____	Plumber/heat	_____	_____
____	Flooring person	_____	_____
____	Painter	_____	_____
____	Carpenter	_____	_____
Lighting			
____	Ceiling fixtures	_____	_____
____	Wall lights	_____	_____
____	Uplights	_____	_____
____	Spotlights	_____	_____
Furniture			
____	Small sofa	_____	_____
____	Bench	_____	_____
____	Hall rack	_____	_____
Floor			
____	Wood	_____	_____
____	Area rugs	_____	_____
____	Carpet	_____	_____
____	Stone/marble	_____	_____
____	Tile	_____	_____
Windows			
____	Sheer curtains	_____	_____
____	Blinds	_____	_____
____	Shutters	_____	_____
____	Shades	_____	_____

The Least You Need to Know

➤ Entryways are small but important spaces for decorating, as they create the first impression for your home.

➤ Practical furnishings for entryways are tables, chairs, and shelving that facilitate entering and leaving the house.

➤ Hallways can be hung with mirrors and set with narrow tables for storage and visual interest.

➤ Entryway lighting can combine window lighting and dramatic ambient lighting from a chandelier.

➤ Hall and stairway lighting should be sufficient for safe passage and provide attractive visual accents.

➤ Small object collections, large mirrors, and art on walls are appropriate and decorative accessories for passageways and foyers.

Part 5

Quick (and Easy-on-the-Budget) Makeovers

One of the exciting things about decorating is the big effect of small changes. Often, when you introduce a new element into a familiar environment—a bit of fresh paint, a set of draperies, or a display of memorabilia—you can put a whole room through a magical mood swing.

In this part of the book, we show you how to use the power of small innovations to quickly revive some tired old spaces. Your kitchen, bathroom, and bedroom get so much use you are probably lucky to keep up with the cleaning. But in each of these hard-working areas—where your family spends so much time—you can easily implement a few changes and revive their fading energy.

Of course, as we have recommended throughout the book, if you have the time and the money, follow the Master Planning List and do a top-to-bottom, fully coordinated renovation on the space. But you don't have to wait for retirement or hit the lottery to enjoy the "instant gratification" of a new decor. Put some of the following ideas into practice and feel better—fast.

Chapter 23

Make the Most of a Small Space ... with Style

In This Chapter

➤ Beginning steps to organizing your small space

➤ Room assessment: the key to small-space decorating

➤ Turning underused spaces into spare rooms or storage

➤ Organizing a versatile living space in one room

As you tackle your house room by room, what can you do if your rooms (or room) are rather small? This chapter will help you create a plan to economize your space and make your small rooms neater and more stylish than you ever thought they could be. A well-designed small room creates an illusion of space, uses appropriately scaled furnishings, and maximizes storage possibilities. But first, to begin any redo, a plan is in order!

Be Like a Pro: Plan and Prepare

Fancy yourself a professional designer for a moment. Pretend you're asking a client (who happens to be you) to name all the items he or she would love to have in the small space you're redesigning. Begin by taking a notebook and writing down some of the ways that you want your room to work.

➤ If your living area needs extra space for people to move around in, remove that large, overscaled sofa and substitute a loveseat instead.

➤ Do you need kitchen storage? Install shelving across the windows to store plates, bowls, and other items.

➤ Replace that bench at the foot of your bed with a convertible ottoman. It doubles as storage as well as seating.

➤ Add a sink skirt to your wall-hung bathroom sink to create storage for extra towels, toilet paper, soap, and cleansers.

Don't forget to consider the way you want to feel when you're in the room you're working on. Do you need a style update? Revisit your Personal Style Assessment (Chapter 1, "You've Got Style: Flaunt It!"), appropriate colors for small spaces (Chapter 4, "Color: The Decorator's Most Powerful Tool"), budgets (Chapter 2, "From Castles in the Air to Down-to-Earth Decorating"), and storage possibilities (Chapter 16, "Living Rooms to Actually Live In"). Once you review your answers, you can begin to maximize your room's space and potential. Be sure to include the following:

➤ What are the room's best points?

➤ What are the room's worst points?

➤ What is your budget?

➤ Do you need more storage in the room?

➤ Who will use the room?

➤ What built-in items do you have to work around (large windows, a fireplace, etc.)?

➤ Do you have ample lighting outlets?

➤ What about natural light?

➤ Are the heating and plumbing adequate? Will they still be after the renovation?

➤ How will you use the room?

Living Well in a Small Living Area

The best feature of a small living space is its great potential for creating a cozy and intimate room for everyday use as well as for entertaining. To make a room livable, you'll need seating, reading and TV areas, storage, and tables. You may be saying to yourself, "What? I can barely fit myself in here, let alone all those items to make the room livable!" Never fear. With a few creative touches, any room can be comfortable and attractive.

Places to Plant Yourself

To avoid a bulky or overcrowded look, the best seating choices for miniscule rooms are chairs with small backs and delicate arms. Small-scale reclining chairs allow you to stretch out your legs but have the advantage of allowing you to return to a compact position. Castors, or wheels, on chairs make seating moveable and therefore make room arrangement more flexible. Folding chairs can be useful for extra guests. Some chairs need not be folded away in a closet if they are finely finished in bamboo or wrought iron. Premade slipcovers are even available to fit a standard metal chair. Both the slipcover and chair can be folded and put away after use. Ottomans and footstools can also double as extra seating. A long, low bench can serve as a coffee table and can seat a few extra guests when necessary.

If you have one uninterrupted wall space, consider a low-backed and curvaceous sofa. Its softer, rounded lines eliminate the boxy feeling that square-edged sofas create and leave the impression of space. Chaise longues are a great way to eliminate bulk and high backs by adding a leisurely, comfortable touch to a room. Loveseats are another wonderful alternative, offering small-scale seating for two.

Expert Advice

A picture-rail molding around a room can serve double duty. It visually adds height to the space and can be used to hold artwork or a collection of plates.

Shelve It!

Most of us have more stuff than we know what to do with! If you hoard objects and have a small living space, you may need to find areas to add shelves for stylish and useful storage.

Floor-to-ceiling shelving can accommodate books, art objects, and general clutter. You can neatly place items on shelves or organize them in coordinated, attractive boxes. Many mail-order catalogs offer stackable kraft paper (brown paper bag) colored boxes that can be neatly labeled for easy identification.

A peg rack with an attached shelf hung around an entire foyer, bathroom, or a section of a bedroom looks clever and adds substantial storage. A shelf placed at the top of a door or window takes advantage of otherwise unused space. In a bathroom, a small ledge placed around the room above sink level can shelve a collection of perfumes, shells, or beach stones.

Built-in or freestanding cupboards with doors and custom shelving can hold and hide hi-tech equipment such as your TV, stereo system, and CDs. A *swivel shelf* for the TV allows everyone a good view from anywhere in the room. An armoire can actually be outfitted with pullout shelves to hold a computer, printer, and keyboard. Attach a bulletin board to the back of the door, and voilà! You're in business!

Discreet and Decorative

Creating clever solutions to your space limitations might include furniture that can do double duty. Desks and bureaus with fold-down writing areas can double as work surfaces and storage areas. Tiny compartments behind the fold-down surface organize everything from pencils to household bills. Trunks and chests can hold things you don't use every day, like extra blankets or games, and can be used as seating or table surfaces. Just be sure the surfaces are flat!

Designer's Dictionary

A TV **swivel shelf** pulls out of an armoire and allows viewers to watch TV from anywhere in the room. When TV viewing is over, the shelf easily slides back into the armoire. The armoire doors can then be closed for a neat, more spacious look to the room.

Ottomans that provide footrests or seating can be converted to hold cushions or throws, or even fill in for a coffee table. Use a large tray to support beverages and snacks.

Glass-topped tables can create an illusion of more space, because you can see right through them. Dark stained wooden tables appear heavier than glass-topped ones of the same size.

Tables with delicate legs take up less visual room. Slim, less-bulky-legged tables will fool your eye into thinking they require less space. Tables with a lower shelf provide valuable extra storage space. And tables that fold or nest can give you three times their usable surface when opened and can then return to a compact arrangement.

Wall and ceiling lights free up valuable table surfaces and floor space. The reflective surfaces of mirrors will double the effect of light if hung near a light source and will open up a room. Review Chapter 14, "Lighting Up Your Life," to properly illuminate your living space.

Uncramp That Kitchen

Kitchens can seem like difficult rooms to pare down. After all, they're expected to accommodate everything from large pots and pans to cutlery, dishes, glassware, dry goods, gadgets galore, and of course, the proverbial kitchen sink. Check out the following suggestions for ways to uncramp your kitchen, create visual space, and increase storage space.

➤ Add windows to let in more light. More light gives the illusion of more space. Of course, this is not an inexpensive or quick solution, but if your budget allows, call a contractor for estimates.

➤ Add a glass panel to a solid door that leads outdoors—or to any door, as a matter of fact—to also add more light and the illusion of space. Again, contractor needed.

➤ Create a serving opening between the kitchen and dining room (if you have a separate dining area). This creates a pass-through window in the wall between the kitchen and dining room.

➤ Position kitchen appliances for the most efficient and practical use. A four-burner apartment-size stove could free up space that a standard-size stove takes up. A small microwave with a fan could be mounted over the stove to free up counter space. Refrigerators made to fit under counters give you valuable extra space. If your sink has to be small, make it a deep one for washing bigger items. (Refer to Chapter 18, "Kitchens to Cook in—Even If You Can't," for more ideas.)

➤ Place a sliding door on a pantry to eliminate the space needed for a standard door swing.

➤ Install pull-up or pull-down worktops or breakfast bars. Push them up or down when they're not in use.

➤ Use a butcher block on castors, with drawer space and a lower shelf for storage.

➤ Install cupboards with lazy Susans and pullout baskets.

➤ Use open shelving without doors over a doorway (or even a window!) for stacking bowls. Install wall hooks for hanging utensils. Mount suspended racks under cupboards to eliminate counter clutter.

➤ Hang an organizer from the ceiling that can be pulled down to retrieve seldom-used large kettles and other cookware.

➤ Put in tiered pot stands. They hold myriad dishes or pots.

➤ Install metal wired shelving in windows to add storage but to still allow light into your kitchen (light adds the illusion of space).

➤ Make clever use of containers, such as crocks or old toolboxes, to hold cutlery and odd cooking utensils.

Expert Advice

Don't forget to use the backs of doors for needed storage! Ready-made shelving adds valuable space for organizing spices and other pantry items.

Double your storage capacity by hanging stemmed glasses under a shelf.

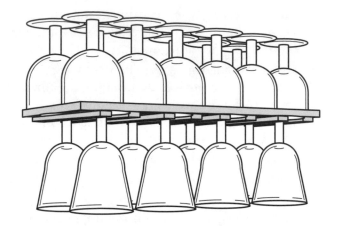

The Big Bedroom Feeling

No matter the size of your bedroom, it can be (and should be) a comfortable retreat. You'll need the basics:

➤ A place to sleep

➤ Seating (hopefully, if you have the room)

➤ Storage

➤ Dressing area

➤ Proper lighting

Now I Lay Me Down to Sleep ...

Since the largest piece of furniture in your bedroom (and, if you're dealing with a small space, probably the one taking up the most room) is the bed itself, take care when selecting it. Be imaginative when choosing a bed. Some good styles for small spaces are ...

➤ **Futons.** Cotton mattresses without springs that are easily folded on frames for use as sofas or unfolded for use as beds.

➤ **Platform beds with storage drawers.** Beds that are raised to accommodate drawers to fit underneath to maximize storage.

➤ **Delicate frames and headboards.** Headboards with a lightweight look, such as iron spindles, tapered two-posters, or fine wicker slipcovered in a sheer fabric.

➤ **Bunk beds.** Twin beds, one placed on top of the other, that provide two sleeping areas in the space of one.

➤ **Sofa beds.** Sofas that convert with the pull of a tab from seating pieces to beds.

➤ *Murphy beds.* Beds that are neatly installed on walls and pulled down when needed.

Clever Concealment, Continued

Organizing your stuff is key to a bedroom that works. Increase your bedroom's storage capacity by using under-the-bed storage drawers with castors attached for easy access.

Built-in wardrobes are fantastic for hiding collections of hats and shoes. Custom-designed shelving for odd angles will help to eliminate clutter and take advantage of otherwise dead space.

Some good ideas to keep your room from getting cluttered are …

➤ **Editing.** Regularly sorting through stuff.

➤ **Storing.** Keeping infrequently used items elsewhere.

➤ **Removing.** Moving bulky winter items to another storage area for the warm months.

➤ **Stacking.** Organizing items in attractive baskets or coordinated boxes.

Designer's Dictionary

A **Murphy bed** is mounted on a wall, freeing up a great deal of wall space when not in use. It can be pulled down easily when needed, and just as easily returned to its wall position.

Let There Be Light …

Proper lighting will greatly affect the look and feel of your bedroom. Wall lights controlled by dimmers are a perfect solution for changing a practical daytime bedroom into a romantic evening hideaway. Ceiling lights emphasize your room's good points. Mirrored walls behind a headboard will make the room grow in size as well as reflect the lighting, creating a lovely atmosphere. Plants tend to imitate nature, adding an airy feel to a room.

Of course, when it comes to a romantic ambiance, there's nothing like candlelight. In the soft glow of candles (especially scented ones), your bedroom will feel like the only place to be!

Makeover Miracles in a Mini Bath

Don't despair if your bathroom is short on space. It doesn't need to be short on function or style! Invest in baskets with covers to store unsightly everyday personal-hygiene products. Install attractive medicine cabinets that are useful, and take advantage of wall spaces to add shelving. Glass shelving appears less obtrusive, whether it be over the sink, the toilet, or at the end of a bath. Hooks and peg rails surrounding a bathroom can hold everything from loofahs to towels. Stacked boxes are super for storing less-attractive paraphernalia. Refer to Chapter 19, "Bathrooms with Practicality and Personality," to put your bathroom and yourself in the best light. Consider the following ideas for making your bathroom feel more spacious:

Expert Advice

Don't settle for a shower stall if you want a bath! Small tubs are available that can be made to look elegant when encased in wooden panels.

➤ Install antique tubs that appear less bulky.

➤ Have a small tub custom-made.

➤ Encase your tub in wood panels for a streamlined effect.

➤ Raise your tub and step up to it.

➤ Open the curtains on a shower/tub to extend the room.

➤ Mount sinks or vanities in a corner.

➤ Use narrow, slim-lined toilets.

➤ Go monochromatic when choosing paint, fixtures, and floor color. The less busy the room is with different colors, the larger it will feel.

Decorator's Diary

Linda's bathroom was so small, I suggested that she splurge on expensive wall covering and tile since she needed so small an amount of each. Both were affordable luxuries that had a great impact on such a small space.

➤ Install a large expanse of wall mirrors or mirror tiles.

➤ Enlarge windows or add a skylight.

➤ Install a proper ventilation fan to relieve that suffocating feeling.

➤ Use waterproof caddies that hang on a showerhead or decorative tub trays to hold soap, shampoos, and loofahs.

Build a simple shelf above the bathroom door to hold towels.

Deck the Halls (and the Stairwells and Closets, Too!)

Often overlooked as useful rooms are the areas we pass through and by every day: halls. If your hall is wide enough, it can double as a dining area if you make use of drop-leaf tables. Shelving a hall with shallow shelves instantly transforms your space into a library. Placing a small chest, a chair, and a phone jack in a hall adds a telephone room to your space. Add a chalkboard and keep track of family messages. Even a desk and chair can be fitted into a hall to create a place to open mail and keep track of bills.

Stairwells can house art objects and create a gallery effect. Add shelves and books, and your stairwell makes an unusual library. Use spotlights to feature treasured art or objects and increase the sense of space in the entire area.

The space under a stairwell makes a perfect cupboard. Use open shelves if you are displaying objects of interest, or use shelves with doors for added storage.

Shelve the "dead" space under a ceiling of a stairwell to accommodate infrequently used books or show off a prized collection. Hang a chandelier from the ceiling to give the dead space life! Add decorative mirrors on the wall, and the area is transformed.

Closets can accommodate entire home offices if set up correctly. Add pullout shelves and hang a bulletin board on the inside of the door. Complete with a roll-out table for a computer and a small chair on castors, and—instant workplace.

Effective lighting and color choices (see Chapters 14 and 4) can accentuate the positive aspects of these areas and help expand their sense of space.

Expert Advice

You can turn a desk into a dining table for four or more in a minute by using a pull-up extension table with four folding chairs that fit neatly with it and can be stored in a one-foot storage compartment.

A Place for Everything: One-Room Living

A one-room living space works hard to service dining, sleeping, relaxing, entertaining, and possibly working. Adapt some of the decorating tips in this chapter for individual rooms to suit your one-room living space. A drop-leaf table can serve as your desk or your dining area. Raise the drop leaf of the table and pull up a dining chair as your seating. Store files in a piece with drawers that can double as a buffet and filing cabinet. A skirted 36-inch round coffee table is perfect for an end table and for a dining table (and it adds valuable storage). Folding chairs are always perfect to pull out when entertaining.

A low coffee table placed in front of a sofa or between two sofas requires no chairs at all. Floor cushions pulled up to the table make for a fun and casual dining spot. A folding game table can make the shift to a dining table and is easily put away (under the bed or in a closet). Hang mirrors to reflect other areas of the room and increase the sense of space.

So you don't become bored with living in one room, you may want to change the atmosphere for special occasions. Here are some quick and instant transformations that can make your one-room space sizzle:

➤ Cover your dining table in a linen or quilted tablecloth that reaches the floor.

➤ Add fresh flowers to the room (several small bunches).

➤ Add tassels to window shades or fun tiebacks to curtains.

➤ Cover dining chairs with slipcovers, or for an instant change, tie on attractive premade seat cushions.

➤ Transform the atmosphere by using easily adjustable track lights and a dimmer.

➤ Use candles throughout instead of electric lighting.

A delicate iron bed doubles as a sofa to maximize space.

(Photo by Laura Ashley)

Now you can stop feeling deprived because your rooms are too small or your entire living quarters consist of a single room. With the advice in this chapter and this book, a pad and pencil, and a little imagination, you can transform cramped and overcrowded spaces into comfortable—even delightful—places to be.

The Least You Need to Know

➤ Small rooms can function beautifully with the right furnishings and color schemes.

➤ Assessing your needs, setting priorities, and creating solutions are the keys to small-space decorating.

➤ Finding a place for everything requires innovative use of unusual spaces, such as halls, stairways, closets, and above doors and windows.

➤ Whether you live in one room, two rooms, or a house with small rooms, properly scaled furniture, creative storage, and thoughtful lighting produce an organized and pleasant space.

➤ To make the most of one-room living, choose versatile furnishings that can be easily moved and serve more than one purpose.

Chapter 24

Give Your Kitchen a Fresh Look—Fast!

In This Chapter

➤ Cook up a quick makeover for a new kitchen feeling

➤ Paint: a fast refresher for walls, cabinets, and more

➤ Soften up the kitchen with soft goods

➤ Chic kitchen projects that everyone can do

➤ Kitchen projects for advanced do-it-yourselfers

If you have come this far in the book, you already know that you need to use a great deal of thought, planning, prioritizing—and lots of your personal passion—to achieve rooms that you'll want to live with for a long time. But decorating does not always have to be a top-to-bottom effort. Sometimes time or money resources just don't allow for the thorough repair, renovating, or refurnishing that your Master Planning List calls for.

But that doesn't mean you have to live with a dingy or dull room, or look at the same old scenery, until that bonus check comes in. With just a few hours of work (and sometimes in no time at all!), you can add life and new personality to your kitchen with a host of quick and easy-on-the-budget makeovers.

Most of the ideas introduced in this chapter are projects you can do yourself with a few hours of work over a weekend. A few of the makeovers are best for accomplished do-it-yourselfers but are within the reach of anyone who can spend some time researching and learning some hands-on techniques. But remember, even if you just add some colorful curtains or wall hangings, you'll brighten all the hours you spend in the busiest room in the house.

Interiors 101

A molding added to the joint where the walls meet the ceiling will add a gentrified air to the kitchen. A simple three-inch molding is sufficient. Have your lumberyard cut the lengths to your measurements and be sure to account for the corner joints (a knowledgeable person at the yard will understand that corners need to be **mitered**). Give the molding a first coat of paint and set it in place with nails every 12 inches.

Paint Is the Most Efficient Method for Makeovers

A new coat of paint on the walls or on other elements in the kitchen is the easiest way to refresh its entire atmosphere.

Paint Those Walls!

This method is the quickest kitchen picker-upper there is. There are some standard wall colors for kitchens that produce reliable and positive effects: Ivory is always a very "clean" color; yellow will make the dullest kitchen bright; and terra cotta will give it an old-world look. But there are many other colors that might work in your kitchen. Refer to Chapter 4, "Color: The Decorator's Most Powerful Tool," and review some of the color profiles; check the kind of light that the room receives. And, of course, test before committing yourself.

The type of paint you use is also important. Use a semigloss or eggshell finish latex paint for durability and better washability, or any paint that is specifically for use in kitchens.

You may choose to do some simple paint techniques like sponging or rag rolling. These techniques provide visual texture and are easy to do, with practice. Refer to Chapter 11, "Walls That Work," for more information.

If your ceiling is stained and needs a fresh coat of paint, here are two easy pick-me-ups:

➤ Repaint the ceiling in white. White is the standard choice for opening up kitchens with low ceilings.

➤ Rag roll your ceiling in shades of brown. This will give the ceiling an aged texture.

When choosing paint, keep in mind that paints in flat-latex finishes are easier to repaint than ones that have an eggshell finish. However, latex finish isn't as scrubbable.

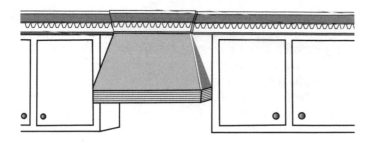

A decorative molding.

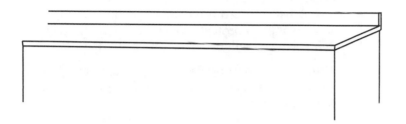

Paint Your Kitchen Cabinets

Reviving old cabinets with a fresh coat of paint will instantly make an impact. Use a latex semigloss or low-lustre enamel for the best durability and washability. Flat paint on cabinets is not durable and will chip and wear quickly with constant use.

You can get a lively, unconventional look by painting the lower cabinets a darker color than the upper ones. Similarly, with open shelving, you can paint the wall background a color that contrasts with the face of the cabinets. If your cabinets have a raised or inset panel, that area can be painted a deeper shade of the main color. Pewter grays and ivories, blacks and natural wood, sage green and dark green, or vibrant greens and yellows are just some of the many tasteful combinations.

Expert Advice

Wall coverings work in kitchens, too. A pattern in bold checks adds a "tavern" feel for eating or entertaining. A wide border of trompe l'oeil jugs and bowls is easy to apply and will add an instant collection of accessories to the space above your cabinets. Choose prepasted vinyl-coated papers for ease of application and washability.

A wall-covered backsplash requires very little paper and time to install. Choose a bold pattern to add color or one that simulates tiles for texture. New fabric-backed prepasted vinyls are the most durable and will easily hide cracks and flaws on old walls.

253

Interiors 101

There are other good ways to re-vive old cabinets. For instance, try sanding and refinishing. You can rent a small sander machine or use sandpaper to rub off the old cabinet finish. Again, this is a little more time-consuming than some projects, but it's not diffi-cult. After you remove the finish, use a pretreated cloth called a **tack cloth** that easily removes traces of sawdust that the sand-ing generates. The success of your refinishing is dependent on a dust-free surface. Next, apply a protective coat of polyurethane. Try to use latex polyurethane, which dries in two hours or so. You can apply three coats within the course of a day. An oil ure-thane is a bit more durable than a latex but requires 24 hours to dry between coats.

If your cabinets are too dark, they can be stripped or whitewashed. Stripping is a little more labor-intensive and a bit of a messy job, but not at all difficult. To perform this, you apply a solvent that "strips" the paint from the wood. Make sure to wear gloves to pro-tect your hands and a mask to limit the fumes you'll breathe that may be given off from the combination of stripper solvents and paint.

If there is any paint color still left in the wood, a wood bleach may be necessary to remove it. Once completed, you can leave the wood natural, but you'll have to apply a protective coat of polyurethane so that the wood will be able to resist stains.

Whitewashing is a process of applying a transparent wash that is made from an equal mix of white enamel paint and paint thinner. (A good paint store will mix it for you.) Brush it on the stripped cabinets, let it set for 15 minutes, and wipe it off. Apply a polyurethane finish to seal and protect the wood. Whitewashing cabinets allows the wood grain or knots to show for a very textural effect. It will also lighten the darkest of kitchens.

You can add character and architectural detail to plain front cabinet doors and drawers by adding molding, which is readily available at lumberyards or home stores. Simple ¹/₂-inch molding can be glued and nailed on the front of cabinet doors and drawers to re-semble custom panels. You can paint them the color of your cabinets after attaching them.

Decorator's Diary

My friend Barbara updated her Colonial Revival kitchen with a combination of new and vintage cabinets. She painted the outside of the cabinets a sage green and the open shelving a black/green. It was stunning!

Other Places to Put That Fresh Paint

As long as you have the paintbrushes out and your overalls on, here are some other kitchen items to redo:

➤ Paint a set of mismatched chairs in a casual kitchen and accent their varied shapes with a lively color like bright red, blue, or yellow. Chairs have flaws? Paint the entire chair flat black!

➤ If you can paint like an artist, fill your kitchen with scenes of farm animals, fresh fruits, or vegetables by painting them on the fronts of some of the doors and drawers or inside the panels. If you aren't a Picasso, try cutting figures or motifs from wall coverings or borders and applying them to the front of the cabinet doors. Then add a protective finish of polyurethane for a decoupage effect.

Expert Advice

You can also embellish cabinets, walls, doors, and drawers with stencils of fruits, vegetables, and other related items. Another simple technique for updating your cabinets, whether you paint or add moldings, is to add new handles, hinges, and pulls. All you'll need for this is a screwdriver.

Decorator's Diary

My kitchen is painted with bright French yellow. I complemented it by stenciling this saying in Old English lettering: "Thou hath nothing under the sun than to eat, drink, and be merry!"

➤ Paint old wooden floors with the spatter technique, as mentioned in Chapter 10, "Possibilities Underfoot." Another good paint technique for floorboards is alternating stripes of ivory and your favorite color or painting a checkerboard motif. Whichever technique you choose, be sure the paint is a floor paint: latex with epoxy reinforcement or an oil-based paint with polyurethane reinforcement.

This kitchen is given a new look with porcelain knobs, stenciled doors, and drawer fronts.

(Photo by Smallbone)

➤ If your appliances are old or the color is just wrong, blend them in with your cabinets by painting them with a metal paint. Your paint dealer can give you advice on the correct type to use.

Soften Up the Kitchen with Soft Goods

Fabric colors and textures are a wonderful contrast to the hard lines and surfaces of a kitchen. You can bring them into your kitchen in many easy ways:

➤ Add a simple valance on the windows. Kitchen windows usually require minimal dressing. A rod-run heading is simple to sew and install. Sew a pocket at the top of your fabric, slide a spring-tension rod through it, and set it in place. Easy and quick, huh? Refer to Chapter 13, "Opening Up the World of Windows," for more ideas.

➤ Put up half curtains of lace panels to give the look and feel of a Parisian bistro. Purchase clip-on rings (they may come with your rod) that grab the top of the fabric panels, and slide the rings on a brass or wrought-iron rod.

➤ For a bit of whimsy, attach a piece of jute from casing to casing at the midpoint of the window. Clothespin pretty kitchen towels as half curtains—you've created a clothesline effect.

➤ You can remove the doors under your sink and replace them with a gathered split skirt hung casually to give the sink a French Country look. Make a pair of gathered rod-run curtains and attach them under the sink on the face of the cabinet with a sash rod.

Interiors 101

Even a small touch like cloth napkins on the table can enhance your kitchen. Find a set of antique linen napkins that match several of your tablecloths.

➤ Add colorful premade seat cushions that tie on to your dining chairs or kitchen stools.

➤ If you have a dining table in your kitchen, use different tablecloths for an instantaneous change of atmosphere. Have tablecloths to use for festive occasions, holiday times, and different seasons. A couple of yards of fabric with edges hemmed will do the trick!

Chic Kitchen Projects Everyone Can Do

No skills necessary to do the following "quick and easies"—all of which will add some flavor to the look of your kitchen. And remember that many accessory displays can be changed seasonally to keep a fresh feel in the kitchen.

➤ Hang a collection of decorative plates with spring plate racks on a empty wall.

➤ Display a collection of antique or uniquely shaped baskets on beams or on top of your cabinets.

➤ Display a collection of old kitchen tools as interesting wall art.

➤ String bunches of herbs and dried flowers with jute and hang in front of the windows.

A generous supply of flowers dry on a rack suspended by a cord-and-pulley system.

(Photo by Smallbone)

➤ Place a large hook in the ceiling over a cooking counter and hang garlic braids, chili peppers, and herbs. This is handy for cooking and is a lovely visual accent.

➤ Spice up the atmosphere! In cold weather, keep a pot simmering with a potpourri of lemon and orange rinds and spices. In warm weather, fill a bowl with lemon peels and herbs and ice-cold water for refreshing scents and hand dipping.

➤ Add a station for cooking and casual entertaining with a freestanding table fitted with a butcher block or a piece of marble. Great for chopping or making pastries.

➤ Add small rugs in front of the sink, the cookstove, and seating area.

Kitchen Projects for the Advanced Do-It-Yourselfers

If you are a handy type, can follow how-to manuals and advice, and especially if you already have carpentry or tiling skills, the following improvement projects will give your kitchen a look you can be proud of. Even if you can't do these renovations yourself, consider finding a professional (or a friend) who can. They are all relatively small and inexpensive touches that will yield big dividends in kitchen enjoyment.

➤ Decorative tiles add a provincial or country touch to the kitchen when installed as a backsplash below the kitchen cabinets and above the counter. Stores that specialize in tile often offer do-it-yourself courses with a discount on purchase of materials.

➤ Replace your cabinet fronts with new doors and drawer panels. Your local kitchen and bath/home store can offer expert advice on the how-tos and what type of fronts you will need to purchase.

➤ Replace countertops with tile. Ask your local tile shop for detailed instructions.

➤ Add shelving with decorative brackets above windows or doors.

➤ Replace some solid doors on cabinets with etched, beveled, or frosted glass doors. You can purchase these through a kitchen/home store and can get advice on installing them.

➤ Install a greenhouse window over the sink or in another kitchen window for growing herbs and other plants. You can order a greenhouse window through a kitchen/home store, and it will come with complete instructions.

➤ Add a hanging fixture that is illuminated with candles over the cooking island or dining table for festive occasions and birthdays. Make your own with an old wagon wheel (available at a flea market or junk shop) hung from a large hook with wrought-iron links. Place large candles around the wheel. It's that easy!

White iron brackets hold up extra display shelves for large platters and soup tureens.

(Photo by Smallbone)

Whether you pick up a paintbrush and brighten the walls or simply place some baskets of fruit or flowers on the countertops, don't delay in giving your kitchen some of these simple, bright touches. They will certainly perk up the time you spend in this busiest room and might even inspire you to cook up some great new dishes.

The Least You Need to Know

➤ For a quick makeover in your kitchen, repaint the walls, cabinets, floors, furnishings, and appliances. Painting surfaces in contrasting colors can have a lively effect.

➤ Refresh cabinet doors and drawers with paint or other surface treatments, and install new hardware.

➤ Adding fabric covering to windows and cabinet openings, and an assortment of table coverings, can provide a distinctive country look to a kitchen.

➤ Some kitchen makeovers require a little bit of experience. Do-it-yourselfers should be able to take on these projects with the right advice from hardware/ kitchen stores.

Chapter 25

Brighten Your Bathroom Without Breaking the Bank

In This Chapter

➤ Painting the bathroom for a fast refresher

➤ Bringing style to the bathroom with stencils

➤ Soft fabric touches: fabulous in your bathroom

➤ Bathroom-beautifying projects that everyone can do

➤ Wall covering, tiling, and other projects for the advanced do-it-yourselfer

You may feel like your tired old bathroom needs more waking up than you do when you enter it first thing in the morning every day. If a complete remodeling project is not in your budget of time and finances, consider some of the many easy cosmetic changes suggested in this chapter. They can have a big impact on this busy space.

Many of these projects can be done in a weekend—or even in a few minutes—and demand no specialized skills. If you are handy, you will also find a host of suggestions that will help you transform the bathroom into a showpiece of affordable home decor. Your fixtures stay fixed, and your costs will be minimal, but you'll create a space that has lots of color and energy for a bright start each morning—and a lovely place to linger while relaxing in a hot bath.

Paint the Bathroom for a Fast Refresher

Once again, paint is the cheapest and easiest renovator's tool. Your choices for wall color in your bathroom are bountiful, but a sure guideline to an effective color scheme begins with your fixtures. (Remember that you will want to coordinate your shower curtain and possibly sink skirt and window dressings with your wall color, too. See the section "Soft Fabric Touches Are Fabulous in Your Bathroom," later in this chapter, for more information.)

Review the lessons on color discussed in Chapter 4, "Color: The Decorator's Most Powerful Tool." If you have colored fixtures, painting walls and choosing fabrics in contrasting colors will make the room seem smaller. On the other hand, if you match the fixtures in a monochromatic color scheme, the room will appear larger.

For fixtures that are white, as is common in most bathrooms, try painting the walls, vanity, and trim in the same white shade for a clean, fresh look. If the floor is wood, you can paint that white as well—colored towels and handcloths, plants, or fresh flowers can provide all the color you need in this scheme.

To create a cool bathroom that has white fixtures, paint your walls in pale blues or greens. For a warmer ambiance, choose pale pinks, peaches, and yellows.

> **Interiors 101**
>
> You can refresh your bath fixtures, too. Even an old-fashioned tub can be repainted on the outside with a high-gloss oil paint and resurfaced by a professional. Ask your paint dealer for more information.

Stencils Bring Style to the Bathroom

> **Expert Advice**
>
> A great way to coordinate and personalize the bathroom is to make your own stencil. Copy and repeat a lovely pattern from your shower curtain or window fabric.

As with kitchens, stencils are a simple paint technique that can liven up your bathroom walls or vanity cabinet. Look for unusual motifs that express your style. Here are some tips to make the most of your stencils:

➤ Copy the pattern in large enough groups (or have a large design) so that the stencil motif really has impact. A small stencil pattern only in one or two spots on a wall will make no impression.

➤ Don't hide your stenciling at the top of the wall, unless it is a large stencil or a lettered saying. More powerful places for stencils are above a midwall molding, right above the sink, or above the baseboard.

Even easier than stencils are stamp kits specially designed for wall decorations. These kits have rubber stamps of alphabet letters, geometric designs, and special motifs; and ink pads with special paints in gold, blue, green, and many other lively colors. Stamps are great for inscribing thoughtful or spirited phrases, names, or even just letters on your walls. With geometric shapes, stamped closely together, you can create walls that look just as though you wall-covered them—and for a lot less money! Stamp kits are available through mail-order catalogs such as Ballard Designs (see the Appendix, "Bibliography and Resources," at the end of this book).

Decorator's Diary

My client Stanley fell head-over-heels for his new bride. He stamped the word "Love" in gold paint—in many different languages and sizes—all over the ivory walls of his bathroom. Corny, but truly unique—and a great statement of personal style!

Soft Fabric Touches Are Fabulous in Your Bathroom

There are a number of easy ways to bring the soft look and feel of fabric to your bathroom. Again, you will want to consider the color of the bathroom fixtures and walls, and further coordinate all your fabric additions—such as shower curtain, sink skirt, and window dressings—through pattern, texture, and color, too.

If you have a wall-hung or pedestal sink, attaching a gathered skirt is a simple project. Measure the sink from one side to the other and from the top of the sink to the floor. Then you can double or triple the dimension of the skirt for desired fullness. The fabric is gathered, attached to a band that is the size of the perimeter of the sink, and hemmed to correct length. To fasten the skirt to the sink, sew loop Velcro to the skirt band and glue the corresponding hook Velcro to the top edge of the sink. For an extra-special effect, try one of the following:

➤ Add ruffles on the bottom of the skirt or several at various lengths.

➤ Attach buttons or bows down the front of the skirt that look like closures but actually provide a decorative effect.

➤ Put a scalloped hem on the bottom.

Fabrics like denim, muslin, and lightweight canvas are smart choices for durability and washability. (Preshrink your fabric before sewing by washing and drying it. This will enable you to wash your skirt later without a lot of shrinkage.) Chintz and linens are equally good-looking but might require dry cleaning.

Decorator's Diary

I once shared a small city apartment with my sisters Mary Kathleen and Mary Frances. The wall-hung sink in our small bathroom had all of the ugly pipes exposed. Since I had no intention of looking at old, rusty pipes, I pulled out of my closet an old, large floral chintz skirt, opened the back seam, and attached it to the sink with Velcro. It fit like a glove!

If you can't find a premade shower curtain that you like, and you're handy, try making one. A standard shower requires a 72-inch × 72-inch curtain. Buy at least five yards of fabric so that two 2^1/$_2$-yard pieces can be sewn together, allowing for side, top, and bottom hems and the repeat of the pattern. For the holes at the top of the curtain, called *grommets,* you will need a grommet tool. These are available at any hardware store in brass or chrome. You will need a dozen grommets per curtain spaced six inches apart. Buttonholes will also provide an opening for curtain-rod rings. The shower curtain tends to get a workout, so use heavy cottons (white can be bleached!). Natural fibers are always appealing. Linens and lighter-weight cottons like chintz will have to be dry-cleaned.

Window Treatments

The bathroom window is another place to add a coordinated fabric dressing. These can either be simple and unfussy or more elaborate. Since the bathroom probably has only one window, you may want to go all out and treat yourself to a luxurious window treatment.

A simple project is to install a valance that coordinates with the shower curtain, along with a shade or blind to pull down for privacy. A quick way to make an ordinary roll-up shade more decorative is to attach a large tassel for the pull. When the shade is up, the tassel will make a delightful focal point of the room. Sew your own valance or purchase a premade one through a mail-order catalog. (Refer to the Appendix for a list of resources.) Choose at least a three- to four-inch tassel for a stylish impression.

Furniture stores with decorative accessories carry tassels, or you can purchase them through a mail-order catalog.

Since many bathroom windows are small and ordinary, you can visually enlarge the window by hanging full curtains from floor to ceiling, extending even beyond the window frame. It's a quick way to add a little grandeur to the room.

For a tailored look (without fabric), consider installing a shutter in your bathroom window. If the shutter and walls are the same color, a clean, streamlined look is achieved. Or you can highlight the shutter by contrasting it with the trim or wall color. Your local lumberyard or home store sells stock shutters that you can stain or paint yourself.

A full-length curtain with a fringed valance and matching sink skirt dress up this bathroom in style.

(Photo by Schumacher)

A clever, inexpensive way to use fabric is to create a "wall" between the bathtub and toilet with a "banner" hung from floor to ceiling the width of the bathtub. Use a transparent fabric like organdy to hint at privacy and lend an airy look to the room. The banner can be attached to a wrought-iron curtain rod or dowel fastened at the top of the wall and can easily be taken down for dry-cleaning.

Of course, the easiest way to bring beautiful color and texture to any bathroom is with a sumptuous display of towels, washcloths, and floor mats. You can be creative and embellish plain towels with flat printed ribbons or pompom fringe. Roll up a glorious assortment of patterned washcloths and hand towels, and set them out in baskets.

Whether they are mismatched vintage linens or new, oversized linen towels with long cotton fringes, they will look fabulous hanging from interesting hooks, or folded and laid in a colorful pile on top of a table.

Bathroom-Beautifying Projects Everyone Can Do

You don't need to be a plumber or a tiling expert to make wonderful, quick improvements to your bathroom. You'll enjoy the big payoff from the following small investments of time and energy:

➤ Turn an old bathroom radiator into an instant shelf by placing a piece of marble on its top. The marble can take the heat and provides a great place for a large mirror or other heavy object.

➤ Decorate an ordinary framed mirror by gluing on natural objects, like shells, dried field flowers, birds' nests, and sea glass.

➤ Towel bars made of tree branches add a rustic touch to any bathroom. You can make hooks for robes by using the "Y" joint of the branch.

➤ Use an assortment of antique hooks for towels, clothes, or robes.

➤ Change your boring plastic shower-curtain hooks to wrought-iron or basic chrome hooks. Even loops of rawhide will work.

➤ Paint the ceiling a pale blue like the sky.

➤ Refresh your vanity cabinet with paint and added moldings or new hardware.

➤ Hang a full-length mirror on an available wall to enlarge the bathroom and serve as your dressing mirror.

➤ Set out many soaps, lotions, bath oils, and perfumes to make a pleasant display— and to make your bathroom smell great.

Bathroom Projects for the Advanced Do-It-Yourselfer

Wall covering can be wonderful in your bathroom: A large-scale pattern in a small bathroom will make it one of the most visually exciting rooms in the house. Wall covering doesn't require a professional to apply, but you must be able to follow directions, have the proper tools, and take your time. Also, you must make sure that your bathroom has good ventilation and that you are using vinyl-coated wall covering. Consult with a knowledgeable salesperson at the store from which you order your wall covering.

If you have some time and good sewing skills, heighten the drama of your bathroom window with a luxurious festoon. Use an eye-catching floral-pattern fabric lined with a small checked pattern and trimmed with a wide triple ruffle of the floral, the check, and a tea-stained lace. Attach the shade at the ceiling to visually lengthen the window.

Tile is, we all know, a perfect material for the bathroom. But you don't always need a professional: A small tiling project such as a decorative backsplash over the sink is well within the reach of a handy homeowner. You may need only a dozen or so tiles and can find beautiful tiles at bargain prices: Mismatched leftovers can give a nice eclectic feel, and vintage tiles will provide a lovely patchwork-quilt effect. You can teach yourself the details of tiling from some of the reliable how-to books listed in the Appendix at the end of this book. And once you have gained confidence by tiling the backsplash, you can go on to do the walls of your bathtub!

Expert Advice

If you become adept at papering the walls, do the ceiling of your bathroom with the same pattern or a coordinating one. It will make your bathroom look magical!

This bathroom is greatly enhanced by mirrors that reflect the wallplates and tiled wall of the bathtub.

(Photo by Smallbone)

Here are some other projects that will satisfy the handy home-improver:

➤ Replace your old faucets with vintage chrome or brass faucets with white porcelain handles that read "H" and "C."

➤ No window? Artistic? Paint a mural of a favorite scene enclosed in a trompe l'oeil window.

➤ Cover old walls—half to three quarters of the way up the wall—with tongue-and-groove bead board. Add a display shelf on top of the board. You can enclose a tub unit in bead board as well for a custom look.

➤ Add shelves at one end of the tub (only if your tub is separate from your shower unit).

➤ Insert glass shelves in the window of your bathroom to display pretty colored bottles.

➤ To make a distinctive vanity, set a small sink into the top of an old small dresser or washstand.

While a bathroom must efficiently serve its eminently practical purposes, it is also a space where design and decor can have notable impact. Artwork, touches of color, and small luxury items can add immeasurably to its feeling of relaxation and personal intimacy—this is one place you can afford to indulge!

The Least You Need to Know

➤ Paint and paint treatments can brighten, enlarge, and warm your bathroom. Coordinate colors with the bathroom fixtures and fabrics in the room.

➤ Simple projects with fabrics can soften the feel of the bathroom. Consider a vanity skirt, a coordinated shower curtain, and various window treatments.

➤ Do-it-yourself improvements for the bathroom include tiling, wall covering, and installing wallboard and shelving.

➤ Many simple projects—even just displaying colorful bath linens—can perk up your bathroom instantly.

Chapter 26

Adding a Touch of Romance to Your Bedroom

In This Chapter

➤ Don't wait to make your bedroom a place to love and linger

➤ A fresh coat of paint can make a setting for your romantic story

➤ A bedroom furnished for relaxing as well as sleeping

➤ The right lighting: more romantic than darkness

➤ Personal accessories: romantic touches

➤ Special projects for serious sewers

In your busy and hectic life, it's easy to neglect the bedroom. Besides, you probably leave it before dawn and don't return to it until your eyes are half-closed, many hours later. However, no place in your home will be more inviting and enjoyed than your bedroom when it's transformed with a touch of romance.

Whether you want the feel of a cozy bedroom in a log cabin or a luxurious suite in a turn-of-the-century mansion, there are some common elements you'll want to have: a comfortable and beautifully dressed bed, intimate lighting, and precious personal objects and pictures. You may also want to change the color of the walls, rearrange the furniture, or embellish the window treatments or bed dressings.

Remember when giving your bedroom a makeover that you don't necessarily need to spend an exorbitant amount of money buying things. In fact, all you might need is a room filled with reminders of the love in your life: your partner, friends, and family. This chapter will help you make the simple additions and changes that can turn your bedroom into a retreat that inspires warm hugs—and perhaps a bit of fantasy.

Creating the Landscape for a Romantic Story ... with a Paintbrush

What colors excite you and stimulate your sense of romance? Does white remind you of summertime sensuality? Do you prefer pale colors to evoke serenity and relaxation? In your bedroom, (almost) anything goes: You can use whatever colors that create the atmosphere you want.

Here are some suggestions for paint and wall-treatment schemes for your bedroom:

➤ Use deep colors on the walls for a sense of drama, such as deep green, cocoa, tan, or apricot.

➤ Paint your ceiling in a contrasting color to the walls. Some interesting combinations are ivory walls with a pale pink, blue, or sage-green ceiling.

➤ It is tantalizing to have a pattern on the ceiling, to view while lying in bed. Consider an unusual motif, such as subtle clouds that you can paint on or stars that you can stamp on in gold ink.

➤ Consider using a special paint technique for your bedroom walls that will create a dramatic atmosphere. One technique that provides a soft visual texture is ragrolling, which you can do yourself. Rag-rolling complements any romantic setting.

➤ Wall covering is a wonderful way to add instant drama to your room. You might choose florals, soft wide stripes, or artsy geometrics. For an overall floral background in your bedroom, repeat the floral pattern on a fabric dust ruffle, and then use a solid denim or a natural linen comforter and solid drapes. Artsy geometrics look good with tailored bedding in colors taken from the prints.

Furnish Your Bedroom for Relaxing as Well as Sleeping

One of the easiest and most delightful ways to romanticize your bedroom is to create a new area for relaxation. A seating spot for the two of you is a perfect invitation for intimate conversation, impromptu candlelight dinners, and indulgent Sunday breakfasts. All you need are two chairs and a small dining table. You can improvise a table by using a luggage rack with a large tray placed on top. And, as the name implies, a loveseat—even an old one—is perfect for morning coffee and private get-togethers.

Add a touch of romantic drama by creating a dressing area set apart from the rest of the room with an exotic folding screen. This alluring area can be complemented with plush boudoir furnishings, such as a vanity, chaise, or small upholstered chairs.

Beds with a Storybook Feeling

Nothing helps us relax from a chaotic day more than sinking into a stylish and luxurious bed. If you already have a four-poster bed, you can create a royal setting with a little bit of ingenuity and easily acquired materials, such as a canopy and full-length side curtains. Netting or gauze is also dreamy. Available and inexpensive at any fabric store, buy lots of it. Drape it around the four posts of your bed or from ceiling-mounted drapery rods for an *Out of Africa* experience every night.

An elevated bed also conveys a sense of privilege and luxury, especially when it is dressed elaborately in rich fabrics and fine trims. Give your bed added height and importance with hidden lengths of PVC pipes! Buy four pieces of a four-inch-diameter pipe (easily found at plumbing supply stores), each 13 inches in height, and place under each leg of a standard metal frame to create a bed 29 inches high. Flank the bedsides with small stools or ottomans to make getting into bed easy. In no time, you'll feel like a sultan (or sultana).

Decorator's Diary

When we acquired a lady's writing desk for my client Diane's bedroom, I had it painted with a trompe l'oeil facsimile of a love-letter envelope sent from Paris by her husband, Nick.

Most bedrooms can always use more storage and surface area. Salvage old furniture, and paint the pieces white for a clean summer look or black for a bit of drama. Add vintage handles of brass to vary the textures.

Ruffled sheer bed drapes add a crowning touch to this elegant bed.

(Photo by Schumacher)

A simply dressed bed with comfortable pillows is the romantic focal point of this room.

(Photo by Laura Ashley)

Decorator's Diary

I will never forget (or let my husband forget) our first date. It was the Fourth of July, and he asked me to go sailing. To remember this sentimental day, I have a long, narrow pillow on my bed that displays the following words: "A curious sailor boy appeared and took my hand and led me only goodness knows where."

Lots of Fabric for the Softest Room in the House

Fill your bedroom with loads of fabric on your furnishings, windows, and bed with fabulous cushions, pillows, and comforters that say "Put your head down and let your cares slip away!" Consider the following for your bedroom:

➤ The ultimate in comfort is a feather bed or a large down-filled "pillow" the size of your bed placed over the mattress for luxurious softness. They are both available at department stores, through specialty-bedding catalogs, and on the World Wide Web.

➤ A bed with many pillows is irresistible. Luxurious combinations of velvets, tapestries, lace, and linen are fun to assemble.

➤ Use antique quilts and linens in a rustic setting. The aged texture lends a feeling of romance and timelessness.

➤ Create an all-white scheme with white linens, bed furnishings, window treatments, and walls. This will allow your artwork (or a cherished piece of furniture) to be the romantic focal point of the room.

➤ Use dust ruffles that are a size bigger than your bed and let them "puddle" on the floor in generous folds.

➤ Make skirts for vanities, desks, and other small pieces from old textiles, quilts, or fringed wool throws. To double or triple the skirts to appear like petticoats on a dress, use several layers of fabric in various lengths, textures, and patterns.

➤ For summertime sleeping, use curtains that are sheer and filmy. They drape well and blow in soft waves with the breeze. Welcome in winter with heavier drapes of tapestry or velvet hanging in deep folds to emphasize their luxury.

Creating More Romance with Light

Sources for intimate lighting are absolutely essential in the bedroom. Recessed lighting in the ceiling is great, if you have it. Place small boudoir lamps with low-wattage bulbs on dressers so you don't have to turn on your reading lamps. Use opaque shades to direct the light downward and create lovely shadows. Another evocative style of lamp is "candlestick lamps," which use incandescent candle bulbs. Put all of these on dimmer switches so that you can set the mood of the room and illuminate the sections you desire. Candles, of course, are the consummately romantic light source. A chandelier-like fixture over the bed is a magnificent mood-maker, if somewhat grand, whether it uses candles or is electrified to take candle bulbs. A beautiful, traditional piece is a candle sconce with an attached mirror behind it. Flickers of reflected candlelight will play all over your bedroom.

Surround Yourself with the Things (and People) You Love

Accessories that appeal to all of your senses are the heart of a truly romantic space. Stir your emotions and your visual sense with pictures of your loved ones in silver frames. Sentimentality is super: Surround your favorite photos with vases of flowers. And add to the good smells with potpourri of your favorite scent placed in several bowls around the room.

Highlight the impact of your visual displays with mirrors hung on the walls and placed on dressers and vanities to reflect the candlelight and the pretty things that your room holds.

Small Touches of Romance Everyone Can Add

You will be delighted with the lovely effects you can create in your bedroom with some of the following easy changes:

➤ Place your bed in a new position—on the diagonal or in the middle of the room—for an airy and exciting look.

➤ Make a fun headboard for your bed from old shutters, doors, or even a section of a pretty wooden fence.

➤ Place your TV behind the closed door of a cabinet.

➤ Use stacked hatboxes, old luggage, and oversized baskets as stylish storage that will reduce bedroom clutter.

➤ Add display space for family portraits, flowers, books, and a pretty lamp by using an old kitchen table covered with a vintage linen tablecloth.

➤ Add a lock to your door for private time—and unplug the telephone (or turn off the ringer)!

Special Projects for Serious Sewers

If you're a whiz with the sewing machine, here are great bedroom touches that you can easily complete:

➤ Sew vintage lace on pillowcase edges. (Dip new lace in tea to achieve an older look.)

➤ Make loose and comfortable-looking slipcovers for loveseats with petticoat hems and faux closures of ties, buttons, or bows.

➤ Add ribbon bindings to the edges of blankets using velvet or ethnic printed ribbon.

➤ Combine cotton lace with a rustic patterned blanket by sewing a three-inch lace trim on the edges.

➤ Sew a duvet cover from vintage cloth or large linen tablecloths. They also make beautiful pillows!

➤ Make up seasonal pillowcases of summer and winter-weight fabrics. Use velvet, damask, and tapestry for cold weather; and linen and chintz for warm-weather months.

➤ Cover a footstool with velvet, tapestry, or damask fabric slipcover. To measure, trace the pattern of the top and measure the sides. Add your seam allowances, cut your pieces, and sew together. Use tacks and a hammer to reupholster and a glue gun for trim pieces to hide the tacks.

One of the wonderful things about making decor changes to your bedroom (a place that is more private than any other) is that they are truly for you and your enjoyment alone. Your bedroom is a place to express your feelings and your dreams—and that's a fabulous and rare opportunity for any decorator. Take advantage of it!

The Least You Need to Know

➤ A romantic bedroom can easily be achieved with a nicely dressed bed, intimate lighting, and a selection of precious personal items.

➤ Using deep colors, painting unusual patterns on the ceiling, and using wall coverings can add drama to bedroom walls and ceilings.

➤ Make intimate sitting, dressing, and relaxing areas in the bedroom with simple furnishing arrangements.

➤ Make abundant use of soft goods like bedclothes, pillows, comforters, vanity skirts, and draperies to create an inviting space with plush and comfortable surfaces.

➤ Use candle lighting, flowers, and potpourri to create a sensual atmosphere.

➤ Sewing enthusiasts can create many lovely accessories for the bedroom with little expense.

➤ Small touches that anyone can do, like using hatboxes for storage or placing your bed in a new position, will create a lovely atmosphere in the bedroom.

Bibliography and Resources

Books

Better Homes and Gardens New Decorating Book. Des Moines: Meredith Corporation, 1990.

Blake, Jill. *Interior Design on Your Own.* New York: Quarto Publishing, 1993.

De Chiara, Joseph, Julius Panero, and Martin Zelnick. *Time-Saver Standards for Interior Design and Space Planning.* New York: McGraw-Hill, 1991.

Fairbanks, Jonathan L., and Elizabeth Bidwell Bates. *American Furniture: 1620 to the Present.* New York: Richard Marek Publishers, 1981.

Faulkner, Sarah. *Planning a Home.* New York: Holt, Rinehart & Winston, 1979.

Gilliat, Mary. *New Guide to Decorating.* Boston: Little Brown & Company, 1988.

Gilliat, Mary. *Period Style.* Boston: Little Brown & Company, 1990.

Hampton, Mark. *On Decorating.* New York: Random House, 1989.

Krasner, Deborah. *Kitchens for Cooks.* New York: Penguin Group, 1994.

Loasby, Wren. *Creative Interiors.* Britain: David Charles, 1992.

Mayer, Barbara. *The Complete Book of Home Decorating.* New York: Friedman/Fairfax Publishers, 1994.

Sloan, Annie, and Kate Gwynn. *Color in Decoration.* Boston: Little Brown & Company, 1990.

Stoddard, Alexandra. *Creating a Beautiful Home.* New York: William Morrow, 1992.

Walton, Stewart. *The Complete Home Decorator.* New York: Rizzoli, 1995.

Wissinger, Joanna. *The Interior Design Handbook.* New York: Henry Holt & Company, 1995.

Magazines

Architectural Digest
High-end designs by top-notch designers

Classic Home
Traditional, timeless interiors

Country Living
Real-life, comfortable, and creative country interiors

Elle Décor
Inspirational and adaptable European design

House Beautiful
As the name implies, beautiful homes with beautiful interiors featuring a variety of styles

Martha Stewart Living
Geared to a little bit of everything—cooking, entertaining, projects, and decorating

Metropolitan Home
Contemporary design

Traditional Home
Tasteful, traditional designs

Victoria
For the homeowner with the romantic touch

How-To Videos

Available at any Benjamin Moore paint dealer:

Faux Finish
Trompe l'oeil paint finishes

Faux Finesse
Several paint effects

Mail Order

Ballard Designs
404-352-1355
Very stylish furnishings, accessories, decorative wall paints, and accents for the garden

Chambers
1-800-334-9790
Tasteful bed linens, garden furniture, bath towels, accessories, and furniture

Country Curtains
1-800-456-0321
Ready-made curtains of lace or print geared for traditional or country homes

Crate & Barrel
1-800-323-5461 (for catalog and store locations)
Great selection of furniture, rugs, kitchenware, and accessories

Edgar B.
1-800-255-6589
Discount brand-name furniture retailer

Gardener's Eden
1-800-822-9600
Decorative accessories for home and garden, furniture for indoor/outdoor use, and gardening supplies

Gardener's Supply
802-863-1700
Selection of compost containers and composting tips, as well as "green" supplies

Garnet Hill
1-800-622-6216
Creative bed linens, throws, rugs, and a small amount of adult and children's bedroom furniture stressing natural elements

Hold Everything
1-800-421-2264
Unique organizing and storage pieces, plus furniture for the home office

Laura Ashley
1-800-429-7678
Tasteful fabrics, custom and premade draperies, furniture, and accessories

Pottery Barn
1-800-922-5507
Great selection of furniture, ready-made window treatments, and accessories

Rue de France
1-800-777-0998
Variety of lace curtains and shades

Smith & Hawken
415-389-8300
Quality indoor/outdoor furniture and garden accents

Spiegel
1-800-345-4500
A large assortment of ready-made draperies and decorative accessories

Williams Sonoma
1-800-541-1262
A cook's catalog with kitchen accessories, utensils, linens, and bonus recipes

Web Sites

www.anthropologie.com
Unusual home accents and clothing

www.baranzelli.com
Exclusive collection of fabrics, furniture, and trimmings

www.countryliving.com
Magazine on the Web with ideas for the home

www.ebay.com
Busy auction site that carries endless supplies of antiques and collectibles

www.furniture.com
Retail furniture site

www.marthastewart.com
An Internet site with goods for the home, such as paint, garden supplies, decorative items, kitchenware, decorating books, and videos

www.pier1.com
Affordable home products from candles to sofas

Wall-Covering Books

American Country Gear

Imperial Designer Stripes and Plaids

Laura Ashley

Ralph Lauren

Raymond Waites

Schumacher

Brochures

American Lighting Association brochures, available by calling 1-800-BRIGHT IDEA or 274-448-4332:

"Lighting Your Life"

"Light Up Your Kitchen and Bath"

Index

O-P

Teach Yourself VISUALLY™

Excel® 2016

by Paul McFedries

Visual
A Wiley Brand

Teach Yourself VISUALLY™ Excel® 2016

Published by
John Wiley & Sons, Inc.
10475 Crosspoint Boulevard
Indianapolis, IN 46256

www.wiley.com

Published simultaneously in Canada

Library of Congress Control Number: 2015943221

ISBN: 978-1-119-07473-1

Manufactured in the United States of America

10 9 8 7 6 5 4 3 2 1

Trademark Acknowledgments

Contact Us

For general information on our other products and services please contact our Customer Care Department within the U.S. at 877-762-2974, outside the U.S. at 317-572-3993 or fax 317-572-4002.

For technical support please visit www.wiley.com/techsupport.

Sales | Contact Wiley at (877) 762-2974 or fax (317) 572-4002.

Credits

Acquisitions Editor
Aaron Black

Project Editor
Lynn Northrup

Technical Editor
Donna Baker

Copy Editor
Lynn Northrup

Production Editor
Barath Kumar Rajasekaran

Manager, Content Development & Assembly
Mary Beth Wakefield

Vice President, Professional Technology Strategy
Barry Pruett

About the Author

Paul McFedries is a full-time technical writer. He has been authoring computer books since 1991 and has more than 85 books to his credit. Paul's books have sold more than four million copies worldwide. These books include the Wiley titles *Teach Yourself VISUALLY Windows 10*, *Windows 10 Simplified*, *The Facebook Guide for People Over 50*, *iPhone 6 Portable Genius*, and *iPad Portable Genius*. Paul is also the proprietor of Word Spy (www.wordspy.com), a website that tracks new words and phrases as they enter the language. Paul invites you to drop by his personal website at www.mcfedries.com or follow him on Twitter @wordspy.

Author's Acknowledgments

It goes without saying that writers focus on text, and I certainly enjoyed focusing on the text that you will read in this book. However, this book is more than just the usual collection of words and phrases designed to educate and stimulate the mind. A quick thumb through the pages will show you that this book is also chock-full of treats for the eye, including copious screenshots, beautiful colors, and sharp fonts. Those sure make for a beautiful book, and that beauty comes from a lot of hard work by the production team at SPi Global. Of course, what you read in this book must also be accurate, logically presented, and free of errors. Ensuring all of this was an excellent group of editors that I got to work with directly, including project and copy editor Lynn Northrup and technical editor Donna Baker. Thanks to both of you for your exceptional competence and hard work. Thanks, as well, to Aaron Black for asking me to write this book.

How to Use This Book

Who This Book Is For

This book is for the reader who has never used this particular technology or software application. It is also for readers who want to expand their knowledge.

The Conventions in This Book

❶ Steps

This book uses a step-by-step format to guide you easily through each task. Numbered steps are actions you must do; bulleted steps clarify a point, step, or optional feature; and indented steps give you the result.

❷ Notes

Notes give additional information — special conditions that may occur during an operation, a situation that you want to avoid, or a cross reference to a related area of the book.

❸ Icons and Buttons

Icons and buttons show you exactly what you need to click to perform a step.

❹ Tips

Tips offer additional information, including warnings and shortcuts.

❺ Bold

Bold type shows command names, options, and text or numbers you must type.

❻ Italics

Italic type introduces and defines a new term.

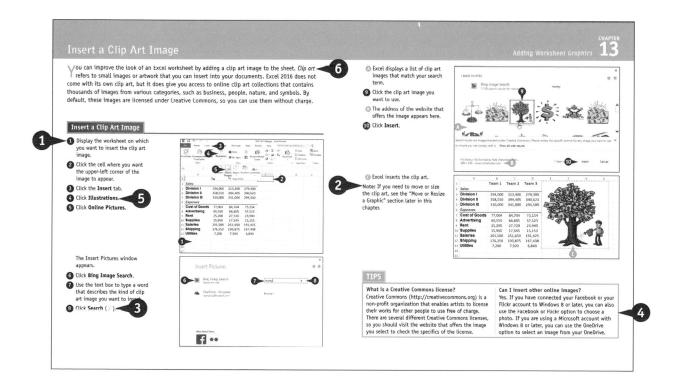

Table of Contents

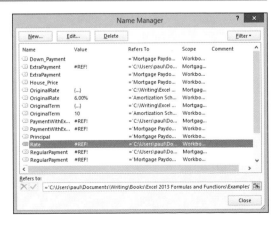

Chapter 3   Formatting Excel Ranges

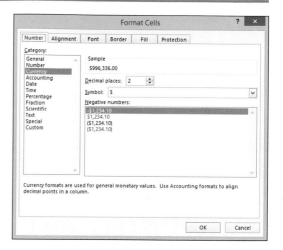

Table of Contents

Chapter 4   Building Formulas

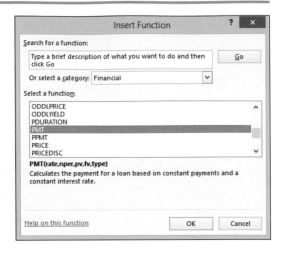

Chapter 5   Manipulating Worksheets

Chapter 6   Dealing with Workbooks

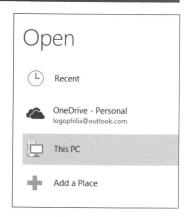

Chapter 7   Formatting Workbooks

Chapter 8   Importing Data into Excel

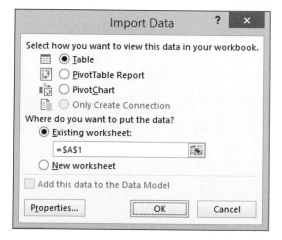

Table of Contents

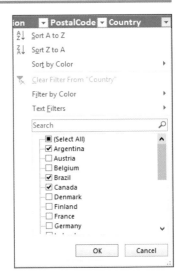

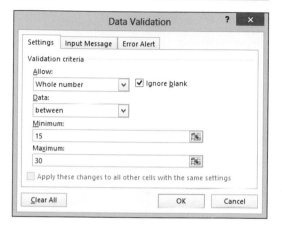

Table of Contents

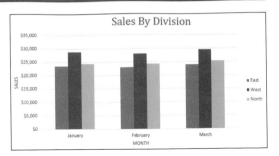

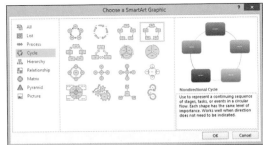

Chapter 14   Collaborating with Others

CHAPTER 1

Working with Ranges

In Excel, a *range* is a collection of two or more cells that you work with as a group rather than separately. This enables you to fill the range with values, move or copy the range, sort the range data, and insert and delete ranges. You learn these and other range techniques in this chapter.

Select a Range

To work with a range in Excel, you must first select the cells that you want to include in the range. After you select the range, you can fill it with data, move it to another part of the worksheet, format the cells, and perform the other range-related tasks that you learn about in this chapter.

You can select a range as a rectangular group of cells, as a collection of individual cells, or as an entire row or column.

Select a Range

Select a Rectangular Range

1 Position the mouse (✛) over the first cell you want to include in the range.

2 Click and drag the ✛ over the cells that you want to include in the range.

A Excel selects the cells.

3 Release the mouse button.

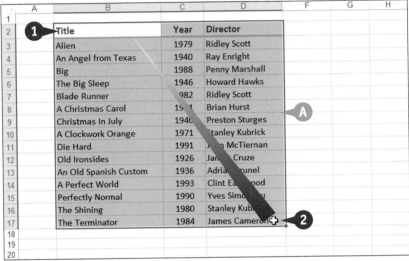

Select a Range of Individual Cells

1 Click in the first cell that you want to include in the range.

2 Hold down Ctrl and click in each of the other cells that you want to include in the range.

B Each time you click in a cell, Excel adds it to the range.

3 Release Ctrl.

4

Select an Entire Row

1 Position the mouse (✛) over the header of the row you want to select (✛ changes to ➡).

2 Click the row header.

C Excel selects the entire row.

To select multiple rows, click and drag across the row headers or hold down **Ctrl** and click each row header.

	A	B	C	D	F	G	H
3		Title	Year	Director			
		Alien	1979	Ridley Scott			
4		An Angel from Texas	1940	Ray Enright			
5		Big	1988	Penny Marshall			
6		The Big Sleep	1946	Howard Hawks			
7		Blade Runner	1982	Ridley Scott			
8		A Christmas Carol	1951	Brian Hurst			
9		Christmas In July	1940	Preston Sturges			
10		A Clockwork Orange	1971	Stanley Kubrick			
11		Die Hard	1991	John McTiernan			
12		Old Ironsides	1926	James Cruze			
13		An Old Spanish Custom	1936	Adrian Brunel			
14		A Perfect World	1993	Clint Eastwood			
15		Perfectly Normal	1990	Yves Simoneau			
16		The Shining	1980	Stanley Kubrick			
17		The Terminator	1984	James Cameron			
18							
19							
20							

Select an Entire Column

1 Position the mouse (✛) over the header of the column you want to select (✛ changes to ⬇).

2 Click the column header.

D Excel selects the entire column.

To select multiple columns, click and drag across the column headers, or hold down **Ctrl** and click each column header.

	A	B	C	D	F	G	H	I
1								
2		Title	Year	Director				
3		Alien	1979	Ridley Scott				
4		An Angel from Texas	1940	Ray Enright				
5		Big	1988	Penny Marshall				
6		The Big Sleep	1946	Howard Hawks				
7		Blade Runner	1982	Ridley Scott				
8		A Christmas Carol	1951	Brian Hurst				
9		Christmas In July	1940	Preston Sturges				
10		A Clockwork Orange	1971	Stanley Kubrick				
11		Die Hard	1991	John McTiernan				
12		Old Ironsides	1926	James Cruze				
13		An Old Spanish Custom	1936	Adrian Brunel				
14		A Perfect World	1993	Clint Eastwood				
15		Perfectly Normal	1990	Yves Simoneau				
16		The Shining	1980	Stanley Kubrick				
17		The Terminator	1984	James Cameron				
18								
19								
20								
21								

TIPS

Are there keyboard techniques I can use to select a range?

Yes. To select a rectangular range, navigate to the first cell that you want to include in the range, hold down **Shift**, and then press ⬅ or ⬇ to extend the selection. To select an entire row, navigate to any cell in the row and press **Shift** + **Spacebar**. To select an entire column, navigate to any cell in the column and then press **Ctrl** + **Spacebar**.

Is there an easy way to select every cell in the worksheet?

Yes. There are two methods you can use. Either press **Ctrl** + **A**, or click the **Select All** button (◢) in the upper-left corner of the worksheet (**A**).

	A	B
1		
2		Title
3		Alien
4		An Angel from Texas

Fill a Range with the Same Data

If you need to fill a range with the same data, you can save time by getting Excel to fill the range for you. The AutoFill feature makes it easy to fill a vertical or horizontal range with the same value, but you can also fill any selected range. This method is much faster than manually entering the same data in each cell.

See the previous section, "Select a Range," to learn how to select a range of cells.

Fill a Range with the Same Data

Fill a Vertical or Horizontal Range

1 In the first cell of the range you want to work with, enter the data you want to fill.

2 Position the mouse (cursor) over the bottom-right corner of the cell (cursor changes to +).

3 Click and drag + down to fill a vertical range or across to fill a horizontal range.

4 Release the mouse button.

A Excel fills the range with the initial cell value.

Fill a Selected Range

1 Select the range you want to fill.

2 Type the text, number, or other data.

3 Press Ctrl + Enter.

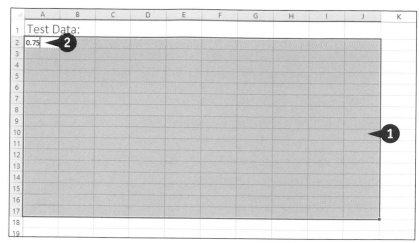

B Excel fills the range with the value you typed.

How do I fill a vertical or horizontal range without also copying the formatting of the original cell?
Follow these steps:

1 Perform steps **1** to **4** to fill the data.

A Excel displays the AutoFill Options smart tag (⊞).

2 Click the **AutoFill Options** ▼.

3 Click **Fill Without Formatting**.

Excel removes the original cell's formatting from the copied cells.

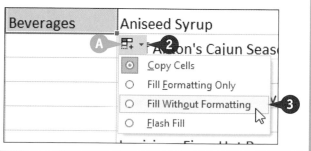

Fill a Range with a Series of Values

If you need to fill a range with a series of values, you can save time by using the AutoFill feature to create the series for you. AutoFill can fill a series of numeric values such as 5, 10, 15, 20, and so on; a series of date values such as January 1, 2016, January 2, 2016, and so on; or a series of alphanumeric values such as Chapter 1, Chapter 2, Chapter 3, and so on.

You can also create your own series with a custom step value, which determines the numeric difference between each item in the series.

Fill a Range with a Series of Values

AutoFill a Series of Numeric, Date, or Alphanumeric Values

1 Click in the first cell and type the first value in the series.

2 Click in an adjacent cell and type the second value in the series.

3 Select the two cells.

4 Position the mouse (⊕) over the bottom-right corner of the second cell (⊕ changes to +).

5 Click and drag + down to fill a vertical range or across to fill a horizontal range.

A As you drag through each cell, Excel displays the series value that it will add to the cell.

6 Release the mouse button.

B Excel fills the range with a series that continues the pattern of the initial two cell values.

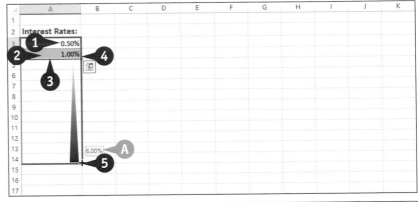

Fill a Custom Series of Values

1 Click in the first cell and type the first value in the series.

2 Select the range you want to fill, including the initial value.

3 Click the **Home** tab.

4 Click **Fill** (⬇).

5 Click **Series**.

The Series dialog box appears.

6 In the Type group, select the type of series you want to fill (○ changes to ◉).

7 If you selected Date in step **6**, select an option in the Date unit group (○ changes to ◉).

8 In the Step value text box, type the value you want to use.

9 Click **OK**.

Ⓒ Excel fills the range with the series you created.

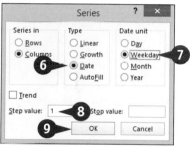

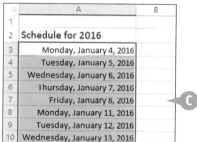

TIP

Can I create my own AutoFill series?
Yes. You can create a *custom list*, which is a series of text values. When you add the first value in your custom list, you can then use AutoFill to fill a range with the rest of the series. Follow these steps:

1 Click the **File** tab.

2 Click **Options**.

The Excel Options dialog box appears.

3 Click **Advanced**.

4 Scroll down to the General section and then click **Edit Custom Lists**.

The Custom Lists dialog box appears.

5 Click **NEW LIST**.

6 In the List entries box, type each item in your list, and press Enter after each item.

7 Click **Add**.

8 Click **OK** to return to the Excel Options dialog box.

9 Click **OK**.

Flash Fill a Range

Y ou can save time and effort by using the Flash Fill feature in Excel to automatically fill a range of data based on a sample pattern that you provide.

Although there are many ways to use Flash Fill, the two most common are flash filling a range with extracted data and flash filling a range with formatted data. For example, if you have a column of full names, you might want to create a new column that includes just the first names extracted from the original column. Similarly, if you have a column of phone numbers in the form 1234567890, you might want a new column that formats the numbers as (123) 456-7890.

Flash Fill a Range

Flash Fill a Range with Extracted Data

1 Make sure the column of original data has a heading.

2 Type a heading for the column of extracted data.

3 Type the first value you want in the new column.

4 Begin typing the second value.

A Excel recognizes the pattern and displays suggestions for the rest of the column.

5 Press **Enter**.

B Excel flash fills the column with the extracted data.

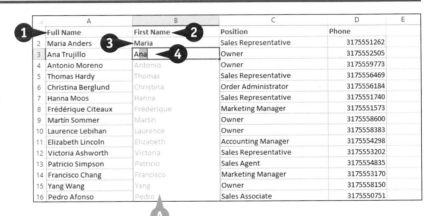

10

Flash Fill a Range with Formatted Data

1 Make sure the column of original data has a heading.

2 Type a heading for the new column of formatted data.

3 Type the first value you want in the new column.

4 Begin typing the second value.

C Excel recognizes the pattern and displays suggestions for the rest of the column.

5 Press Enter.

D Excel flash fills the column with the formatted data.

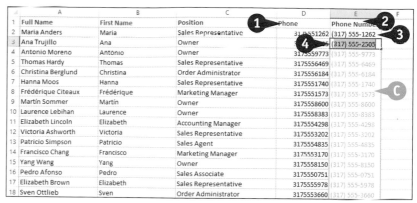

Why do I not see the automatic Flash Fill suggestions when I type the sample data?

For Flash Fill's automatic suggestions to appear, you must have headings at the top of both the column of original data and the column you are using for the filled data. Also, the flash fill column must be adjacent to the original column and the sample entries you make in the fill column must occur one after the other. Finally, note that Flash Fill's automatic suggestions usually only work with text data, not numeric data.

Can I still use Flash Fill even though I do not see the automatic suggestions?

Yes, you can still invoke Flash Fill on any range by running the Ribbon command. In the fill range, type the first value, then select that value and the rest of the fill range. Click the **Data** tab and then click **Flash Fill** (📝). Excel flash fills the selected range.

Move or Copy a Range

If your worksheet is not set up the way you want, you can restructure or reorganize the worksheet by moving an existing range to a different part of the sheet.

You can also make a copy of a range, which is a useful technique if you require a duplicate of the range elsewhere, or if you require a range that is similar to an existing range. In the latter case, after you copy the range, you can then edit the copied version of the data as needed.

Move or Copy a Range

Move a Range

1 Select the range you want to move.

2 Position the mouse (⊕) over any outside border of the range (⊕ changes to ⊹).

3 Click and drag the range to the new location (⊹ changes to ⬚).

A Excel displays an outline of the range.

B Excel displays the address of the new location.

4 Release the mouse button.

C Excel moves the range to the new location.

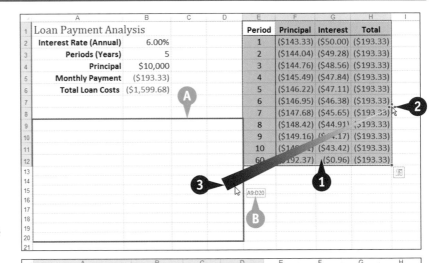

Copy a Range

1 Select the range you want to copy.

2 Press and hold **Ctrl**.

3 Position the mouse (✥) over any outside border of the range (✥ changes to ↘).

4 Click and drag the range to the location where you want the copy to appear.

Ⓓ Excel displays an outline of the range.

Ⓔ Excel displays the address of the new location.

5 Release the mouse button.

6 Release **Ctrl**.

Ⓕ Excel creates a copy of the range in the new location.

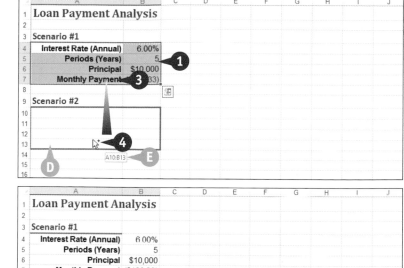

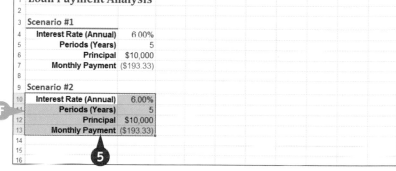

Can I move or copy a range to another worksheet?

Yes. Click and drag the range as described in this section. Remember to hold down **Ctrl** if you are copying the range. Press and hold **Alt** and then drag the mouse pointer over the tab of the sheet you want to use as the destination. Excel displays the worksheet. Release **Alt** and then drop the range on the worksheet.

Can I move or copy a range to another workbook?

Yes. If you can see the other workbook on-screen, click and drag the range as described in this section, and then drop it on the other workbook. Remember to hold down **Ctrl** if you are copying the range. Otherwise, select the range, click the **Home** tab, click **Cut** (✂) to move the range or **Copy** (🗐) to copy it, switch to the other workbook, select the cell where you want the range to appear, click **Home**, and then click **Paste** (📋).

Insert a Row or Column

You can insert a row or column into your existing worksheet data to accommodate more information. The easiest way to add more information to a worksheet is to add it to the right or at the bottom of your existing data. However, you will often find that the new information you need to add fits naturally within the existing data. In such cases, you first need to insert a new row or column in your worksheet at the place where you want the new data to appear, and then add the new information in the blank row or column.

Insert a Row or Column

Insert a Row

1 Click any cell in the row below where you want to insert the new row.

2 Click the **Home** tab.

3 Click the **Insert** ▼.

4 Click **Insert Sheet Rows**.

Ⓐ Excel inserts the new row.

Ⓑ The rows below the new row are shifted down.

5 Click the **Insert Options** smart tag (✔).

6 Select a formatting option for the new row (◯ changes to ◉).

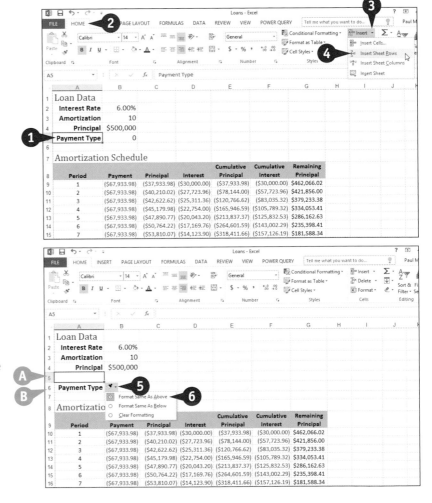

Insert a Column

1 Click any cell in the row to the right of where you want to insert the new column.

2 Click the **Home** tab.

3 Click the **Insert** ▼.

4 Click **Insert Sheet Columns**.

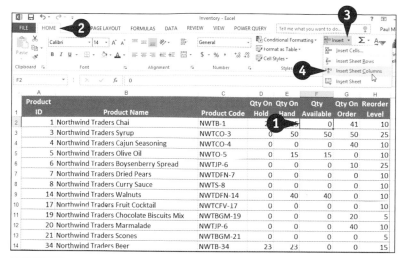

C Excel inserts the new column.

D The columns to the right of the new column are shifted to the right.

5 Click the **Insert Options** smart tag (✔).

6 Select a formatting option for the new column (○ changes to ●).

TIP

Can I insert more than one row or column at a time?

Yes. You can insert as many new rows or columns as you need. First, select the same number of rows or columns that you want to insert. (See the "Select a Range" section earlier in this chapter to learn how to select rows and columns.) For example, if you want to insert four rows, select four existing rows. For rows, be sure to select existing rows below where you want the new rows inserted and then follow steps **2** to **4** in the "Insert a Row" subsection. For columns, be sure to select existing columns to the right of where you want to insert the new columns and then follow steps **2** to **4** in the "Insert a Column" subsection.

Insert a Cell or Range

If you need to add data to an existing range, you can insert a single cell or a range of cells within that range. When you insert a cell or range, Excel shifts the existing data to accommodate the new cells.

Although it is often easiest to create room for new data within a range by inserting an entire row or column, as explained in the previous section, "Insert a Row or Column," this causes problems for some types of worksheet layouts. (See the first tip to learn more.) You can work around such problems by inserting just a cell or range.

Insert a Cell or Range

1 Select the cell or range where you want the inserted cell or range to appear.

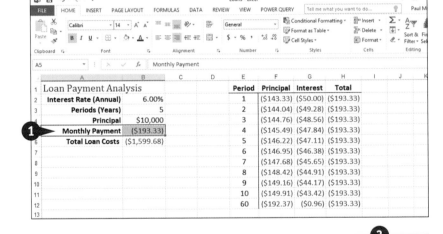

2 Click the **Home** tab.

3 Click the **Insert** ▼.

4 Click **Insert Cells**.

Note: You can also press
Ctrl + Shift + =.

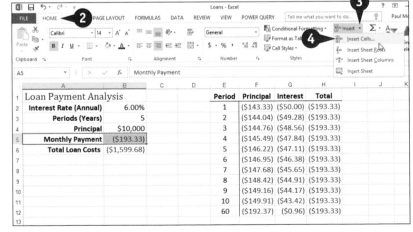

The Insert dialog box appears.

5 Select the option that corresponds to how you want Excel to shift the existing cells to accommodate your new cells (○ changes to ◉).

Note: In most cases, if you selected a horizontal range, you should click the **Shift cells down** option; if you selected a vertical range, you should click the **Shift cells right** option.

6 Click **OK**.

Ⓐ Excel inserts the cell or range.

Ⓑ The existing data is shifted down (in this case) or to the right.

7 Click the **Insert Options** smart tag (✋).

8 Select a formatting option for the new row (○ changes to ◉).

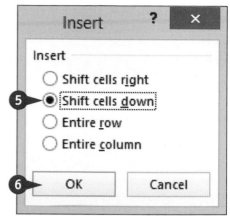

	A	B	C	D	E
1	Loan Payment Analysis				**Period**
2	**Interest Rate (Annual)**	6.00%			1
3	**Periods (Years)**	5			2
4	**Principal**	$10,000			3
5					4
6	**Monthly Payment**	($193.33)			5
7	**Total Loan Costs**	($1,599.68)	◉ Format Same As Above		7
8			○ Format Same As Below		7
9			○ Clear Formatting		8
10					9

TIPS

Under what circumstances would I insert a cell or range instead of inserting an entire row or column?

In most cases, it is better to insert a cell or range when you have other data either to the left or right of the existing range, or above or below the range. For example, if you have data to the left or right of the existing range, inserting an entire row would create a gap in the other data.

How do I know which cells to select to get my inserted cell or range in the correct position?

The easiest way to do this is to select the existing cell or range that is exactly where you want the new cell or range to appear. For example, if you want the new range to be A5:B5 as shown in this section's example, you first select the existing A5:B5 range. When you insert the new range, Excel shifts the existing cells (down in this case) to accommodate it.

Delete Data from a Range

If your worksheet has a range that contains data you no longer need, you can delete that data. This helps to reduce worksheet clutter and makes your worksheet easier to read.

Note that deleting cell data does not adjust the structure of your worksheet in any way. That is, after you delete the cell data, the rest of your worksheet data remains intact and in the same place that it was before the data deletion. If you want to delete cells and not just the data within the cells, see the following section, "Delete a Range."

Delete Data from a Range

Delete Range Data

1 Select the range that contains the data you want to delete.

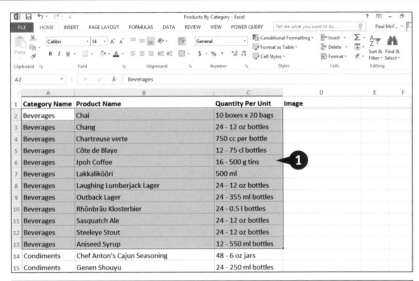

2 Click the **Home** tab.

3 Click **Clear** (🖉).

4 Click **Clear Contents**.

A If you want to delete the range data and its formatting, click **Clear All** instead.

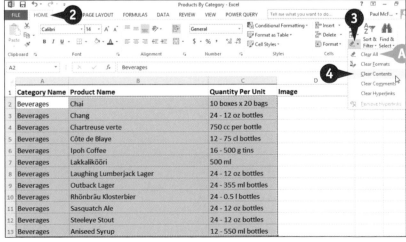

B Excel removes the range data.

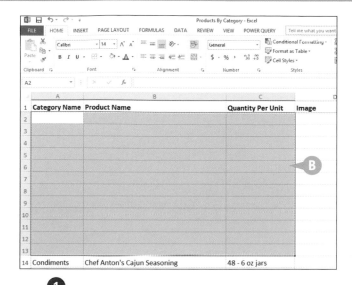

Undo Range Data Deletion

1 Click the **Undo** ▼.

2 Click **Clear**.

Note: If the data deletion was the most recent action you performed, you can undo it by pressing <kbd>Ctrl</kbd>+<kbd>Z</kbd> or by clicking **Undo** (↩).

C Excel restores the data to the range.

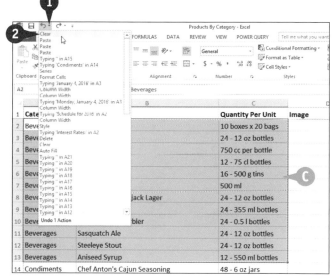

Are there faster ways to delete the data from a range?

Yes. Probably the fastest method is to select the range and then press <kbd>Delete</kbd>. You can also select the range, right-click any part of the range, and then click **Clear Contents**.

Is it possible to delete a cell's numeric formatting?

Yes. Select the range with the formatting that you want to remove, click **Home**, click ◆, and then click **Clear Formats**. Excel removes all the formatting from the selected range. If you prefer to delete only the numeric formatting, click **Home**, click the **Number Format** ▼, and then click **General**.

Delete a Range

If your worksheet contains a range that you no longer need, you can delete that range. Note that this is not the same as deleting the data within a cell or range, as described in the previous section, "Delete Data from a Range." When you delete a range, Excel deletes not just the data within the range, but also the range of cells. Excel then shifts the remaining worksheet data to replace the deleted range. Excel displays a dialog box that enables you to choose whether the data is shifted up or to the left.

Delete a Range

1 Select the range that you want to delete.

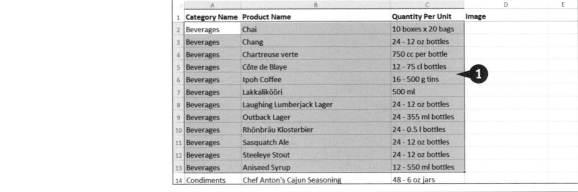

2 Click the **Home** tab.

3 Click the **Delete** ▼.

4 Click **Delete Cells**.

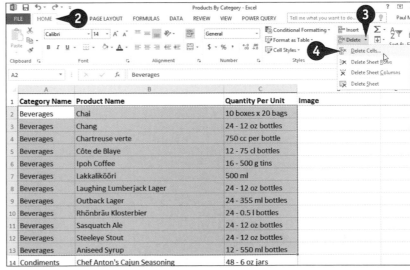

The Delete dialog box appears.

5 Select the option that corresponds to how you want Excel to shift the remaining cells after it deletes the range (○ changes to ◉).

Note: In most cases, if you have data below the selected range, you should click the **Shift cells up** option; if you have data to the right of the selected range, you should click the **Shift cells left** option.

6 Click **OK**.

Ⓐ Excel deletes the range and shifts the remaining data.

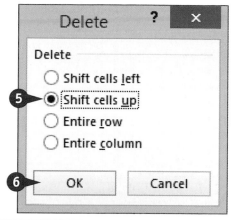

	A	B	C	
1	Category Name	Product Name	Quantity Per Unit	Image
2	Condiments	Chef Anton's Cajun Seasoning	48 - 6 oz jars	
3	Condiments	Genen Shouyu	24 - 250 ml bottles	
4	Condiments	Grandma's Boysenberry Spread	12 - 8 oz jars	
5	Condiments	Gula Malacca	20 - 2 kg bags	
6	Condiments	Louisiana Fiery Hot Pepper Sauce	32 - 8 oz bottles	
7	Condiments	Louisiana Hot Spiced Okra	24 - 8 oz jars	
8	Condiments	Northwoods Cranberry Sauce	12 - 12 oz jars	
9	Condiments	Original Frankfurter grüne Soße	12 boxes	
10	Condiments	Sirop d'érable	24 - 500 ml bottles	
11	Condiments	Vegie-spread	15 - 625 g jars	
12	Confections	Chocolade	10 pkgs.	
13	Confections	Gumbär Gummibärchen	100 - 250 g bags	

TIPS

Are there faster ways to delete a range?
Yes. Probably the fastest method is to select the range and then press `Ctrl`+`-`. You can also select the range, right-click any part of the range, and then click **Delete**. Both methods display the Delete dialog box.

How do I delete a row or column?
To delete a row, select any cell in the row, click the **Home** tab, click the **Delete** ▼, and then click **Delete Sheet Rows**. To delete a column, select any cell in the column, click the **Home** tab, click the **Delete** ▼, and then click **Delete Sheet Columns**. Note, too, that you can delete multiple rows or columns by selecting at least one cell in each row or column.

Hide a Row or Column

If you do not need to see or work with a row or column temporarily, you can make your worksheet easier to read and to navigate by hiding the row or column. Hiding a row or column is also useful if you are showing someone a worksheet that contains private or sensitive data that you do not want the person to see.

Hiding a row or column does not affect other parts of your worksheet. In particular, formulas that use or rely on data in the hidden rows and columns still display the same results.

Hide a Row or Column

Hide a Row

1. Click in any cell in the row you want to hide.

2. Click the **Home** tab.

3. Click **Format**.

4. Click **Hide & Unhide**.

5. Click **Hide Rows**.

Note: You can also hide a row by pressing Ctrl + 9.

Ⓐ Excel removes the row from the worksheet display.

Ⓑ Excel displays a double-line border between the surrounding row headers to indicate that a hidden row lies between them.

Another way to hide a row is to move the mouse (🖑) over the bottom edge of the row heading (🖑 changes to ✛), and then click and drag the edge up until the height displays 0.

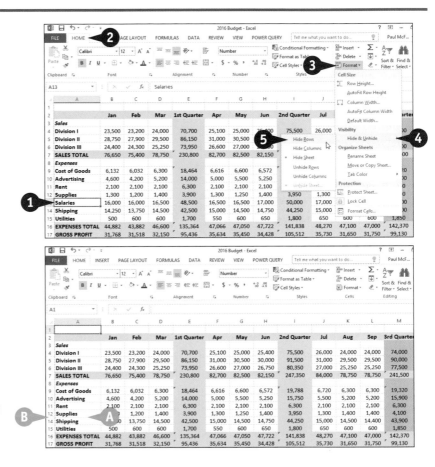

Hide a Column

1 Click in any cell in the column you want to hide.

2 Click the **Home** tab.

3 Click **Format**.

4 Click **Hide & Unhide**.

5 Click **Hide Columns**.

Note: You can also hide a column by pressing `Ctrl` + `0`.

C Excel removes the column from the worksheet display.

D Excel displays a slightly thicker heading border between the surrounding columns to indicate that a hidden column lies between them.

Another way to hide a column is to move the mouse (⊕) over the right edge of the column heading (⊕ changes to ◂▸), and then click and drag the edge left until the width displays 0.

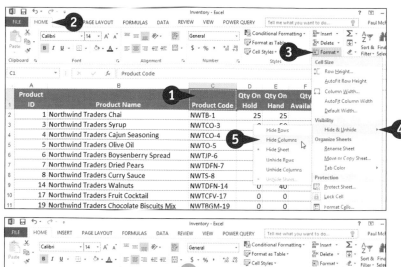

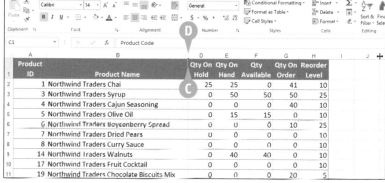

TIP

How do I display a hidden row or column?

To display a hidden row, select the row above and the row below the hidden row, click **Home**, click **Format**, click **Hide & Unhide**, and then click **Unhide Rows**. Alternatively, move the mouse (⊕) between the headings of the selected rows (⊕ changes to ⬍) and then double-click. To unhide row 1, right-click the top edge of the row 2 header and then click **Unhide**.

To display a hidden column, select the column to the left and the column to the right of the hidden column, click **Home**, click **Format**, click **Hide & Unhide**, and then click **Unhide Columns**. Alternatively, move the ⊕ between the headings of the selected columns (⊕ changes to ◂▸) and then double-click. To unhide column A, right-click the left edge of the column B header and then click **Unhide**.

Freeze Rows or Columns

You can keep your column labels in view as you scroll the worksheet by freezing the row or rows that contain the labels. This makes it easier to review and add data to the worksheet because you can always see the column labels.

If your worksheet also includes row labels, you can keep those labels in view as you horizontally scroll the worksheet by freezing the column or columns that contain the labels.

Freeze Rows or Columns

Freeze Rows

1. Scroll the worksheet so that the row or rows that you want to freeze are visible.

2. Select the cell in column A that is one row below the last row you want to freeze.

   For example, if you want to freeze row 1, select cell A2.

3. Click the **View** tab.

4. Click **Freeze Panes**.

5. Click **Freeze Panes**.

   Excel freezes the rows.

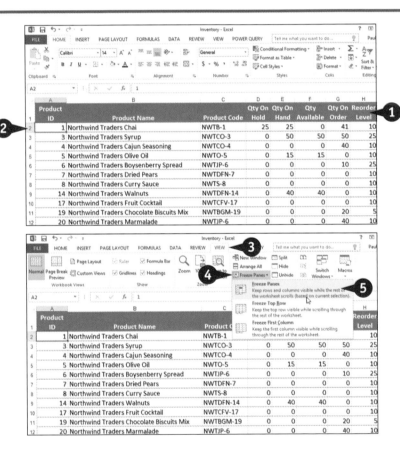

Freeze Columns

1 Scroll the worksheet so that the column or columns that you want to freeze are visible.

2 Select the cell in row 1 that is one row to the right of the last column you want to freeze.

For example, if you want to freeze column A, select cell B1.

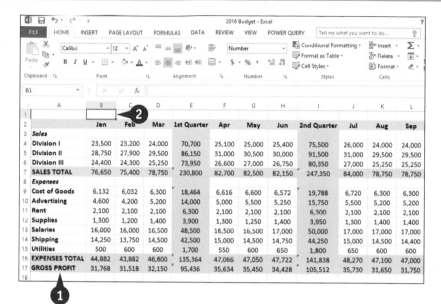

3 Click the **View** tab.

4 Click **Freeze Panes**.

5 Click **Freeze Panes**.

Excel freezes the columns.

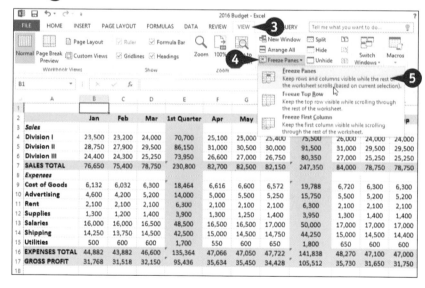

TIPS

Are there easier methods I can use to freeze just the top row or the first column?
Yes. To freeze just the top row, click **View**, click **Freeze Panes**, and then click **Freeze Top Row**. To freeze just the first column, click **View**, click **Freeze Panes**, and then click **Freeze First Column**. Note that in both cases you do not need to select a cell in advance.

How do I unfreeze a row or column?
If you no longer require a row or column to be frozen, you can unfreeze it by clicking **View**, clicking **Freeze Panes**, and then clicking **Unfreeze Panes**.

Merge Two or More Cells

You can create a single large cell by merging two or more cells. For example, it is common to merge several cells in the top row to use as a worksheet title.

Another common reason for merging cells is to create a label that applies to multiple columns of data. For example, if you have three columns labeled *January*, *February*, and *March*, you could select the three cells in the row above these labels, merge them, and then use the merged cell to add the label *First Quarter*.

Merge Two or More Cells

1 Select the cells that you want to merge.

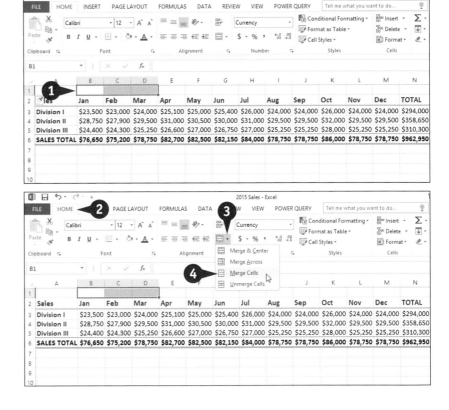

2 Click the **Home** tab.

3 Click the **Merge & Center** ▼.

4 Click **Merge Cells**.

Ⓐ Excel merges the selected cells into a single cell.

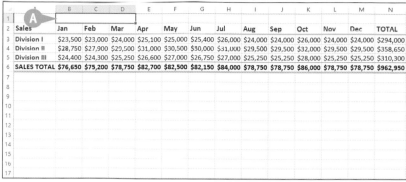

5 Type your text in the merged cell.

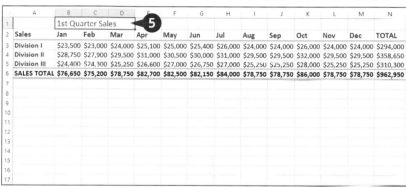

How do I center text across multiple columns?

This is a useful technique for your worksheet titles or headings. You can center a title across the entire worksheet, or you can center a heading across the columns that it refers to. Follow steps **1** to **3** and then click **Merge & Center**. Excel creates the merged cell and formats the cell with the Center alignment option. Any text you enter into the merged cell appears centered within the cell.

Transpose Rows and Columns

You can use the Transpose command in Excel to easily turn a row of data into a column of data, or a column of data into a row of data.

The Transpose command is useful when you enter data into a row (or column) or receive a worksheet from another person that has data in a row (or column), and you decide the data would be better presented as a column (or row). You can also transpose rows and columns together in a single command, which is handy when you need to restructure a worksheet.

Transpose Rows and Columns

1 Select the range that includes the data you want to transpose.

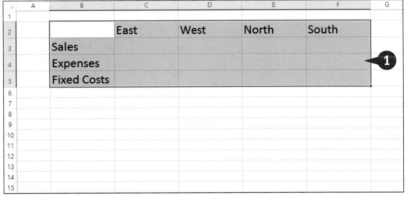

2 Click the **Home** tab.

3 Click **Copy** (⧉).

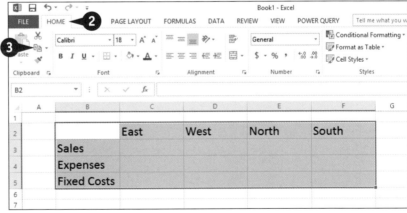

4 Click where you want the transposed range to appear.

5 Click the **Paste** ⌄.

6 Click **Transpose** (📋).

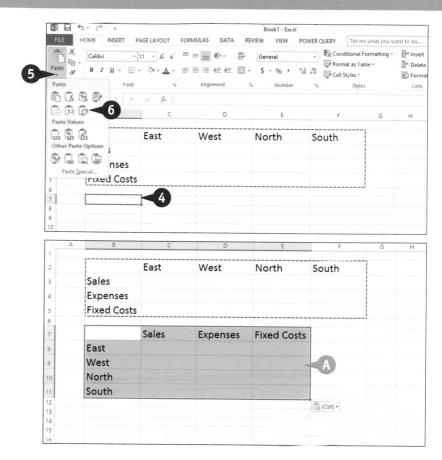

Ⓐ Excel transposes the data and then pastes it to the worksheet.

How do I know which cells to select?

The range you select before copying depends on what you want to transpose. If you want to transpose a single horizontal or vertical range of cells, then select just that range. If you want to transpose a horizontal range of cells and a vertical range of cells at the same time, select the range that includes all the cells, as shown in this section's example.

Can I transpose range values as well as range labels?

Yes. The Transpose command works with text, numbers, dates, formulas, and any other data that you can add to a cell. So if you have a rectangular region of data that includes row labels, column labels, and cell values within each row and column, you can select the entire range and transpose it.

Select and Enter Data Using Touch Gestures

If you will also be working with the Excel app on a touchscreen device, such as an iPad or Surface, you need to know how to use touch gestures to select, enter, and edit data. Although you can attach external keyboards to these devices, most of the time you might not have access to a physical keyboard. In such cases, you need to use touch gestures — tapping, sliding, and so on — to manipulate the data that you see on the Excel screen.

Select and Enter Data Using Touch Gestures

Select Data

1 Tap the first cell you want to select.

2 Tap and hold the lower-right selector, and then slide down and/or to the right to extend the selection.

3 Tap and hold the upper-left selector, and then slide up and/or to the left to extend the selection.

Enter and Edit Data

1 Double-tap the cell you want to use to enter or edit data.

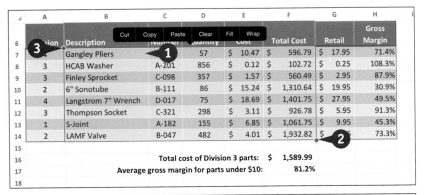

The Excel app opens the Formula bar for editing and displays the on-screen keyboard.

2 Using the on-screen keyboard, add or edit the cell data.

Note: To position the cursor within the Formula bar, tap and hold inside the Formula bar, then slide left or right.

Ⓐ Tap **Abc** or **123** to toggle the keyboard between letters and numbers.

3 To confirm the cell entry or edit, tap **OK** (✓).

Ⓑ If you do not want to accept the changes to the cell, tap **Cancel** (✕).

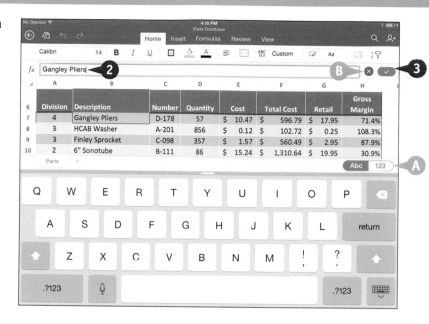

TIPS

Is there an easier way to enter a long list of items in a column or a row of cells?

Yes. Rather than tapping **OK** (✓) after each entry, tap **123** to display the numeric keyboard, and then tap an arrow key. The active cell moves in the direction of the arrow or to the cell you tapped, and Excel leaves the Formula bar open for editing.

Is there an easier way to enter several items randomly in a worksheet?

Yes. Instead of tapping **OK** (✓) after each entry, tap the next cell you want to use. The active cell moves to the cell you tapped, and Excel leaves the Formula bar open for editing.

CHAPTER 2

Working with Range Names

You can make it easier to navigate Excel worksheets and build Excel formulas by applying names to your ranges. This chapter explains range names and shows you how to define, edit, and use range names.

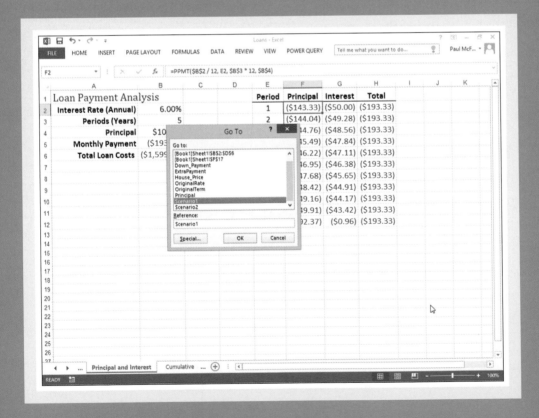

Understanding the Benefits of Using Range Names

A *range name* is a text label that you apply to a single cell or to a range of cells. Once you have defined a name for a range, you can use that name in place of the range coordinates, which has several benefits. These benefits include making your worksheets more intuitive and making your work more accurate. In addition, a range name is easier to remember than range coordinates, it does not change when you move the underlying range, and it makes it easier to navigate your worksheets.

More Intuitive

Range names are more intuitive than range coordinates, particularly in formulas. For example, if you see the range B2:B10 in a formula, the only way to know what

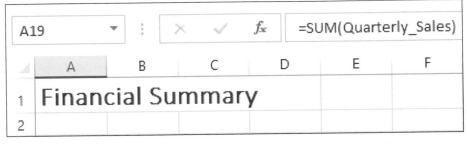

the range refers to is to look at the data. However, if you see the name Quarterly_Sales in the formula, then you already know what the range refers to.

More Accurate

Range names are more accurate than range coordinates. For example, consider the range address A1:B3, which consists of four different pieces of information: the column (A) and row (1) of the cell in the upper-left corner of the range, and the column

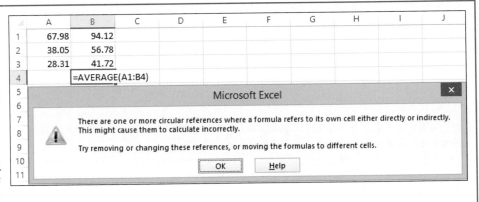

(B) and row (3) of the cell in the lower-right corner. If you get even one of these values wrong, it can cause errors throughout a spreadsheet. By contrast, with a range name you need only reference the actual name.

Easier to Remember

Range names are easier to remember than range coordinates. For example, if you want to use a particular range in a formula, but that range is not currently visible, to get the coordinates you must scroll until you can see the range and then

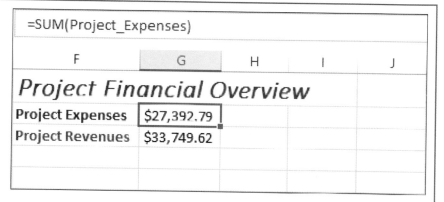

determine the range's coordinates. However, if you have already assigned the range an intuitive name such as Project_Expenses, you can add that name directly without having to view the range.

Names Do Not Change

Range names do not change when you adjust the position of a range, as they do with range coordinates. For example, if you move the range A1:B5 to the right by five columns, the range coordinates change to F1:G5. If you have a formula that references that range, Excel updates the formula with the

new range coordinates, which could confuse someone examining the worksheet. By contrast, a range name does not change when you move the range.

Easier Navigation

Range names make it easier to navigate a worksheet. For example, Excel has a Go To command that enables you to choose a range name, and Excel takes you directly to the range. You can also use the Name box to select a range name and navigate to that range. You can also use Go To and the Name box to specify range coordinates, but range coordinates are much more difficult to work with.

Define a Range Name

Before you can use a range name in your formulas or to navigate a worksheet, you must first define the range name. You can define as many names as you need, and you can even define multiple names for the same range.

You can create range names manually, or you can get Excel to create the names for you automatically based on the existing text labels in a worksheet. To do this, see the following section, "Using Worksheet Text to Define a Range Name."

Define a Range Name

1 Select the range you want to name.

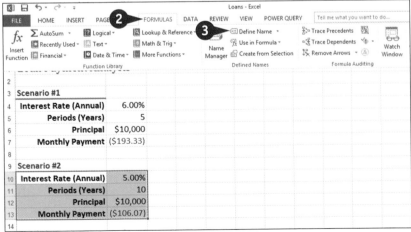

2 Click the **Formulas** tab.

3 Click **Define Name**.

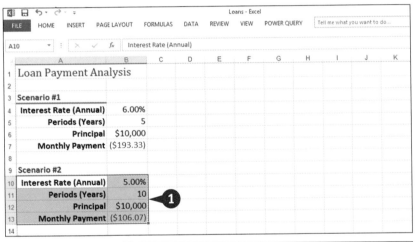

The New Name dialog box appears.

④ Type the name you want to use in the **Name** text box.

Note: The first character of the name must be a letter or an underscore (_). The name cannot include spaces or cell references, and it cannot be any longer than 255 characters.

Note: You can only use a particular range name once in a workbook.

⑤ Click **OK**.

Excel assigns the name to the range.

Ⓐ The new name appears in the Name box whenever you select the range.

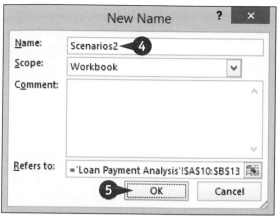

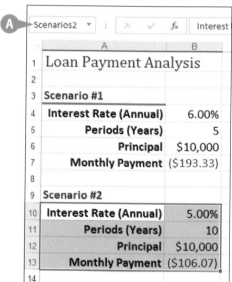

Is there an easier way to define a range name?

Yes, you can follow these steps to bypass the New Name dialog box:

① Select the range you want to name.

② Click inside the **Name** box.

③ Type the name you want to use.

④ Press **Enter**.

Excel assigns the name to the range.

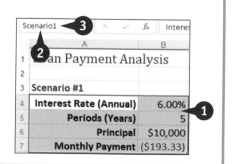

Using Worksheet Text to Define a Range Name

If you have several ranges to name, you can speed up the process by getting Excel to create the names for you automatically based on each range's text labels.

You can create range names from worksheet text when the labels are in the top or bottom row of the range, or the left or right column of the range. For example, if you have a column named Company, using the technique in this section results in that column's data being assigned the range name "Company."

Using Worksheet Text to Define a Range Name

1 Select the range or ranges you want to name.

A Be sure to include the text labels you want to use for the range names.

2 Click the **Formulas** tab.

3 Click **Create from Selection**.

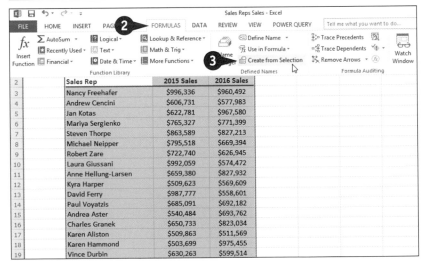

The Create Names from Selection dialog box appears.

4 Select the setting or settings that correspond to where the text labels are located in the selected range (☐ changes to ✔).

If Excel has activated a check box that does not apply to your data, deselect it (✔ changes to ☐).

5 Click **OK**.

Excel assigns the text labels as range names.

B When you select one of the ranges, the range name assigned by Excel appears in the Name box.

Note: If the label text contains any illegal characters, such as a space, Excel replaces each of those characters with an underscore (_).

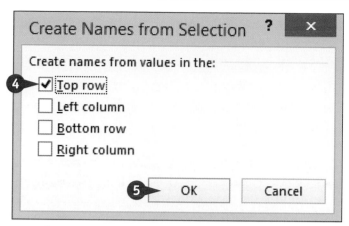

Create Names from Selection

Create names from values in the:

4 ✔ Top row
☐ Left column
☐ Bottom row
☐ Right column

5 OK   Cancel

B Sales_Rep   fx   Nancy Freehafer

	A	B	C	D
1				
2		Sales Rep	2015 Sales	2016 Sales
3		Nancy Freehafer	$996,336	$960,492
4		Andrew Cencini	$606,731	$577,983
5		Jan Kotas	$622,781	$967,580
6		Mariya Sergienko	$765,327	$771,399
7		Steven Thorpe	$863,589	$827,213
8		Michael Neipper	$795,518	$669,394
9		Robert Zare	$722,740	$626,945
10		Laura Giussani	$992,059	$574,472
11	**B**	Anne Hellung-Larsen	$659,380	$827,932
12		Kyra Harper	$509,623	$569,609
13		David Ferry	$987,777	$558,601
14		Paul Voyatzis	$685,091	$602,182
15		Andrea Aster	$540,484	$693,762
16		Charles Granek	$650,733	$823,034
17		Karen Aliston	$509,863	$511,569
18		Karen Hammond	$503,699	$975,455
19		Vince Durbin	$630,263	$599,514
20		Paul Sellars	$779,722	$596,353
21		Gregg O'Donoghue	$592,802	$652,171
22				

TIPS

Is there a faster way to run the Create from Selection command?

Yes, Excel offers a keyboard shortcut for the command. Select the range or ranges you want to work with and then press `Ctrl`+`Shift`+`F3`. Excel displays the Create Names from Selection dialog box. Follow steps **4** and **5** to create the range names.

Given a table with labels in the top row and left column, is there a way to automatically assign a name to the table data?

Yes. The table data refers to the range of cells that does not include the table headings in the top row and left column. To assign a name to the data range, type a label in the top-left corner of the table. When you run the Create from Selection command on the entire table, Excel assigns the top-left label to the data range, as shown here.

GDP_Growth

	A	B	C	D
1	GDP Growth	2009	2010	2011
2	Canada	-2.8	3.2	2.5
3	France	-3.1	1.7	1.7
4	Germany	-5.1	3.7	3.0
5	United Kindom	-4.4	2.1	0.7
6	United States	-3.5	3.0	1.7

Navigate a Workbook Using Range Names

One of the big advantages of defining range names is that they make it easier to navigate a workbook. You can choose a range name from a list and Excel automatically selects the associated range. This works even if the named range exists in a different worksheet of the same workbook.

Excel offers two methods for navigating a workbook using range names: the Name box and the Go To command.

Navigate a Workbook Using Range Names

Use the Name Box

1 Open the workbook that contains the range you want to work with.

2 Click the **Name** box ▼.

3 Click the name of the range you want to select.

A Excel selects the range.

Use the Go To Command

1 Open the workbook that contains the range you want to work with.

2 Click the **Home** tab.

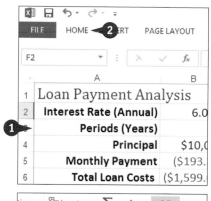

3 Click **Find & Select** (🔍).

4 Click **Go To**.

Note: You can also select the Go To command by pressing Ctrl+G.

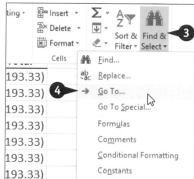

The Go To dialog box appears.

5 Click the name of the range you want to select.

6 Click **OK**.

Excel selects the range.

TIP

Is it possible to navigate to a named range in a different workbook?

Yes, but it is not easy or straightforward:

1 Follow steps **1** to **4** in the "Use the Go To Command" subsection to display the Go To dialog box.

2 In the **Reference** text box, type the following: **'[*workbook*]*worksheet*'!*name***

Replace *workbook* with the filename of the workbook; replace *worksheet* with the name of the worksheet that contains the range; and replace *name* with the range name.

3 Click **OK**.

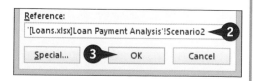

Change a Range Name

You can change any range name to a more suitable or accurate name. Changing a range name is useful if you are no longer satisfied with the original name you applied to a range or if the existing name no longer accurately reflects the contents of the range. You might also want to change a range name if you do not like the name that Excel generated automatically from the worksheet labels.

If you want to change the range coordinates associated with a range name, see the second tip.

Change a Range Name

1 Open the workbook that contains the range name you want to change.

2 Click the **Formulas** tab.

3 Click **Name Manager**.

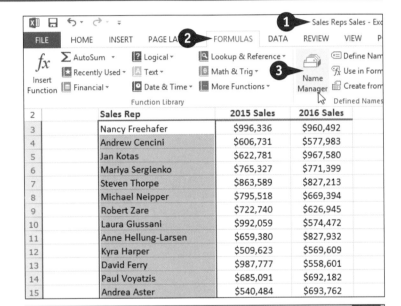

The Name Manager dialog box appears.

4 Click the name you want to change.

5 Click **Edit**.

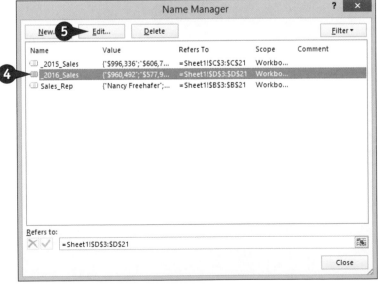

The Edit Name dialog box appears.

6 Use the **Name** text box to edit the name.

7 Click **OK**.

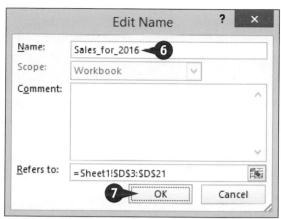

A The new name appears in the Name Manager dialog box.

8 Click **Close**.

Excel closes the dialog box and returns you to the worksheet.

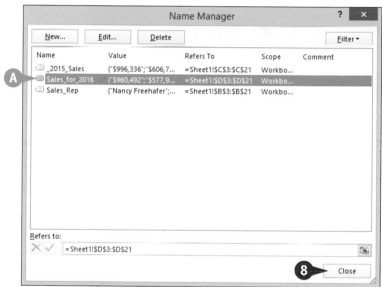

TIPS

Is there a faster method I can use to open the Name Manager dialog box?
Yes, Excel offers a shortcut key that enables you to bypass steps **2** and **3**. Open the workbook that contains the range name you want to change, and then press Ctrl+F3. Excel opens the Name Manager dialog box.

Can I assign a name to a different range?
Yes. If you add another range to your workbook and you feel that an existing name would be more suited to that range, you can modify the name to refer to the new range. Follow steps **1** to **5** to open the Edit Name dialog box. Click inside the **Refers to** reference box, click and drag the mouse (⊕) on the worksheet to select the new range, and then press Enter. Click **Close**.

Delete a Range Name

If you have a range name that you no longer need, you should delete it. This reduces clutter in the Name Manager dialog box, and makes the Name box easier to navigate.

Note, however, that deleting a range name will generate an error in any formula that uses the name. This occurs because when you delete a range name, Excel does not convert the name to its range coordinates in formulas that use the name. Therefore, before deleting a range name, you should convert that name to its range coordinates in every formula that uses the name.

Delete a Range Name

1 Open the workbook that contains the range name you want to delete.

2 Click the **Formulas** tab.

3 Click **Name Manager**.

Note: You can also open the Name Manager dialog box by pressing Ctrl+F3.

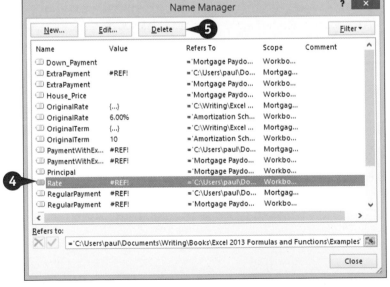

The Name Manager dialog box appears.

4 Click the name you want to delete.

5 Click **Delete**.

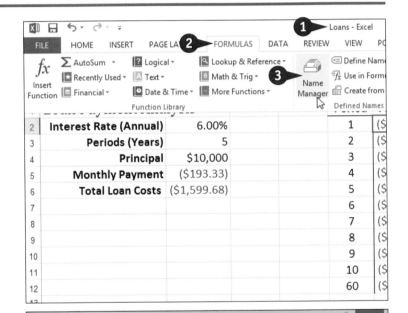

Excel asks you to confirm the deletion.

6 Click **OK**.

A Excel deletes the range name.

7 Click **Close**.

Excel closes the dialog box and returns you to the worksheet.

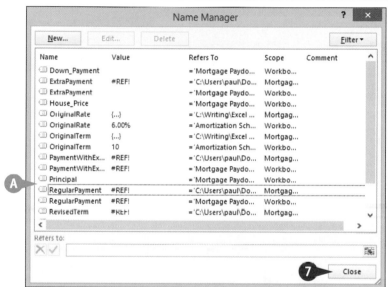

TIP

Is there a faster way to delete multiple range names?
Yes, you can delete two or more range names at once. First, follow steps **1** to **3** to display the Name Manager dialog box. Next, select the range names you want to delete: To select consecutive names, click the first name you want to delete, hold down Shift, and then click the last name you want to delete; to select nonconsecutive names, hold down Ctrl and click each name you want to delete. When you have selected the names you want to remove, click **Delete** and then click **OK** when Excel asks you to confirm the deletion. Click **Close** to return to the worksheet.

Paste a List of Range Names

To make your workbook easier to use, particularly for other people who are not familiar with the names you have defined, you can paste a list of the workbook's range names to a worksheet. This is also useful for a workbook you have not used in a while. Examining the list of range names can help you familiarize yourself once again with the workbook's contents.

The pasted list contains two columns: one for the range names and one for the range coordinates associated with each name.

Paste a List of Range Names

1 Open the workbook that contains the range names you want to paste.

2 Select the cell where you want the pasted list to appear.

Note: Excel will overwrite existing data, so select a location where there is no existing cell data or where it is okay to delete the existing cell data.

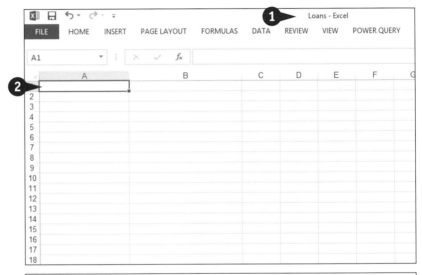

3 Click the **Formulas** tab.

4 Click **Use in Formula**.

5 Click **Paste Names**.

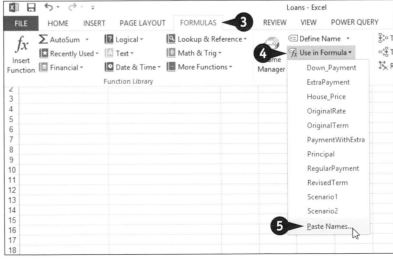

The Paste Name dialog box appears.

6 Click **Paste List**.

Paste Name

Paste _name_

Down_Payment
ExtraPayment
House_Price
OriginalRate
OriginalTerm
PaymentWithExtra
Principal
RegularPayment

6 Paste List   OK   Cancel

Excel closes the Paste Name dialog box.

Ⓐ Excel pastes the list of range names to the worksheet.

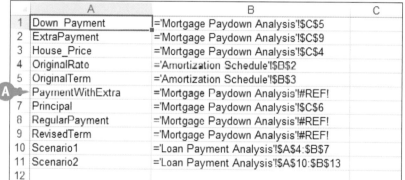

	A	B	C
1	Down_Payment	='Mortgage Paydown Analysis'!$C$5	
2	ExtraPayment	='Mortgage Paydown Analysis'!$C$9	
3	House_Price	='Mortgage Paydown Analysis'!$C$4	
4	OriginalRate	='Amortization Schedule'!$B$2	
5	OriginalTerm	='Amortization Schedule'!$B$3	
6	PaymentWithExtra	='Mortgage Paydown Analysis'!#REF!	
7	Principal	='Mortgage Paydown Analysis'!$C$6	
8	RegularPayment	='Mortgage Paydown Analysis'!#REF!	
9	RevisedTerm	='Mortgage Paydown Analysis'!#REF!	
10	Scenario1	='Loan Payment Analysis'!$A$4:$B$7	
11	Scenario2	='Loan Payment Analysis'!$A$10:$B$13	
12			

TIP

Is there a faster method I can use to paste a list of range names?
Yes, Excel offers a handy keyboard shortcut that you can use. Open the workbook that contains the range names you want to paste, and then select the cell where you want the pasted list to appear. Press **F3** to open the Paste Name dialog box, and then click **Paste List**.

CHAPTER 3

Formatting Excel Ranges

Microsoft Excel 2016 offers many commands and options for formatting ranges, including the font, text color, text alignment, background color, number format, column width, row height, and more.

Change the Font and Font Size

When you work in an Excel worksheet, you can add visual appeal to a cell or range by changing the font. In this section and throughout this book, the term *font* is synonymous with *typeface*, and both terms refer to the overall look of each character.

You can also make labels and other text stand out from the rest of the worksheet by changing the font size. The font size is measured in *points*, where there are roughly 72 points in an inch.

Change the Font and Font Size

Change the Font

1 Select the range you want to format.

2 Click the **Home** tab.

3 Click ▼ in the **Font** list.

A When you use the mouse ▷ to point to a typeface, Excel temporarily changes the selected text to that typeface.

4 Click the typeface you want to apply.

B Excel applies the font to the text in the selected range.

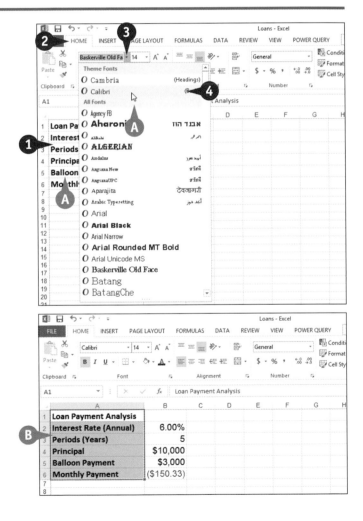

Change the Font Size

1 Select the range you want to format.

2 Click the **Home** tab.

3 Click ▼ in the **Font Size** list.

C When you use the mouse ▷ to point to a font size, Excel temporarily changes the selected text to that size.

4 Click the size you want to apply.

D You can also type the size you want in the Size text box.

E Excel applies the font size to the text in the selected range.

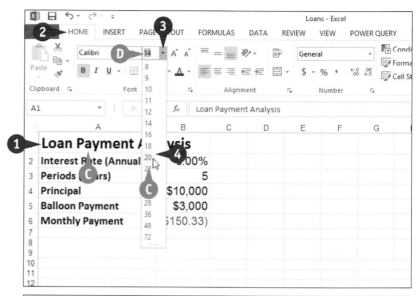

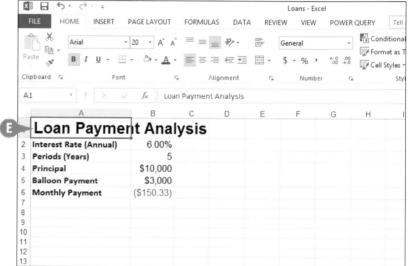

TIPS

In the Theme Fonts section of the Font list, what do the designations Body and Headings mean?

When you create a workbook, Excel automatically applies a document theme to the workbook, and that theme includes predefined fonts. The theme's default font is referred to as Body, and it is the font used for regular worksheet text. Each theme also defines a Headings font, which Excel uses for cells formatted with a heading or title style.

Can I change the default font and font size?

Yes. Click the **File** tab and then click **Options** to open the Excel Options dialog box. Click the **General** tab, click the **Use this as the default font** ▼, and then click the typeface you want to use as the default. Click the **Font size** ▼ and then click the size you prefer to use as the default. Click **OK**.

Apply Font Effects

You can improve the look and impact of text in an Excel worksheet by applying font effects to a cell or to a range.

Font effects include common formatting such as **bold**, which is often used to make labels stand out from regular text; *italic*, which is often used to add emphasis to text; and underline, which is often used for worksheet titles and headings. You can also apply special effects such as ~~strikethrough~~, superscripts (for example, x^2+y^2), and subscripts (for example, H_2O).

Apply Font Effects

1 Select the range you want to format.

2 Click the **Home** tab.

3 To format the text as bold, click the **Bold** button (**B**).

A Excel applies the bold effect to the selected range.

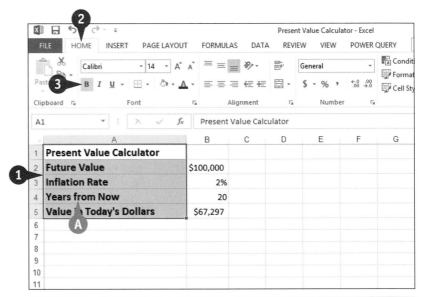

4 To format the text as italic, click the **Italic** button (*I*).

5 To format the text as underline, click the **Underline** button (**U**).

B Excel applies the effects to the selected range.

6 Click the **Font** dialog box launcher (⌐).

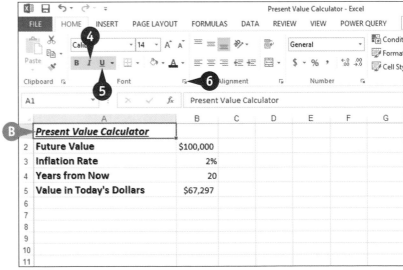

The Format Cells dialog box appears with the Font tab displayed.

⑦ To format the text as strikethrough, click **Strikethrough** (☐ changes to ☑).

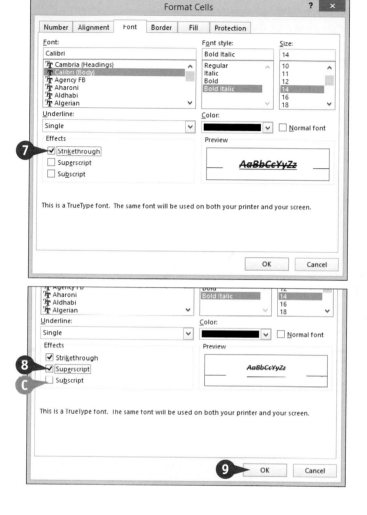

⑧ To format the text as a superscript, click **Superscript** (☐ changes to ☑).

⑨ To format the text as a subscript, click **Subscript** (☐ changes to ☑).

⑨ Click **OK**.

Excel applies the font effects.

TIP

Are there any font-related keyboard shortcuts I can use?
Yes. Excel supports the following font shortcuts:

Press	To
Ctrl + B	Toggle the selected range as bold
Ctrl + I	Toggle the selected range as italic
Ctrl + U	Toggle the selected range as underline
Ctrl + 5	Toggle the selected range as strikethrough
Ctrl + 1	Display the Format Cells dialog box

Change the Font Color

When you work in an Excel worksheet, you can add visual interest by changing the font color. Most worksheets are meant to convey specific information, but that does not mean the sheet has to be plain. By adding a bit of color to your text, you make your worksheets more appealing. Adding color can also make the worksheet easier to read by, for example, differentiating titles, headings, and labels from regular text.

You can change the font color by applying a color from the workbook's theme, from the Excel palette of standard colors, or from a custom color that you create.

Change the Font Color

Select a Theme or Standard Color

1. Select the range you want to format.

2. Click the **Home** tab.

3. Click ▼ in the **Font Color** list (**A**).

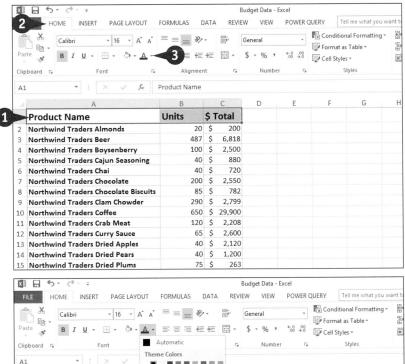

4. Click a theme color.

Ⓐ Alternatively, click one of the Excel standard colors.

Ⓑ Excel applies the color to the selected range.

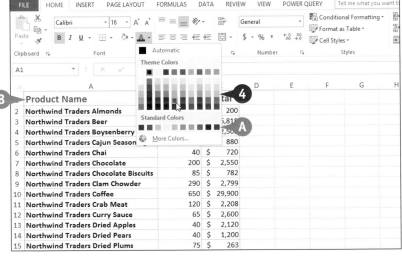

Select a Custom Color

1 Select the range you want to format.

2 Click the **Home** tab.

3 Click ▼ in the **Font Color** list (**A**).

4 Click **More Colors**.

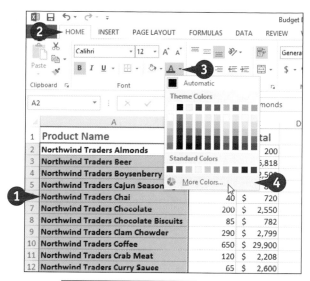

The Colors dialog box appears.

5 Click the color you want to use.

C You can also click the **Custom** tab and then either click the color you want or enter the values for the Red, Green, and Blue components of the color.

6 Click **OK**.

Excel applies the color to the selected range.

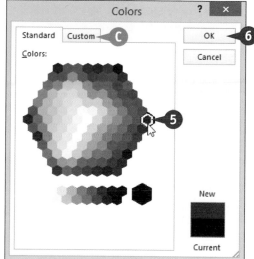

Align Text Within a Cell

You can make your worksheets easier to read by aligning text and numbers within each cell. By default, Excel aligns numbers with the right side of the cell, and it aligns text with the left side of the cell. You can also align numbers or text with the center of each cell.

Excel also allows you to align your data vertically within each cell. By default, Excel aligns all data with the bottom of each cell, but you can also align text with the top or middle.

Align Text Within a Cell

Align Text Horizontally

1 Select the range you want to format.

2 Click the **Home** tab.

3 In the Alignment group, click the horizontal alignment option you want to use:

Click **Align Text Left** (≡) to align data with the left side of each cell.

Click **Center** (≡) to align data with the center of each cell.

Click **Align Text Right** (≡) to align data with the right side of each cell.

Excel aligns the data horizontally within each selected cell.

A In this example, the data in the cells is centered.

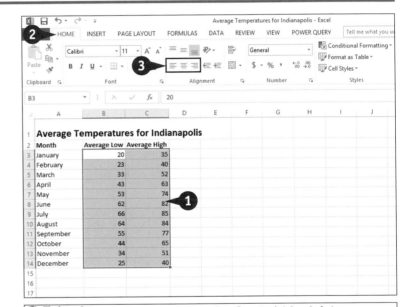

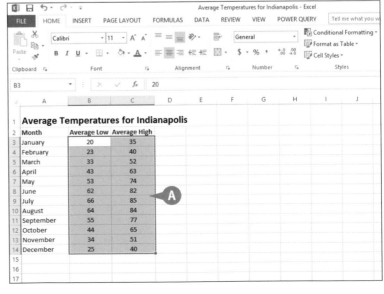

Align Text Vertically

1 Select the range you want to format.

2 Click the **Home** tab.

3 In the Alignment group, click the vertical alignment option you want to use:

Click **Top Align** (≡) to align data with the top of each cell.

Click **Middle Align** (≡) to align data with the middle of each cell.

Click **Bottom Align** (≡) to align data with the bottom of each cell.

Excel aligns the data vertically within each selected cell.

B In this example, the text is aligned with the middle of the cell.

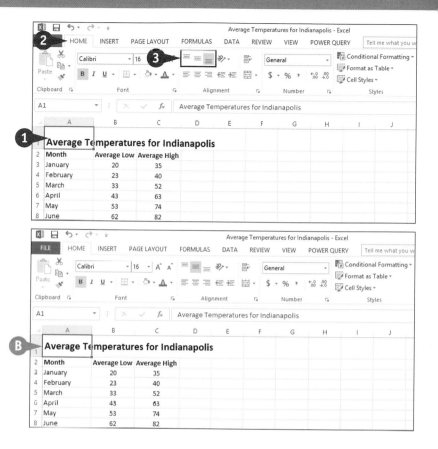

TIPS

How do I format text so that it aligns with both the left and right sides of the cell?

This is called *justified* text, and it is useful if you have a lot of text in one or more cells. Select the range, click the **Home** tab, and then click the dialog box launcher (▫) in the Alignment group. The Format Cells dialog box appears with the Alignment tab displayed. In the **Horizontal** list, click ▾ and then click **Justify**. Click **OK** to justify the cells.

How do I indent cell text?

Select the range you want to indent, click the **Home** tab, and then click the Alignment group's dialog box launcher (▫). In the Alignment tab, click the **Horizontal** list ▾ and then click **Left (Indent)**. Use the **Indent** text box to type the indent, in characters, and then click **OK**. You can also click the **Increase Indent** (≡) or **Decrease Indent** (≡) button in the Home tab's Alignment group.

Center Text Across Multiple Columns

You can make a worksheet more visually appealing and easier to read by centering text across multiple columns. This feature is most useful when you have text in a cell that you use as a label or title for a range. Centering the text across the range makes it easier to see that the label or title applies to the entire range.

Center Text Across Multiple Columns

1 Select a range that consists of the text you want to work with and the cells across which you want to center the text.

2 Click the **Home** tab.

3 In the **Alignment** group, click the dialog box launcher ( ).

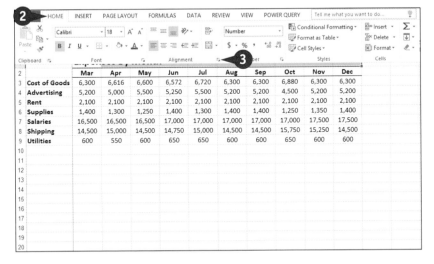

Excel opens the Format Cells dialog box with the Alignment tab displayed.

④ Click the **Horizontal** ▼ and then click **Center Across Selection**.

⑤ Click **OK**.

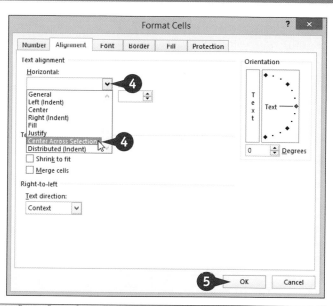

Ⓐ Excel centers the text across the selected cells.

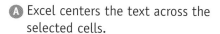

	Mar	Apr	May	Jun	Jul	Aug	Sep	Oct	Nov	Dec
Expenses By Month										
Cost of Goods	6,300	6,616	6,600	6,572	6,720	6,300	6,300	6,880	6,300	6,300
Advertising	5,200	5,000	5,500	5,250	5,500	5,200	5,200	4,500	5,200	5,200
Rent	2,100	2,100	2,100	2,100	2,100	2,100	2,100	2,100	2,100	2,100
Supplies	1,400	1,300	1,250	1,400	1,300	1,400	1,400	1,250	1,350	1,400
Salaries	16,500	16,500	16,500	17,000	17,000	17,000	17,000	17,000	17,500	17,500
Shipping	14,500	15,000	14,500	14,750	15,000	14,500	14,500	15,750	15,250	14,500
Utilities	600	550	600	650	650	600	600	650	600	600

TIP

Is there an easier way to center text across multiple columns?

Yes, although this technique also merges the selected cells into a single cell. (See Chapter 1 to learn more about merging cells.) Follow these steps:

① Repeat steps **1** and **2**.

② In the Alignment group, click the **Merge & Center** button (▦).

Excel merges the selected cells into a single cell and centers the text within that cell.

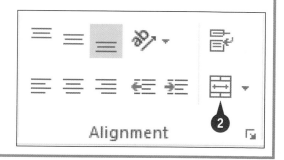

Alignment

Rotate Text Within a Cell

You can add visual interest to your text by slanting the text upward or downward in the cell. You can also use this technique to make a long column heading take up less horizontal space on the worksheet.

You can choose a predefined rotation, or you can make cell text angle upward or downward by specifying the degrees of rotation.

Rotate Text Within a Cell

1 Select the range containing the text you want to angle.

2 Click the **Home** tab.

3 Click **Orientation** (📐).

Ⓐ If you want to use a predefined orientation, click one of the menu items and skip the rest of the steps.

4 Click **Format Cell Alignment**.

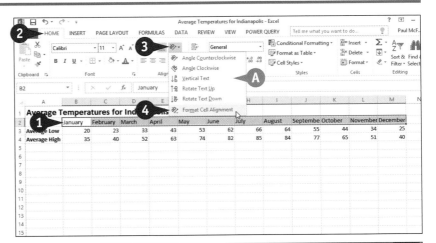

The Format Cells dialog box appears with the Alignment tab displayed.

5 Click an orientation marker.

Ⓑ You can also use the Degrees spin box to type or click a degree of rotation (see the tip).

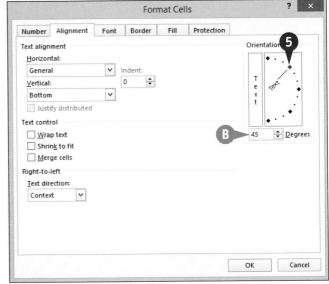

60

C You can click the vertical text area to display your text vertically instead of horizontally in the cell.

6 Click **OK**.

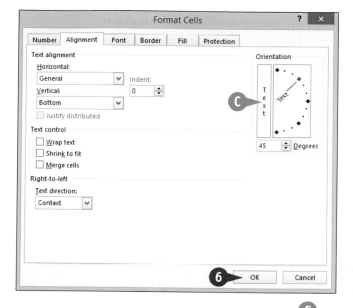

D Excel rotates the cell text.

E The row height automatically increases to contain the slanted text.

F You can reduce the column width to free up space and make your cells more presentable.

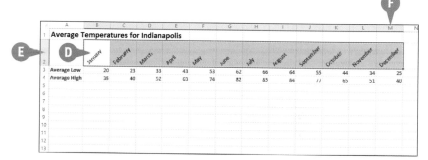

TIP

How does the Degrees spin box work?

If you use the Degrees spin box to set the text orientation, you can set the orientation to a positive number, such as 25, and Excel angles the text in an upward (counterclockwise) direction. If you set the text orientation to a negative number, such as –40, Excel angles the text in a downward (clockwise) direction.

You can specify values in the range from 90 degrees (which is the same as clicking the Rotate Text Up command in the Orientation menu) to –90 degrees (which is the same as clicking the Rotate Text Down command).

Add a Background Color to a Range

You can make a range stand out from the rest of the worksheet by applying a background color to the range. Note, however, that if you want to apply a background color to a range based on the values in that range — for example, red for negative values and green for positive — it is easier to apply a conditional format, as described in the "Apply a Conditional Format to a Range" section, later in this chapter.

You can change the background color by applying a color from the workbook's theme, from the Excel palette of standard colors, or from a custom color that you create.

Add a Background Color to a Range

Select a Theme or Standard Color

1. Select the range you want to format.

2. Click the **Home** tab.

3. Click ▼ in the **Fill Color** list (🖋).

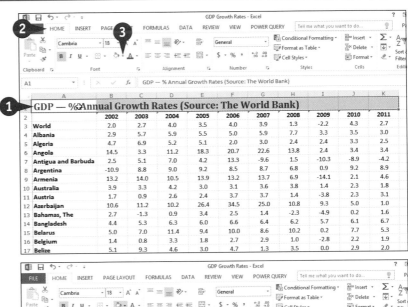

4. Click a theme color.

Ⓐ Alternatively, click one of the standard Excel colors.

Ⓑ Excel applies the color to the selected range.

Ⓒ To remove the background color from the range, click **No Fill**.

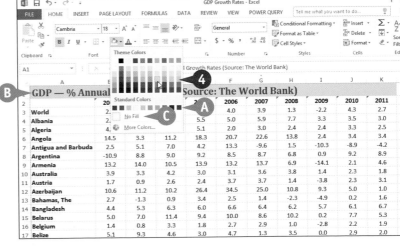

Select a Custom Color

1 Select the range you want to format.

2 Click the **Home** tab.

3 Click ▼ in the **Fill Color** list (🖍).

4 Click **More Colors**.

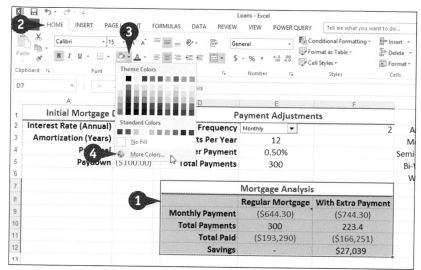

The Colors dialog box appears.

5 Click the color you want to use.

D You can also click the **Custom** tab and then either click the color you want or enter the values for the Red, Green, and Blue components of the color.

6 Click **OK**.

Excel applies the color to the selected range.

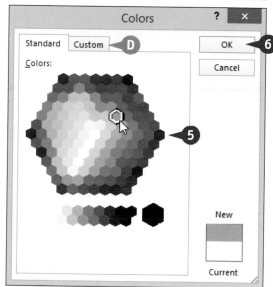

Are there any pitfalls to watch out for when I apply background colors?

Yes. The biggest pitfall is applying a background color that clashes with the range text. For example, the default text color is black, so if you apply any dark background color, the text will be very difficult to read. Always use either a light background color with dark-colored text, or a dark background color with light-colored text.

Can I apply a background that fades from one color to another?

Yes. This is called a *gradient* effect. Select the range, click the **Home** tab, and then click the Font group's dialog box launcher (🔲). Click the **Fill** tab and then click **Fill Effects**. In the Fill Effects dialog box, use the **Color 1** ▼ and the **Color 2** ▼ to choose your colors. Click an option in the **Shading styles** section (◯ changes to ◉), and then click **OK**.

Apply a Number Format

You can make your worksheet easier to read by applying a number format to your data. For example, if your worksheet includes monetary data, you can apply the Currency format to display each value with a dollar sign and two decimal places.

Excel offers ten number formats, most of which apply to numeric data. However, you can also apply the Date format to date data, the Time format to time data, and the Text format to text data.

Apply a Number Format

1. Select the range you want to format.

2. Click the **Home** tab.

3. Click the **Number Format** ▼.

4. Click the number format you want to use.

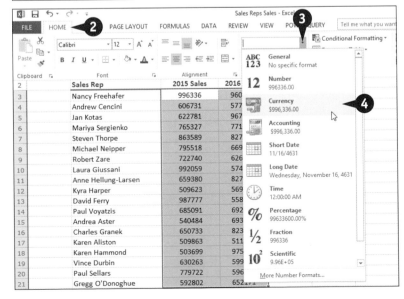

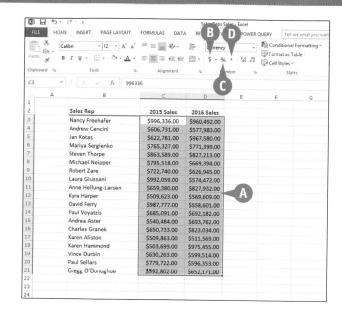

A Excel applies the number format to the selected range.

B For monetary values, you can also click **Accounting Number Format** ($).

C For percentages, you can also click **Percent Style** (%).

D For large numbers, you can also click **Comma Style** (,).

TIP

Is there a way to get more control over the number formats?

Yes. You can use the Format Cells dialog box to control properties such as the display of negative numbers, the currency symbol used, and how dates and times appear. Follow these steps:

1 Select the range you want to format.

2 Click the **Home** tab.

3 Click the **Number** group's dialog box launcher (⌐).

The Format Cells dialog box appears with the Number tab displayed.

4 In the **Category** list, click the type of number format you want to apply.

5 Use the controls that Excel displays to customize the number format.

The controls you see vary, depending on the number format you chose in step **4**.

6 Click **OK**.

Excel applies the number format.

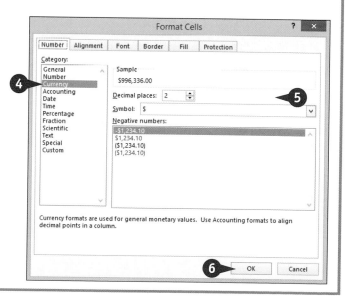

Change the Number of Decimal Places Displayed

You can make your numeric values easier to read and interpret by adjusting the number of decimal places that Excel displays. For example, you might want to ensure that all dollar-and-cent values show two decimal places, while dollar-only values show no decimal places. Similarly, you can adjust the display of percentage values to suit your audience by showing more decimals (greater accuracy but more difficult to read) or fewer decimals (less accuracy but easier to read).

You can either decrease or increase the number of decimal places that Excel displays.

Change the Number of Decimal Places Displayed

Decrease the Number of Decimal Places

1 Select the range you want to format.

2 Click the **Home** tab.

3 Click the **Decrease Decimal** button (.00→.0).

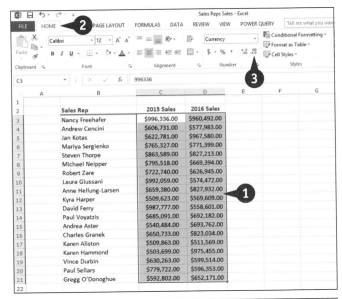

Ⓐ Excel decreases the number of decimal places by one.

4 Repeat step **3** until you get the number of decimal places you want.

Increase the Number of Decimal Places

1 Select the range you want to format.

2 Click the **Home** tab.

3 Click the **Increase Decimal** button (⬅.0/.00).

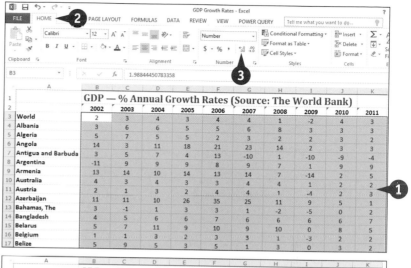

B Excel increases the number of decimal places by one.

4 Repeat step **3** until you get the number of decimal places you want.

My range currently has values that display different numbers of decimal places. What happens when I change the number of decimal places?

In this situation, Excel uses the value that has the most displayed decimal places as the basis for formatting all the values. For example, if the selected range has values that display no, one, two, or four decimal places, Excel uses the value with four decimals as the basis. If you click **Decrease Decimal**, Excel displays every value with three decimal places; if you click **Increase Decimal**, Excel displays every value with five decimal places.

Apply an AutoFormat to a Range

You can save time when formatting your Excel worksheets by using the AutoFormat feature. This feature offers a number of predefined formatting options that you can apply to a range all at once. The formatting options include the number format, font, cell alignment, borders, patterns, row height, and column width.

The AutoFormats are designed for data in a tabular format, particularly where you have headings in the top row and left column, numeric data in the rest of the cells, and a bottom row that shows the totals for each column.

Apply an AutoFormat to a Range

1 Select the range you want to format.

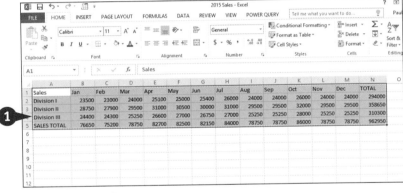

2 Click **AutoFormat** (⊞).

Note: See the second tip to learn how to add a button to the Quick Access Toolbar. In this case, you must add the AutoFormat button.

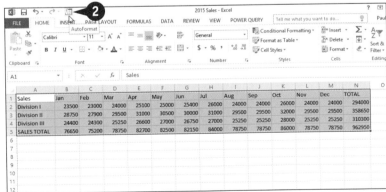

The AutoFormat dialog box appears.

③ Click the AutoFormat you want to use.

④ Click **OK**.

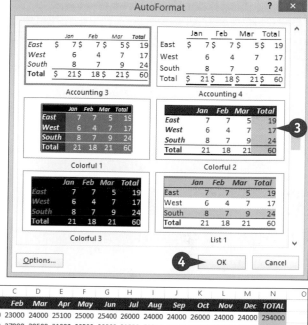

Ⓐ Excel applies the AutoFormat to the selected range.

Note: If you do not like or no longer need the AutoFormat you applied to the cells, you can revert them to a plain, unformatted state. Select the range and then click 📊 to display the AutoFormat dialog box. At the bottom of the format list, click **None**, and then click **OK**. Excel removes the AutoFormat from the selected range.

	A	B	C	D	E	F	G	H	I	J	K	L	M	N	O
1	Sales	Jan	Feb	Mar	Apr	May	Jun	Jul	Aug	Sep	Oct	Nov	Dec	TOTAL	
2	Division I	23500	23000	24000	25100	25000	25400	26000	24000	24000	26000	24000	24000	294000	
3	Division II	28750	27900	29500	31000	30500	30000	31000	29500	29500	32000	29500	29500	358650	
4	Division III	24400	24300	25250	26600	27000	26750	27000	25250	25250	28000	25250	25250	310300	
5	SALES TOTAL	76650	75200	78750	82700	82500	82150	84000	78750	78750	86000	78750	78750	962950	
6															
7															

TIPS

Is there a way to apply an AutoFormat without using some of its formatting?

Yes. Follow steps **1** to **3** to choose the AutoFormat you want to apply. Click **Options** to expand the dialog box and display the Formats to apply group. Deselect the option for each format you do not want to apply (☑ changes to ☐), and then click **OK**.

How do I add a button to the Quick Access Toolbar?

Click the **Customize Quick Access Toolbar** button (▾). If you see the command you want, click it; otherwise, click **More Commands**. Click the **Choose commands from** ▾, click the category you want to use, click the command you want to add, click **Add**, and then click **OK**.

Apply a Conditional Format to a Range

You can make a worksheet easier to analyze by applying a conditional format to a range. A *conditional format* is formatting that Excel applies only to cells that meet the condition you specify. For example, you can tell Excel to apply the formatting only if a cell's value is greater than some specified amount.

When you set up your conditional format, you can specify the font, border, and background pattern, which helps to ensure that the cells that meet your criteria stand out from the other cells in the range.

Apply a Conditional Format to a Range

1 Select the range you want to work with.

2 Click the **Home** tab.

3 Click **Conditional Formatting**.

4 Click **Highlight Cells Rules**.

5 Click the operator you want to use for your condition.

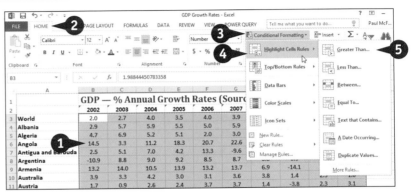

An operator dialog box appears, such as the Greater Than dialog box shown here.

6 Type the value you want to use for your condition.

Ⓐ You can also click the **Collapse Dialog** button (⊞) and then click a worksheet cell.

Depending on the operator, you may need to specify two values.

7 Click the **with** ▼ and then click the formatting you want to use.

Ⓑ To create your own format, click **Custom Format**.

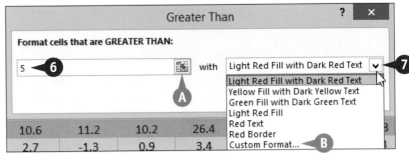

8 Click **OK**.

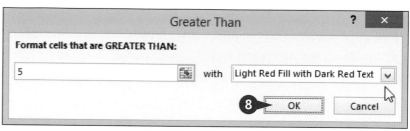

| Greater Than | ? | ✕ |

Format cells that are GREATER THAN:

| 5 | 📊 | with | Light Red Fill with Dark Red Text ▾ |

8 → OK   Cancel

C Excel applies the formatting to cells that meet your condition.

	A	B	C	D	E	F	G	H	I	J	K
1		GDP — % Annual Growth Rates (Source: The World Bank)									
2		2002	2003	2004	2005	2006	2007	2008	2009	2010	2011
3	World	2.0	2.7	4.0	3.5	4.0	3.9	1.3	-2.2	4.3	2.7
4	Albania	2.9	5.7	5.9	5.5	5.0	5.9	7.7	3.3	3.5	3.0
5	Algeria	4.7	6.9	5.2	5.1	2.0	3.0	2.4	2.4	3.3	2.5
6	Angola	14.5	3.3	11.2	18.3	20.7	22.6	13.8	2.4	3.4	3.4
7	Antigua and Barbuda	2.5	5.1	7.0	4.2	13.3	-9.6	1.5	-10.3	-8.9	-4.2
8	Argentina	-10.9	8.8	9.0	9.2	8.5	8.7	6.8	0.9	9.2	8.9
9	Armenia	13.2	14.0	10.5	13.9	13.2	13.7	6.9	-14.1	2.1	4.6
10	Australia	3.9	3.3	4.2	3.0	3.1	3.6	3.8	1.4	2.3	1.8
11	Austria	1.7	0.9	2.6	2.4	3.7	3.7	1.4	-3.8	2.3	3.1
12	Azerbaijan	10.6	11.2	10.2	26.4	34.5	25.0	10.8	9.3	5.0	1.0
13	Bahamas, The	2.7	-1.3	0.9	3.4	2.5	1.4	-2.3	-4.9	0.2	1.6
14	Bangladesh	4.4	5.3	6.3	6.0	6.6	6.4	6.2	5.7	6.1	6.7
15	Belarus	5.0	7.0	11.4	9.4	10.0	8.6	10.2	0.2	7.7	5.3
16	Belgium	1.4	0.8	3.3	1.8	2.7	2.9	1.0	-2.8	2.2	1.9
17	Belize	5.1	9.3	4.6	3.0	4.7	1.3	3.5	0.0	2.9	2.0
18	Benin	4.5	3.9	3.1	2.9	4.1	4.6	5.1	3.8	3.0	3.1
19	Bhutan	8.9	8.6	8.0	8.8	6.8	17.9	4.7	6.7	7.4	8.4
20	Bolivia	2.5	2.7	4.2	4.4	4.8	4.6	6.1	3.4	4.1	5.1
21	Bosnia and Herzegovir	5.3	4.0	6.1	5.0	6.2	6.8	5.4	-2.9	0.8	1.7
22	Botswana	9.0	6.3	6.0	1.6	5.1	4.8	2.9	-4.8	7.0	5.1
23	Brazil	2.7	1.1	5.7	3.2	4.0	6.1	5.2	-0.3	7.5	2.7

TIPS

Can I set up more than one condition for a single range?

Yes. Excel enables you to specify multiple conditional formats. For example, you could set up one condition for cells that are greater than some value, and a separate condition for cells that are less than some other value. You can apply unique formats to each condition. Follow steps **1** to **8** to configure the new condition.

How do I remove a conditional format from a range?

If you no longer require a conditional format, you can delete it. Follow steps **1** to **3** to select the range and display the Conditional Formatting menu, and then click **Manage Rules**. Excel displays the Conditional Formatting Rules Manager dialog box. Click the **Show formatting rules for** ▾ and then click **This Worksheet**. Click the conditional format you want to remove and then click **Delete Rule**. Click **OK** to return to the worksheet.

Apply a Style to a Range

You can reduce the time it takes to format your worksheets by applying the predefined Excel styles to your ranges. Excel comes with more than 20 predefined styles for different worksheet elements such as headings, numbers, calculations, and special range types such as explanatory text, worksheet notes, and warnings. Excel also offers two dozen styles associated with the current document theme.

Each style includes the number format, cell alignment, font typeface and size, border, and fill color.

Apply a Style to a Range

1 Select the range you want to format.

2 Click the **Home** tab.

3 Click **Cell Styles**.

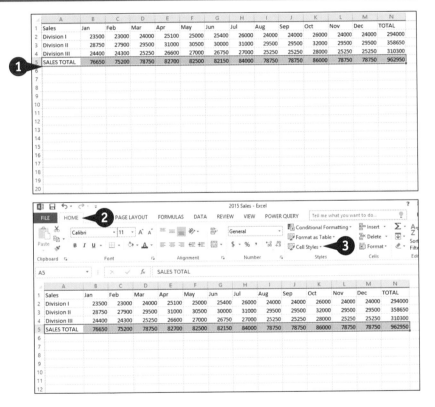

Excel displays the Cell Styles gallery.

④ Click the style you want to apply.

Note: If the style is not exactly the way you want, you can right-click the style, click **Modify**, and then click **Format** to customize the style.

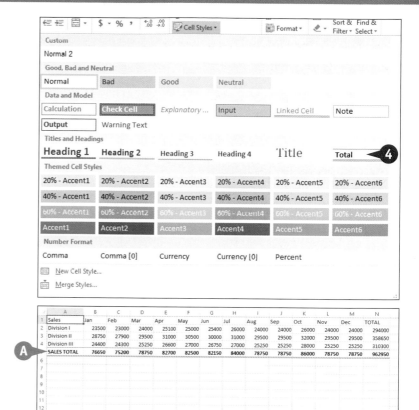

Ⓐ Excel applies the style to the range.

Are there styles I can use to format tabular data?

Yes. Excel comes with a gallery of table styles that offer formatting options that highlight the first row, apply different formats to alternating rows, and so on. Select the range that includes your data, click the **Home** tab, and then click **Format as Table**. In the gallery that appears, click the table format you want to apply.

Can I create my own style?

Yes. This is useful if you find yourself applying the same set of formatting options over and over. By saving those options as a custom style, you can apply it by following steps **1** to **4**. Apply your formatting to a cell or range, and then select that cell or range. Click **Home**, click **Cell Styles**, and then click **New Cell Style**. In the Style dialog box, type a name for your style, and then click **OK**.

Change the Column Width

You can make your worksheets neater and more readable by adjusting the column widths to suit the data contained in each column.

For example, if you have a large number or a long line of text in a cell, Excel may display only part of the cell value. To avoid this, you can increase the width of the column. Similarly, if a column only contains a few characters in each cell, you can decrease the width to fit more columns on the screen.

Change the Column Width

1 Click in any cell in the column you want to resize.

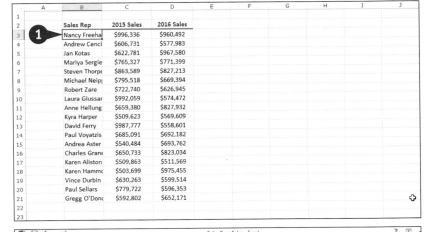

2 Click the **Home** tab.

3 Click **Format**.

4 Click **Column Width**.

The Column Width dialog box appears.

5 In the Column width text box, type the width you want to use.

6 Click **OK**.

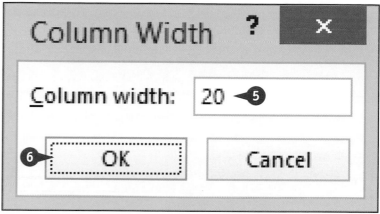

A Excel adjusts the column width.

B You can also move ✛ over the right edge of the column heading (✛ changes to ↔) and then click and drag the edge to set the width.

	A	B	C	D	E
1					
2		Sales Rep		2015 Sales	2016 Sales
3		Nancy Freehafer		$996,336	$960,492
4		Andrew Cencini		$606,731	$577,983
5		Jan Kotas		$622,781	$967,580
6		Mariya Sergienko		$765,327	$771,399
7		Steven Thorpe		$863,589	$827,213
8		Michael Neipper		$795,518	$669,394
9		Robert Zare		$722,740	$626,945
10		Laura Giussani		$992,059	$574,472
11		Anne Hellung-Larsen		$659,380	$827,932
12		Kyra Harper		$509,623	$569,609
13		David Ferry		$987,777	$558,601
14		Paul Voyatzis		$685,091	$692,182
15		Andrea Aster		$540,484	$693,762
16		Charles Granek		$650,733	$823,034
17		Karen Aliston		$509,863	$511,569
18		Karen Hammond		$503,699	$975,455
19		Vince Durbin		$630,263	$599,514
20		Paul Sellars		$779,722	$596,353
21		Gregg O'Donoghue		$592,802	$652,171
22					

TIPS

Is there an easier way to adjust the column width to fit the contents of a column?

Yes. You can use the Excel AutoFit feature, which automatically adjusts the column width to fit the widest item in a column. Click any cell in the column, click **Home**, click **Format**, and then click **AutoFit Column Width**. Alternatively, move ✛ over the right edge of the column heading (✛ changes to ↔) and then double-click.

Is there a way to change all the column widths at once?

Yes. Click ◢ to select the entire worksheet, and then follow the steps in this section to set the width you prefer. If you have already adjusted some column widths and you want to change all the other widths, click **Home**, click **Format**, and then click **Default Width** to open the Standard Width dialog box. Type the new standard column width, and then click **OK**.

Change the Row Height

You can make your worksheet more visually appealing by increasing the row heights to create more space. This is particularly useful in worksheets that are crowded with text. Changing the row height is also useful if the current height is too small and your cell text is cut off at the bottom.

If you want to change the row height to display multiline text within a cell, you must also turn on text wrapping within the cell. See the following section, "Wrap Text Within a Cell."

Change the Row Height

1 Select a range that includes at least one cell in every row you want to resize.

2 Click the **Home** tab.

3 Click **Format**.

4 Click **Row Height**.

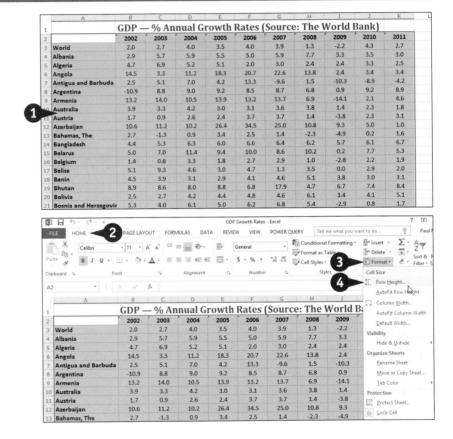

The Row Height dialog box appears.

5 In the Row height text box, type the height you want to use.

6 Click **OK**.

Row Height ? ✕

Row height: 18 ◄ **5**

6 ► OK   Cancel

A Excel adjusts the row heights.

B You can also move ✛ over the bottom edge of a row heading (✛ changes to ✚) and then click and drag the bottom edge to set the height.

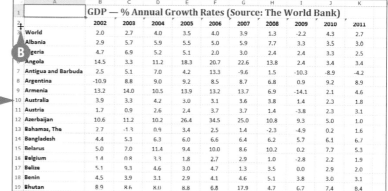

	A	B	C	D	E	F	G	H	I	J	K
1		GDP — % Annual Growth Rates (Source: The World Bank)									
2		2002	2003	2004	2005	2006	2007	2008	2009	2010	2011
3	World	2.0	2.7	4.0	3.5	4.0	3.9	1.3	-2.2	4.3	2.7
4	Albania	2.9	5.7	5.9	5.5	5.0	5.9	7.7	3.3	3.5	3.0
5	Algeria	4.7	6.9	5.2	5.1	2.0	3.0	2.4	2.4	3.3	2.5
6	Angola	14.5	3.3	11.2	18.3	20.7	22.6	13.8	2.4	3.4	3.4
7	Antigua and Barbuda	2.5	5.1	7.0	4.2	13.3	-9.6	1.5	-10.3	-8.9	-4.2
8	Argentina	-10.9	8.8	9.0	9.2	8.5	8.7	6.8	0.9	9.2	8.9
9	Armenia	13.2	14.0	10.5	13.9	13.2	13.7	6.9	-14.1	2.1	4.6
10	Australia	3.9	3.3	4.2	3.0	3.1	3.6	3.8	1.4	2.3	1.8
11	Austria	1.7	0.9	2.6	2.4	3.7	3.7	1.4	-3.8	2.3	3.1
12	Azerbaijan	10.6	11.2	10.2	26.4	34.5	25.0	10.8	9.3	5.0	1.0
13	Bahamas, The	2.7	-1.3	0.9	3.4	2.5	1.4	-2.3	-4.9	0.2	1.6
14	Bangladesh	4.4	5.3	6.3	6.0	6.6	6.4	6.2	5.7	6.1	6.7
15	Belarus	5.0	7.0	11.4	9.4	10.0	8.6	10.2	0.2	7.7	5.3
16	Belgium	1.4	0.8	3.3	1.8	2.7	2.9	1.0	-2.8	2.2	1.9
17	Belize	5.1	9.3	4.6	3.0	4.7	1.3	3.5	0.0	2.9	2.0
18	Benin	4.5	3.9	3.1	2.9	4.1	4.6	5.1	3.8	3.0	3.1
19	Bhutan	8.9	8.6	8.0	8.8	6.8	17.9	4.7	6.7	7.4	8.4

TIPS

Is there an easier way to adjust the row height to fit the contents of a row?

Yes. You can use the Excel AutoFit feature, which automatically adjusts the row height to fit the tallest item in a row. Click in any cell in the row, click **Home**, click **Format**, and then click **AutoFit Row Height**. Alternatively, move ✛ over the bottom edge of the row heading (✛ changes to ✚) and then double-click.

Is there a way to change all the row heights at once?

Yes. Click ◢ to select the entire worksheet. You can then either follow the steps in this section to set the height manually, or move ✛ over the bottom edge of any row heading (✛ changes to ✚) and then click and drag the edge to set the height of all the rows.

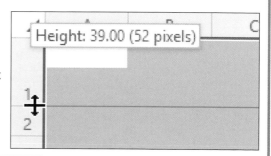

Height: 39.00 (52 pixels)

Wrap Text Within a Cell

You can make a long text entry in a cell more readable by formatting the cell to wrap the text. *Wrapping* cell text means that the text is displayed on multiple lines within the cell instead of just a single line.

If you type more text in a cell than can fit horizontally, Excel either displays the text over the next cell if it is empty or displays only part of the text if the next cell contains data. To prevent Excel from showing only truncated cell data, you can format the cell to wrap text within the cell.

Wrap Text Within a Cell

1 Select the cell that you want to format.

2 Click the **Home** tab.

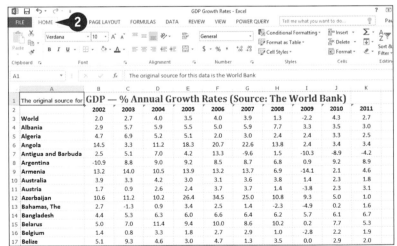

3 Click **Wrap Text** (⬚).

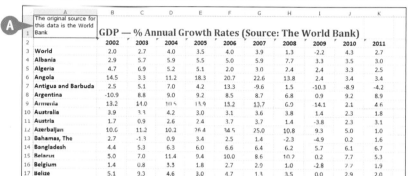

Excel turns on text wrapping for the selected cell.

A If the cell has more text than can fit horizontally, Excel wraps the text onto multiple lines and increases the row height to compensate.

TIP

My text is only slightly bigger than the cell. Is there a way to view all of the text without turning on text wrapping?

Yes. There are several things you can try. For example, you can widen the column until you see all your text; see the "Change the Column Width" section, earlier in this chapter.

Alternatively, you can try reducing the cell font size. One way to do this is to choose a smaller value in the **Font Size** list of the Home tab's Font group. However, an easier way is to click the Alignment group's dialog box launcher (⬚) to open the Format Cells dialog box with the Alignment tab displayed. Select the **Shrink to fit** check box (☐ changes to ☑) and then click **OK**.

Add Borders to a Range

You can make a range stand out from the rest of your worksheet data by adding a border around the range. For example, if you have a range of cells that are used as the input values for one or more formulas, you could add a border around the input cells to make it clear the cells in that range are related to each other.

You can also use borders to make a range easier to read. For example, if your range has totals on the bottom row, you can add a double border above the totals.

Add Borders to a Range

1 Select the range that you want to format.

2 Click the **Home** tab.

3 Click the **Borders** ▼.

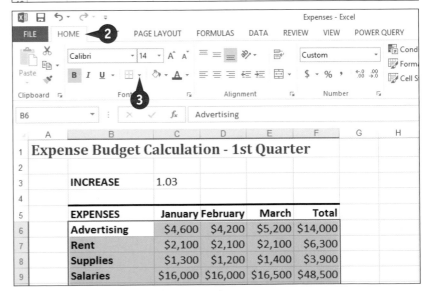

④ Click the type of border you want to use.

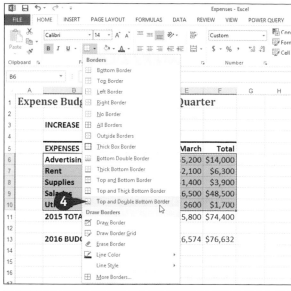

Ⓐ Excel applies the border to the range.

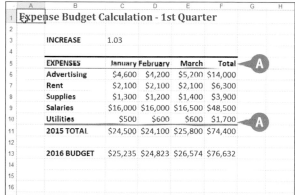

TIPS

How do I get my borders to stand out from the worksheet gridlines?

One way to make your borders stand out is to click the **Borders** ▼, click **Line Style**, and then click a thicker border style. You can also click **Line Color** and then click a color that is not a shade of gray. However, perhaps the most effective method is to turn off the worksheet gridlines. Click the **View** tab, and then in the Show group, select the **Gridlines** check box (☑ changes to ☐).

None of the border types is quite right for my worksheet. Can I create a custom border?

Yes. You can draw the border manually. Click the **Borders** ▼ and then click **Draw Border**. Use the **Line Style** and **Line Color** lists to configure your border. Click a cell edge to add a border to that edge; click and drag a range to add a border around that range. If you prefer to create a grid where the border surrounds every cell, click the **Draw Border Grid** command instead.

Copy Formatting from One Cell to Another

You can save yourself a great deal of time by copying existing formatting to other areas of a worksheet.

As you have seen in this chapter, although formatting cells is not difficult, it can be time-consuming to apply the font, color, alignment, number format, and other options. After you spend time formatting text or data, rather than spending time repeating the steps for other data, you can use the Format Painter tool to copy the formatting with a couple of mouse clicks.

Copy Formatting from One Cell to Another

1 Select the cell that has the formatting you want to copy.

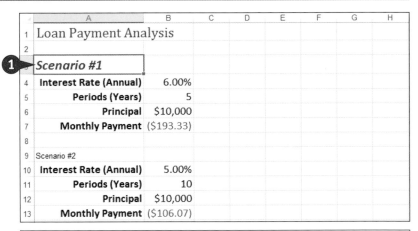

2 Click the **Home** tab.

3 Click **Format Painter** ().

⊕ changes to ⊕🖌.

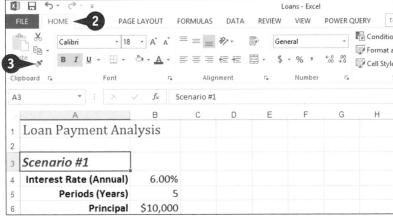

4 Click the cell to which you want to copy the formatting.

Note: If you want to apply the formatting to multiple cells, click and drag ⊹🖌 over the cells.

	A	B	C	D	E	F	G	H
1	Loan Payment Analysis							
2								
3	*Scenario #1*							
4	Interest Rate (Annual)	6.00%						
5	Periods (Years)	5						
6	Principal	$10,000						
7	Monthly Payment	($193.33)						
8								
9	Scenario #2 ⊹🖌 ◄ 4							
10	Interest Rate (Annual)	5.00%						
11	Periods (Years)	10						
12	Principal	$10,000						
13	Monthly Payment	($106.07)						

A Excel copies the formatting to the cell.

	A	B	C	D	E	F	G	H
1	Loan Payment Analysis							
2								
3	*Scenario #1*							
4	Interest Rate (Annual)	6.00%						
5	Periods (Years)	5						
6	Principal	$10,000						
7	Monthly Payment	($193.33)						
8								
9	*Scenario #2* ◄ A							
10	Interest Rate (Annual)	5.00%						
11	Periods (Years)	10						
12	Principal	$10,000						
13	Monthly Payment	($106.07)						

TIP

Is there an easy way to copy formatting to multiple cells or ranges?

Yes. If the cells are together, you can click and drag over the cells to apply the copied formatting. If the cells or ranges are not together, Excel offers a shortcut that means you do not have to select the Format Painter multiple times to copy formatting to multiple ranges.

Click the cell that contains the formatting you want to copy, click the **Home** tab, and then double-click 🖌. Click each cell to which you want to copy the formatting, or click and drag over each range that you want to format. When you are done, click 🖌 to cancel the Format Painter command.

CHAPTER 4

Building Formulas

Are you ready to start creating powerful and useful worksheets by building your own formulas? This chapter explains formulas, shows you how to build them, and shows you how to incorporate the versatile worksheet functions in Excel into your formulas.

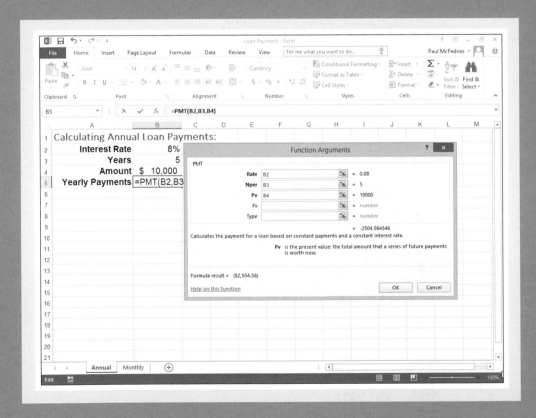

Understanding Excel Formulas

Although you can use Excel to create simple databases to store text, numbers, dates, and other data, the spreadsheets you create are also designed to analyze data and make calculations. Therefore, to get the most out of Excel, you need to understand formulas so that you can use them to analyze and perform calculations on your worksheet data.

To build accurate and useful formulas, you need to know the components of a formula, including operators and operands. You also need to understand arithmetic and comparison formulas and you need to understand the importance of precedence when building a formula.

Formulas

A *formula* is a set of symbols and values that perform some kind of calculation and produce a result. All Excel formulas have the same general structure: an equal sign (=) followed by one or more operands and operators. The equal sign tells Excel to interpret everything that follows in the cell as a formula. For example, if you type **=5+8** into a cell, Excel interprets the 5+8 text as a formula, and displays the result (13) in the cell.

Operands

Every Excel formula includes one or more *operands*, which are the data that Excel uses in the calculation. The simplest type of operand is a constant value, which is usually a number. However, most Excel formulas include references to worksheet data, which can be a cell address (such as A1), a range address (such as B1:B5), or a range name. Finally, you can also use any of the built-in Excel functions as an operand.

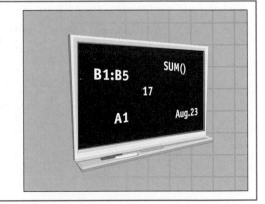

Operators

In an Excel formula that contains two or more operands, each operand is separated by an *operator*, which is a symbol that combines the operands in some way, usually mathematically. Example operators include the plus sign (+) and the multiplication sign (*). For example, the formula =B1+B2 adds the values in cells B1 and B2.

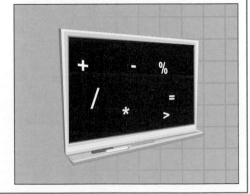

Arithmetic Formulas

An arithmetic formula combines numeric operands — numeric constants, functions that return numeric results, and fields or items that contain numeric values — with mathematical operators to perform a calculation. Because Excel worksheets primarily deal with numeric data, arithmetic formulas are by far the most common formulas used in worksheet calculations.

The following table lists the seven arithmetic operators that you can use to construct arithmetic formulas:

Operator	Name	Example	Result
+	Addition	=10 + 5	15
–	Subtraction	=10 – 5	5
–	Negation	=−10	−10
*	Multiplication	=10 * 5	50
/	Division	=10 / 5	2
%	Percentage	=10%	0.1
^	Exponentiation	=10 ^ 5	100000

Comparison Formulas

A comparison formula combines numeric operands — numeric constants, functions that return numeric results, and fields or items that contain numeric values — with special operators to compare one operand with another.

A comparison formula always returns a logical result. This means that if the comparison is true, then the formula returns the value 1, which is equivalent to the logical value TRUE; if the comparison is false, then the formula returns the value 0, which is equivalent to the logical value FALSE.

The following table lists the six operators that you can use to construct comparison formulas:

Operator	Name	Example	Result
=	Equal to	=10 = 5	0
<	Less than	=10 < 5	0
< =	Less than or equal to	=10 < = 5	0
>	Greater than	=10 > 5	1
> =	Greater than or equal to	=10 > = 5	1
< >	Not equal to	=10 < > 5	1

Operator Precedence

Most of your formulas include multiple operands and operators. In many cases, the order in which Excel performs the calculations is crucial. For example, consider the formula =3 + 5 ^ 2. If you calculate from left to right, the answer you get is 64 (3 + 5 equals 8, and 8 ^ 2 equals 64). However, if you perform the exponentiation first and then the addition, the result is 28 (5 ^ 2 equals 25, and 3 + 25 equals 28). Therefore, a single formula can produce multiple answers, depending on the order in which you perform the calculations.

To solve this problem, Excel evaluates a formula according to a predefined order of precedence, which is determined by the formula operators, as shown in the following table:

Operator	Operation	Precedence
( )	Parentheses	1st
–	Negation	2nd
%	Percentage	3rd
^	Exponentiation	4th
* and /	Multiplication and division	5th
+ and –	Addition and subtraction	6th
= < < = > > = < >	Comparison	7th

Build a Formula

You can add a formula to a worksheet cell using a technique similar to adding data to a cell. To ensure that Excel treats the text as a formula, be sure to begin with an equal sign (=) and then type your operands and operators.

When you add a formula to a cell, Excel displays the formula result in the cell, not the actual formula. For example, if you add the formula =C3+C4 to a cell, that cell displays the sum of the values in cells C3 and C4. To see the formula, click the cell and examine the Formula bar.

Build a Formula

1 Click in the cell in which you want to build the formula.

2 Type =.

A Your typing also appears in the Formula bar.

Note: You can also type the formula into the Formula bar.

3 Type or click an operand. For example, to reference a cell in your formula, click in the cell.

B Excel inserts the address of the clicked cell into the formula.

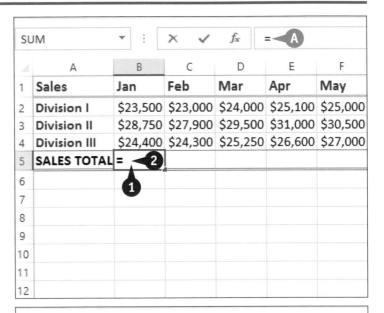

4 Type an operator.

5 Repeat steps **3** and **4** to add other operands and operators to your formula.

6 Click ✓ or press **Enter**.

| B4 | | ▾ | : | ✕ | ✓ | *fx* | =B2 + B3 + B4 |

	A	B	C	D	E	F
1	Sales	Jan	Feb	Mar	Apr	May
2	Division I	$23,500	$23,000	$24,000	$25,100	$25,000
3	Division II	$28,750	$27,900	$29,500	$31,000	$30,500
4	Division III	$24,400	$24,300	$25,250	$26,600	$27,000
5	SALES TOTAL	=B2 + B3 + B4				
6						
7						
8						
9						
10						
11						
12						

C Excel displays the formula result in the cell.

| B5 | | ▾ | : | ✕ | ✓ | *fx* | =B2 + B3 + B4 |

	A	B	C	D	E	F
1	Sales	Jan	Feb	Mar	Apr	May
2	Division I	$23,500	$23,000	$24,000	$25,100	$25,000
3	Division II	$28,750	$27,900	$29,500	$31,000	$30,500
4	Division III	$24,400	$24,300	$25,250	$26,600	$27,000
5	SALES TOTAL	$76,650				
6						
7						
8						
9						
10						
11						
12						

TIPS

If Excel displays only the result of the formula, how do I make changes to the formula?

Excel displays the formula result in the cell, but it still keeps track of the original formula. To display the formula again, you have two choices: Click the cell and then edit the formula using the Formula bar, or double-click the cell to display the original formula in the cell and then edit the formula. In both cases, click ✓ or press **Enter** when you finish editing the formula.

If I have many formulas, is there an easy way to view them?

Yes. You can configure the worksheet to show the formulas instead of their results. Click **File** and then click **Options** to open the Excel Options dialog box. Click the **Advanced** tab, scroll to the **Display options for this worksheet** section, select the **Show formulas in cells instead of their calculated results** check box (☐ changes to ☑), and then click **OK**. You can also toggle between formulas and results by pressing **Ctrl**+**`**.

Understanding Excel Functions

To build powerful and useful formulas, you often need to include one or more Excel functions as operands. To get the most out of functions and to help you build formulas quickly and easily, you need to understand a few things about functions. For example, you need to understand the advantages of using functions and you need to know the basic structure of every function. To get a sense of what is available and how you might use functions, you need to review the Excel function types.

Functions

A *function* is a predefined formula that performs a specific task. For example, the SUM function calculates the total of a list of numbers, and the PMT (payment) function calculates a loan or mortgage payment. You can use functions on their own, preceded by =, or as part of a larger formula.

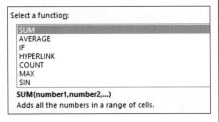

Function Advantages

Functions are designed to take you beyond the basic arithmetic and comparison formulas by offering two main advantages. First, functions make simple but cumbersome formulas easier to use. For example, calculating a loan payment requires a complex formula, but the Excel PMT function makes this easy. Second, functions enable you to include complex mathematical expressions in your worksheets that otherwise would be difficult or impossible to construct using simple arithmetic operators.

=PMT(D5, D6, D7)

C	D
Interest Rate (Monthly)	0.50%
Periods (Months)	60
Principal	$10,000
Monthly Payment	($193.33)

Function Structure

Every worksheet function has the same basic structure: NAME(Argument1, Argument2, . . .). The NAME part identifies the function. In worksheet formulas and custom PivotTable formulas, the function name always appears in uppercase letters: PMT, SUM, AVERAGE, and so on. The items that appear within the parentheses are the functions' *arguments*. The arguments are the inputs that functions use to perform calculations. For example, the function SUM(B2, B3, B4) adds the values in cells B2, B3, and B4.

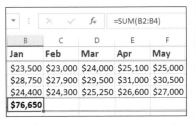

Mathematical Functions

The following table lists some common mathematical functions:

Function	Description
MOD(number,divisor)	Returns the remainder of a number after dividing by the divisor
PI( )	Returns the value Pi
PRODUCT(number1, number2, . . .)	Multiplies the specified numbers
RAND( )	Returns a random number between 0 and 1
RANDBETWEEN (number1,number2)	Returns a random number between the two numbers
ROUND(number,digits)	Rounds the number to a specified number of digits
SQRT(number)	Returns the positive square root of the number
SUM(number1, number2, . . .)	Adds the arguments

Statistical Functions

The following table lists some common statistical functions:

Function	Description
AVERAGE(number1,number2, . . .)	Returns the average of the arguments
COUNT(number1,number2, . . .)	Counts the numbers in the argument list
MAX(number1,number2, . . .)	Returns the maximum value of the arguments
MEDIAN(number1,number2, . . .)	Returns the median value of the arguments
MIN(number1,number2, . . .)	Returns the minimum value of the arguments
MODE(number1,number2, . . .)	Returns the most common value of the arguments
STDEV(number1,number2, . . .)	Returns the standard deviation based on a sample
STDEVP(number1,number2, . . .)	Returns the standard deviation based on an entire population

Financial Functions

Most of the Excel financial functions use the following arguments:

Argument	Description
rate	The fixed rate of interest over the term of the loan or investment
nper	The number of payments or deposit periods over the term of the loan or investment
pmt	The periodic payment or deposit
pv	The present value of the loan (the principal) or the initial deposit in an investment
fv	The future value of the loan or investment
type	The type of payment or deposit: 0 (the default) for end-of-period payments or deposits; 1 for beginning-of-period payments or deposits

The following table lists some common financial functions:

Function	Description
FV(rate,nper,pmt,pv,type)	Returns the future value of an investment or loan
IPMT(rate,per,nper,pv,fv,type)	Returns the interest payment for a specified period of a loan
NPER(rate,pmt,pv,fv,type)	Returns the number of periods for an investment or loan
PMT(rate,nper,pv,fv,type)	Returns the periodic payment for a loan or investment
PPMT(rate,per,nper,pv,fv,type)	Returns the principal payment for a specified period of a loan
PV(rate,nper,pmt,fv,type)	Returns the present value of an investment
RATE(nper,pmt,pv,fv,type,guess)	Returns the periodic interest rate for a loan or investment

Add a Function to a Formula

To get the benefit of an Excel function, you need to use it within a formula. You can use a function as the only operand in the formula, or you can include the function as part of a larger formula. To make it easy to choose the function you need and to add the appropriate arguments, Excel offers the Insert Function feature. This is a dialog box that enables you to display functions by category and then choose the function you want from a list. You then see the Function Arguments dialog box that enables you to easily see and fill in the arguments used by the function.

Add a Function to a Formula

1 Click in the cell in which you want to build the formula.

2 Type =.

3 Type any operands and operators you need before adding the function.

4 Click the **Insert Function** button (f_x).

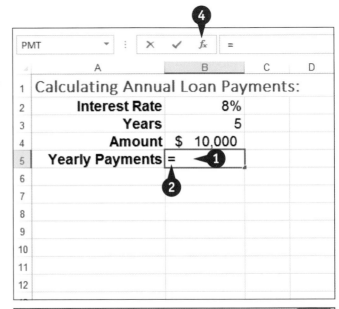

The Insert Function dialog box appears.

5 Click ▼ and then click the category that contains the function you want to use.

6 Click the function.

7 Click **OK**.

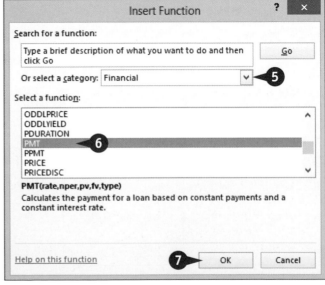

The Function Arguments dialog box appears.

8 Click inside an argument box.

9 Click the cell that contains the argument value.

You can also type the argument value.

10 Repeat steps **8** and **9** to fill as many arguments as you need.

A The function result appears here.

11 Click **OK**.

B Excel adds the function to the formula.

C Excel displays the formula result.

Note: In this example, the result appears in the parentheses to indicate a negative value. In loan calculations, money that you pay out is always a negative amount.

Note: If your formula requires any other operands and operators, press F2 and then type what you need to complete your formula.

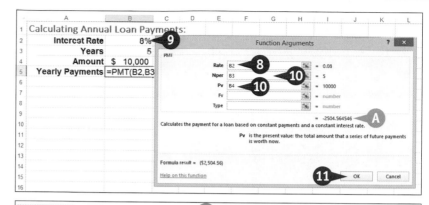

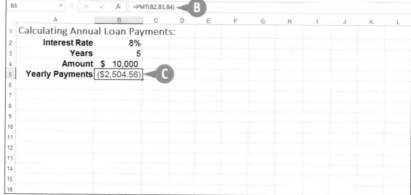

TIPS

Do I have to specify a value for every function argument?

Not necessarily. Some function arguments are required to obtain a result, but others are optional. In the PMT function, for example, the rate, nper, and pv arguments are required, but the fv and type arguments are optional. When the Function Arguments dialog box displays a result for the function, you know you have entered all of the required arguments.

How do I calculate a monthly financial result if I only have yearly values?

This is a common problem. For example, if your loan payment worksheet contains an annual interest rate and a loan term in years, how do you calculate the monthly payment using the PMT function? You need to convert the rate and term to monthly values. That is, you divide the annual interest rate by 12, and you multiply the term by 12. For example, if the annual rate is in cell B2, the term in years is in B3, and the loan amount is in B4, then the function PMT(B2/12, B3*12, B4) calculates the monthly payment.

Add a Row or Column of Numbers

You can quickly add worksheet numbers by building a formula that uses the Excel SUM function. When you use the SUM function in a formula, you can specify as the function's arguments a series of individual cells. For example, SUM(A1, B2, C3) calculates the total of the values in cells A1, B2, and C3.

However, you can also use the SUM function to specify just a single argument, which is a range reference to either a row or a column of numbers. For example, SUM(C3:C21) calculates the total of the values in all the cells in the range C3 to C21.

Add a Row or Column of Numbers

1 Click in the cell where you want the sum to appear.

2 Type **=sum(**.

A When you begin a function, Excel displays a banner that shows you the function's arguments.

Note: In the function banner, bold arguments are required, and arguments that appear in square brackets are optional.

3 Use the mouse ✛ to click and drag the row or column of numbers that you want to add.

B Excel adds a reference for the range to the formula.

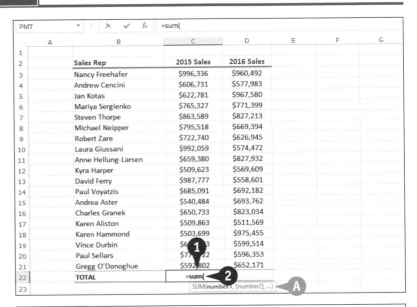

4 Type **)**.

5 Click ✔ or press Enter.

5

| C22 | ▼ : ✕ ✔ fx | =sum(C3:C21) |

	A	B	C	D	E	F	G
1							
2		Sales Rep	2015 Sales	2016 Sales			
3		Nancy Freehafer	$996,336	$960,492			
4		Andrew Cencini	$606,731	$577,983			
5		Jan Kotas	$622,781	$967,580			
6		Mariya Sergienko	$765,327	$771,399			
7		Steven Thorpe	$863,589	$827,213			
8		Michael Neipper	$795,518	$669,394			
9		Robert Zare	$722,740	$626,945			
10		Laura Glussani	$992,059	$574,472			
11		Anne Hellung-Larsen	$659,380	$827,932			
12		Kyra Harper	$509,623	$569,609			
13		David Ferry	$987,777	$558,601			
14		Paul Voyatzis	$685,091	$692,182			
15		Andrea Aster	$540,484	$693,762			
16		Charles Granek	$650,733	$823,034			
17		Karen Aliston	$509,863	$511,569			
18		Karen Hammond	$503,699	$975,455			
19		Vince Durbin	$630,263	$599,514			
20		Paul Sellars	$779,722	$596,353			
21		Gregg O'Donoghue	$592,802	$652,171			
22		TOTAL	=sum(C3:C21)	**4**			
23							

C Excel displays the formula.

D Excel displays the sum in the cell.

| C22 | ▼ : ✕ ✔ fx | =SUM(C3:C21) **C** |

	A	B	C	D	E	F	G
1							
2		Sales Rep	2015 Sales	2016 Sales			
3		Nancy Freehafer	$996,336	$960,492			
4		Andrew Cencini	$606,731	$577,983			
5		Jan Kotas	$622,781	$967,580			
6		Mariya Sergienko	$765,327	$771,399			
7		Steven Thorpe	$863,589	$827,213			
8		Michael Neipper	$795,518	$669,394			
9		Robert Zare	$722,740	$626,945			
10		Laura Giussani	$992,059	$574,472			
11		Anne Hellung-Larsen	$659,380	$827,932			
12		Kyra Harper	$509,623	$569,609			
13		David Ferry	$987,777	$558,601			
14		Paul Voyatzis	$685,091	$692,182			
15		Andrea Aster	$540,484	$693,762			
16		Charles Granek	$650,733	$823,034			
17		Karen Aliston	$509,863	$511,569			
18		Karen Hammond	$503,699	$975,455			
19		Vince Durbin	$630,263	$599,514			
20		Paul Sellars	$779,722	$596,353			
21		Gregg O'Donoghue	$592,802	$652,171			
22		TOTAL	$13,414,518	**D**			
23							

TIPS

Can I use the SUM function to total rows and columns at the same time?

Yes, the SUM function works not only with simple row and column ranges, but with any rectangular range. After you type **=sum(**, use the mouse ✛ to click and drag the entire range that you want to sum.

Can I use the SUM function to total only certain values in a row or column?

Yes. The SUM function can accept multiple arguments, so you can enter as many cells or ranges as you need. After you type **=sum(**, hold down Ctrl and either click each cell that you want to include in the total, or use the mouse ✛ to click and drag each range that you want to sum.

Build an AutoSum Formula

You can reduce the time it takes to build a worksheet as well as reduce the possibility of errors by using the Excel AutoSum feature. This tool adds a SUM function formula to a cell and automatically adds the function arguments based on the structure of the worksheet data. For example, if there is a column of numbers above the cell where you want the SUM function to appear, AutoSum automatically includes that column of numbers as the SUM function argument.

Build an AutoSum Formula

1 Click in the cell where you want the sum to appear.

Note: For AutoSum to work, the cell you select should be below or to the right of the range you want to sum.

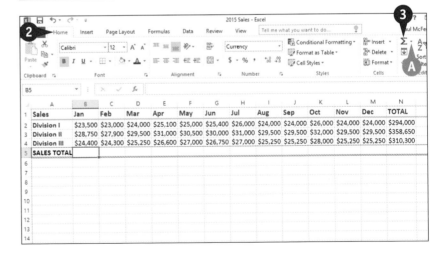

2 Click the **Home** tab.

3 Click the **Sum** button (∑).

A If you want to use a function other than SUM, click the **Sum** ▼ and then click the operation you want to use: **Average**, **Count Numbers**, **Max**, or **Min**.

B Excel adds a SUM function formula to the cell.

Note: You can also press Alt + = instead of clicking Σ.

C Excel guesses that the range above (or to the left of) the cell is the one you want to add.

If Excel guessed wrong, you can select the correct range manually.

4 Click ✓ or press Enter.

D Excel displays the formula.

E Excel displays the sum in the cell.

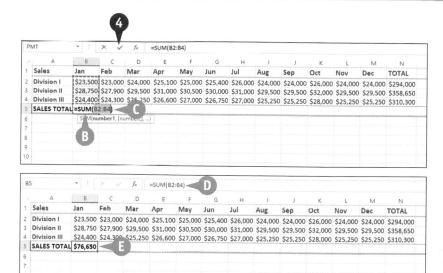

TIPS

Is there a way to see the sum of a range without adding an AutoSum formula?

Yes. You can use the Excel status bar to do this. When you select any range, Excel adds the range's numeric values and displays the result in the middle of the status bar — for example, SUM: 76,650. By default, Excel also displays the Average and Count. If you want to see a different calculation, right-click the result in the status bar and then click the operation you want to use: Numerical Count, Maximum, or Minimum.

Is there a faster way to add an AutoSum formula?

Yes. If you know the range you want to sum, and that range is either a vertical column with a blank cell below it or a horizontal row with a blank cell to its right, select the range (including the blank cell) and then click Σ or press Alt + =. Excel populates the blank cell with a SUM formula that totals the selected range.

Add a Range Name to a Formula

You can make your formulas easier to build, more accurate, and easier to read by using range names as operands instead of cell and range addresses. For example, the formula =SUM(B2:B10) is difficult to decipher on its own, particularly if you cannot see the range B2:B10 to examine its values. However, if you use the formula =SUM(Expenses), instead, it becomes immediately obvious what the formula is meant to do.

See Chapter 2 to learn how to define names for ranges in Excel.

Add a Range Name to a Formula

1 Click in the cell in which you want to build the formula, type **=**, and then type any operands and operators you need before adding the range name.

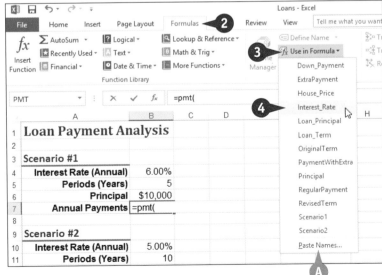

2 Click the **Formulas** tab.

3 Click **Use in Formula**.

Ⓐ Excel displays a list of the range names in the current workbook.

4 Click the range name you want to use.

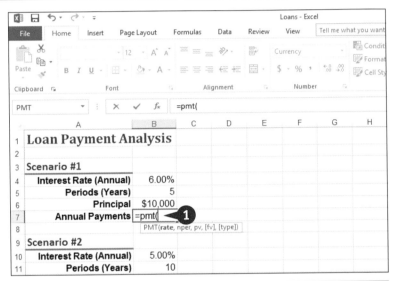

98

B Excel inserts the range name into the formula.

5 Type any operands and operators you need to complete your formula.

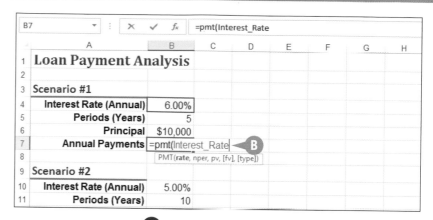

C If you need to insert other range names into your formula, repeat steps **2** to **5** for each name.

6 Click ✔ or press **Enter**.

Excel calculates the formula result.

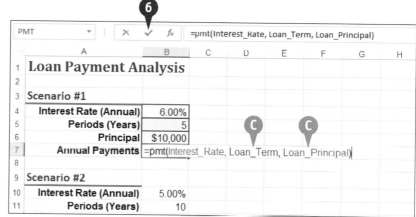

TIPS

If I create a range name after I build my formula, is there an easy way to convert the range reference to the range name?
Yes. Excel offers an Apply Names feature that replaces range references with their associated range names throughout a worksheet. Click the **Formulas** tab, click the **Define Name** ▼, and then click **Apply Names** to open the Apply Names dialog box. In the Apply names list, click the range name you want to use, and then click **OK**. Excel replaces the associated range references with the range name in each formula in the current worksheet.

Do I have to use the list of range names to insert range names into my formula?
No. As you build your formula, you can type the range name manually, if you know it. Alternatively, as you build your formula, click the cell or select the range that has the defined name, and Excel adds the name to your formula instead of the range address. If you want to work from a list of defined range names, click an empty area of the worksheet, click **Formulas**, click **Use in Formula**, click **Paste Names**, and then click **Paste List**.

Reference Another Worksheet Range in a Formula

You can add flexibility to your formulas by adding references to ranges that reside in other worksheets. This enables you to take advantage of work you have done in other worksheets, so you do not have to waste time repeating your work in the current worksheet.

Referencing a range in another worksheet also gives you the advantage of having automatically updated information. For example, if the data in the other worksheet range changes, Excel automatically updates your formula to include the changed data when you save your work.

Reference Another Worksheet Range in a Formula

1 Click in the cell in which you want to build the formula, type =, and then type any operands and operators you need before adding the range reference.

	A	I	J	K	L	M	N	O	P	Q	R
1		2nd Quarter	Jul	Aug	Sep	3rd Quarter	Oct	Nov	Dec	4th Quarter	TOTAL
2	*Sales*										
3	Division I	75,500	26,000	24,000	24,000	74,000	26,000	24,000	24,000	74,000	294,000
4	Division II	91,500	31,000	29,500	29,500	90,000	32,000	29,500	29,500	91,000	358,550
5	Division III	80,350	27,000	25,250	25,250	77,500	28,000	25,250	25,250	78,500	310,000
6	**SALES TOTAL**	247,350	84,000	78,750	78,750	241,500	86,000	78,750	78,750	243,500	962,550
7	*Expenses*										
8	**Cost of Goods**	19,788	6,720	6,300	6,300	19,320	6,880	6,300	6,300	19,480	77,004
9	Advertising	15,750	5,500	5,200	5,200	15,900	4,500	5,200	5,200	14,900	60,550
10	Rent	6,300	2,100	2,100	2,100	6,300	2,100	2,100	2,100	6,300	25,200
11	Supplies	3,950	1,300	1,400	1,400	4,100	1,250	1,350	1,400	4,000	15,950
12	Salaries	50,000	17,000	17,000	17,000	51,000	17,000	17,500	17,500	52,000	201,500
13	Shipping	44,250	15,000	14,500	14,500	44,000	15,750	15,250	14,500	45,500	176,250
14	Utilities	1,800	650	600	600	1,850	650	600	600	1,850	7,200
15	**EXPENSES TOTAL**	141,838	48,270	47,100	47,100	142,470	48,130	48,300	47,600	144,030	563,654
16	**GROSS PROFIT**	105,512	35,730	31,650	31,650	99,030	37,870	30,450	31,150	99,470	398,896
17										Difference from Last Year's Profit:	=R16
18											

2 Press Ctrl + Page down until the worksheet you want to use appears.

	A	I	J	K	L	M	N	O	P	Q	R
6	**SALES TOTAL**	70,518	68,816	72,450	211,784	76,084	75,900	75,578	227,562	77,280	7
7	*Expenses*										
8	**Cost of Goods**	5,924	5,781	6,086	17,790	6,391	6,376	6,349	19,115	6,492	6
9	Advertising	4,830	4,410	5,460	14,700	5,250	5,775	5,513	16,538	5,775	5
10	Rent	2,205	2,205	2,205	6,615	2,205	2,205	2,205	6,615	2,205	2
11	Supplies	1,365	1,260	1,470	4,095	1,365	1,313	1,470	4,148	1,365	1
12	Salaries	16,800	16,800	17,325	50,925	17,325	17,325	17,850	52,500	17,850	17
13	Shipping	14,963	14,438	15,225	44,625	15,750	15,225	15,488	46,463	15,750	15
14	Utilities	525	630	630	1,785	578	630	683	1,890	683	
15	**EXPENSES TOTAL**	46,611	45,523	48,401	140,535	48,864	48,848	49,556	147,268	50,119	48
16	**GROSS PROFIT**	23,907	23,293	24,049	71,249	27,220	27,052	26,022	80,294	27,161	23
17											
18											
19											
20											
21											
22											
23											

Budget | Assumptions | Projections | 2015-2016 Final | Gross Margin

3 Select the range you want to use.

4 Press Ctrl + Page up until you return to the original worksheet.

75,578	227,562	77,280	72,450	72,450	222,180	79,120	72,450	72,450	224,020	885,546
6,349	19,115	6,492	6,086	6,086	18,663	6,646	6,086	6,086	18,818	74,386
5,513	16,538	5,775	5,460	5,460	16,695	4,725	5,460	5,460	15,645	63,578
2,205	6,615	2,205	2,205	2,205	6,615	2,205	2,205	2,205	6,615	26,460
1,470	4,148	1,365	1,470	1,470	4,305	1,313	1,418	1,470	4,200	16,748
17,850	52,500	17,850	17,850	17,850	53,550	17,850	18,375	18,375	54,600	211,575
15,488	46,463	15,750	15,225	15,225	46,200	16,538	16,013	15,225	47,775	185,063
683	1,890	683	630	630	1,943	683	630	630	1,943	7,560
49,556	147,268	50,119	48,926	48,926	147,971	49,959	50,186	49,451	149,595	585,368
26,022	80,294	27,161	23,524	23,524	74,209	29,161	22,264	22,999	74,425	300,178

Budget   Projections   2015-2016 Final   Estimates   Gross Margin

A A reference to the range on the other worksheet appears in your formula.

5 Type any operands and operators you need to complete your formula.

6 Click ✓ or press Enter.

Excel calculates the formula result.

=R16 - '2015-2016 Final'!R16

	Jul	Aug	Sep	3rd Quarter	Oct	Nov	Dec	4th Quarter	TOTAL
Sales									
Division I	26,000	24,000	24,000	74,000	26,000	24,000	24,000	74,000	294,000
Division II	31,000	29,500	29,500	90,000	32,000	29,500	29,500	91,000	358,550
Division III	27,000	25,250	25,250	77,500	28,000	25,250	25,250	78,500	310,000
SALES TOTAL	84,000	78,750	78,750	241,500	86,000	78,750	78,750	243,500	962,550
Expenses									
Cost of Goods	6,720	6,300	6,300	19,320	6,880	6,300	6,300	19,480	77,004
Advertising	5,500	5,200	5,200	15,900	4,500	5,200	5,200	14,900	60,550
Rent	2,100	2,100	2,100	6,300	2,100	2,100	2,100	6,300	25,200
Supplies	1,300	1,400	1,400	4,100	1,250	1,350	1,400	4,000	15,950
Salaries	17,000	17,000	17,000	51,000	17,000	17,500	17,500	52,000	201,500
Shipping	15,000	14,500	14,500	44,000	15,750	15,250	14,500	45,500	176,250
Utilities	650	600	600	1,850	650	600	600	1,850	7,200
EXPENSES TOTAL	48,270	47,100	47,100	147,470	48,130	48,300	47,600	144,030	563,654
GROSS PROFIT	35,730	31,650	31,650	99,030	37,870	30,450	31,150	99,470	398,896

Difference from Last Year's Profit: =R16 - '2015-2016 Final'!R16

TIPS

Can I manually reference a range in another worksheet?

Yes. Rather than selecting the other worksheet range with your mouse, you can type the range reference directly into your formula. Type the worksheet name, surrounded by single quotation marks (') if the name contains a space; type an exclamation mark (!); then type the cell or range address. Here is an example: **'Expenses 2013'!B2:B10**.

Can I reference a range in another workbook in my formula?

Yes. First make sure the workbook you want to reference is open. When you reach the point in your formula where you want to add the reference, click the Excel icon (▣) in the Windows taskbar, and then click the other workbook to switch to it. Click the worksheet that has the range you want to reference, and then select the range. Click ▣ and then click the original workbook to switch back to it. Excel adds the other workbook range reference to your formula.

Move or Copy a Formula

You can restructure or reorganize a worksheet by moving an existing formula to a different part of the worksheet. When you move a formula, Excel preserves the formula's range references.

Excel also enables you to make a copy of a formula, which is a useful technique if you require a duplicate of the formula elsewhere or if you require a formula that is similar to an existing formula. When you copy a formula, Excel adjusts the range references to the new location.

Move or Copy a Formula

Move a Formula

1 Click the cell that contains the formula you want to move.

2 Position ✛ over any outside border of the cell (✛ changes to ⬚).

3 Click and drag the cell to the new location (⬚ changes to ⬚).

Ⓐ Excel displays an outline of the cell.

Ⓑ Excel displays the address of the new location.

4 Release the mouse button.

Ⓒ Excel moves the formula to the new location.

Ⓓ Excel does not change the formula's range references.

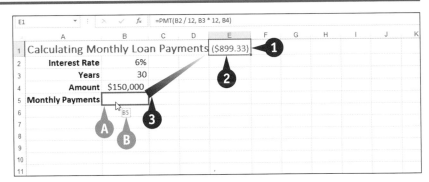

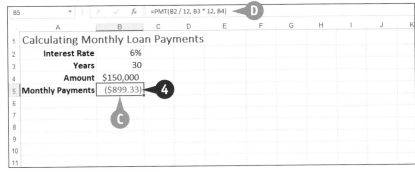

102

Copy a Formula

1 Click the cell that contains the formula you want to copy.

2 Press and hold **Ctrl**.

3 Position ✛ over any outside border of the cell (✛ changes to ⬚).

4 Click and drag the cell to the location where you want the copy to appear.

E Excel displays an outline of the cell.

F Excel displays the address of the new location.

5 Release the mouse button.

6 Release **Ctrl**.

G Excel creates a copy of the formula in the new location.

H Excel adjusts the range references.

Note: You can make multiple copies by dragging the bottom-right corner of the cell. Excel fills the adjacent cells with copies of the formula. See the following section, "Switch to Absolute Cell References," for an example.

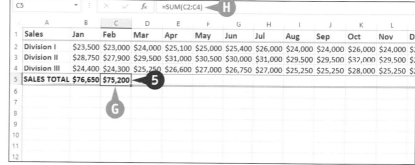

TIP

Why does Excel adjust the range references when I copy a formula?

When you make a copy of a formula, Excel assumes that you want that copy to reference different ranges than in the original formula. In particular, Excel assumes that the ranges you want to use in the new formula are positioned relative to the ranges used in the original formula, and that the relative difference is equal to the number of rows and columns you dragged the cell to create the copy.

For example, suppose your original formula references cell A1, and you make a copy of the formula in the cell one column to the right. In that case, Excel also adjusts the cell reference one column to the right, so it becomes B1 in the new formula. To learn how to control this behavior, see the following section, "Switch to Absolute Cell References."

Switch to Absolute Cell References

You can make some formulas easier to copy by switching to absolute cell references. When you use a regular cell address — called a *relative cell reference* — such as A1 in a formula, Excel adjusts that reference when you copy the formula to another location. To prevent that reference from changing, you must change it to the *absolute cell reference* format: $A$1.

See the first tip at the end of this section to learn more about the difference between relative and absolute cell references.

Switch to Absolute Cell References

1 Double-click the cell that contains the formula you want to edit.

2 Select the cell reference you want to change.

3 Press **F4**.

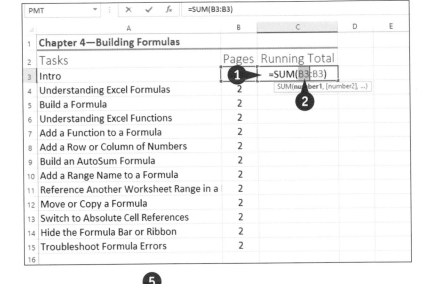

A Excel switches the address to an absolute cell reference.

4 Repeat steps **2** and **3** to switch any other cell addresses that you require in the absolute reference format.

5 Click ✓ or press **Enter**.

B Excel adjusts the formula.

6 Copy the formula.

Note: See the previous section, "Move or Copy a Formula," to learn how to copy a formula.

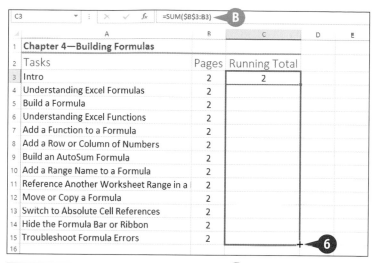

C Excel preserves the absolute cell references in the copied formulas.

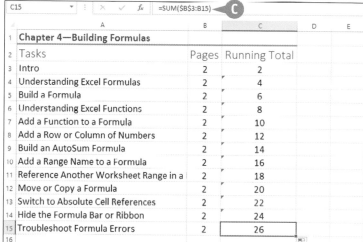

What is the difference between absolute cell references and relative cell references?

When you use a cell reference in a formula, Excel treats that reference as being relative to the formula's cell. For example, if the formula is in cell B5 and it references cell A1, Excel effectively treats A1 as the cell four rows up and one column to the left. If you copy the formula to cell D10, then the cell four rows up and one column to the left now refers to cell C6, so in the copied formula Excel changes A1 to C6. If the original formula instead refers to $A$1, then the copied formula in cell D10 also refers to $A$1.

How do I restore a cell address back to a relative cell reference?

You can use the F4 keyboard technique, which actually runs the address through four different reference formats. Press F4 once to switch to the absolute cell reference format, such as $A$1. Press F4 again to switch to a mixed reference format that uses a relative column and absolute row (A$1). Press F4 a third time to switch to a mixed reference format that uses an absolute column and relative row ($A1). Finally, press F4 a fourth time to return to the relative cell reference (A1).

Hide the Formula Bar or Ribbon

You can give yourself a bit more room in the Excel window by hiding the Formula bar or Ribbon. Hiding the Formula bar is a good idea if you never use the Formula bar to enter or edit cell data and you never use Formula bar features such as the Name box, the Enter button, and the Insert Function button. After hiding the Formula bar, if you find that you need it, you can quickly restore it to the Excel window. You can also gain more worksheet room by hiding the Ribbon. When you hide the Ribbon, Excel keeps the tabs visible, so you can still access the commands.

Hide the Formula Bar or Ribbon

Hide the Formula Bar

1 Click the **View** tab.

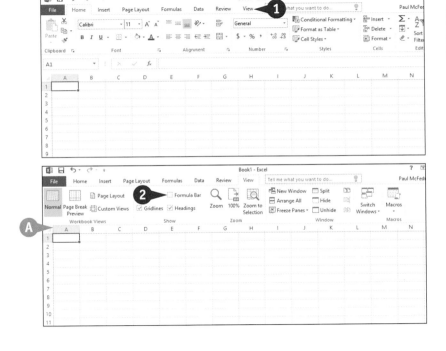

2 Click **Formula Bar**
(☑ changes to ☐).

Ⓐ Excel removes the Formula bar from the window.

Note: To restore the Formula bar, repeat steps **1** and **2** (☐ changes to ☑).

Hide the Ribbon

1 Click **Unpin the Ribbon** (⬈).

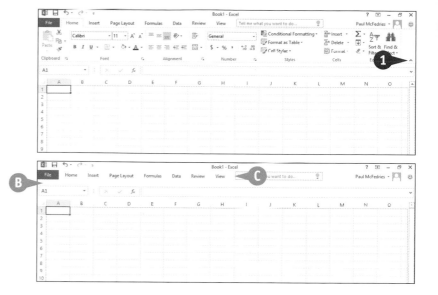

B Excel hides the Ribbon.

C Excel keeps the Ribbon tabs visible.

Note: To restore the Ribbon, click any tab and then click **Pin the Ribbon** (📌).

Note: You can also hide and display the Ribbon by pressing Ctrl + F1.

TIP

If I have a long entry in a cell, I only see part of the entry in the Formula bar. Can I fix that?

Yes, you can use the Expand Formula Bar feature in Excel to expand the formula to show multiple lines of data instead of just a single line. On the right side of the Formula bar, click the **Expand Formula Bar** button (▼) or press Ctrl + Shift + U to increase the size of the Formula bar as shown here. If you still cannot see the entire cell entry, either click and drag the bottom edge of the Formula bar to expand it even further, or click ▼ and ▲ to scroll through the entry.

When you are done, click the **Collapse Formula Bar** button (⬈) or press Ctrl + Shift + U to return the Formula bar to its normal state.

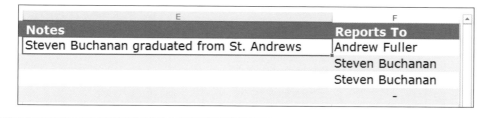

Troubleshoot Formula Errors

Despite your best efforts, a formula may return an inaccurate or erroneous result. To help you fix such problem formulas, there are a few troubleshooting techniques you can use, such as checking for incorrect range references or function arguments, confirming your data, and checking for punctuation errors such as missing colons or parentheses.

If Excel displays an error such as #DIV/0 instead of a result, then you also need to understand these error messages so that you can troubleshoot and correct the problem.

Confirm Range References

If your formula is returning an unexpected or inaccurate result, the first thing to check is your range and cell references. For example, if your data is in the range A1:A10, but your formula uses A1:A9, then the result will be inaccurate. The easiest way to check the range and cell references is to double-click the cell containing the formula. Excel highlights the range referenced by the formula, so you can see at a glance which range your formula is using.

	A	B	C	D
7	**Expenses**			
8	**Cost of Goods**	5,924	5,781	6,086
9	**Advertising**	4,830	4,410	5,460
10	**Rent**	2,205	2,205	2,205
11	**Supplies**	1,365	1,260	1,470
12	**Salaries**	16,800	16,800	17,325
13	**Shipping**	14,963	14,438	15,225
14	**Utilities**	525	630	630
15	**EXPE**	=SUM(B8:B11)		48,401
16	**GROSS PROFIT**	SUM(**number1**, [number2], ...)		24,049

Confirm Range Data

If your formula is correct but it is still producing unexpected results, the problem might lie with the data instead of the formula. Double-check your range data to make sure that it is accurate and up to date.

C6		▼	⋮	✕	✓	f_x	=SUM(C3:C5)

	A	B	C	D
1		**Jan**	**Feb**	**Mar**
2	**Sales**			
3	**Division I**	21,620	1	22,080
4	**Division II**	26,450	1	27,140
5	**Division III**	22,448	1	23,230
6	**SALES TOTAL**	70,518	3	72,450

Confirm Punctuation

Many formulas produce inaccurate or erroneous results because of incorrect punctuation. Look for missing colons in range references; missing or misplaced quotation marks in string data or links to other worksheets or workbooks; and missing commas in function arguments. Also check parentheses to make sure you have one closing parenthesis for each opening parenthesis, and that your parentheses are in the correct locations within the formula.

| PMT | ▼ | : | ✕ | ✓ | f_x | =PMT(B2 / 12 B3 * 12, B4) |

	A	B	C
1	Loan Payment Analysis		
2	Interest Rate (Annual)	6.00%	
3	Periods (Years)	5	
4	Principal	$10,000	
5	Monthly Payment	=PMT(B2 / 12 B3 * 12, B4)	
6		PMT(**rate**, nper, pv, [fv], [type])	
7			

Confirm Operator Precedence

The order in which Excel calculates numeric formulas can make a big difference to the final result, particularly if you are mixing addition and subtraction with multiplication and division. Confirm the correct order of precedence that your formula requires; compare this with the natural order of operator precedence in Excel, as described in the "Understanding Excel Formulas" section earlier in this chapter; and then use parentheses to force the correct order if necessary.

	A	B	C	D	E
1					
2	Calculating the Pre-Tax Cost of an Item				
3					
4	Variables:		Pre-Tax Cost Calculation:		
5	Total Cost	$10.65		Result	Formula in D
6	Tax Rate	7%	Without controlling precedence →	$10.72	=B5 / 1 + B6
7			Controlling precedence →	$9.95	=B5 / (1 + B6)
8					

Understand the Excel Error Values

Excel may display an error value instead of a formula result. Here are descriptions of the six main error types:

Error	Description
#DIV/0	Your formula is dividing by zero. Check the divisor input cells for values that are either zero or blank.
#N/A	Your formula cannot return a legitimate result. Check that your function arguments are appropriate for each function.
#NAME?	Your formula uses a name that Excel does not recognize. Check your range names and function names.
#NUM!	Your formula uses a number inappropriately. Check the arguments for your mathematical functions to make sure they use the correct types of numbers.
#REF#	Your formula contains an invalid cell reference. This usually occurs when you delete a cell referenced by a formula. Adjust the formula to use a different cell.
#VALUE!	Your formula uses an inappropriate value in a function argument. Check your function arguments to make sure they use the correct data type.

CHAPTER 5

Manipulating Worksheets

An Excel worksheet is where you enter your headings and data and build your formulas. You will spend most of your time in Excel operating within a worksheet, so you need to know how to navigate and perform worksheet tasks such as renaming, moving, copying, and deleting.

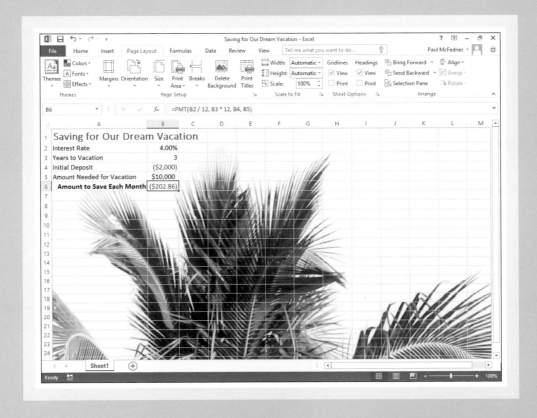

Navigate a Worksheet

You can use a few keyboard techniques that make it easier to navigate data after you have entered it in a worksheet.

It is usually easiest to use your mouse to click in the next cell you want to work with. If you are using Excel on a tablet or PC that has a touchscreen, then you can tap the next cell you want to use. However, if you are entering data, then using the keyboard to navigate to the next cell is often faster because your hands do not have to leave the keyboard.

Keyboard Techniques for Navigating a Worksheet	
Press	**To move**
←	Left one cell
→	Right one cell
↑	Up one cell
↓	Down one cell
Home	To the beginning of the current row
Page down	Down one screen
Page up	Up one screen
Alt + Page down	One screen to the right
Alt + Page up	One screen to the left
Ctrl + Home	To the top-left corner of the worksheet (cell A1)
Ctrl + End	To the bottom-right corner of the used portion of the worksheet
Ctrl + arrow keys	In the direction of the arrow to the next non-blank cell if the current cell is blank, or to the last non-blank cell if the current cell is not blank

Rename a Worksheet

You can make your Excel workbooks easier to understand and navigate by providing each worksheet with a name that reflects the contents of the sheet.

Excel provides worksheets with generic names such as Sheet1 and Sheet2, but you can change these to more descriptive names such as Sales 2013, Amortization, or Budget Data. Note, however, that although worksheet names can include any combination of letters, numbers, symbols, and spaces, they cannot be longer than 31 characters.

Rename a Worksheet

1 Display the worksheet you want to rename.

2 Click the **Home** tab.

3 Click **Format**.

4 Click **Rename Sheet**.

A You can also double-click the worksheet's tab.

B Excel opens the worksheet name for editing and selects the text.

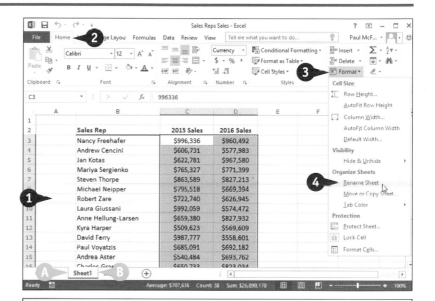

5 If you want to edit the existing name, press either ← or → to deselect the text.

6 Type the new worksheet name.

7 Press **Enter**.

Excel assigns the new name to the worksheet.

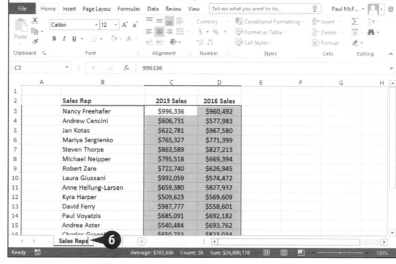

Create a New Worksheet

When you create a new workbook, Excel includes a single worksheet that you can use to build a spreadsheet model or store data. If you want to build a new model or store a different set of data, and this new information is related to the existing data in the workbook, you can create a new worksheet to hold the new information. Excel supports multiple worksheets in a single workbook, so you can add as many worksheets as you need for your project or model.

In most cases, you will add a blank worksheet, but Excel also comes with several predefined worksheet templates that you can use.

Create a New Worksheet

Insert a Blank Worksheet

1 Open the workbook to which you want to add the worksheet.

2 Click the **Home** tab.

3 Click the **Insert** ▼.

4 Click **Insert Sheet**.

A Excel inserts the worksheet.

Note: You can also insert a blank worksheet by pressing Shift + F11.

B Another way to add a blank worksheet is to click the **Insert Worksheet** button (⊕).

Insert a Worksheet from a Template

1 Open the workbook to which you want to add the worksheet.

2 Right-click a worksheet tab.

3 Click **Insert**.

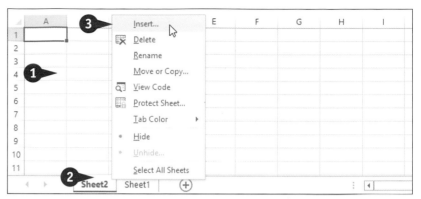

The Insert dialog box appears.

4 Click the **Spreadsheet Solutions** tab.

5 Click the type of worksheet you want to add.

C You can also click **Templates on Office.com** to download worksheet templates from the web.

6 Click **OK**.

D Excel inserts the worksheet.

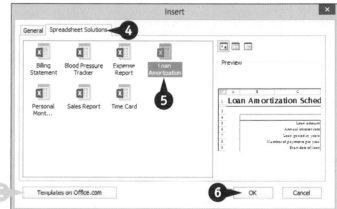

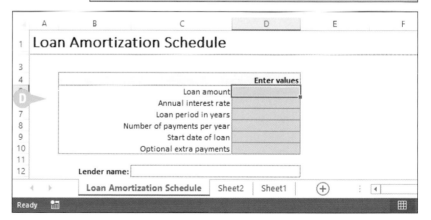

How do I navigate from one worksheet to another?

The easiest way is to click the tab of the worksheet you want to use. You can also click the following controls:

◀	Move to the previous worksheet.	Ctrl + ◀	Move to the first worksheet.
▶	Move to the next worksheet.	Ctrl + ▶	Move to the last worksheet.

Move a Worksheet

You can organize an Excel workbook and make it easier to navigate by moving your worksheets to different positions within the workbook. You can also move a worksheet to another workbook.

When you add a new worksheet to a workbook, Excel adds the sheet to the left of the existing sheets. However, it is unlikely that you will add each new worksheet in the order you want them to appear in the workbook. For example, in a budget-related workbook, you might prefer to have all the sales-related worksheets together, all the expense-related worksheets together, and so on.

Move a Worksheet

1 If you want to move the worksheet to another workbook, open that workbook and then return to the current workbook.

2 Click the tab of the worksheet you want to move.

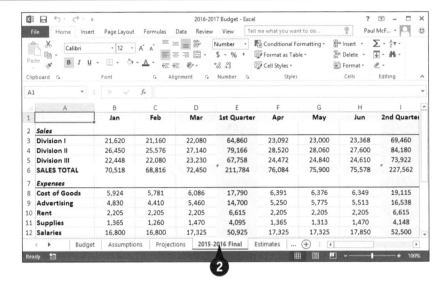

3 Click the **Home** tab.

4 Click **Format**.

5 Click **Move or Copy Sheet**.

A You can also right-click the tab and then click **Move or Copy Sheet**.

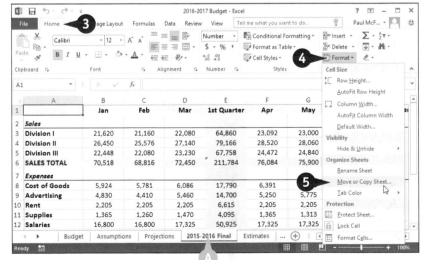

The Move or Copy dialog box appears.

6 If you want to move the sheet to another workbook, click the **To book** ▼ and then click the workbook.

7 Use the **Before sheet** list to click a destination worksheet.

When Excel moves the worksheet, it will appear to the left of the sheet you selected in step **7**.

8 Click **OK**.

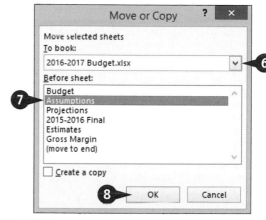

Move or Copy ? ✕

Move selected sheets
To book:

2016-2017 Budget.xlsx ⌄ **6**

Before sheet:

Budget
7 Assumptions
Projections
2015-2016 Final
Estimates
Gross Margin
(move to end)

☐ Create a copy

8 OK   Cancel

B Excel moves the worksheet.

⊿	A	B	C	D	E	F
1		Jan	Feb	Mar	1st Quarter	Apr
2	*Sales*					
3	**Division I**	21,620	21,160	22,080	64,860	23,092
4	**Division II**	26,450	25,576	27,140	79,166	28,520
5	**Division III**	22,448	22,080	23,230	67,758	24,472
6	**SALES TOTAL**	70,518	68,816	72,450	211,784	76,084
7	*Expenses*					
8	**Cost of Goods**	5,924	5,781	6,086	17,790	6,391
9	**Advertising**	4,830	4,410	5,460	14,700	5,250
10	**Rent**	2,205	2,205	2,205	6,615	2,205
11	**Supplies**	1,365	1,260	1,470	4,095	1,365
12	**Salaries**	16,800	16,800	17,325	50,925	17,325

◀ ▶ │ Budget │ **2015-2016 Final** │ Assumptions │ Projections │ Estimates

B

TIP

Is there an easier way to move a worksheet within the same workbook?
Yes. It is usually much easier to use your mouse to move a worksheet within the same workbook:

1 Move ▷ over the tab of the workbook you want to move.

2 Click and drag the worksheet tab left or right to the new position within the workbook (▷ changes to ▷).

A As you drag, an arrow shows the position of the worksheet.

3 When you have the worksheet positioned where you want it, drop the worksheet tab.

Excel moves the worksheet.

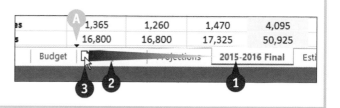

es	1,365	1,260	1,470	4,095
s	16,800	16,800	17,325	50,925
	Budget		Projections	2015-2016 Final	Esti

A   **3** **2**   **1**

Copy a Worksheet

Excel enables you to make a copy of a worksheet, which is a useful technique if you require a new worksheet that is similar to an existing worksheet. You can copy the sheet to the same workbook or to another workbook.

One of the secrets of productivity in Excel is to not repeat work that you have already done. For example, if you have already created a worksheet and you find that you need a second sheet that is very similar, then you should not create the new worksheet from scratch. Instead, you should copy the existing worksheet and then edit the new sheet as needed.

Copy a Worksheet

1 If you want to copy the worksheet to another workbook, open that workbook and then return to the current workbook.

2 Click the tab of the worksheet you want to copy.

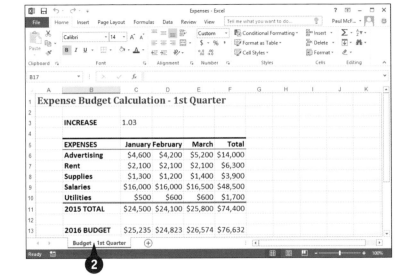

3 Click the **Home** tab.

4 Click **Format**.

5 Click **Move or Copy Sheet**.

Ⓐ You can also right-click the tab and then click **Move or Copy Sheet**.

The Move or Copy dialog box appears.

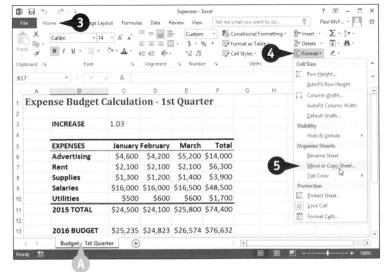

6 If you want to copy the sheet to another workbook, click the **To book** ⬇ and then click the workbook.

7 Use the **Before sheet** list to click a destination worksheet.

When Excel copies the worksheet, the copy will appear to the left of the sheet you selected in step **7**.

8 Select the **Create a copy** check box (☐ changes to ✔).

9 Click **OK**.

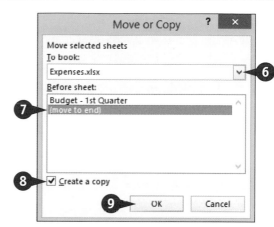

Move or Copy   ? ✕

Move selected sheets
To book:

Expenses.xlsx — **6**

Before sheet:

Budget - 1st Quarter
7 (move to end)

8 ✔ Create a copy

9   OK   Cancel

Ⓑ Excel copies the worksheet.

Ⓒ Excel gives the new worksheet the same name as the original, but with (2) appended.

Note: See the "Rename a Worksheet" section earlier in this chapter to learn how to edit the name of the copied worksheet.

⊿	A	B	C	D	E	F	G
1	**Expense Budget Calculation - 1st Quarter**						
2							
3		**INCREASE**	1.03				
4							
5		**EXPENSES**	**January**	**February**	**March**	**Total**	
6		**Advertising**	$4,600	$4,200	$5,200	$14,000	
7		**Rent**	$2,100	$2,100	$2,100	$6,300	
8		**Supplies**	$1,300	$1,200	$1,400	$3,900	
9		**Salaries**	$16,000	$16,000	$16,500	$48,500	
10		**Utilities**	$500	$600	$600	$1,700	
11		**2015 TOTAL**	$24,500	$24,100	$25,800	$74,400	
12							
13		**2016 BUDGET**	$25,235	$24,823	$26,574	$76,632	

◂ ▸   Budget - 1st Quarter | Budget - 1st Quarter (2) **Ⓒ**

Ready   **Ⓑ**

TIP

Is there an easier way to copy a worksheet within the same workbook?
Yes. It is usually much easier to use your mouse to copy a worksheet within the same workbook:

1 Move ⬚ over the tab of the workbook you want to copy.

2 Hold down `Ctrl`.

3 Click and drag the worksheet tab left or right (⬚ changes to ⬚).

Ⓐ As you drag, an arrow shows the position of the worksheet.

4 When you have the worksheet positioned where you want it, drop the worksheet tab.

Excel copies the worksheet.

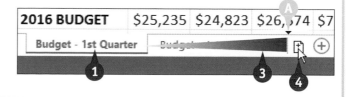

2016 BUDGET $25,235 $24,823 $26,574 $7

Budget - 1st Quarter   Budget   ⬚ ⊕

1   **3**   **4**

Delete a Worksheet

If you have a worksheet that you no longer need, you can delete it from the workbook. This reduces the size of the workbook and makes the workbook easier to navigate.

You cannot undo a worksheet deletion, so check the worksheet contents carefully before proceeding with the deletion. To be extra safe, save the workbook before performing the worksheet deletion. If you delete the wrong sheet accidentally, close the workbook without saving your changes.

Delete a Worksheet

1 Click the tab of the worksheet you want to delete.

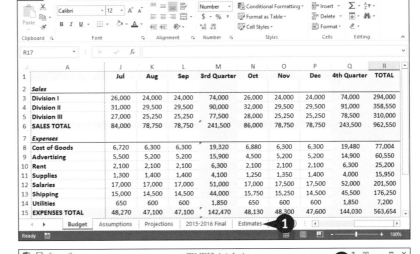

2 Click the **Home** tab.

3 Click the **Delete** ▼.

4 Click **Delete Sheet**.

Ⓐ You can also right-click the tab and then click **Delete Sheet**.

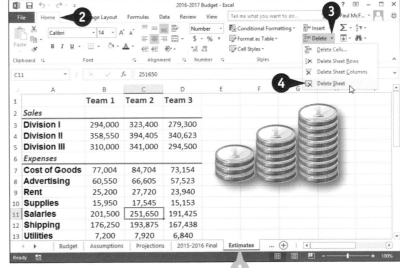

120

If the worksheet contains data, Excel asks you to confirm that you want to delete the worksheet.

⑤ Click **Delete**.

Ⓑ Excel removes the worksheet.

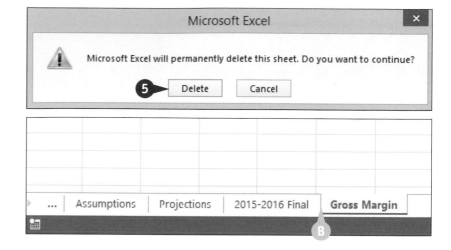

TIP

I have several worksheets that I need to delete. Do I have to delete them individually?

No. You can select all the sheets you want to remove and then run the deletion. To select multiple worksheets, click the tab of one of the worksheets, hold down Ctrl, and then click the tabs of the other worksheets.

If your workbook has many worksheets and you want to delete most of them, an easy way to select the sheets is to right-click any worksheet tab and then click **Select All Sheets**. Hold down Ctrl, and then click the tabs of the worksheets that you do not want to delete.

After you have selected your worksheets, follow steps **3** to **5** to delete all the selected worksheets at once.

Change the Gridline Color

You can add some visual interest to your worksheet by changing the color that Excel uses to display the gridlines. The default color is black, but Excel offers a palette of 56 colors that you can choose from.

Changing the gridline color also has practical value because it enables you to differentiate between the gridlines and the borders that you add to a range or a table. See Chapter 3 to learn how to add borders to your worksheet ranges.

Change the Gridline Color

1 Click the tab of the worksheet you want to customize.

2 Click the **File** tab.

3 Click **Options**.

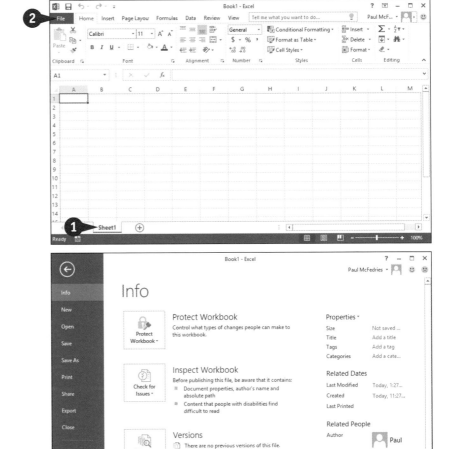

The Excel Options dialog box appears.

④ Click **Advanced**.

⑤ Scroll down to the **Display options for this worksheet** section.

Ⓐ The worksheet you selected in step **1** appears here.

⑥ Click the **Gridline color** ▼.

⑦ Click the color you want to use.

⑧ Click **OK**.

Ⓑ Excel displays the gridlines using the color you selected.

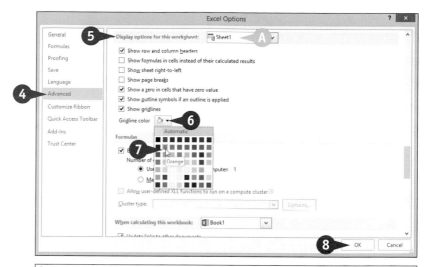

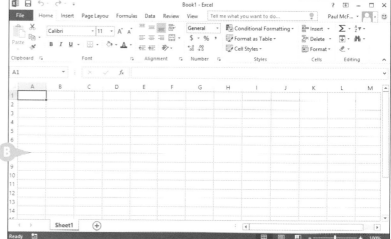

Toggle Worksheet Gridlines On and Off

Y ou can make your worksheet look cleaner and make the worksheet text easier to read by turning off the sheet gridlines. When you do this, Excel displays the worksheet with a plain white background, which often makes the worksheet easier to read. This is particularly true on a worksheet where you have added numerous borders to your ranges, as described in Chapter 3.

If you find you have trouble selecting ranges with the gridlines turned off, you can easily turn them back on again.

Toggle Worksheet Gridlines On and Off

Turn Gridlines Off

1 Click the tab of the worksheet you want to work with.

2 Click the **View** tab.

3 Click **Gridlines** (☑ changes to ☐).

A Excel turns off the gridline display.

Turn Gridlines On

B To turn the gridlines back on, click **Gridlines** (☐ changes to ☑).

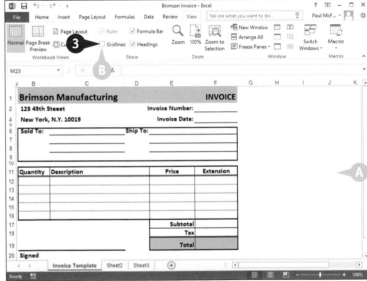

Toggle Worksheet Headings On and Off

You can give yourself a bit more room to work by turning off the worksheet's row headings — the numbers 1, 2, and so on to the left of the worksheet — and column headings — the letters A, B, and so on above the worksheet.

If you find you have trouble reading your worksheet or building formulas with the headings turned off, you can easily turn them back on again.

Toggle Worksheet Headings On and Off

Turn Headings Off

1 Click the tab of the worksheet you want to work with.

2 Click the **View** tab.

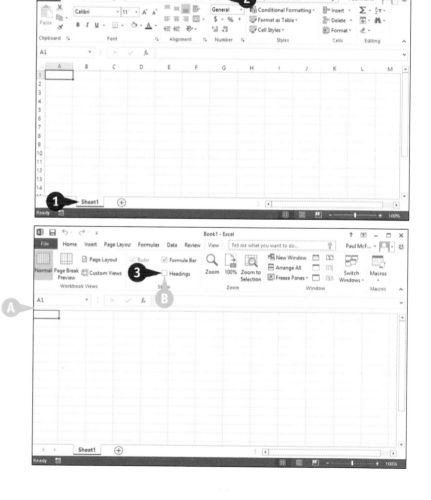

3 Click **Headings** (☑ changes to ☐).

A Excel turns off the headings.

Turn Headings On

B To turn the headings back on, click **Headings** (☐ changes to ☑).

Set the Worksheet Tab Color

You can make a workbook easier to navigate by color-coding the worksheet tabs. For example, if you have a workbook with sheets associated with several projects, you could apply a different tab color for each project. Similarly, you could format the tabs of incomplete worksheets with one color, and completed worksheets with another color.

Excel offers 10 standard colors as well as 60 colors associated with the current workbook theme. You can also apply a custom color if none of the standard or theme colors suits your needs.

Set the Worksheet Tab Color

1 Click the tab of the worksheet you want to format.

2 Click the **Home** tab.

3 Click **Format**.

4 Click **Tab Color**.

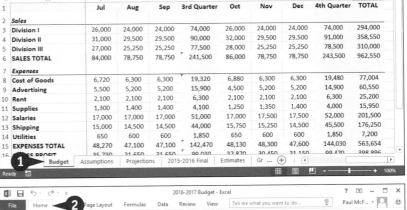

Excel displays the Tab Color palette.

5 Click the color you want to use for the current tab.

A To apply a custom color, click **More Colors** and then use the Colors dialog box to choose the color you want.

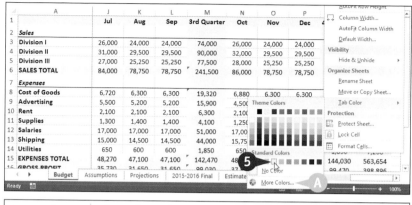

B Excel applies the color to the tab.

Note: You can also right-click the tab, click **Tab Color**, and then click the color you want to apply.

Note: The tab color appears very faintly when the tab is selected, but the color appears quite strongly when any other tab is selected.

If I want to apply the same color to several worksheets, do I have to format them individually?

No. You can select all the sheets you want to format and then apply the tab color. To select multiple worksheets, click the tab of one of the worksheets, hold down Ctrl, and then click the tabs of the other worksheets. After you have selected your worksheets, follow steps **2** to **5** to apply the tab color to all the selected worksheets at once.

How do I remove a tab color?

If you no longer require a worksheet to have a colored tab, you can remove the color. Follow steps **1** to **4** to select the worksheet and display the Tab Color palette, and then click **No Color**. Excel removes the color from the worksheet's tab.

Set the Worksheet Background

You can add visual interest to a worksheet by replacing the standard white sheet background with a photo, drawing, or other image. For example, a worksheet that tracks the amount needed for a future vacation could show a photo from the proposed destination as the background.

When choosing the image you want to use as the background, be sure to select a picture that will not make the worksheet text difficult to read. For example, if your sheet text is a dark color, choose a light-colored image as the background.

Set the Worksheet Background

① Click the tab of the worksheet you want to customize.

② Click the **Page Layout** tab.

③ Click **Background** (▨).

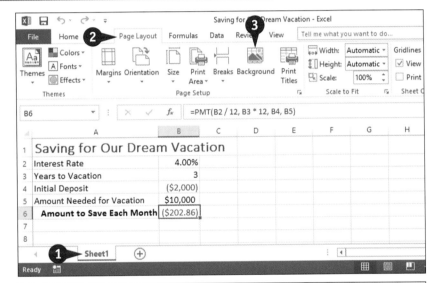

The Insert Pictures dialog box appears.

④ Click **From a file**.

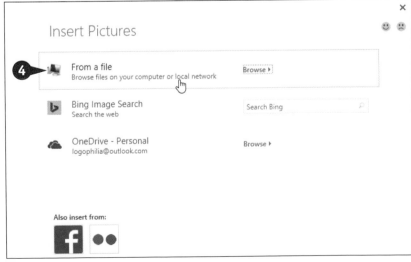

The Sheet Background dialog
box appears.

⑤ Select the location of the image
you want to use.

⑥ Click the image.

⑦ Click **Insert**.

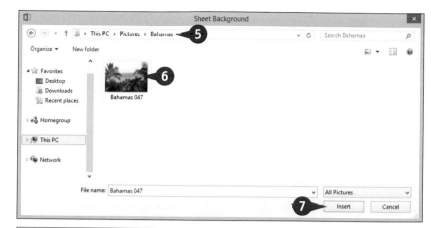

Ⓐ Excel formats the worksheet
background with the image you
selected.

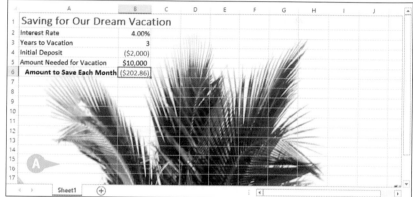

TIPS

**How do I apply a background color instead of a
background image?**
Excel does not have a command that changes the
background color of the entire worksheet. Instead, you
must first select all the cells in the worksheet by
clicking **Select All** (▲). Click the **Home** tab, click the
Fill Color ▼, and then click the color you want to use.
Excel applies the color to the background of every cell.

**How do I remove the background image from
the worksheet?**
If you find that having the background image
makes it difficult to read the worksheet text, then
you should remove the background. Click the tab
of the worksheet, click **Page Layout**, and then
click **Delete Background** (▣). Excel removes the
background image from the worksheet.

Zoom In on or Out of a Worksheet

Y ou can get a closer look at a portion of a worksheet by zooming in on that range. When you zoom in on a range, Excel increases the magnification of the range, which makes it easier to see the range data, particularly when the worksheet font is quite small.

On the other hand, if you want to get a sense of the overall structure of a worksheet, you can also zoom out. When you zoom out, Excel decreases the magnification, so you see more of the worksheet.

Zoom In on or Out of a Worksheet

1 Click the tab of the worksheet you want to zoom.

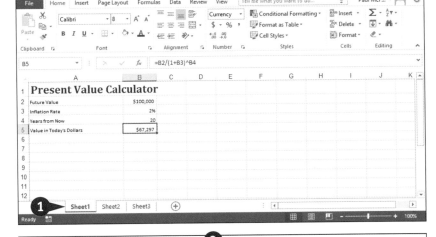

2 Click the **View** tab.

3 Click **Zoom** (🔍).

Ⓐ You can also run the Zoom command by clicking the zoom level in the status bar.

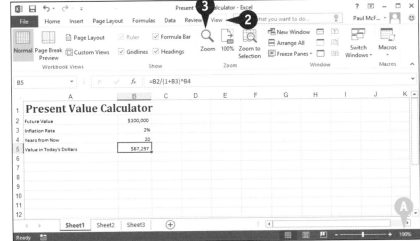

The Zoom dialog box appears.

④ Click the magnification level you want to use (○ changes to ◉).

Ⓑ You can also click **Custom** (○ changes to ◉) and then type a magnification level in the text box.

Note: Select a magnification level above 100% to zoom in on the worksheet; select a level under 100% to zoom out of the worksheet.

⑤ Click **OK**.

Excel changes the magnification level and redisplays the worksheet.

Ⓒ You can click **100%** ( ) to return to the normal zoom level.

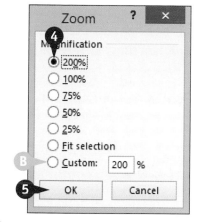

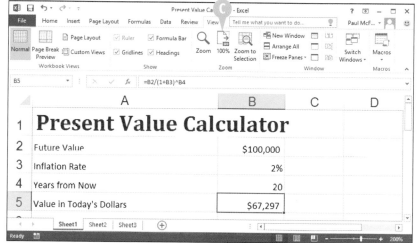

TIPS

How can I zoom in on a particular range?
Excel offers the Zoom to Selection feature that enables you to quickly and easily zoom in on a range. First, select the range that you want to magnify. Click the **View** tab and then click **Zoom to Selection** ( ). Excel magnifies the selected range to fill the entire Excel window.

Is there an easier way to zoom in and out of a worksheet?
Yes, you can use the Zoom slider, which appears on the far-right side of the Excel status bar. Drag the slider 🔳 to the right to zoom in on the worksheet, or drag 🔳 to the left to zoom out. You can also click the **Zoom In** (➕) or **Zoom Out** (➖) button to change the magnification.

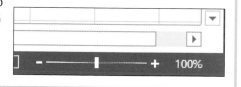

Split a Worksheet into Two Panes

Y| ou can make it easier to examine your worksheet data by splitting the worksheet into two scrollable panes that each show different parts of the worksheet. This is useful if you have cell headings at the top of the worksheet that you want to keep in view as you scroll down the worksheet.

Splitting a worksheet into two panes is also useful if you want to keep some data or a formula result in view while you scroll to another part of the worksheet.

Split a Worksheet into Two Panes

1 Click the tab of the worksheet you want to split.

2 Select a cell in column A that is below the point where you want the split to occur.

For example, if you want to place the first five rows in the top pane, select cell A6.

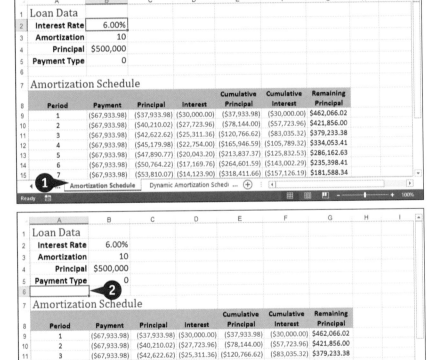

③ Click the **View** tab.

④ Click **Split** (⬚).

Ⓐ Excel splits the worksheet into two horizontal panes at the selected cell.

Ⓑ You can adjust the size of the panes by clicking and dragging the split bar up or down.

To remove the split, either click ⬚ again, or double-click the split bar.

TIPS

Can I split a worksheet into two vertical panes?
Yes. To do this, you must first select a cell in the top row of the worksheet. Specifically, select the top cell in the column to the right of where you want the split to occur. For example, if you want to show only column A in the left pane, select cell B1. When you click ⬚, Excel splits the worksheet into two vertical panes.

Can I split a worksheet into four panes?
Yes. This is useful if you have three or four worksheet areas that you want to examine separately. To perform a four-way split, first select the cell where you want the split to occur. Note that this cell must not be in either row 1 or column A. When you click ⬚, Excel splits the worksheet into four panes. The cell you selected becomes the upper-left cell in the bottom-right pane.

Hide and Unhide a Worksheet

You can hide a worksheet so that it no longer appears in the workbook. This is useful if you need to show the workbook to other people, but the workbook contains a worksheet with sensitive or private data that you do not want others to see. You might also want to hide a worksheet if it contains unfinished work that is not ready for others to view.

To learn how to protect a workbook so that other people cannot unhide a worksheet, see Chapter 14.

Hide and Unhide a Worksheet

Hide a Worksheet

1. Click the tab of the worksheet you want to hide.

2. Click the **Home** tab.

3. Click **Format**.

4. Click **Hide & Unhide**.

5. Click **Hide Sheet**.

Ⓐ You can also right-click the worksheet tab and then click **Hide Sheet**.

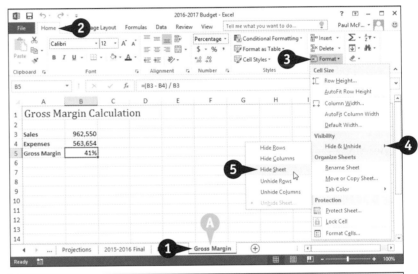

Ⓑ Excel temporarily removes the worksheet from the workbook.

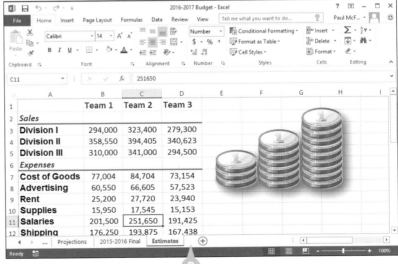

Unhide a Worksheet

1 Click the **Home** tab.

2 Click **Format**.

3 Click **Hide & Unhide**.

4 Click **Unhide Sheet**.

🅒 You can also right-click any worksheet tab and then click **Unhide Sheet**.

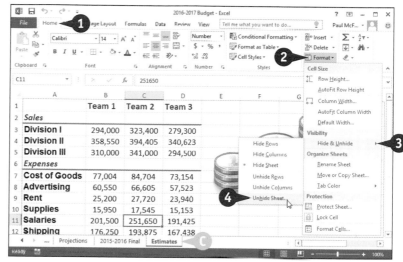

The Unhide dialog box appears.

5 Click the worksheet you want to restore.

6 Click **OK**.

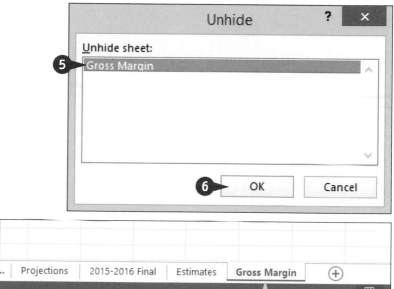

🅓 Excel returns the worksheet to the workbook.

I have several worksheets that I need to hide. Do I have to hide them individually?

No. You can select all the sheets you want to work with and then hide them. To select multiple worksheets, click the tab of one of the worksheets, hold down Ctrl, and then click the tabs of the other worksheets.

If your workbook has many worksheets and you want to hide most of them, an easy way to select the sheets is to right-click any worksheet tab and then click **Select All Sheets**. Hold down Ctrl, and then click the tabs of the worksheets that you do not want to hide.

After you have selected your worksheets, follow steps **3** to **5** to hide all the selected worksheets at once.

CHAPTER 6

Dealing with Workbooks

Everything you do in Excel takes place within a *workbook*, which is the standard Excel file. This chapter shows you how to get more out of workbooks by creating new files; saving, opening, and closing files; checking spelling; and more.

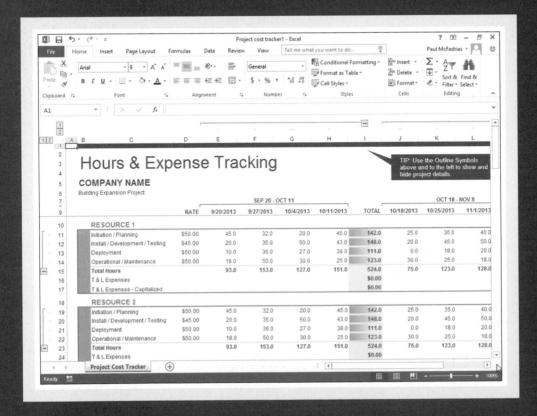

Create a New Blank Workbook

To perform new work in Excel, you need to first create a new, blank Excel workbook. When you launch Excel, it prompts you to create a new workbook and you can click Blank Workbook to start with a blank file that contains a single empty worksheet. However, for subsequent files you must use the File tab to create a new blank workbook.

If you prefer to create a workbook based on one of the Excel templates, see the following section, "Create a New Workbook from a Template."

Create a New Blank Workbook

1 Click the **File** tab.

2 Click **New**.

3 Click **Blank Workbook.**

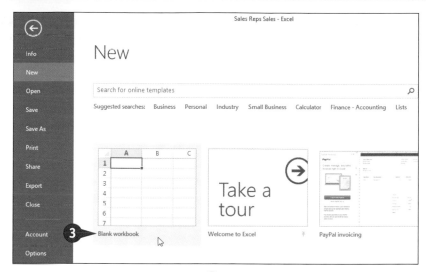

A Excel creates the blank workbook and displays it in the Excel window.

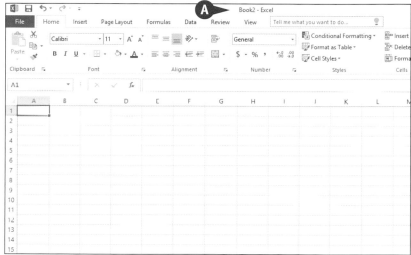

TIPS

Is there a faster method I can use to create a new workbook?

Yes. Excel offers a keyboard shortcut for faster workbook creation. From the keyboard, press Ctrl + N.

When I start Excel and then open an existing workbook, Excel often removes the new, blank workbook that it opened automatically. How can I prevent this?

Excel assumes that you want to use a fresh workbook when you start the program, so it prompts you to create a new workbook. However, if you do not make any changes to the blank workbook and then open an existing file, Excel assumes you do not want to use the new workbook, so it closes it. To prevent this from happening, make a change to the blank workbook before opening another file.

Create a New Workbook from a Template

You can save time and effort by creating a new workbook based on one of the Excel template files. Each template includes a working spreadsheet model that contains predefined headings, labels, and formulas, as well as preformatted colors, fonts, styles, borders, and more. In many cases, you can use the new workbook as is and just fill in your own data.

Excel 2016 offers more than two dozen templates, and many more are available through Microsoft Office Online.

Create a New Workbook from a Template

1 Click the **File** tab.

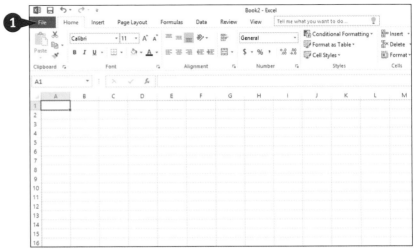

2 Click **New**.

A To use an Office Online template, use the Search Online Templates text box to type a word or two that defines the type of template you want to use.

3 Click the template you want to use.

B A preview of the template appears.

4 Click **Create**.

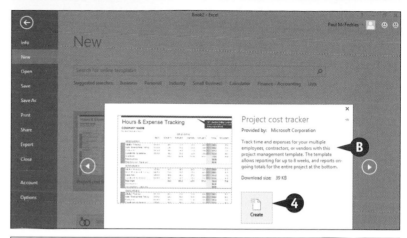

C Excel creates the new workbook and displays it in the Excel window.

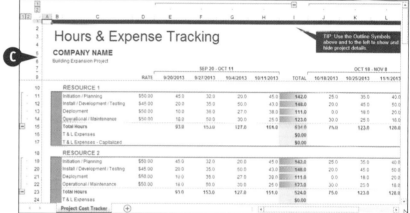

TIP

Can I create my own template?

Yes. If you have a specific workbook structure that you use frequently, you should save it as a template so that you do not have to re-create the same structure from scratch each time. Open the workbook, click **File**, and then click **Save as**. In the Save As dialog box, click **Computer**, and then click **Browse**. Click the **Save as type** ▼ and then click **Excel Template**. Type a name in the **File name** text box and then click **Save**. To use the template, click **File** and click **Open**; then, in the Open dialog box, click **Computer**, click **Browse**, and then click your template file.

Save a Workbook

After you create a workbook in Excel and make changes to it, you can save the document to preserve your work. When you edit a workbook, Excel stores the changes in your computer's memory, which is erased each time you shut down your computer. Saving the document preserves your changes on your computer's hard drive. To ensure that you do not lose any work if your computer crashes or Excel freezes up, you should save your work frequently: at least every few minutes.

Save a Workbook

1 Click **Save** (💾).

You can also press Ctrl + S.

If you have saved the document previously, your changes are now preserved, and you do not need to follow the rest of the steps in this section.

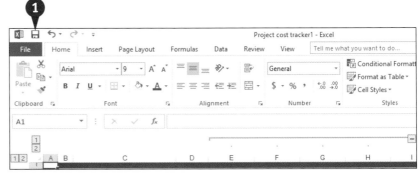

The Save As tab appears.

2 Click **This PC**.

3 Click **Browse**.

The Save As dialog box appears.

4 Select a folder in which to store the file.

5 Click in the **File name** text box and type the name that you want to use for the document.

6 Click **Save**.

Excel saves the file.

Note: To learn how to save a workbook in an older Excel format, see Chapter 14.

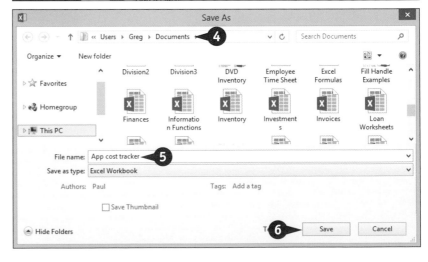

Open a Workbook

To view or make changes to an Excel workbook that you have saved in the past, you must open the workbook in Excel. To open a workbook, you must first locate it in the folder you used when you originally saved the file.

If you have used the workbook recently, you can save time by opening the workbook from the Excel Recent Workbooks menu, which displays a list of the 25 workbooks that you have used most recently.

Open a Workbook

1 Click the **File** tab (not shown).

2 Click **Open**.

The Open tab appears.

A You can click **Recent** to see a list of your recently used workbooks. If you see the file you want, click it and then skip the rest of these steps.

3 Click **This PC**.

4 Click **Browse**.

You can also press `Ctrl`+`O`.

The Open dialog box appears.

5 Select the folder that contains the workbook you want to open.

6 Click the workbook.

7 Click **Open**.

The workbook appears in a window.

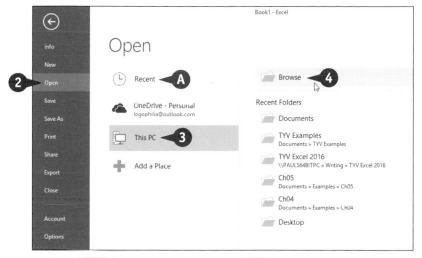

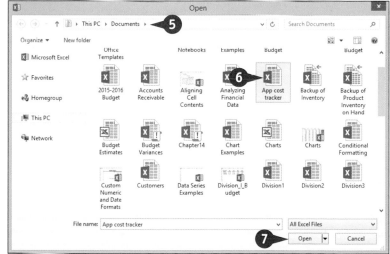

Arrange Workbook Windows

You can view two or more workbooks at once by arranging the workbook windows on the Windows desktop. This is useful if, for example, you want to compare or contrast data in two or more workbooks. By arranging the workbooks so that they do not overlap each other, you can see the workbooks' data without having to switch from one window to another.

Excel offers four view modes for arranging workbook windows: Tiled, Horizontal, Vertical, and Cascade.

Arrange Workbook Windows

1 Open the workbooks you want to view.

2 Click the **View** tab.

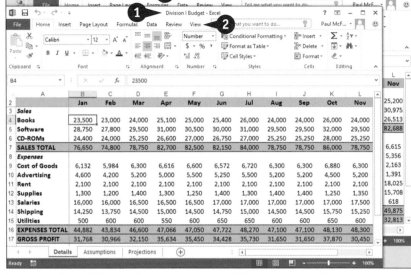

3 Click **Arrange All** (□).

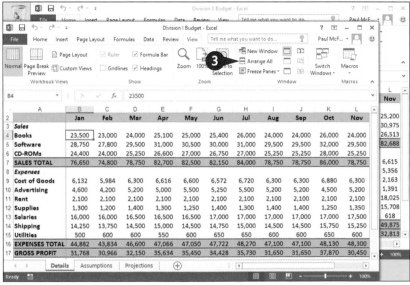

The Arrange Windows dialog box appears.

④ Click a view mode (○ changes to ◉).

Tiled arranges the workbooks evenly on the Windows desktop.

Horizontal stacks the workbooks one above the other.

Vertical displays the workbooks side by side.

Cascade arranges the workbooks in an overlapping cascade pattern.

⑤ Click **OK**.

Ⓐ Excel arranges the workbook windows.

This example shows two workbooks arranged with the Vertical view mode.

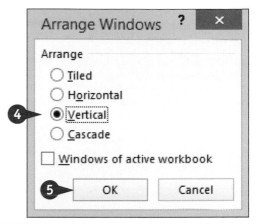

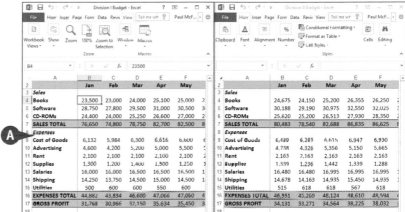

TIPS

How do I return to viewing one workbook at a time?

Click the workbook you want to use, and then click the workbook window's **Maximize** button (☐). This maximizes the workbook on the Windows desktop, so you only see that workbook. To switch to another open workbook, click the Excel icon (☒) in the taskbar to display thumbnail versions of the open workbooks, and then click the one you want to view.

Is it possible to view two different sections of a single workbook at the same time?

Yes. Excel enables you to create a second window for a workbook and you can then arrange the two windows as described in this section. Switch to the workbook you want to view, click the **View** tab, and then click **New Window** (⊟). Follow steps **1** to **3** to open the Arrange Windows dialog box and select a view option. Select the **Windows of active workbook** check box (☐ changes to ☑), and then click **OK**.

Find Text in a Workbook

Most spreadsheet models require at most a screen or two in a single worksheet, so locating the text you want is usually not difficult. However, you might be working with a large spreadsheet model that takes up either multiple screens in a single worksheet or multiple worksheets. In such large workbooks, locating specific text can be difficult and time-consuming. You can make this task easier and faster using the Excel Find feature, which searches the entire workbook in the blink of an eye.

Find Text in a Workbook

1 Click the **Home** tab.

2 Click **Find & Select**.

3 Click **Find**.

Note: You can also run the Find command by pressing **Ctrl** + **F**.

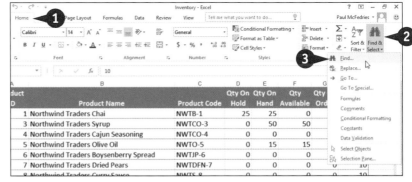

The Find and Replace dialog box appears.

4 Click in the **Find what** text box and type the text you want to find.

5 Click **Find Next**.

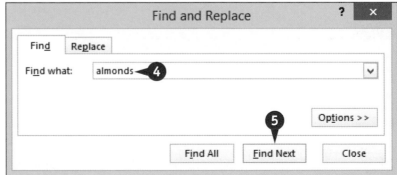

(A) Excel selects the next cell that contains an instance of the search text.

Note: If the search text does not exist in the document, Excel displays a dialog box to let you know.

(6) If the selected instance is not the one you want, click **Find Next** until Excel finds the correct instance.

(7) Click **Close** to close the Find and Replace dialog box.

(B) Excel leaves the cell selected.

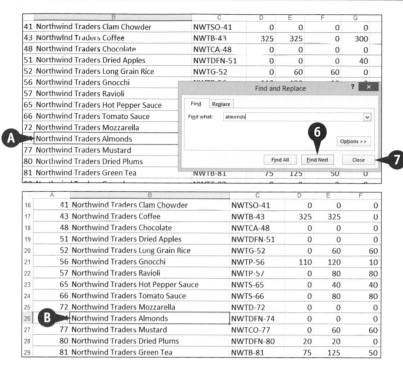

TIPS

When I search for a particular term, Excel only looks in the current worksheet. How can I get Excel to search the entire workbook?

In the Find and Replace dialog box, click **Options** to expand the dialog box. Click the **Within** ⬇ and then click **Workbook**. This option tells Excel to examine the entire workbook for your search text.

When I search for a name such as *Bill*, Excel also matches the non-name *bill*. Is there a way to fix this?

Yes. In the Find and Replace dialog box, click **Options** to expand the dialog box. Select the **Match case** check box (☐ changes to ☑). This option tells Excel to match the search text only if it has the same mix of uppercase and lowercase letters that you specify in the **Find what** text box. If you type **Bill**, for example, the program matches only *Bill* and not *bill*.

Replace Text in a Workbook

Do you need to replace a word or part of a word with some other text? If you only need to replace one or two instances of the text, you can usually perform the replacement quickly and easily. However, if you have many instances of the text to replace, the replacement can take a long time and the more instances there are, the more likely it is that you will make a mistake. You can save time and do a more accurate job if you let the Excel Replace feature replace the text for you.

Replace Text in a Workbook

1 Click the **Home** tab.

2 Click **Find & Select**.

3 Click **Replace**.

Note: You can also run the Replace command by pressing Ctrl + H.

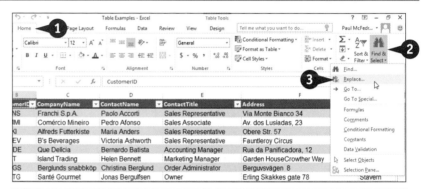

The Find and Replace dialog box appears.

4 In the **Find what** text box, type the text you want to find.

5 Click in the **Replace with** text box and type the text you want to use as the replacement.

6 Click **Find Next**.

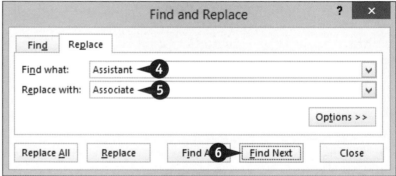

A Excel selects the cell that contains the next instance of the search text.

Note: If the search text does not exist in the document, Excel displays a dialog box to let you know.

7 If the selected instance is not the one you want, click **Find Next** until Excel finds the correct instance.

8 Click **Replace**.

B Excel replaces the selected text with the replacement text.

C Excel selects the next instance of the search text.

9 Repeat steps **7** and **8** until you have replaced all the instances you want to replace.

10 Click **Close** to close the Find and Replace dialog box.

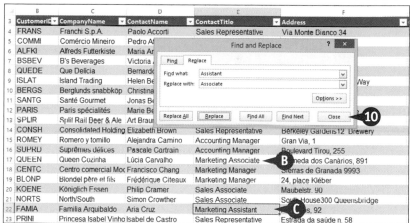

Check Spelling and Grammar

Although Excel workbooks are mostly concerned with numbers, formulas, and data, a workbook that contains misspelled words might not be taken as seriously as one that is free of jarring typos. You can eliminate any text errors in your Excel workbooks by taking advantage of the spell-checker, which identifies potentially misspelled words and offers suggested corrections.

When the spell-checker flags a word as misspelled, you can correct the word, tell the spell-checker to ignore it, or add it to the spell-checker's dictionary.

Check Spelling and Grammar

1 Click the **Review** tab.

2 Click **Spelling** (ABC✓).

Note: You can also press F7.

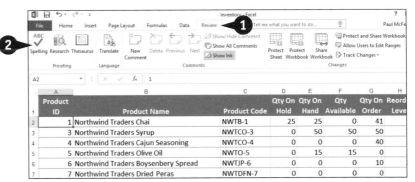

A The Spelling dialog box appears and selects the cell that contains the first error.

3 Click the correction you want to use.

4 Click **Change**.

B Click **Change All** to correct every instance of the error.

C The spell-checker displays the next error.

5 If you want to correct the word, repeat step **4**.

D If you do not want to correct the word, click one of the following buttons:

Click **Ignore Once** to skip this instance of the error.

Click **Ignore All** to skip all instances of the error.

Click **Add to Dictionary** to include the word in the spell-checker's dictionary.

6 When the check is complete, click **OK**.

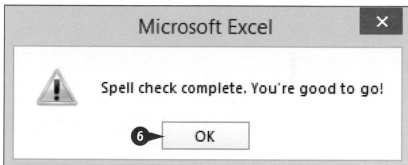

TIP

Can I remove a word that I added to the spell-checker's dictionary?

Yes. Follow these steps:

1 Click **File**.

2 Click **Options** to open the Excel Options dialog box.

3 Click **Proofing**.

4 Click **Custom Dictionaries** to open the Custom Dictionaries dialog box.

5 Click the dictionary marked as **Default** and then click **Edit Word List**.

6 Click the term you want to remove.

7 Click **Delete**.

8 Click **OK** to return to the Custom Dictionaries dialog box.

9 Click **OK** to return to the Excel Options dialog box.

10 Click **OK**.

CHAPTER 7

Formatting Workbooks

Excel offers several settings that enable you to control the look of a workbook, including the workbook colors, fonts, and special effects. You can also apply a workbook theme and add a header and footer to a workbook.

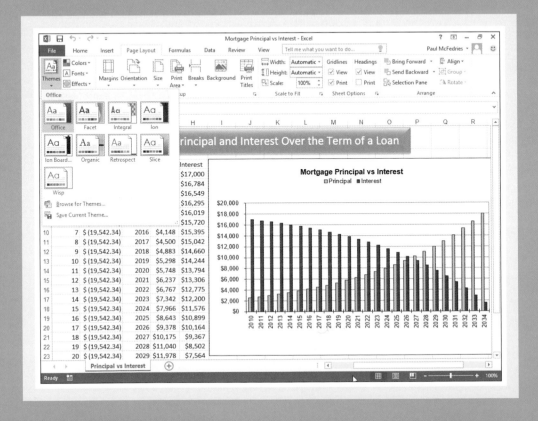

Modify the Workbook Colors

You can give your workbook a new look by selecting a different color scheme. Each color scheme affects a dozen workbook elements, including the workbook's text colors, background colors, border colors, chart colors, and more. Excel offers more than 20 color schemes. However, if none of these predefined schemes suits your needs, you can also create your own custom color scheme.

To get the most out of the Excel color schemes, you must apply styles to your ranges, as described in Chapter 3.

Modify the Workbook Colors

1 Open or switch to the workbook you want to format.

2 Click the **Page Layout** tab.

3 Click **Colors** ( ).

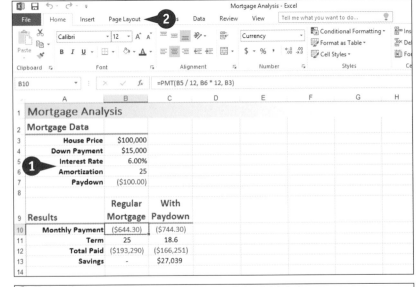

④ Click the color scheme you want to apply.

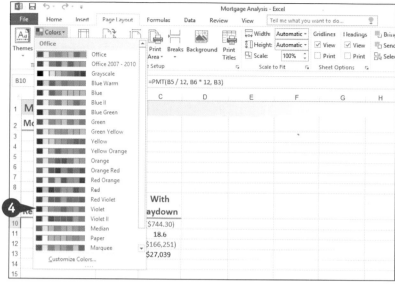

Ⓐ Excel applies the color scheme to the workbook.

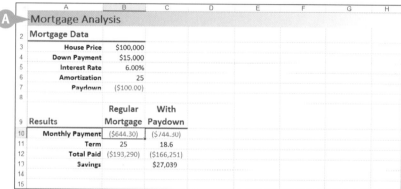

Can I create my own color scheme?
Yes, by following these steps:

① Click the **Page Layout** tab.

② Click ▣.

③ Click **Customize Colors**.

The Create New Theme Colors dialog box appears.

④ For each theme color, click ▼ and then click the color you want to use.

Ⓐ The Sample area shows what your theme colors look like.

⑤ Type a name for the custom color scheme.

⑥ Click **Save**.

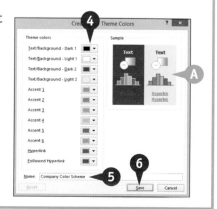

Set the Workbook Fonts

You can add visual appeal to your workbook by selecting a different font scheme. Each font scheme has two defined fonts: a *heading font* for the titles and headings, and a *body font* for the regular worksheet text. Excel offers more than 20 font schemes. However, if none of the predefined schemes is suitable, you can create a custom font scheme.

To get the most out of the Excel font schemes, particularly the heading fonts, you must apply styles to your ranges, as described in Chapter 3.

Set the Workbook Fonts

1 Open or switch to the workbook you want to format.

2 Click the **Page Layout** tab.

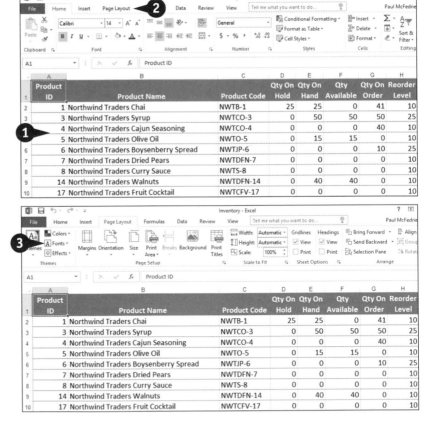

3 Click **Fonts** (A).

④ Click the font scheme you want to apply.

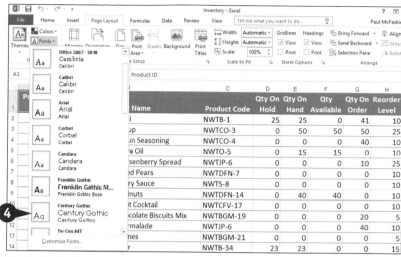

Ⓐ Excel applies the heading font to the workbook's headings.

Ⓑ Excel applies the body font to the workbook's regular text.

Can I create my own font scheme?

Yes, by following these steps:

❶ Click the **Page Layout** tab.

❷ Click $\boxed{A}$.

❸ Click **Customize Fonts**.

The Create New Theme Fonts dialog box appears.

❹ Click the **Heading font** ▼ and then click the font you want to use for titles and headings.

❺ Click the **Body font** ▼ and then click the font you want to use for regular sheet text.

Ⓐ The Sample area shows what your theme fonts look like.

❻ Type a name for the custom font scheme.

❼ Click **Save**.

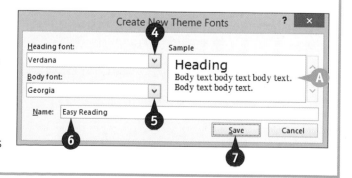

Choose Workbook Effects

You can enhance the look of your workbook by selecting a different effect scheme. The effect scheme applies to charts and graphic objects, and each scheme defines a border style, fill style, and added effect such as a drop shadow or glow. Excel offers more than 20 effect schemes.

To get the most out of the Excel effect schemes, you must apply a style to your chart, as described in Chapter 12, or to your graphic object, as described in Chapter 13.

Choose Workbook Effects

1. Open or switch to the workbook you want to format.

2. Click the **Page Layout** tab.

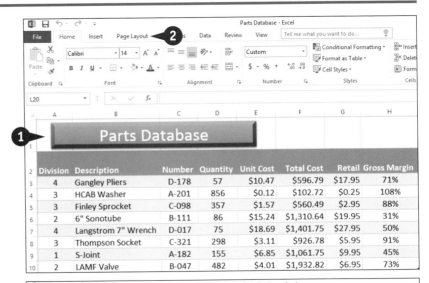

3. Click **Effects** (⊙).

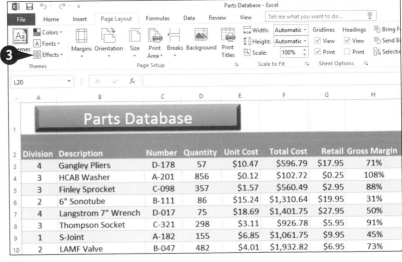

④ Click the effect scheme you want to apply.

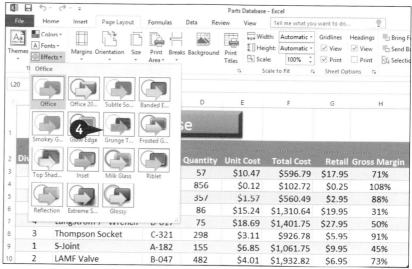

Ⓐ Excel applies the effect scheme to the workbook's charts and graphics.

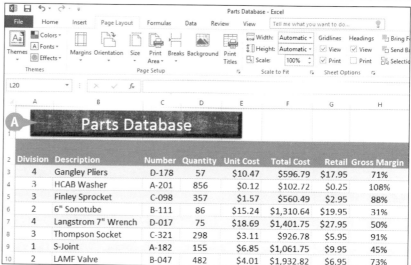

Can I create a custom effect scheme?

No. Unlike with the color schemes and font schemes described earlier in this chapter, Excel does not have a feature that enables you to create your own effect scheme.

Why are all the effect schemes the same color?

The color you see in the effect schemes depends on the color scheme you have applied to your workbook. If you apply a different color scheme, as described in the "Modify the Workbook Colors" section earlier in the chapter, you will see a different color in the effect schemes. If you want to use a custom effect color, create a custom color scheme and change the Accent 1 color to the color you want.

Apply a Workbook Theme

You can give your workbook a completely new look by selecting a different workbook theme. Each theme consists of the workbook's colors, fonts, and effects. Excel offers ten predefined workbook themes.

To get the most out of the Excel workbook themes, you must apply styles to your ranges, as described in Chapter 3; to your charts, as described in Chapter 12; and to your graphic objects, as described in Chapter 13.

Apply a Workbook Theme

1 Open or switch to the workbook you want to format.

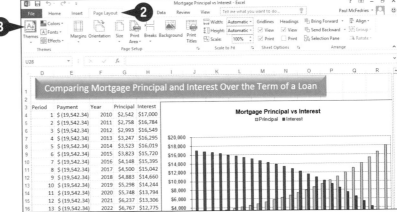

2 Click the **Page Layout** tab.

3 Click **Themes** (Aa).

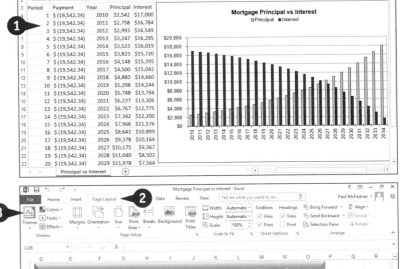

④ Click the workbook theme you
want to apply.

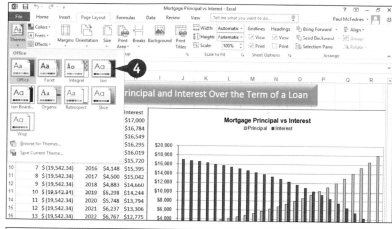

Ⓐ Excel applies the theme to the
workbook.

Note: After you apply the theme, the
new font size might require you to
adjust the column widths to see your
data properly.

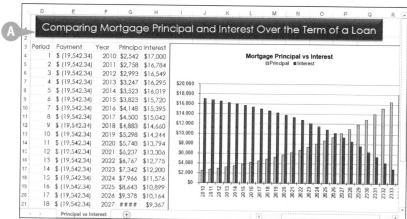

TIP

Can I create my own workbook theme?

Yes, by following these steps:

① Format the workbook with a color scheme,
font scheme, and effect scheme, as described
in the previous three sections.

② Click the **Page Layout** tab.

③ Click Ⓐ.

④ Click **Save Current Theme**.

The Save Current Theme dialog box appears.

⑤ Type a name for the custom theme.

⑥ Click **Save**.

Add a Workbook Header

If you will be printing a workbook, you can enhance the printout by building a custom header that includes information such as the page number, date, filename, or even a picture.

The *header* is an area on the printed page between the top of the page text and the top margin. Excel offers a number of predefined header items that enable you to quickly add data to the workbook header. If none of the predefined header items suits your needs, Excel also offers tools that make it easy to build a custom header.

Add a Workbook Header

1 Click the **View** tab.

2 Click **Page Layout** (📄).

Excel switches to Page Layout view.

Ⓐ You can also click the **Page Layout** button (📄).

3 Click the **Add header** text.

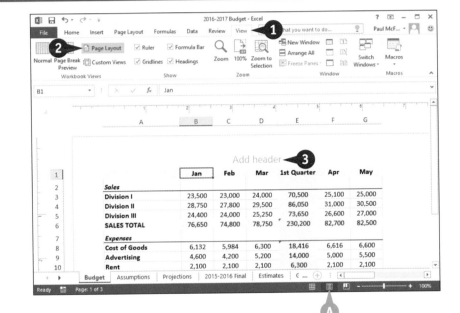

Ⓑ Excel opens the header area for editing.

Ⓒ Excel adds the Header & Footer Tools tab.

4 Click the **Design** tab.

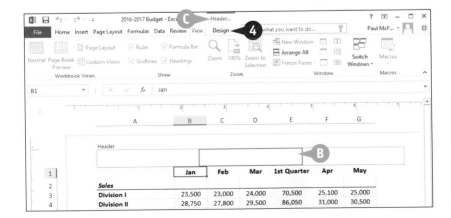

⑤ Type your text in the header.

⑥ If you want to include a predefined header item, click **Header** and then click the item.

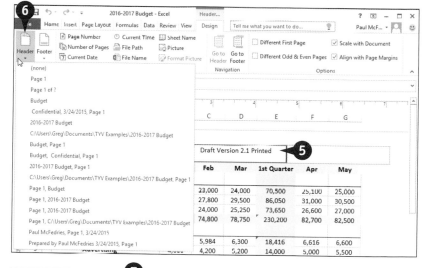

⑦ Click a button in the Header & Footer Elements group to add that element to the header.

Ⓓ Excel inserts a code into the header, such as &[Date] for the Current Date element, as shown here.

⑧ Repeat steps **5** to **7** to build the header.

⑨ Click outside the header area.

Excel applies the header. When you are in Page Layout view, you see the current values for elements such as the date.

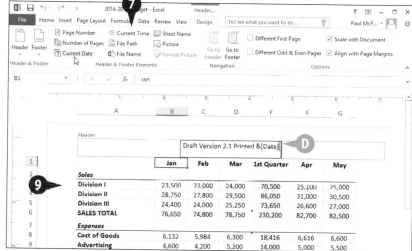

TIP

Can I have multiple headers in a workbook?

Yes. You can have a different header and footer on the first page, which is useful if you want to add a title or explanatory text to the first page. In the Design tab, select the **Different First Page** check box (☐ changes to ☑).

You can also have different headers and footers on the even and odd pages of the printout, such as showing the filename on the even pages and the page numbers on the odd pages. In the Design tab, select the **Different Odd & Even Pages** check box (☐ changes to ☑).

Add a Workbook Footer

If you will be printing a workbook, you can enhance the printout by building a custom footer that includes information such as the current page number, the total number of pages, the worksheet name, and more.

The *footer* is an area on the printed page between the bottom of the page text and the bottom margin. Excel offers a number of predefined footer items that enable you to quickly add data to the workbook footer. If none of the predefined footer items suits your needs, Excel also offers tools that make it easy to build a custom footer.

Add a Workbook Footer

1 Click the **View** tab.

2 Click **Page Layout** (⊞).

Excel switches to Page Layout view.

Ⓐ You can also click the **Page Layout** button (▣).

3 Scroll down to the bottom of the page and click the **Add footer** text.

Note: You can also click the **Add header** text and then click the Design tab's **Go to Footer** command (▤).

Ⓑ Excel opens the footer area for editing.

Ⓒ Excel adds the Header & Footer Tools tab.

4 Click the **Design** tab.

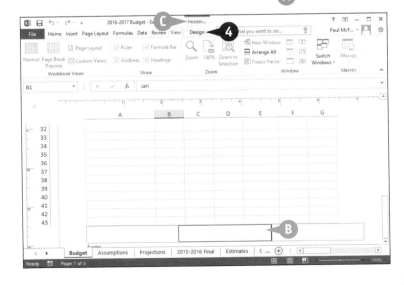

5 Type your text in the footer.

6 If you want to include a predefined footer item, click **Footer** and then click the item.

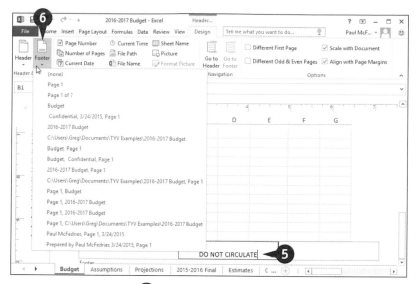

7 Click a button in the Header & Footer Elements group to add that element to the footer.

Ⓓ Excel inserts a code into the footer, such as &[Pages] for the Number of Pages element, as shown here.

8 Repeat steps **5** to **7** to build the footer.

9 Click outside the footer area.

Excel applies the footer. When you are in Page Layout view, you see the current values for elements such as the page number.

TIP

Can I view my headers and footers before I print the workbook?

Yes. Follow these steps:

1 Click the **File** tab.

2 Click **Print**.

Ⓐ The right side of the Print tab shows you a preview of the workbook printout.

Ⓑ The header appears here.

Ⓒ The footer appears here.

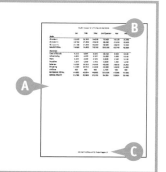

CHAPTER 8

Importing Data into Excel

Excel offers a number of tools that enable you to import external data into the program. Excel can access a wide variety of external data types. However, this chapter focuses on the six most common types: data source files, Access tables, Word tables, text files, web pages, and XML files.

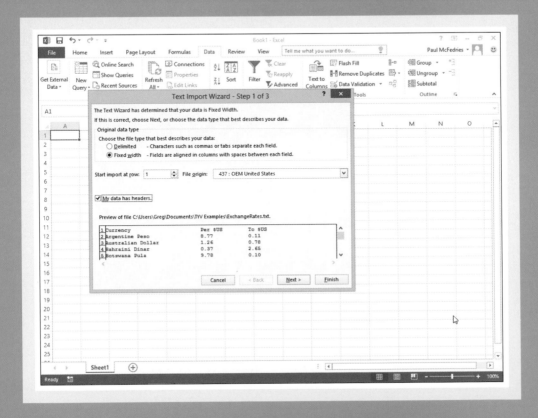

Understanding External Data

*E*xternal data is data that resides outside of Excel in a file, database, server, or website. You can import external data directly into an Excel PivotTable or worksheet for additional types of data analysis.

Before you learn the specifics of importing external data into your Excel workbooks, you need to understand the various types of external data that you are likely to encounter. For the vast majority of applications, external data comes in one of the following six formats: data sources, Access tables, Word tables, text files, web pages, and XML files.

Data Source File

Open Database Connectivity (ODBC) data sources give you access to data residing in databases such as Access and dBase, or on servers such as SQL Server and Oracle. However, there are many other data-source types that connect to specific objects in a data source. For more information, see the next section, "Import Data from a Data Source."

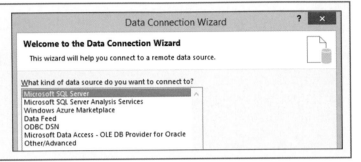

Access Table

Microsoft Access is the Office suite's relational database management system, and so it is often used to store and manage the bulk of the data used by a person, team, department, or company. For more information, see the section "Import Data from an Access Table."

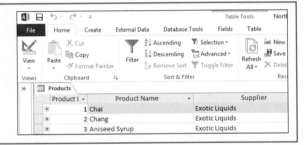

Word Table

Some simple data is often stored in a table embedded in a Word document. You can only perform so much analysis on that data within Word, and so it is often useful to import the data from the Word table into an Excel worksheet. For more information, see the section "Import Data from a Word Table."

Text File

Text files often contain useful data. If that data is formatted properly — for example, where each line has the same number of items, all separated by spaces, commas, or tabs — then it is possible to import that data into Excel for further analysis. For more information, see the section "Import Data from a Text File."

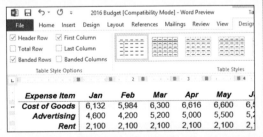

Web Page

People and companies often store useful data on web pages that reside either on the Internet or on company Intranets. This data is often a combination of text and tables, but you cannot analyze web-based data in any meaningful way in your web browser. Fortunately, Excel enables you to create a web query that lets you import text and tables from a web page. For more information, see the section "Import Data from a Web Page."

XML

XML — Extensible Markup Language — is redefining how data is stored. This is reflected in the large number of tools that Excel now has for dealing with XML data, particularly tools for importing XML data into Excel. For more information, see the section "Import Data from an XML File."

Access to External Data

To use external data, you must have access to it. This usually means knowing at least one of the following: the location of the data or the login information required to authorize your use of the data.

Connect to ODBC Data Source

Choose the ODBC data source you want to connect to.

ODBC data sources:

Excel Files
MS Access Database

Location

To access external data, you must at least know where it is located. Here are the most common possibilities: in a file on your computer; in a file on your network; on a network server, particularly as part of a large, server-based database management system, such as SQL Server or Oracle; on a web page; or on a web server.

Login

Knowing where the data is located is probably all that you require if you are dealing with a local file or database or, usually, a web page. However, after you start accessing data remotely — on a network, database server, or web server — you will also require authorization to secure that access. See the administrator of the resource to obtain a username or login ID as well as a password.

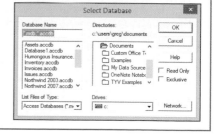

Import Data from a Data Source

You can quickly import data into just about any format by importing the data from a defined data source file.

In this section, you learn how to import data from a *data connection file*. This is a data source that connects you to a wide variety of data, including ODBC, SQL Server, SQL Server OLAP Services, Oracle, and web-based data retrieval services. You can also read the tip to learn how to create a data connection file.

Import Data from a Data Source

1 Click the **Data** tab.

2 Click **Get External Data**.

3 Click **Existing Connections**.

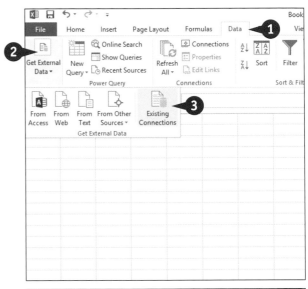

The Existing Connections dialog box appears.

4 Click the data source you want to import.

5 Click **Open**.

The Import Data dialog box appears.

6 Click **Table** (◯ changes to ◉).

A To import the data directly into a PivotTable, click **PivotTable Report** (◯ changes to ◉).

7 Click **Existing worksheet** (◯ changes to ◉).

8 Click the cell where you want the imported data to appear.

B To import the data to a new sheet, click **New worksheet** (◯ changes to ◉).

9 Click **OK**.

Excel imports the data into the worksheet.

How do I create a data connection file?

To create your own data connection (.odc) file, click the **Data** tab, click **Get External Data**, click **From Other Sources**, and then click **From Data Connection Wizard**. Click the data source you want, and then click **Next**.

The next steps depend on the data source. For example, for Microsoft SQL Server or Oracle, you specify the server name or address and your server login data; similarly, for ODBC DSN (Database Source Name) you choose the ODBC data source, specify the location of the file, and select the table or query to which you want to connect.

When you get to the Import Data dialog box, click **OK** to import the data or click **Cancel** if you just want to create the data source file for now.

Import Data from an Access Table

If you want to use Excel to analyze data from a table within an Access database, you can import the table to an Excel worksheet.

In Excel, you can use Microsoft Query to create a database query to extract records from a database, to filter and sort the records, and then to return the results to your worksheet. Excel offers tools creating a database query for any ODBC data source, including an Access database. However, Excel also gives you an easier way to do this: You can import the table directly from the Access database.

Import Data from an Access Table

1. Click the **Data** tab.
2. Click **Get External Data**.
3. Click **From Access**.

   The Select Data Source dialog box appears.

4. Open the folder that contains the database.
5. Click the file.
6. Click **Open**.

Note: If the Data Link Properties dialog box appears, make sure the login information is correct, and then click **Test Connection** until you can connect. Click **OK**.

   The Select Table dialog box appears.

7. Click the table or query you want to import.
8. Click **OK**.

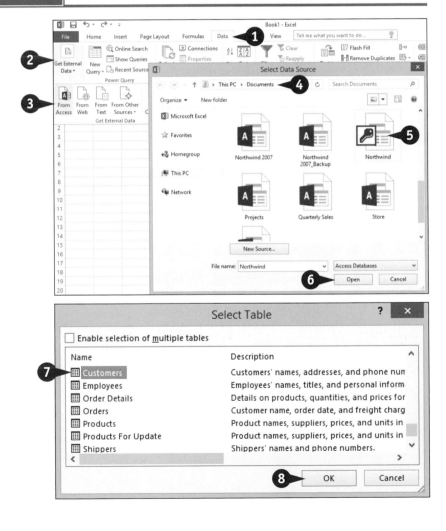

The Import Data dialog box appears.

9 Click **Table** (○ changes to ◉).

A To import the data directly into a PivotTable, click **PivotTable Report** (○ changes to ◉).

10 Select **Existing worksheet** (○ changes to ◉).

11 Click the cell where you want the imported data to appear.

B To import the data to a new sheet, click **New worksheet** (○ changes to ◉).

12 Click **OK**.

Excel imports the data to the worksheet.

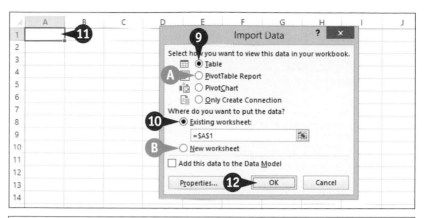

TIP

Why am I prompted multiple times for my password?

To avoid this extra step, tell Excel to save the database password along with the external data. Click the **Data** tab, click the **Refresh All** drop-down arrow (▼), and then click **Connection Properties**. In the Connection Properties dialog box, click the **Definition** tab, and then select the **Save password** check box (☐ changes to ☑). Click **Yes**, and then click **OK**.

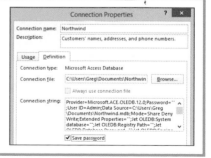

Import Data from a Word Table

Word tables are collections of rows, columns, and cells that look like Excel ranges. You can insert fields into Word table cells to perform calculations. In fact, Word fields support cell references, built-in functions such as SUM and AVERAGE, and operators such as addition (+) and multiplication (*), to build formulas that calculate results based on the table data.

However, even the most powerful Word formulas cannot perform the tasks available to you in Excel, which offers much more sophisticated data analysis tools. Therefore, to analyze your Word table data properly, you should import the table into an Excel worksheet.

Import Data from a Word Table

1. Launch Microsoft Word and open the document that contains the table.

2. Click a cell inside the table you want to import.

3. Click the **Layout** tab.

4. Click **Select**.

5. Click **Select Table**.

   Ⓐ You can also select the table by clicking the table selection handle (⊞).

6. Click the **Home** tab.

7. Click **Copy** (📋).

   You can also press Ctrl + C.

   Word copies the table to the Clipboard.

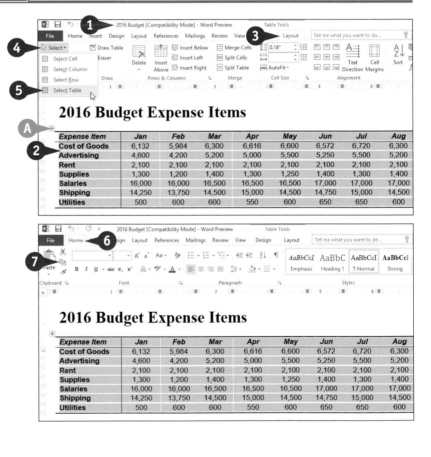

174

8 Switch to the Excel workbook into which you want to import the table.

9 Click the cell where you want the table to appear.

10 Click the **Home** tab.

11 Click **Paste** ( ).

You can also press Ctrl + V .

Excel pastes the Word table data.

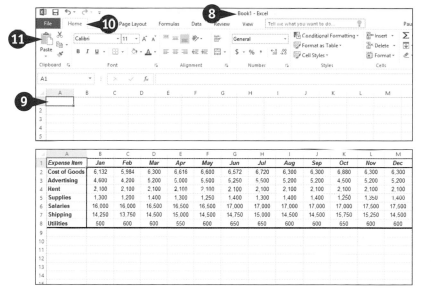

TIP

If I make changes to the Word data, are those changes automatically reflected in the Excel data?

No. If this is a concern, a better approach is to shift the data's container application from Word to Excel. That is, after you paste the table data into Excel, copy the Excel range, switch to Word, click the **Home** tab, click the **Paste** drop-down arrow ( ), and then click **Paste Special**. In the Paste Special dialog box, click **HTML Format** in the **As** list, and then click **Paste link** (changes to). Click **OK**, and the resulting table is linked to the Excel data. This means that any changes you make to the data in Excel automatically appear in the Word table. Note, however, that if you change the data in Word, you cannot update the original data in Excel.

Import Data from a Text File

Today, most data resides in some kind of special format, such as an Excel workbook, Access database, or web page. However, it is still relatively common to find data stored in simple text files because text is a universal format that works on any system and a wide variety of programs. You can analyze the data contained in certain text files by importing the data into an Excel worksheet.

Note, however, that although you can import any text file into Excel, you will get the best results if you only import *delimited* or *fixed-width* text files. See the tip to learn more.

Import Data from a Text File

Start the Text Import Wizard

1. Click the cell where you want the imported data to appear.

2. Click the **Data** tab.

3. Click **Get External Data**.

4. Click **From Text**.

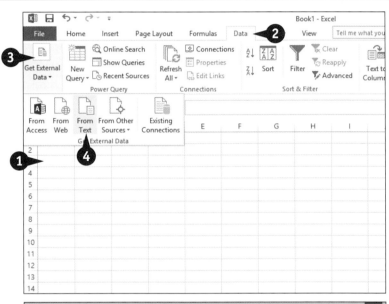

The Import Text File dialog box appears.

5. Open the folder that contains the text file.

6. Click the text file.

7. Click **Import**.

The Text Import Wizard – Step 1 of 3 dialog box appears.

Note: For delimited text, continue with the subsection "Import Delimited Data"; for fixed-width text, skip to the subsection "Import Fixed-Width Data."

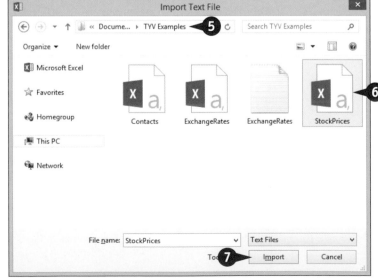

Import Delimited Data

1 Click **Delimited** (○ changes to ◉).

2 Use the **Start import at row** spin box
(↕) to set the first row you want to
import.

3 If the first import row consists of
column headers, select the **My data has
headers** check box (☐ changes to ☑).

4 Click **Next**.

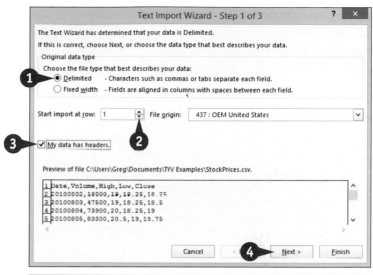

The Text Import Wizard – Step 2 of 3
dialog box appears.

5 Select the check box beside the
delimiter character that your text data
uses (☐ changes to (☑).

Ⓐ If you choose the correct delimiter,
the data appears in separate columns.

6 Click **Next**.

The Text Import Wizard – Step 3 of 3
dialog box appears.

Note: To complete this section, follow the
steps in the subsection "Finish the Text
Import Wizard."

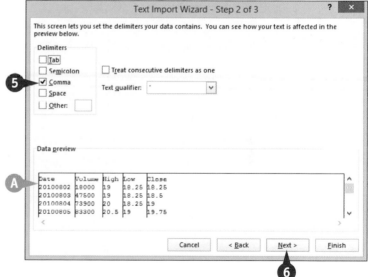

TIP

What are delimited and fixed-width text files?

A *delimited* text file uses a text structure in which each item on a line of text is separated by a character
called a *delimiter*. The most common text delimiter is the comma (,). A delimited text file is imported into
Excel by treating each line of text as a record and each item between the delimiter as a field.

A *fixed-width* text file uses a text structure in which all the items on a line of text use a set amount of
space — say, 10 or 20 characters — and these fixed widths are the same on every line of text. A fixed-width
text file is imported into Excel by treating each line of text as a record and each fixed-width item as a field.

continued ►

If you are importing data that uses the fixed-width structure, you need to tell Excel where the separation between each field occurs.

In a fixed-width text file, each column of data is a constant width. The Text Import Wizard is usually quite good at determining the width of each column, and in most cases, the wizard automatically sets up *column break lines*, which are vertical lines that separate one field from the next. However, titles or introductory text at the beginning of the file can impair the wizard's calculations. Make sure the proposed break lines are accurate.

Import Data from a Text File (continued)

Import Fixed-Width Data

Note: You need to have run through the steps in the subsection "Start the Text Import Wizard" before continuing with this section.

1 Click **Fixed width** (○ changes to ●).

2 Use the **Start import at row** spin box (⟰) to set the first row you want to import.

3 If the first import row consists of column headers, select the **My data has headers** check box (☐ changes to ☑).

4 Click **Next**.

The Text Import Wizard – Step 2 of 3 dialog box appears.

5 Click and drag a break line to set the width of each column.

Ⓑ To create a break line, you can click the ruler at the point where you want the break to appear.

Ⓒ To delete a break line, you can double-click it.

6 Click **Next**.

The Text Import Wizard – Step 3 of 3 dialog box appears.

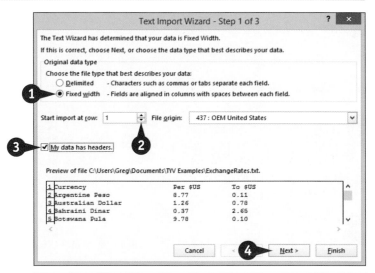

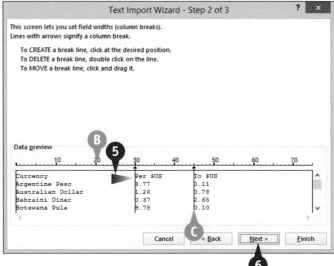

Finish the Text Import Wizard

1 Click a column.

2 Click the radio button of the data format you want Excel to apply to the column (○ changes to ◉).

D If you select the Date option, you can use this drop-down list to select the date format your data uses.

3 Repeat steps **1** and **2** to set the data format for all the columns.

4 Click **Finish**.

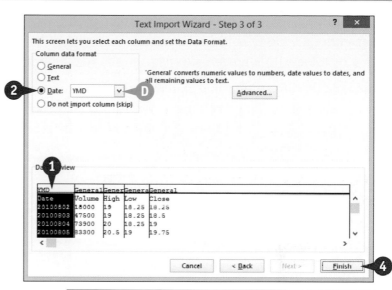

The Import Data dialog box appears.

5 Click **Existing worksheet** (○ changes to ◉).

E If you want the data to appear in a new sheet, click **New worksheet** (○ changes to ◉).

6 Click **OK**.

Excel imports the data to the worksheet.

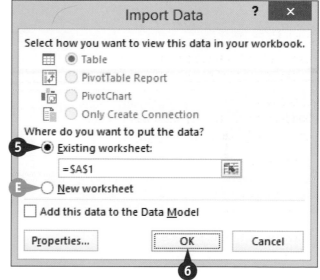

What do I do when my data uses a comma instead of a dot as the decimal separator?

To import such data, click **Advanced** in the Text Import Wizard – Step 3 of 3 dialog box to display the Advanced Text Import Settings dialog box. Click the **Decimal separator** drop-down arrow (▼), and then click the text's decimal separator. You can also click the **Thousands separator** drop-down arrow (▼), and then click the text's thousands separator.

If I make a mistake when importing a text file, do I have to start over?

No. Click any cell in the imported data, click the **Data** tab, click the **Refresh All** drop-down arrow (▼), and then click **Connection Properties**. Click the **Definition** tab, and then click **Edit Query**. The Import Text File dialog box appears. Click the file you want, and then click **Import**. Excel launches the Import Text Wizard so you can run through the options again.

Import Data from a Web Page

Data is often available on web pages. Although this data is usually text, some web page data comes as either a table (a rectangular array of rows and columns) or as preformatted text (text that has been structured with a predefined spacing used to organize data into columns with fixed widths).

Both types are suitable for import into Excel so that you can perform more extensive data analysis. To import web page data, the file must reside on your computer or on your network.

Import Data from a Web Page

1 Click the cell where you want the imported data to appear.

2 Click the **Data** tab.

3 Click **Get External Data**.

4 Click **From Web**.

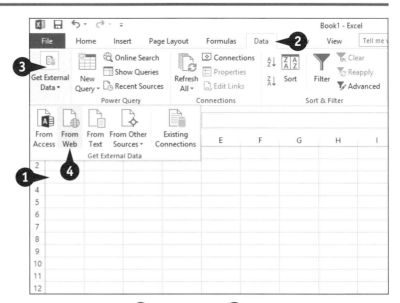

The New Web Query dialog box appears.

5 Type the address of the web page.

6 Click **Go**.

A Excel loads the page into the dialog box.

7 Click the **Select Table** icon (→) beside the table that you want to import.

B Excel selects the table.

8 Click **Import**.

The Import Data dialog box appears.

9 Click **Existing worksheet** (○ changes to ◉).

C If you want the data to appear in a new sheet, click **New worksheet** (○ changes to ◉).

10 Click **OK**.

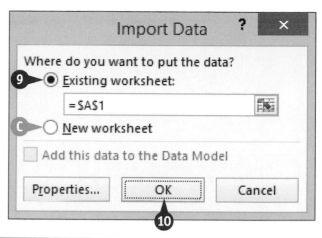

Excel imports the data to the worksheet.

	A	B		C	D	E	F	G
1	Products							
2	Beverages	Chai		10 boxes x 20 bags	$18.00	39	10	0
3	Beverages	Chang		24 - 12 oz bottles	$19.00	17	25	0
4	Beverages	Chartreuse verte		750 cc per bottle	$18.00	69	5	0
5	Beverages	Côte de Blaye		12 - 75 cl bottles	$263.50	17	15	0
6	Beverages	Ipoh Coffee		16 - 500 g tins	$46.00	17	25	0
7	Beverages	Lakkalikööri		500 ml	$18.00	57	20	0
8	Beverages	Laughing Lumberjack Lager		24 - 12 oz bottles	$14.00	52	10	0
9	Beverages	Outback Lager		24 - 355 ml bottles	$15.00	15	30	0
10	Beverages	Rhönbräu Klosterbier		24 0.5 l bottles	$7.75	125	25	0
11	Beverages	Sasquatch Ale		24 - 12 oz bottles	$14.00	111	15	0
12	Beverages	Steeleye Stout		24 - 12 oz bottles	$18.00	20	15	0
13	Condiments	Aniseed Syrup		12 - 550 ml bottles	$10.00	13	25	0

TIP

Are there other ways to import a web page into Excel?

Yes. Excel gives you two other methods for creating web queries. Both of these alternative methods assume that you already have the web page open in Internet Explorer:

- Right-click the page, and then click **Export to Microsoft Excel**.
- Copy the web page text, switch to Excel, and then paste the text. When the Paste Options smart tag appears, click the smart tag drop-down arrow (▼), and then click **Refreshable Web Query**.

Each of these methods opens the New Web Query dialog box and automatically loads the web page.

If you want to save the web query for future use in other workbooks, click **Save Query** (⊞) in the New Web Query dialog box, and then use the Save Workspace dialog box to save the query file.

Import Data from an XML File

You can analyze data that currently resides in XML format by importing that data into Excel and then manipulating and analyzing the resulting table.

XML, or extensible markup language, is a standard that enables the management and sharing of structured data using simple text files. These XML files organize data using *tags* that specify the equivalent of a table name and field names. Because XML is just text, if you want to perform data analysis on the XML file, you must import the XML file into an Excel table.

Import Data from an XML File

1 Click the cell where you want the imported data to appear.

2 Click the **Data** tab.

3 Click **Get External Data**.

4 Click **From Other Sources**.

5 Click **From XML Data Import**.

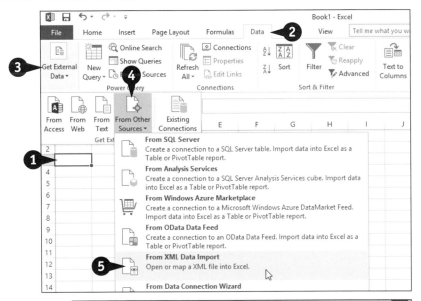

The Select Data Source dialog box appears.

6 Select the folder that contains the XML file you want to import.

7 Click the XML file.

8 Click **Open**.

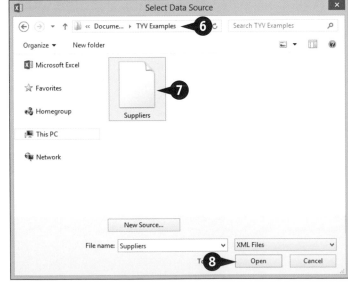

Note: If you see a dialog box that says there is a problem with the data, click **OK**.

The Import Data dialog box appears.

9 Click **XML table in existing worksheet** (○ changes to ◉).

10 Click **OK**.

Excel imports the data into the worksheet as an XML table.

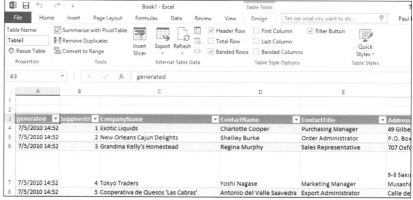

TIPS

What does an XML file look like?

An XML file is a text file that uses a specific structure. Here is a simple XML example that constitutes a single record in a table named *Products:*

```
<Products>
<ProductName>Chai</ProductName>
<CompanyName>Exotic Liquids</CompanyName>
<ContactName>Charlotte Cooper</ContactName>
</Products>
```

Can I remove a field in the XML table?

Yes. Right-click the XML table, click **XML**, and then click **XML Source** to display the XML Source pane. The XML Source pane displays a list of the fields — called *elements* in the XML table. To remove an element, right-click it and then click **Remove element.** To add an element back into the XML list, right-click the element and then click **Map element.**

Refresh Imported Data

External data often changes; you can ensure that you are working with the most up-to-date version of the information by refreshing the imported data.

Refreshing the imported data means retrieving the most current version of the source data. This is usually a straightforward operation. However, it is possible to construct a query that accesses confidential information or destroys some or all of the external data. Therefore, when you refresh imported data, Excel always lets you know the potential risks and asks if you are sure the query is safe.

Refresh Imported Data

Refresh Non-Text Data

1 Click any cell inside the imported data.

2 Click the **Data** tab.

3 Click the **Refresh All** drop-down arrow (▼).

4 Click **Refresh**.

Note: You can also refresh the current data by pressing Alt + F5.

A To refresh all the imported data in the current workbook, you can click **Refresh All**, or press Ctrl + Alt + F5.

Excel refreshes the imported data.

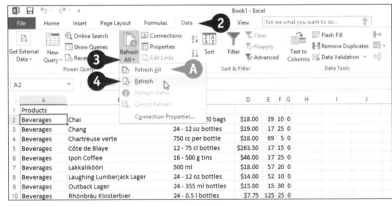

Refresh Text Data

1. Click any cell inside the imported text data.

2. Click the **Data** tab.

3. Click the **Refresh All** drop-down arrow (▼).

4. Click **Refresh**.

Note: You can also refresh the current data by pressing `Alt` + `F5`.

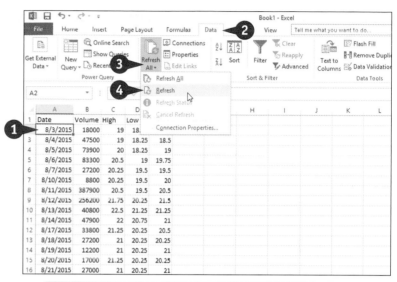

The Import Text File dialog box appears.

5. Open the folder that contains the text file.

6. Click the text file.

7. Click **Import**.

Excel refreshes the imported text data.

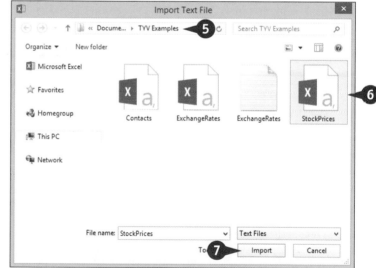

TIPS

Is there an easier way to refresh data regularly?
In most cases, you can set up a schedule that automatically refreshes the data at a specified interval. Follow steps **1** to **3** in the subsection "Refresh Non-Text Data," and then click **Connection Properties**. Select the **Refresh Every** check box (☐ changes to ☑). Use the spin box (🔼) to specify the refresh interval in minutes (not every type of imported data supports this feature).

Why does my refresh not seem to be working?
The refresh may take a long time. To check the status of the refresh, follow steps **1** to **3** in the subsection "Refresh Non-Text Data," and then click **Refresh Status** to display the External Data Refresh Status dialog box; click **Close** to continue the refresh. If the refresh is taking too long, repeat steps **1** to **3**, and then click **Cancel Refresh** to stop it.

Separate Cell Text into Columns

You can make imported data easier to analyze by separating the text in each cell into two or more columns of data.

An imported data column may contain multiple items of data. In imported contact data, for example, a column might contain each person's first and last name, separated by a space. This is problematic when sorting the contacts by last name, so you need to organize the names into separate columns. Excel makes this easy with the Text to Columns feature, which examines a column of data and then separates it into two or more columns.

Separate Cell Text into Columns

1 Insert a column to the right of the column you want to separate.

Note: If the data will separate into three or more columns, you can insert as many new columns as you need to hold the separated data.

2 Select the data you want to separate.

3 Click the **Data** tab.

4 Click **Text to Columns** (⊞).

The Convert Text to Columns Wizard – Step 1 of 3 dialog box appears.

5 Click **Delimited** (○ changes to ⊙).

6 Click **Next**.

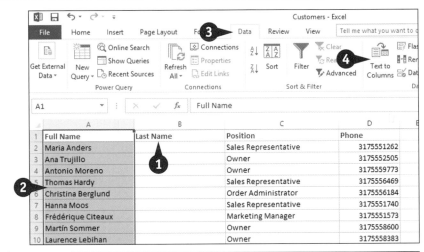

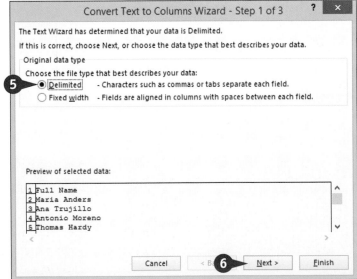

The Convert Text to Columns Wizard –
Step 2 of 3 dialog box appears.

7 Select the check box beside the delimiter
character that your text data uses
(☐ changes to ✔).

Ⓐ If you choose the correct delimiter, the
data appears in separate columns.

8 Click **Next**.

The Convert Text to Columns Wizard –
Step 3 of 3 dialog box appears.

9 Click a column.

10 Click the radio button of the data format
you want Excel to apply to the column
(○ changes to ●).

Ⓑ If you click the **Date** option, you can use
this list to click the date format your
data uses.

11 Repeat steps **9** and **10** to set the data
format for all the columns.

12 Click **Finish**.

Excel asks if you want to replace the
contents of the destination cells.

13 Click **OK** (not shown).

Excel separates the data.

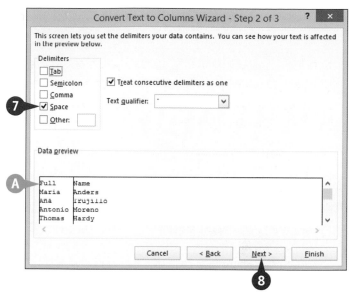

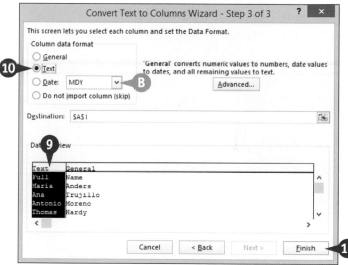

TIPS

What do I do if my column contains fixed-width text?

Follow steps **1** to **4** to start the Convert
Text to Columns Wizard. Click the **Fixed
width** radio button (○ changes to ●).
Click **Next**, and then click and drag a break
line to set the width of each column. Click
Next, and then follow steps **9** to **13** to
complete the wizard.

Does Excel always create only one extra column from the data?

No, not always. For example, in a column of contact names,
if any of those names use three words, Excel assumes that
you want to create two extra columns for all the data.
Unfortunately, this might cause Excel to overwrite some of
your existing data. Therefore, before separating data into
columns, check the data to see exactly how many columns
Excel will create.

CHAPTER 9

Printing
Workbooks

If you want to distribute hard copies of one or more worksheets or an entire workbook, you can use the Excel Print feature. Before you print, you can adjust print-related options such as the margins, page orientation, and paper size.

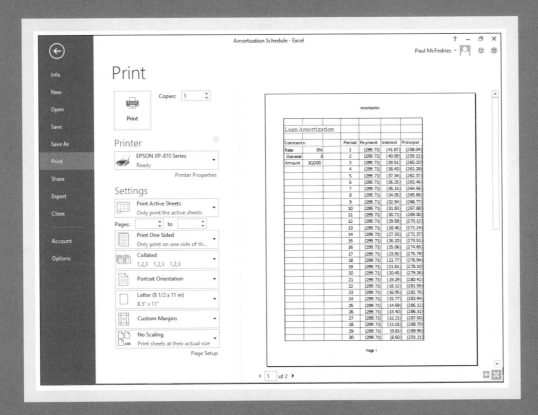

Adjust the Workbook Margins

You can get more space on the printed page to display your worksheet data by using smaller page margins. The *margins* are the blank areas that surround the printed data. For example, if you find that Excel is printing extra pages because your data is a bit too wide or a bit too long to fit on a single page, you can reduce either the left and right margins or the top and bottom margins.

If you or another person will be writing notes on the printouts, consider using wider margins to allow more room for the notes.

Adjust the Workbook Margins

Use the Ribbon

1 Open the workbook you want to print.

2 Click the **Page Layout** tab.

3 Click **Margins** (⊞).

Ⓐ If you see a margin setting you want to use, click the setting and skip the rest of these steps.

4 Click **Custom Margins**.

The Page Setup dialog box appears with the Margins tab selected.

5 Use the spin boxes to specify the margin sizes in inches.

Note: Do not make the margins too small or your document may not print properly. Most printers cannot handle margins smaller than about 0.25 inch, although you should consult your printer manual to confirm this. In particular, see if your printer offers a "borderless" printing option.

6 Click **OK**.

Excel adjusts the margin sizes.

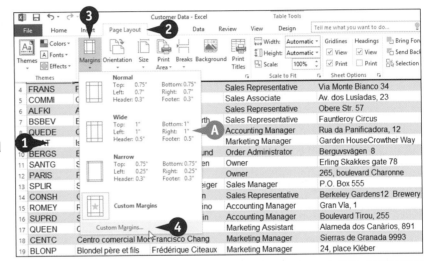

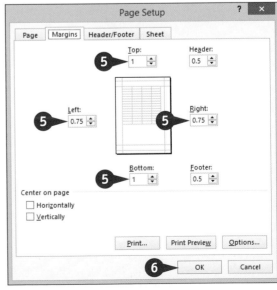

Use the Ruler

1 Open the workbook you want to print.

2 Click **Page Layout** (▤).

3 Move the ▷ over the right edge of the ruler's left margin area (▷ changes to ↔).

4 Click and drag the edge of the margin to set the left margin width.

5 Click and drag the left edge of the right margin area to set the margin width.

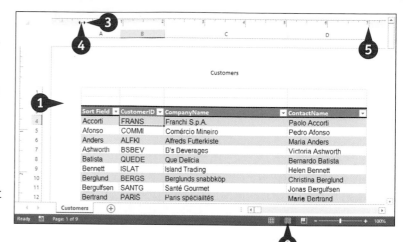

6 Move the ▷ over the bottom edge of the ruler's top margin area (▷ changes to ↕).

7 Click and drag the edge of the margin to set the top margin width.

8 Click and drag the top edge of the bottom margin area (not shown) to set the bottom margin width.

Note: You need to scroll down to the bottom of the page to see the bottom margin.

Excel adjusts the margin sizes.

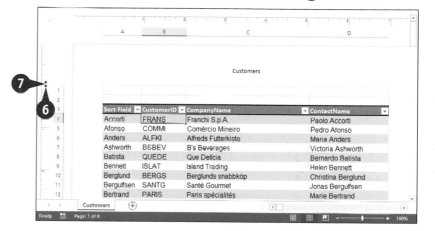

TIPS

I increased my margin sizes to get more room around the text. Is there a way to center the text on the page?
Yes. This is a good idea if you want to ensure that you have the same amount of whitespace above and below the text, and to the left and right of the text. Follow steps **1** to **4** in the "Use the Ribbon" subsection to open the Page Setup dialog box with the Margins tab selected. Click **Horizontally** (☐ changes to ☑), click **Vertically** (☐ changes to ☑), and then click **OK**.

What are the header and footer margins?
The header margin is the space between the workbook header and the top of the page, and the footer margin is the space between the workbook footer and the bottom of the page. (See Chapter 7 to learn how to add a header and footer to your workbook.) In the Margins tab of the Page Setup dialog box, use the **Header** and **Footer** spin boxes to set these margins.

Change the Page Orientation

You can improve the look of your printout by changing the page orientation to suit your data. The page orientation determines whether Excel prints more rows or columns on a page. Portrait orientation is taller, so it prints more rows; landscape orientation is wider, so it prints more columns.

Choose the orientation based on your worksheet data. If your worksheet has many rows and only a few columns, choose portrait; if your worksheet has many columns but just a few rows, choose landscape.

Change the Page Orientation

1 Open the workbook you want to print.

2 Click the **Page Layout** tab.

3 Click **Orientation** (📄).

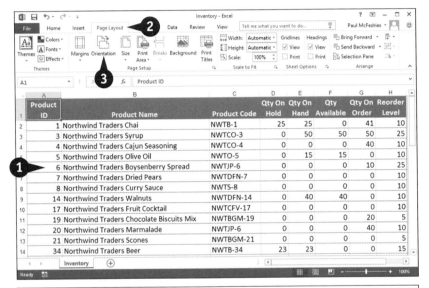

4 Click the orientation you want to use.

Ⓐ Excel adjusts the orientation.

Ⓑ Click 📄 to see the orientation.

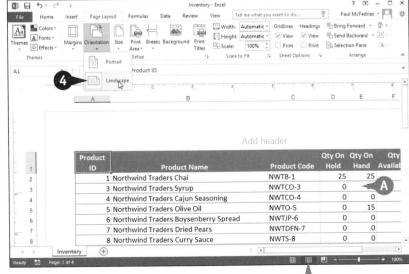

192

Insert a Page Break

You can control what data appears on each printed page by inserting a page break in your worksheet. A *page break* is a location within a worksheet where Excel begins a new printed page. Excel normally inserts its own page breaks based on the number and height of rows in the sheet, the number and width of the sheet columns, the margin widths, and the page orientation.

A vertical page break starts a new page at a particular column; a horizontal page break starts a new page at a particular row.

Insert a Page Break

1 Open the workbook you want to print.

2 Select the cell to the right of and below where you want the vertical and horizontal page breaks to appear.

Note: Select a cell in row 1 to create just a vertical page break; select a cell in column A to create just a horizontal page break.

3 Click the **Page Layout** tab.

4 Click **Breaks** (⊬).

5 Click **Insert Page Break**.

Ⓐ Excel inserts the page breaks and indicates the breaks with thicker horizontal and vertical lines.

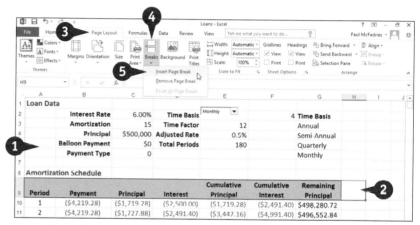

Choose a Paper Size

You can customize your print job by choosing a paper size that is appropriate for your printout. For example, if your worksheet has many rows, you might prefer to print it on a longer sheet of paper, such as a legal-size page (8½ inches wide by 14 inches long). Similarly, if your worksheet has many columns, you might also want to use a longer sheet of paper, but switch to landscape mode, as described in the "Change the Page Orientation" section earlier in the chapter.

Check your printer manual to make sure your printer can handle the paper size you select.

Choose a Paper Size

1 Open the workbook you want to print.

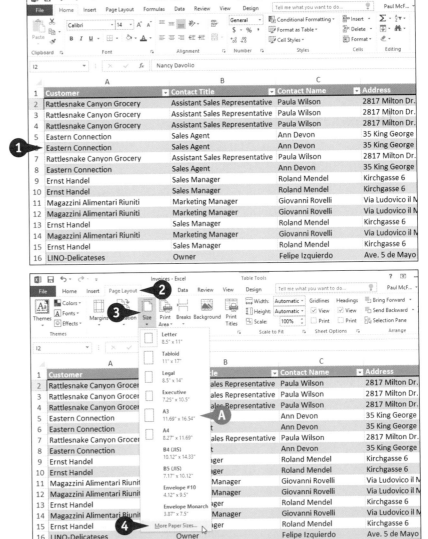

2 Click the **Page Layout** tab.

3 Click **Size** (🗋).

Ⓐ If you see a page size you want to use, click the size and skip the rest of these steps.

4 Click **More Paper Sizes**.

The Page Setup dialog box appears with the Page tab selected.

5 Click the **Paper size** ▼ and then click the size you want to use.

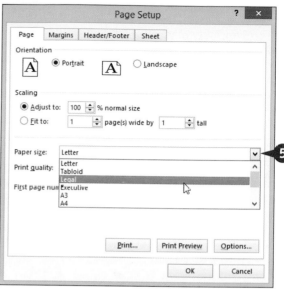

6 Click **OK**.

Excel uses the new paper size option when you print the workbook.

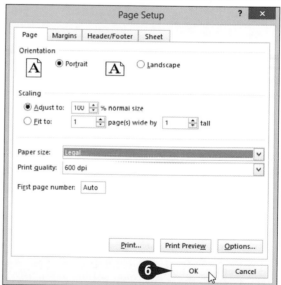

TIP

Is there a way to ensure that all my worksheet columns fit onto a single page?
Yes. First, try selecting a wider page size as described in this section. You can also try reducing the left and right margins, as described in the "Adjust the Workbook Margins" section earlier in the chapter. Alternatively, switch to the landscape orientation, as described in the "Change the Page Orientation" section earlier in the chapter. You can also follow steps **1** to **4** to display the Page Setup dialog box with the Page tab selected. Click **Fit to** (◯ changes to ◉), and set the **page(s) wide by** spin box to 1. Set the **tall** spin box to a number large enough that all your printed rows will fit on a single page. (If you are not sure about the correct number, you can click **Print Preview** to check.) Click **OK**.

Set the Print Area

You can control the cells that Excel includes in the printout by setting the print area for the worksheet. The print area is a range of cells that you select. When Excel prints the workbook, it prints only the cells within the print area.

You normally define a single range of cells as the print area, but it is possible to set up two or more ranges as the print area. See the first tip for more information.

Set the Print Area

1 Open the workbook you want to print.

2 Select the range that you want to print.

3 Click the **Page Layout** tab.

4 Click **Print Area** (🖨).

5 Click **Set Print Area**.

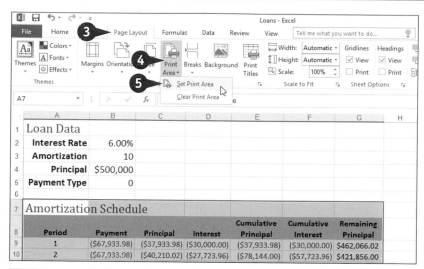

A Excel displays a border around the print area.

When you print the worksheet, Excel prints only the cells within the print area.

Can I define two different ranges as the print area?

Yes. The easiest way to do this is to follow the steps in this section to set the first range as the print area. Next, select the second range, click the **Page Layout** tab, click 🖨, and then click **Add to Print Area**. You can repeat this procedure to add as many ranges as you require to the print area.

How do I remove an existing print area?

First, note that if you just want to set a new print area, you do not need to remove the existing print area first. Instead, select the range you want to use and then follow steps **3** to **5**. Excel replaces the original print area with the new one. If you no longer want a print area defined, click the **Page Layout** tab, click 🖨, and then click **Clear Print Area**.

Configure Titles to Print on Each Page

You can make your printout easier to read by configuring the worksheet to print the range titles on each page of the printout. For example, if your data has a row of headings at the top, you can configure the worksheet to display those headings at the top of each printout page.

Similarly, if your data has a column of headings at the left, you can configure the worksheet to display those headings on the left side of each printout page.

Configure Titles to Print on Each Page

1 Open the workbook you want to print.

2 Click the tab of the worksheet you want to configure.

3 Click the **Page Layout** tab.

4 Click **Print Titles** (🖼).

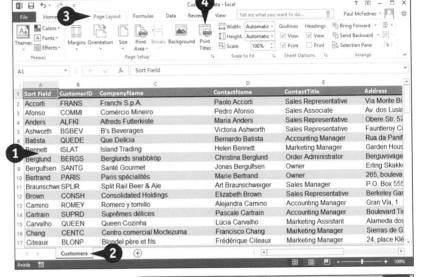

Excel opens the Page Setup dialog box with the Sheet tab displayed.

5 Click inside the **Rows to repeat at top** range box.

6 Click **Collapse Dialog** (🖾).

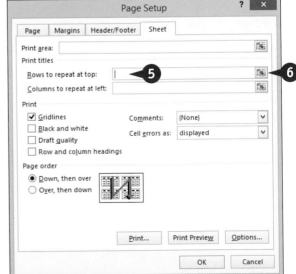

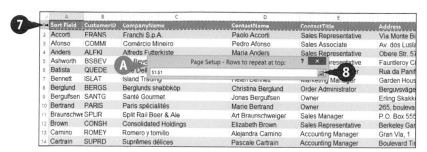

Ⓐ Excel collapses the Page Setup dialog box.

The mouse pointer changes from ▷ to ➡.

7 Use the mouse ➡ to click the row that you want to appear at the top of each printed page.

If you want more than one row to repeat at the top of each page, use the mouse ➡ to click the last row that you want to repeat.

8 Click **Restore Dialog** (🖳).

Ⓑ The address of the row appears in the **Rows to repeat at top** box.

9 Click **OK**.

When you print this worksheet, Excel displays the selected row at the top of each page.

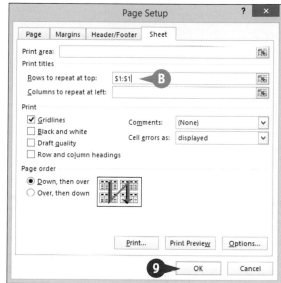

TIP

How do I configure my worksheet to print a column of headings on each page?

If your headings appear in a column rather than a row, you can still configure the sheet to print them on each page. Follow these steps:

1 Follow steps **1** to **4** to open the Page Setup dialog box with the Sheet tab displayed.

2 Click inside the **Columns to repeat at left** range box.

3 Click 🖳.

4 Use the mouse ⬇ to click the column that you want to appear on the left of each printed page.

5 Click 🖳.

6 Click **OK**.

Preview the Printout

You can save time and paper by using the Print Preview feature to examine your printout on-screen before you send it to the printer. You can use Print Preview to make sure settings such as margins, page orientation, page breaks, print areas, and sheet titles all result in the printout you want.

If you see a problem in the preview, you can use the Print Preview screen to make adjustments to some printout options.

Preview the Printout

1 Open the workbook you want to print.

2 Click the tab of the worksheet you want to preview.

3 Click the **File** tab.

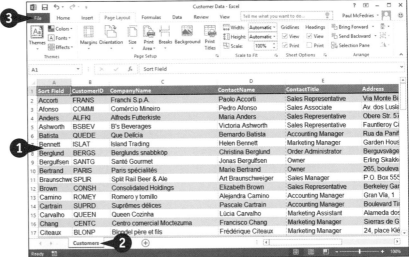

4 Click **Print**.

The Print window appears.

A Excel displays a preview of the printout.

Note: If you do not see the preview, click **Show Print Preview**.

5 Click **Print Preview Next Page** (▶) to scroll through the printout pages.

6 Click **Print Preview Previous Page**
(◀) to return to a printout page.

B You can click the **Page Orientation** ▼ to change the page orientation.

C You can click the **Page Size** ▼ to change the page size.

D You can click the **Margins** ▼ to change the margins.

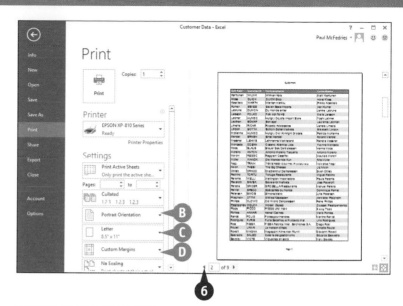

7 When you are done, click **Back**
(⬅) to return to the workbook.

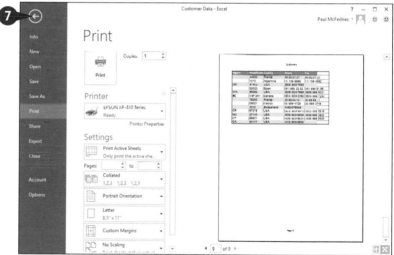

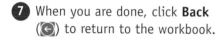

TIP

Can I fine-tune the margins in Print Preview?

Yes. The Margins list only offers a few predefined margin sets. To define custom margins in Print Preview, follow these steps:

1 Click **Show Margins** (▦).

A Print Preview augments the preview with lines that indicate the margins.

2 Click and drag a line to adjust that margin.

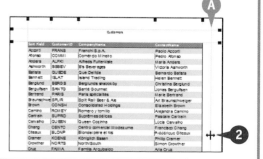

Print a Workbook

When you need a hard copy of your document, either for your files or to distribute to someone else, you can send the document to your printer.

This section assumes that you have a printer connected to your computer and that the printer is turned on. Also, before printing you should check that your printer has enough paper to complete the print job.

Print a Workbook

1 Open the workbook you want to print.

2 If you only want to print a single worksheet, click the tab of that worksheet.

Note: To print multiple worksheets, hold down **Ctrl** and click the tab of each sheet you want to print.

3 Click the **File** tab.

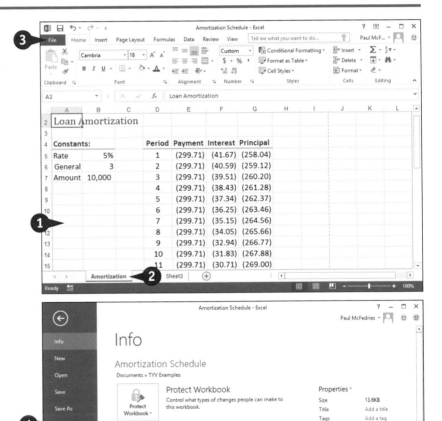

4 Click **Print**.

Note: You can also press **Ctrl**+**P**.

The Print window appears.

5 Type the number of copies you want to print in the **Copies** text box.

A If you have more than one printer, click the **Printer** ▼ and then click the printer that you want to use.

B By default, Print Active Sheets appears in the Print What list, which tells Excel to print only the selected sheets. If you want to print all the sheets in the workbook, click the **Print What** ▼ and then click **Print Entire Workbook**.

6 Click **Print**.

Excel prints the document.

C The printer icon (🖨) appears in the taskbar's notification area while the document prints.

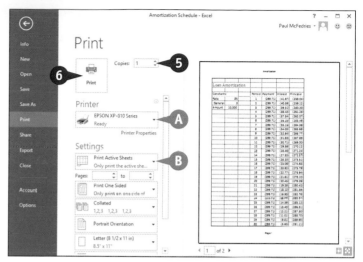

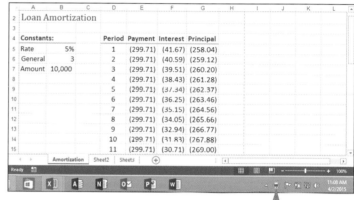

TIPS

Is there a faster way to print?
Yes. To print a single copy of the selected worksheet, you can use the Excel Quick Print command to send the worksheet directly to your default printer. Click ▼ in the Quick Access Toolbar, and then click **Quick Print** to add this command to the toolbar. You can then click **Quick Print** (🖨) to print the current worksheet without having to go through the Print window.

Can I print just part of a worksheet?
Yes, you can tell Excel to print just a range. Begin by selecting the range or ranges you want to print. (See Chapter 1 to learn how to select a range.) Follow steps **3** and **4** to open the Print window and choose the number of copies. Click the **Print What** ▼ and then click **Print Selection**. Click **Print**.

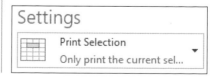

CHAPTER 10

Working with Tables

The forte of Excel is spreadsheet work, of course, but its row-and-column layout also makes it a natural flat-file database manager. That is, instead of entering data and then using the Excel tools to build formulas and analyze that data, you can also use Excel simply to store data in a special structure called a table.

Understanding Tables

In Excel, a *table* is a rectangular range of cells used to store data. The table is a collection of related information with an organizational structure that makes it easy to find or extract data from its contents. To get the most out of Excel tables, you need to understand a few basic concepts, such as how a table is like a database, the advantages of tables, and how tables help with data analysis.

A Table Is a Database

A table is a type of database where the data is organized into rows and columns: Each column represents a database field, which is a single type of information, such as a name, address, or phone number; each row represents a database record, which is a collection of associated field values, such as the information for a specific contact.

	ContactName	ContactTitle	Address
1	ContactName	ContactTitle	Address
2	Paolo Accorti	Sales Representative	Via Monte Bianco 34
3	Pedro Afonso	Sales Associate	Av. dos Lusíadas, 23
4	Maria Anders	Sales Representative	Obere Str. 57
5	Victoria Ashworth	Sales Representative	Fauntleroy Circus
6	Bernardo Batista	Accounting Manager	Rua da Panificadora, 12
7	Helen Bennett	Marketing Manager	Garden HouseCrowther Way
8	Christina Berglund	Order Administrator	Berguvsvägen 8
9	Jonas Bergulfsen	Owner	Erling Skakkes gate 78
10	Marie Bertrand	Owner	265, boulevard Charonne
11	Art Braunschweiger	Sales Manager	P.O. Box 555
12	Elizabeth Brown	Sales Representative	Berkeley Gardens12 Brewer
13	Alejandra Camino	Accounting Manager	Gran Vía, 1

Advantages of a Table

A table differs from a regular Excel range in that Excel offers a set of tools that makes it easier for you to work with the data within a table. As you see in this chapter, these tools make it easy to convert existing worksheet data into a table, add new records and fields to a table, delete existing records and fields, insert rows to show totals, and apply styles.

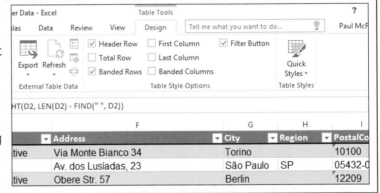

Data Analysis

Tables are also useful tools for analyzing your data. For example, as you see later in this chapter in the "Create a PivotTable" section, you can easily use a table as the basis of a PivotTable, which is a special object for summarizing and analyzing data. In Chapter 11, you also learn how to sort table records and how to filter table data to show only specific records.

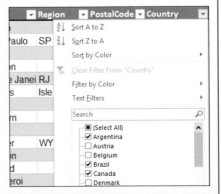

Get to Know Table Features

Although a table looks much like a regular Excel range, it offers a number of features that differentiate it from a range. To understand these differences and make it as easy as possible to learn how to build and use tables, you need to know the various features in a typical table, such as the table rows and columns, the table headers, and the filter buttons.

A Table Column

A single type of information, such as names, addresses, or phone numbers. In an Excel table, each column is the equivalent of a database field.

B Column Headers

The unique names you assign to every table column that serve to label the type of data in each column. These names are always found in the first row of the table.

C Table Cell

An item in a table column that represents a single instance of that column's data, such as a name, address, or phone number. In an Excel table, each cell is equivalent to a database field value.

D Table Row

A collection of associated table cells, such as the data for a single contact. In Excel tables, each row is the equivalent of a database record.

E Column Filter Button

A feature that gives you access to a set of commands that perform various actions on a column, such as sorting or filtering the column data.

CompanyName	ContactName	ContactTitle	Address	City
Franchi S.p.A.	Paolo Accorti	Sales Representative	Via Monte Bianco 34	Torino
Comércio Mineiro	Pedro Afonso	Sales Associate	Av. dos Lusíadas, 23	São Paulo
Alfreds Futterkiste	Maria Anders	Sales Representative	Obere Str. 57	Berlin
B's Beverages	Victoria Ashworth	Sales Representative	Fauntleroy Circus	London
Que Delicia	Bernardo Batista	Accounting Manager	Rua da Panificadora, 12	Rio de Janei
Island Trading	Helen Bennett	Marketing Manager	Garden HouseCrowther Way	Cowes
Berglunds snabbköp	Christina Berglund	Order Administrator	Berguvsvägen 8	Luleå
Santé Gourmet	Jonas Bergulfsen	Owner	Erling Skakkes gate 78	Stavern
Paris spécialités	Marie Bertrand	Owner	265, boulevard Charonne	Paris
Split Rail Beer & Ale	Art Braunschweiger	Manager	P.O. Box 555	Lander
Consolidated Holdings	Elizabeth Brown	Sales Representative	Berkeley Gardens12 Brewery	London
Romero y tomillo	Alejandra Camino	Accounting Manager	Gran Via, 1	Madrid
Suprêmes délices	Pascale Cartrain	Accounting Manager	Boulevard Tirou, 255	Charleroi
Queen Cozinha	Lúcia Carvalho	Marketing Assistant	Alameda dos Canàrios, 891	São Paulo
Centro comercial Moctezuma	Francisco Chang	Marketing Manager	Sierras de Granada 9993	México D.F.
Blondel père et fils	Frédérique Citeaux	Marketing Manager	24, place Kléber	Strasbourg
Königlich Essen	Philip Cramer	Sales Associate	Maubelstr. 90	Brandenburg
North/South	Simon Crowther	Sales Associate	South House300 Queensbridge	London

Convert a Range to a Table

In Excel 2016, you cannot create a table from scratch and then fill that table with data. Instead, you must first create a range that includes at least some of the data you want in your table and then convert that range to a table.

Note that you do not need to enter all your data before converting the range to a table. Once you have the table, you can add new rows and columns as needed, as described later in this chapter. However, it is best to decide up front whether you want your table to have column headers.

Convert a Range to a Table

1 Click a cell within the range that you want to convert to a table.

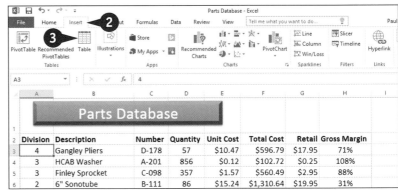

2 Click the **Insert** tab.

3 Click **Table** (▦).

Note: You can also choose the Table command by pressing `Ctrl` + `T`.

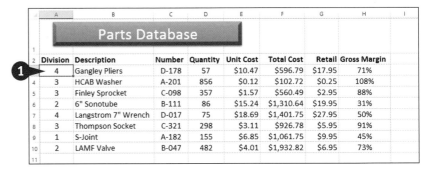

The Create Table dialog box appears.

Ⓐ Excel selects the range that it will convert to a table.

Ⓑ If you want to change the range, click 🔳, drag the mouse ✛ over the new range, and then click 🔳.

④ If your range has labels that you want to use as column headers, click **My table has headers** (☐ changes to ✔).

⑤ Click **OK**.

Excel converts the range to a table.

Ⓒ Excel applies a table format to the range.

Ⓓ The Table Tools contextual tab appears.

Ⓔ Filter buttons appear in each column heading.

⑥ Click the **Design** tab to see the Excel table design tools.

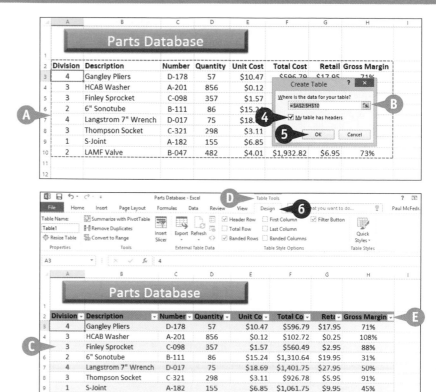

TIPS

Do I need to add labels to the top of each column before converting my range to a table?
No, you do not need to add labels before performing the conversion. In this case, follow steps **1** to **3** to display the Create Table dialog box, then click **My table has headers** (✔ changes to ☐). After you click **OK**, Excel converts the range to a table and automatically adds headers to each column. These headers use the generic names Column1, Column2, and so on.

If I selected the wrong range for my table, is there a way to tell Excel the correct range?
Yes, although you cannot change the location of the headers. To redefine the range used in the table, first select any cell in the table. Under the Table Tools contextual tab, click the **Design** tab and then click **Resize Table** (⊞) to open the Resize Table dialog box. Drag the mouse ✛ over the new range and then click **OK**.

Select Table Data

If you want to work with part of a table, you first need to select that part of the table. For example, if you want to apply a format to an entire column or copy an entire row, you first need to select that column or row.

The normal range-selection techniques in Excel often do not work well with a table. For example, selecting an entire worksheet column or row does not work because no table uses up an entire worksheet column or row. Instead, Excel provides several tools for selecting a table column (just the data or the data and the header), a table row, or the entire table.

Select Table Data

Select a Table Column

1 Right-click any cell in the column you want to select.

2 Click **Select**.

3 Click **Table Column Data**.

Excel selects all the column's data cells.

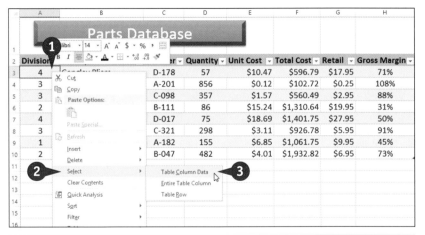

Select a Table Column and Header

1 Right-click any cell in the column you want to select.

2 Click **Select**.

3 Click **Entire Table Column**.

Excel selects the column's data and header.

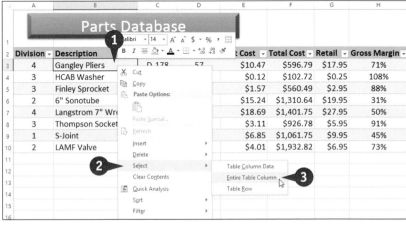

Select a Table Row

1 Right-click any cell in the row you want to select.

2 Click **Select**.

3 Click **Table Row**.

Excel selects all the data within the row.

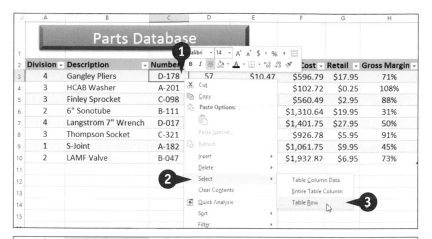

Select the Entire Table

1 Click any cell within the table.

2 Press **Ctrl** + **A**.

Excel selects the entire table.

Division	Description	Number	Quantity	Unit Cost	Total Cost	Retail	Gross Margin
4	Gangley Pliers	D-178	57	$10.47	$596.79	$17.95	71%
3	HCAB Washer	A-201	856	$0.12	$102.72	$0.25	108%
3	Finley Sprocket	C-098	357	$1.57	$560.49	$2.95	88%
2	6" Sonotube	B-111	86	$15.24	$1,310.64	$19.95	31%
4	Langstrom 7" Wrench	D-017	75	$18.69	$1,401.75	$27.95	50%
3	Thompson Socket	C-321	298	$3.11	$926.78	$5.95	91%
1	S-Joint	A-182	155	$6.85	$1,061.75	$9.95	45%
2	LAMF Valve	B-047	482	$4.01	$1,932.82	$6.95	73%

TIP

Can I select multiple columns or rows in a table?

Yes. To select two or more table columns, first select one cell in each of the columns that you want to include in your selection. If the columns are not side-by-side, click the first cell and then hold down **Ctrl** as you click each of the other cells. Right-click any selected cell, click **Select**, and then click **Table Column Data** (or **Entire Table Column** if you also want to include the column headers in the selection).

To select two or more table rows, first select one cell in each of the rows that you want to include in your selection. Again, if the rows are not adjacent, click the first cell and then hold down **Ctrl** as you click each of the other cells. Right-click any selected cell, click **Select**, and then click **Table Row**.

Insert a Table Row

You can add a new record to your Excel table by inserting a new row. You can insert a row either within the table or at the end of the table.

Once you have entered the initial set of data into your table, you will likely add most new records within the table by inserting a new row above a current row. However, when you are in the initial data entry phase, you will most likely prefer to add new records by adding a row to the end of the table.

Insert a Table Row

1 Select a cell in the row below which you want to insert the new row.

2 Click the **Home** tab.

3 Click **Insert** (⊞).

4 Click **Insert Table Rows Above**.

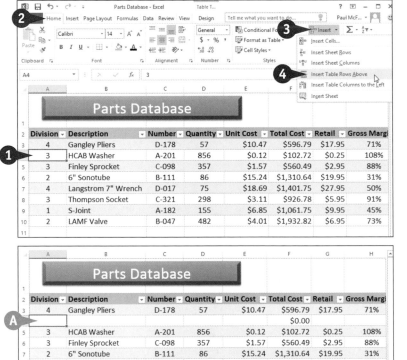

Ⓐ Excel inserts the new row.

Ⓑ To insert a new row at the end of the table, select the lower-right table cell and then press Tab .

Insert a Table Column

Y ou can add a new field to your Excel table by inserting a new column. You can insert a column either within the table or at the end of the table.

To make data entry easier and more efficient, you should decide in advance all the fields you want to include in the table. However, if later on you realize you forgot a particular field, you can still add it to the table. Inserting a table column is also useful if you imported or inherited the data from elsewhere and you see that the data is missing a field that you require.

Insert a Table Column

1 Select a cell in the column to the left of which you want to insert the new column.

A If you want to insert the new column at the end of the table, select a cell in the last table column.

2 Click the **Home** tab.

3 Click **Insert** (⊞).

4 Click **Insert Table Columns to the Left**.

To insert a column at the end of the table instead, click **Insert Table Columns to the Right** (not shown).

B Excel inserts the new column.

5 Name the new field by editing the column header.

Delete a Table Row

If your table contains a record that includes inaccurate, outdated, or unnecessary data, you should delete that row to preserve your table's data integrity.

An Excel table is a repository of data that you can use as a reference source or to analyze or summarize the data. However you use the table, it is only as beneficial as its data is accurate, so you should take extra care to ensure the data you enter is correct. If you find that an entire record is inaccurate or no longer needed, Excel enables you to quickly delete that row.

Delete a Table Row

1 Select a cell in the row you want to delete.

Note: To delete multiple rows, select a cell in each row you want to delete.

2 Click the **Home** tab.

3 Click **Delete** (🗑).

4 Click **Delete Table Rows**.

Ⓐ Excel deletes the row.

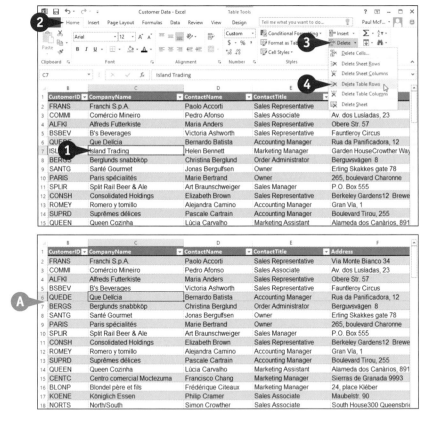

214

Delete a Table Column

If your table contains a field that you do not require, you should delete that column to make your table easier to work with and manage.

As you see later in this chapter and in Chapter 11, you analyze and summarize your table information based on the data in one or more fields. If your table contains a field that you never look at and that you never use for analysis or summaries, consider deleting that column to reduce table clutter and make your table easier to navigate.

Delete a Table Column

1 Select a cell in the column you want to delete.

Note: To delete multiple columns, select a cell in each column you want to delete.

2 Click the **Home** tab.

3 Click **Delete** (📷).

4 Click **Delete Table Columns**.

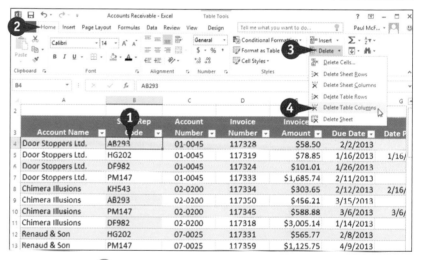

A Excel deletes the column.

Add a Column Subtotal

You can get more out of your table data by summarizing a field with a subtotal that appears at the bottom of the column.

Although the word *subtotal* implies that you are summing the numeric values in a column, Excel uses the term more broadly. That is, a subtotal can be not only a numeric sum, but also an average, a maximum or minimum, or a count of the values in the field. You can also choose more esoteric subtotals such as a standard deviation or a variance.

Add a Column Subtotal

1 Select all the data in the column you want to total.

Note: See the "Select Table Data" section earlier in the chapter to learn how to select column data.

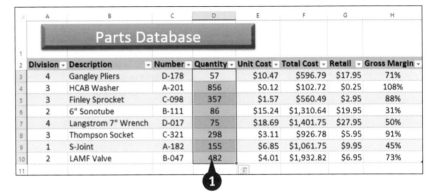

2 Click the **Quick Analysis** smart tag (📋).

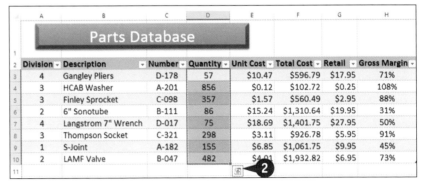

The Quick Analysis options appear.

③ Click **Totals**.

④ Click the type of calculation you want to use.

Division	Description	Number	Quantity	Unit Cost	Total Cost	Retail	Gross Margin
4	Gangley Pliers	D-178	57	$10.47	$596.79	$17.95	71%
3	HCAB Washer	A-201	856	$0.12	$102.72	$0.25	108%
3	Finley Sprocket	C-098	357	$1.57	$560.49	$2.95	88%
2	6" Sonotube	B-111	86	$15.24	$1,310.64	$19.95	31%
4	Langstrom 7" Wrench	D-017	75	$18.69	$1,401.75	$27.95	50%
3	Thompson Socket	C-321	298	$3.11	$926.78	$5.95	91%
1	S-Joint	A-182	155	$6.85	$1,061.75	$9.95	45%
2	LAMF Valve	B-047	482	$4.01	$1,932.82	$6.95	73%

Formatting   Charts   **Totals**   Sparklines

Sum   Average   Count   % Total   Running...   Sum

Formulas automatically calculate totals for you.

A Excel adds a Total row to the bottom of the table.

B Excel inserts a SUBTOTAL function to perform the calculation you chose in step **4**.

C Click the cell's ▼ to choose a different type of subtotal.

D11   =SUBTOTAL(109,[Quantity]) — **B**

Parts Database

Division	Description	Number	Quantity	Unit Cost	Total Cost	Retail	Gross Margin
4	Gangley Pliers	D-178	57	$10.47	$596.79	$17.95	71%
3	HCAB Washer	A-201	856	$0.12	$102.72	$0.25	108%
3	Finley Sprocket	C-098	357	$1.57	$560.49	$2.95	88%
2	6" Sonotube	B-111	86	$15.24	$1,310.64	$19.95	31%
4	Langstrom 7" Wrench	D-017	75	$18.69	$1,401.75	$27.95	50%
3	Thompson Socket	C-321	298	$3.11	$926.78	$5.95	91%
1	S-Joint	A-182	155	$6.85	$1,061.75	$9.95	45%
2	LAMF Valve	B-047	482	$4.01	$1,932.82	$6.95	73%
			A 2366	**C**			

TIP

Is there a quick way to insert a total row in my table?

Yes. If the column you want to total is the last column in the table, you can add the total row and include a SUBTOTAL function for that column with just a few mouse clicks:

① Click any cell within the table.

② Click the **Design** tab.

③ Select the **Total Row** check box (☐ changes to ☑).

A Excel automatically inserts a row named Total at the bottom of the table.

B Excel adds a SUBTOTAL function below the last column.

④ Click the cell's ▼ and then click the type of subtotal you want to use.

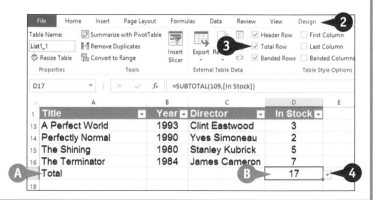

Title	Year	Director	In Stock
A Perfect World	1993	Clint Eastwood	3
Perfectly Normal	1990	Yves Simoneau	2
The Shining	1980	Stanley Kubrick	5
The Terminator	1984	James Cameron	7
Total			17

Convert a Table to a Range

If you no longer require the Excel table tools, you can convert a table to a normal range.

Tables are extremely useful Excel features, but they can occasionally be bothersome. For example, if you click a table cell, click the Design tab, and then click a cell outside the table, Excel automatically switches to the Home tab. If you then click a table cell again, Excel automatically switches back to the Design tab. If you are not using the table features in the Design tab, this behavior can be annoying, but you can prevent it from happening by converting the table to a normal range.

Convert a Table to a Range

① Click a cell inside the table.

② Click the **Design** tab.

③ Click **Convert to Range** (▣).

Excel asks you to confirm.

④ Click **Yes.**

Excel converts the table to a normal range.

Apply a Table Style

You can give an Excel table more visual appeal and make it easier to read by applying a table style.

A table style is a combination of formatting options that Excel applies to 13 different table elements, including the first and last columns, the header row, the total row, and the entire table. For each element, Excel applies one or more of the following formatting options: the font, including the typeface, style, size, color, and text effects; the border; and the background color and fill effects.

Apply a Table Style

1 Click a cell inside the table.

2 Click the **Design** tab.

3 Click **Table Quick Styles**.

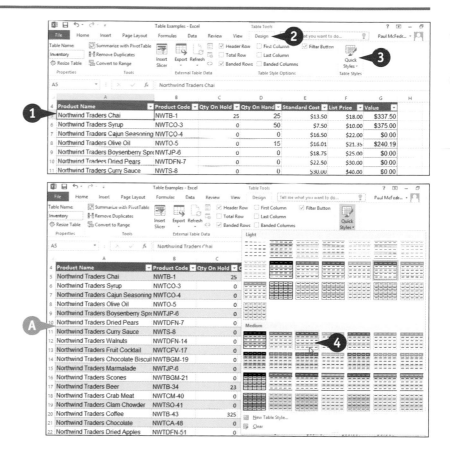

The Table Quick Styles gallery appears.

4 Click the table style you want to use.

A Excel applies the style to the table.

Build a Custom Table Style

You can make it easier to format tables the way you prefer by creating a custom table style.

Excel comes with dozens of predefined table styles, all of which vary with the document theme. If none of the predefined table styles is right for your needs, you can use the Format Cells dialog box to apply your own formatting to the various table elements. If you want to reuse this formatting in other workbooks, you can save the formatting options as a custom table style.

Build a Custom Table Style

1. Click a cell inside the table.

2. Click the **Design** tab.

3. Click **Table Quick Styles**.

A. The Table Styles gallery appears.

4. Click **New Table Style**.

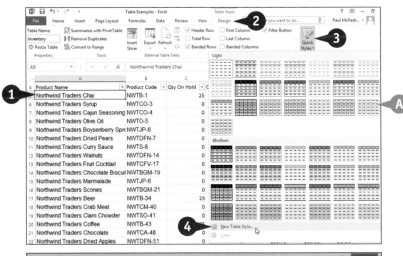

The New Table Style dialog box appears.

5. Type a name for the style.

6. Click the table element you want to format.

7. Click **Format**.

The Format Cells dialog box appears.

8 Use the tabs to select the formatting options you want in your cell style.

Note: Depending on the table element you are working with, some of the formatting options may be disabled.

9 Click **OK**.

10 Repeat steps **5** to **8** to set the formatting for the other table elements, as needed.

11 Click **OK** in the New Table Style dialog box (not shown).

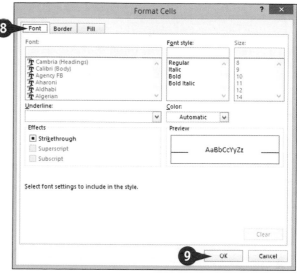

12 Click **Table Quick Styles**.

B Your table style appears in the Custom section of the Table Styles gallery.

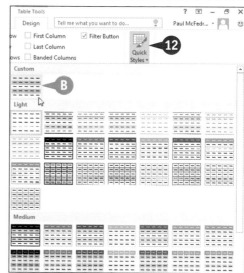

Is there an easy way to use the custom style for all the tables I create?

Yes. If you want to use your custom table style for all or most of the tables you create, you should set the custom style as the default. When you are creating a new custom table style, follow steps **1** to **10** and then select the **Set as default table style for this document** check box (☐ changes to ☑). For an existing custom table style, click a table cell, click the **Design** tab, click the **Table Styles** ▼, right-click the custom style, and then click **Set As Default**.

How do I make changes to a custom table style?

To change the formatting for a custom table style, click a table cell, click the **Design** tab, and then click the **Table Styles** ▼ to display the Table Styles gallery. Right-click the custom style, click **Modify**, and then follow steps **6** to **11**.

221

Create a PivotTable

You can more easily analyze a large amount of data by creating a PivotTable from that data. A PivotTable is a powerful data analysis tool because it automatically groups large amounts of data into smaller, more manageable categories, and it displays summary calculations for each group.

You can also manipulate the layout of — or *pivot* — the PivotTable to see different views of your data. Although you can create a PivotTable from a normal range, for best results, you should convert your range to a table before creating the PivotTable (see the "Convert a Range to a Table" section earlier in the chapter).

Create a PivotTable

1 Click a cell within the table that you want to use as the source data.

2 Click the **Design** tab.

3 Click **Summarize with PivotTable** (📊).

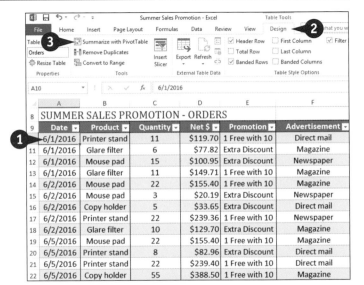

The Create PivotTable dialog box appears.

4 Click **New Worksheet** (◯ changes to ◉).

A If you want to place the PivotTable in an existing location, click **Existing Worksheet** (◯ changes to ◉) and then use the **Location** range box to select the worksheet and cell where you want the PivotTable to appear.

5 Click **OK**.

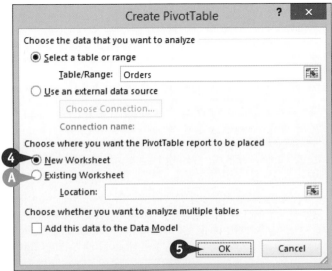

B Excel creates a blank PivotTable.

C Excel displays the PivotTable Fields list.

6 Click and drag a field and drop it inside the ROWS area.

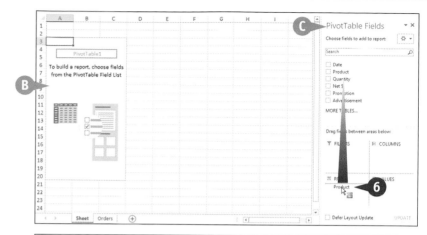

D Excel adds the field's unique values to the PivotTable's row area.

7 Click and drag a numeric field and drop it inside the VALUES area.

E Excel sums the numeric values based on the row values.

8 If desired, click and drag fields and drop them in the COLUMNS area and the FILTERS area.

Each time you drop a field in an area, Excel updates the PivotTable to include the new data.

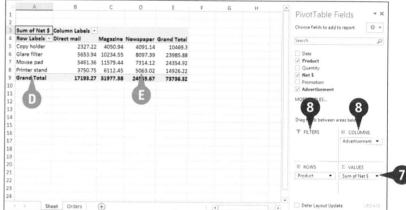

TIPS

Are there faster ways to build a PivotTable?

Yes. In the PivotTable Fields list, if you select a check box for a text or date field (☐ changes to ☑), Excel adds the field to the ROWS area; if you select a check box for a numeric field (◯ changes to ◉), Excel adds the field to the VALUES area. You can also right-click a field and then click the area you want to use.

Can I add multiple fields to each area?

Yes. You can add as many fields as you like to each area. You can also move a PivotTable's fields from one area of the PivotTable to another. This enables you to view your data from different perspectives, which can greatly enhance the analysis of the data. Moving a field within a PivotTable is called *pivoting* the data. To move a field, use the PivotTable Fields list to click and drag a field from one area and drop it on another.

CHAPTER 11

Analyzing Data

You can get more out of Excel by performing *data analysis*, which is the application of tools and techniques to organize, study, and reach conclusions about a specific collection of information. In this chapter, you learn data analysis techniques such as sorting and filtering a range, setting validation rules, and using subtotals and scenarios.

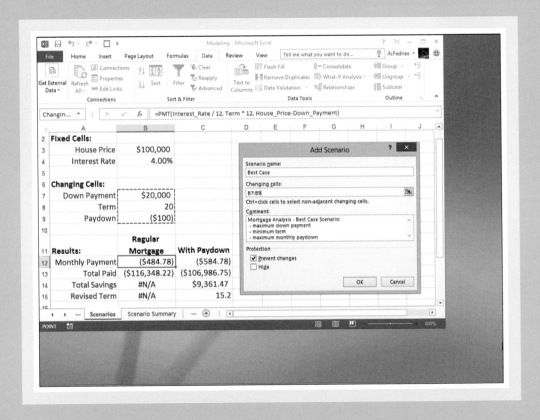

Sort a Range or Table

You can make a range or table easier to read and analyze by sorting the data based on the values in one or more columns.

You can sort the data in either ascending or descending order. An ascending sort arranges the values alphabetically from A to Z, or numerically from 0 to 9; a descending sort arranges the values alphabetically from Z to A, or numerically from 9 to 0.

Sort a Range or Table

1. Click any cell in the range you want to sort.

2. Click the **Data** tab.

3. Click **Sort** (ᶻₐᴬᵤ).

The Sort dialog box appears.

4. Click the **Sort by** ▼ and then click the field you want to use for the main sort level.

5. Click the **Order** ▼ and then click a sort order for the field.

6. To sort on another field, click **Add Level**.

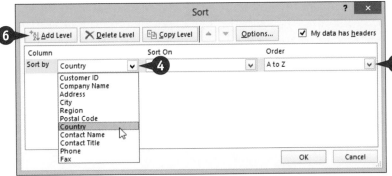

Ⓐ Excel adds another sort level.

7 Click the **Then by** ▼ and then click the field you want to use for the sort level.

8 Click the **Order** ▼ and then click a sort order for the field.

9 Repeat steps **6** to **8** to add more sort levels as needed.

10 Click **OK**.

Ⓑ Excel sorts the range.

TIPS

Is there a faster way to sort a range?
Yes, as long as you only need to sort your range on a single column. First, click in any cell inside the column you want to use for the sort. Click the **Data** tab and then click one of the following buttons in the Sort & Filter group:

A↓Z	Click for an ascending sort.
Z↓A	Click for a descending sort.

How do I sort a range using the values in a row instead of a column?
Excel normally sorts a range from top to bottom based on the values in one or more columns. However, you can tell Excel to sort the range from left to right based on the values in one or more rows. Follow steps **1** to **3** to display the Sort dialog box. Click **Options** to display the Sort Options dialog box, select the **Sort left to right** option (○ changes to ●), and then click **OK**.

Filter a Range or Table

You can analyze table data much faster by only viewing those table records that you want to work with. In Excel, this is called *filtering* a range.

The easiest way to filter a range is to use the Filter buttons, each of which presents you with a list of check boxes for each unique value in a column. You filter the data by selecting the check boxes for the rows you want to see. If you have converted the range to a table, as described in Chapter 10, the Filter buttons for each column are displayed automatically.

Filter a Range or Table

Display the Filter Buttons

Note: If you are filtering a table, you can skip directly to the "Filter the Data" subsection.

1 Click inside the range.

2 Click the **Data** tab.

3 Click **Filter** (⊽).

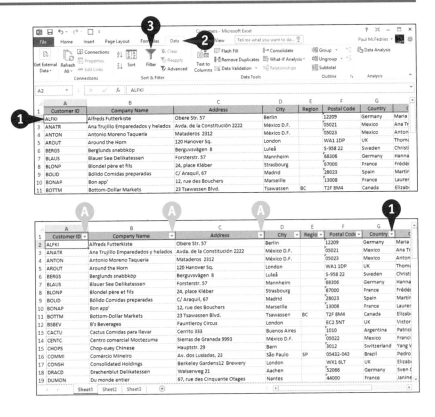

A Excel adds a Filter button (⌄) to each field.

Filter the Data

1 Click ⌄ for the field you want to use as the filter.

B Excel displays a list of the unique values in the field.

2 Select the check box for each value you want to see (☐ changes to ☑).

C You can toggle all the check boxes on and off by clicking **Select All**.

3 Click **OK**.

D Excel filters the table to show only those records that have the field values you selected.

E Excel displays the number of records found.

F The field's drop-down list displays a filter icon (🔽).

To remove the filter, click the **Data** tab and then click **Clear** (🔽; not shown).

TIP

Can I create more sophisticated filters?
Yes, by using a second technique called *quick filters*, which enables you to specify criteria for a field:

1 Click 🔽 for the field you want to use as the filter.

2 Click **Number Filters**.

Note: If the field is a date field, click **Date Filters**; if the field is a text field, click **Text Filters**.

3 Click the filter you want to use.

4 Enter the value you want to use.

5 Click **OK**.

Set Data Validation Rules

You can make Excel data entry more efficient by setting up data entry cells to accept only certain values. To do this, you can set up a cell with data validation criteria that specify the allowed value or values. This is called a *data validation rule*.

Excel also lets you tell the user what to enter by defining an input message that appears when the user selects the cell. You can also configure the data validation rule to display a message when the user tries to enter an invalid value.

Set Data Validation Rules

1 Click the cell you want to restrict.

2 Click the **Data** tab.

3 Click **Data Validation** (≣◎).

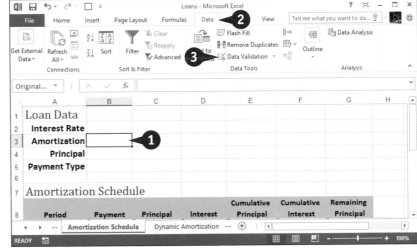

The Data Validation dialog box appears.

4 Click the **Settings** tab.

5 In the **Allow** list, click ▼ and select the type of data you want to allow in the cell.

6 In the **Data** list, click ▼ and select the operator you want to use to define the allowable data.

7 Specify the validation criteria, such as the **Maximum** and **Minimum** allowable values shown here.

Note: The criteria boxes you see depend on the operator you chose in step **6**.

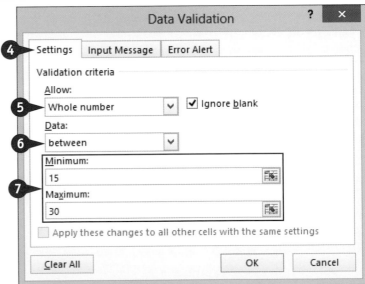

8 Click the **Input Message** tab.

9 Make sure the **Show input message when cell is selected** check box is selected (☑).

10 Type a message title in the **Title** text box.

11 Type the message you want to display in the **Input Message** text box.

12 Click **OK**.

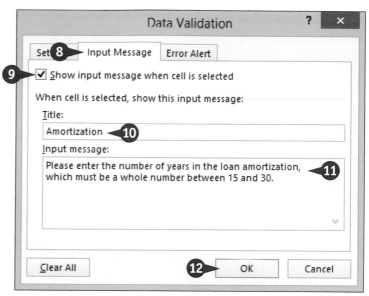

Excel configures the cell to accept only values that meet your criteria.

A When the user selects the cell, the input message appears.

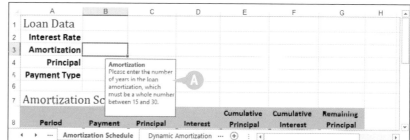

TIPS

Can I configure the cell to display a message if the user tries to enter an invalid value?

Yes. Follow steps **1** to **3** to open the Data Validation dialog box, and then click the **Error Alert** tab. Make sure the **Show error alert after invalid data is entered** check box is selected (☑), and then specify the **Style**, **Title**, and **Error Message**. Click **OK**.

How do I remove data validation from a cell?

If you no longer need to use data validation on a cell, you should clear the settings. Follow steps **1** to **3** to display the Data Validation dialog box and then click **Clear All**. Excel removes all the validation criteria, as well as the input message and the error alert. Click **OK**.

Create a Data Table

If you are interested in studying the effect a range of values has on the formula, you can set up a *data table*. This is a table that consists of the formula you are using, and multiple input values for that formula. Excel automatically creates a solution to the formula for each different input value.

Do not confuse data tables with the Excel tables that you learned about in Chapter 10. A data table is a special range that Excel uses to calculate multiple solutions to a formula.

Create a Data Table

1 Type the input values:

To enter the values in a column, start the column one cell down and one cell to the left of the cell containing the formula, as shown here.

To enter the values in a row, start the row one cell up and one cell to the right of the cell containing the formula.

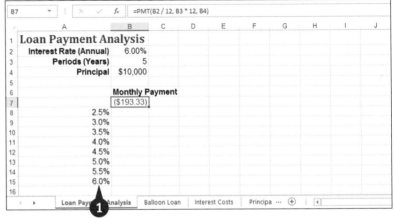

2 Select the range that includes the input values and the formula.

3 Click the **Data** tab.

4 Click **What-If Analysis** (⊞).

5 Click **Data Table**.

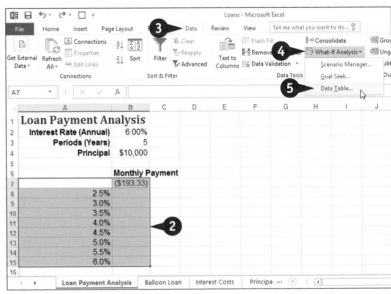

The Data Table dialog box appears.

6 Specify the formula cell you want to use as the data table's input cell:

If the input values are in a column, enter the input cell's address in the **Column input cell** text box.

If you entered the input values in a row, enter the input cell's address in the **Row input cell** text box.

7 Click **OK**.

Ⓐ Excel displays the results.

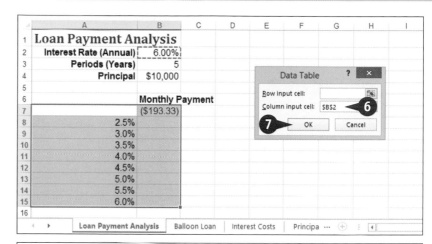

TIPS

What is what-if analysis?

The technique called *what-if analysis* is perhaps the most basic method for analyzing worksheet data. With what-if analysis, you first calculate a formula D, based on the input from variables A, B, and C. You then say, "What happens to the result if I change the value of variable A?", "What happens if I change B or C?", and so on.

When I try to delete part of the data table, I get an error. Why?

The data table results are created as an *array formula*, which is a special formula that Excel treats as a unit. This means that you cannot move or delete part of the results. If you need to work with the data table results, you must first select the entire results range.

Summarize Data with Subtotals

Although you can use formulas and worksheet functions to summarize your data in various ways, including sums, averages, counts, maximums, and minimums, if you are in a hurry, or if you just need a quick summary of your data, you can get Excel to do most of the work for you. The secret here is a feature called *automatic subtotals*, which are formulas that Excel adds to a worksheet automatically.

Summarize Data with Subtotals

1 Click a cell within the range you want to subtotal.

2 Click the **Data** tab.

3 Click **Subtotal** ().

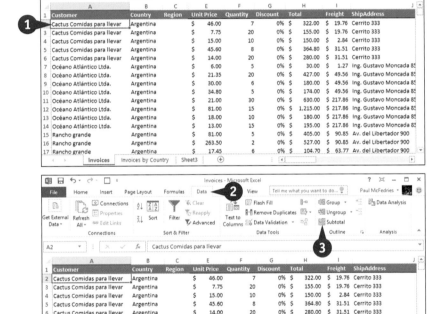

The Subtotal dialog box appears.

4 Click the **At each change in** ▼ and then click the column you want to use to group the subtotals.

5 In the **Add subtotal to** list, select the check box for the column you want to summarize (☐ changes to ☑).

6 Click **OK**.

Ⓐ Excel calculates the subtotals and adds them into the range.

Ⓑ Excel adds outline symbols to the range.

Note: See the next section, "Group Related Data," to learn more about outlining in Excel.

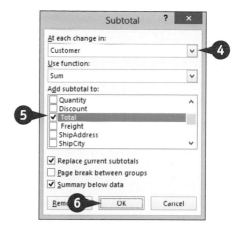

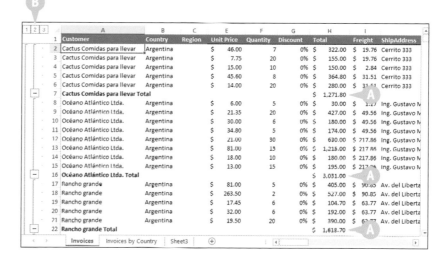

TIPS

Do I need to prepare my worksheet to use subtotals?

Yes. Excel sets up automatic subtotals based on data groupings in a selected field. For example, if you ask for subtotals based on the Customer field, Excel runs down the Customer column and creates a new subtotal each time the name changes. To get useful summaries, you need to sort the range on the field containing the data groupings you are interested in.

Can I only calculate totals?

No. The word *subtotal* here is a bit misleading because you can summarize more than just totals. You can also count values, calculate the average of the values, determine the maximum or minimum value, and more. To change the summary calculation, follow steps **1** to **4**, click the **Use function** ▼, and then click the function you want to use for the summary.

Group Related Data

Y ou can control a worksheet range display by grouping the data based on the worksheet formulas and data.

Grouping the data creates a worksheet outline, which you can use to "collapse" sections of the sheet to display only summary cells, or "expand" hidden sections to show the underlying detail. Note that when you add subtotals to a range as described in the previous section, "Summarize Data with Subtotals," Excel automatically groups the data and displays the outline tools.

Group Related Data

Create the Outline

1 Display the worksheet you want to outline.

2 Click the **Data** tab.

3 Click the **Group** ▼.

4 Click **Auto Outline**.

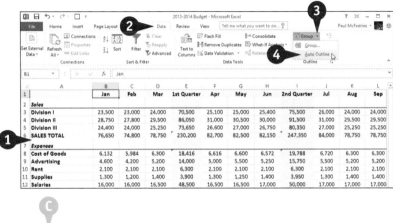

A Excel outlines the worksheet data.

B Excel uses level bars to indicate the grouped ranges.

C Excel displays level symbols to indicate the various levels of the detail that are available in the outline.

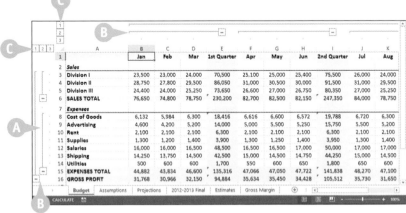

Use the Outline to Control the Range Display

1 Click a **Collapse** symbol ([–]) to hide the range indicated by the level bar.

D You can also collapse multiple ranges that are on the same outline level by clicking the appropriate level symbol.

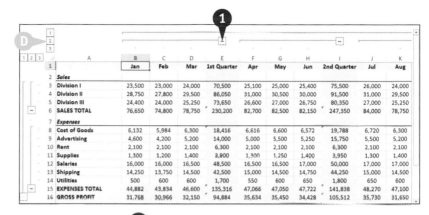

E Excel collapses the range.

2 Click the **Expand** symbol ([+]) to view the range again.

F You can also show multiple ranges that are on the same outline level by clicking the appropriate level symbol.

Do I have to prepare my worksheet before I can group the data?

Yes. Not all worksheets can be grouped, so you need to make sure your worksheet is a candidate for outlining. First, the worksheet must contain formulas that reference cells or ranges directly adjacent to the formula cell. Worksheets with SUM( ) functions that subtotal cells above or to the left are particularly good candidates for outlining.

Second, there must be a consistent pattern to the direction of the formula references. For example, a worksheet with formulas that always reference cells above or to the left can be outlined. Excel will not outline a worksheet with, say, SUM( ) functions that reference ranges above and below a formula cell.

Analyze Data with Goal Seek

I f you already know the formula result you want, but you must find an input value that produces that result, you can use the Excel Goal Seek tool to solve the problem. You tell Goal Seek the final value you need and which variable to change, and it finds a solution for you.

For example, you might know that you want to have $50,000 saved to purchase new equipment five years from now, so you need to calculate how much to invest each year.

Analyze Data with Goal Seek

1 Set up your worksheet model.

Note: See the first tip to learn more about setting up a worksheet for Goal Seek.

2 Click the **Data** tab.

3 Click **What-If Analysis** (⊞?).

4 Click **Goal Seek**.

The Goal Seek dialog box appears.

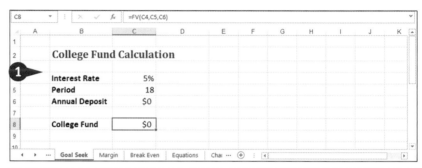

5 Click inside the **Set cell** box.

6 Click the cell that contains the formula you want Goal Seek to work with.

7 Use the **To value** text box to type the value that you want Goal Seek to find.

8 Click in the **By changing cell** box.

9 Click the cell that you want Goal Seek to modify.

10 Click **OK**.

A Goal Seek adjusts the changing cell value until it reaches a solution.

B The formula now shows the value you entered in step **7**.

11 Click **OK**.

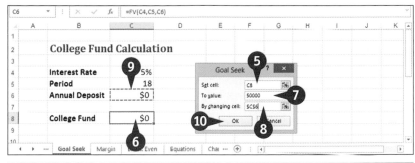

TIPS

How do I set up my worksheet to use Goal Seek?

Setting up your worksheet model for Goal Seek means doing three things. First, set up one cell as the *changing cell*, which is the value that Goal Seek will manipulate to reach the goal. Enter an initial value (such as 0) into the cell. Second, set up the other input values for the formula and give them proper initial values. Third, create a formula for Goal Seek to use to reach the goal.

What other types of problems can Goal Seek solve?

One common problem is called a *break-even analysis*, where you determine the number of units you have to sell of a product so that your total profits are 0. In this case, the changing cell is the number of units sold, and the formula is the profit calculation. You can also use Goal Seek to determine which price (the changing cell) is required to return a particular profit margin (the formula).

Analyze Data with Scenarios

You can analyze the result of a formula by creating sets of values that enable you to quickly use those values as the inputs for a formula.

For example, one set of values might represent a best-case approach, while another might represent a worst-case approach. In Excel, each of these coherent sets of input values — known as *changing cells* — is called a *scenario*. By creating multiple scenarios, you can easily apply these different value sets to analyze how the result of a formula changes under different conditions.

Analyze Data with Scenarios

Create a Scenario

1 Set up your worksheet model.

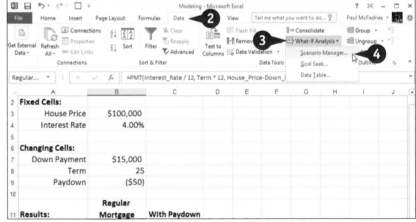

2 Click the **Data** tab.

3 Click **What-If Analysis** (📊).

4 Click **Scenario Manager**.

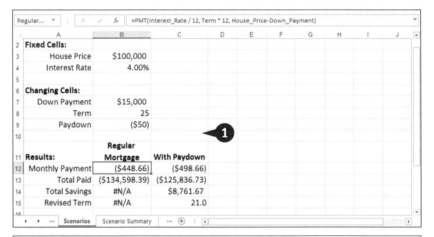

The Scenario Manager dialog box appears.

5 Click **Add**.

The Add Scenario dialog box appears.

6 Type a name for the scenario.

7 Click in the **Changing cells** box.

8 Select the cells you want to change in the scenario.

9 Type a description for the scenario.

10 Click **OK**.

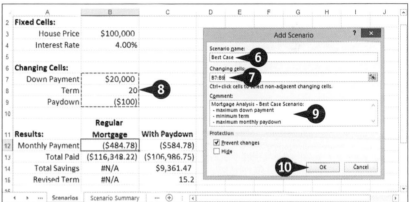

TIPS

Are there any restrictions on the changing cells?

When you are building a worksheet model for use with scenarios, make sure that each changing cell is a constant value. If you use a formula for a changing cell, Excel replaces that formula with a constant value defined in the scenario, so you lose your formula.

Do I need to add a description to each scenario?

Yes. As you see in the next section, once you have one or more scenarios defined, they appear in the Scenario Manager, and for each scenario you see its changing cells and its description. The description is often very useful, particularly if you have several scenarios defined, so be sure to write a detailed description in step **9** to help you differentiate your scenarios later on.

continued ▶

Analyze Data with Scenarios (continued)

xcel stores your scenarios in the Scenario Manager. You can use the Scenario Manager to perform a number of scenario-related tasks. For example, you can select one of your scenarios and then click a button to display the scenario's values in your worksheet. You can also use the Scenario Manager to edit existing scenarios and to delete scenarios you no longer need.

Analyze Data with Scenarios (continued)

The Scenario Values dialog box appears.

⑪ Use the text boxes to specify a value for each changing cell.

Ⓐ To add more scenarios, click **Add** and then repeat steps **6** to **11**.

⑫ Click **OK**.

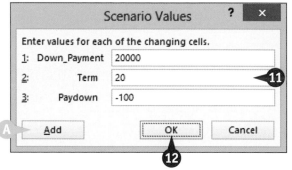

⑬ Click **Close**.

Display Scenarios

1 Click the **Data** tab.

2 Click ⊞.

3 Click **Scenario Manager**.

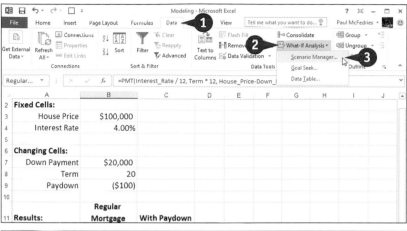

The Scenario Manager dialog box appears.

4 Click the scenario you want to display.

5 Click **Show**.

Ⓑ Excel enters the scenario values into the changing cells and displays the formula result.

6 Repeat steps **4** and **5** to display other scenarios.

7 Click **Close**.

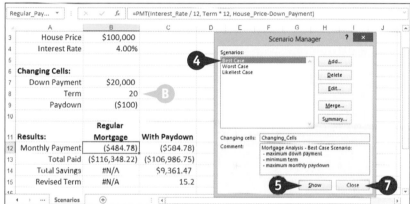

How do I edit a scenario?

If you need to make changes to a scenario, you can edit the name, the changing cells, the description, and the scenario's input values. Click the **Data** tab, click ⊞, and then click **Scenario Manager**. In the Scenario Manager dialog box, click the scenario you want to modify, and then click **Edit**.

How do I remove a scenario?

If you have a scenario that you no longer need, you should delete it to reduce clutter in the Scenario Manager. Click the **Data** tab, click ⊞, and then click **Scenario Manager**. Click the scenario you want to delete. Note that Excel does not ask you to confirm the deletion, so double-check that you have selected the correct scenario. Click **Delete** and then click **Close**.

Remove Duplicate Values from a Range or Table

You can make your Excel data more accurate for analysis by removing any duplicate records. Duplicate records throw off your calculations by including the same data two or more times. To prevent this, you should delete duplicate records. However, rather than looking for duplicates manually, you can use the Remove Duplicates command, which can quickly find and remove duplicates in even the largest ranges or tables.

Before you use the Remove Duplicates command, you must decide what defines a duplicate record in your data. That is, does every field have to be identical or is it enough that only certain fields are identical?

Remove Duplicate Values from a Range or Table

1 Click a cell inside the range or table.

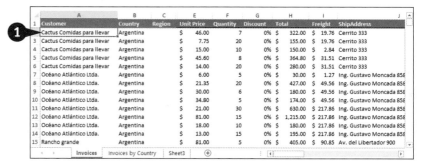

2 Click the **Data** tab.

3 Click **Remove Duplicates** (▐→▐).

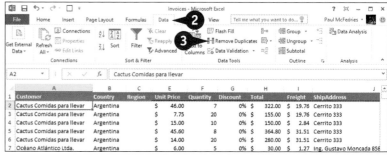

The Remove Duplicates dialog box appears.

4 Select the check box beside each field that you want Excel to check for duplication values (☐ changes to ✔).

Note: Excel does not give you a chance to confirm the deletion of the duplicate records, so be sure you want to do this before proceeding.

5 Click **OK**.

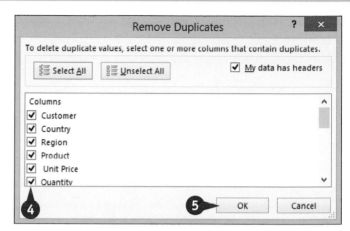

Excel deletes any duplicate records that it finds.

Ⓐ Excel tells you the number of duplicate records that it deleted.

6 Click **OK**.

If I have a lot of columns, is there a quick way to check for duplicates based on just a couple of those fields?

Yes. If your table has many fields, you may want Excel to use only one or two of those fields to look for duplicate records. Rather than deselecting all the other check boxes manually, first click **Unselect All** in the Remove Duplicates dialog box to clear all the check boxes (✔ changes to ☐). You can then select just the check boxes you want Excel to use (☐ changes to ✔).

Can I remove duplicates even if my range does not have column headers?

Yes. Excel can still examine the column data even if there are no headers. In this case, follow steps **1** to **3** to open the Remove Duplicates dialog box, then make sure the **My data has headers** check box is deselected (☐). Use the check boxes labeled Column A, Column B, and so on to choose the columns that you want Excel to check for duplicate values (☐ changes to ✔) and then click **OK**.

Highlight Cells That Meet Some Criteria

A *conditional format* is formatting that Excel applies only to cells that meet the criteria you specify. For example, you can tell Excel to apply the formatting only if a cell's value is greater or less than some specified amount, between two specified values, or equal to some value. You can also look for cells that contain specified text, dates that occur during a specified timeframe, and more.

You can specify the font, border, and background pattern, which helps to ensure that the cells that meet your criteria stand out from the other cells in the range.

Highlight Cells That Meet Some Criteria

1 Select the range with which you want to work.

2 Click the **Home** tab.

3 Click **Conditional Formatting** (⊞).

4 Click **Highlight Cells Rules**.

5 Click the operator you want to use for the condition.

A dialog box appears, the name of which depends on the operator you clicked in step **5**.

6 Type the value you want to use for the condition.

Ⓐ You can also click **Collapse Dialog** (▦), click a worksheet cell, and then click **Restore Dialog** (▦).

Depending on the operator, you may need to specify two values.

7 Click this drop-down arrow (▼), and then click the formatting you want to use.

Ⓑ To create your own format, click **Custom Format**.

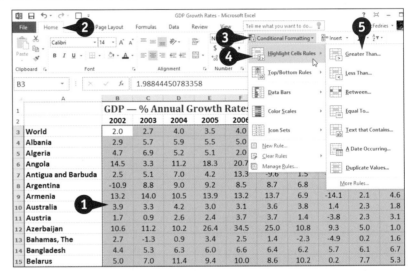

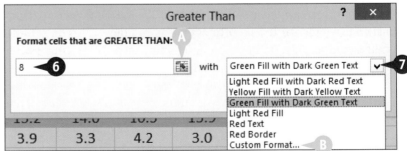

8 Click **OK**.

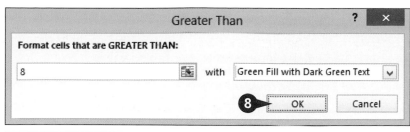

Greater Than ? ✕

Format cells that are GREATER THAN:

| 8 | with | Green Fill with Dark Green Text ▾ |

8 → OK   Cancel

C Excel applies the formatting to cells that meet the condition you specified.

	A	B	C	D	E	F	G	H	I	J	K
1		GDP — % Annual Growth Rates (Source: The World Bank)									
2		2002	2003	2004	2005	2006	2007	2008	2009	2010	2011
3	World	2.0	2.7	4.0	3.5	4.0	3.9	1.3	-2.2	4.3	2.7
4	Albania	2.9	5.7	5.9	5.5	5.0	5.9	7.7	3.3	3.5	3.0
5	Algeria	4.7	6.9	5.2	5.1	2.0	3.0	2.4	2.4	3.3	2.5
6	Angola	14.5	3.3	11.2	18.3	20.7	22.6	13.8	2.4	3.4	3.4
7	Antigua and Barbuda	2.5	5.1	7.0	4.2	13.3	-9.6	1.5	-10.3	-8.9	-4.2
8	Argentina	-10.9	8.8	9.0	9.2	8.5	8.7	6.8	0.9	9.2	8.9
9	Armenia	13.2	14.0	10.5	13.9	13.2	13.7	6.9	-14.1	2.1	4.6
10	Australia	3.9	3.3	4.2	3.0	3.1	3.6	3.8	1.4	2.3	1.8
11	Austria	1.7	0.9	2.6	2.4	3.7	3.7	1.4	-3.8	2.3	3.1
12	Azerbaijan	10.6	11.2	10.2	26.4	34.5	25.0	10.8	9.3	5.0	1.0
13	Bahamas, The	2.7	-1.3	0.9	3.4	2.5	1.4	-2.3	-4.9	0.2	1.6
14	Bangladesh	4.4	5.3	6.3	6.0	6.6	6.4	6.2	5.7	6.1	6.7
15	Belarus	5.0	7.0	11.4	9.4	10.0	8.6	10.2	0.2	7.7	5.3

TIPS

Can I set up more than one conditional format on a range?

Yes, Excel enables you to specify multiple conditional formats. For example, you could set up one condition for cells that are greater than some value, and a separate condition for cells that are less than some other value. You can apply unique formats to each condition. Follow steps **1** to **8** to configure the new condition.

How do I remove a conditional format?

If you no longer require a conditional format, you can delete it. Follow steps **1** to **3** to select the range and display the Conditional Formatting drop-down menu, and then click **Manage Rules**. Excel displays the Conditional Formatting Rules Manager dialog box. Click the conditional format you want to remove and then click **Delete Rule**.

Highlight the Top or Bottom Values in a Range

When analyzing worksheet data, it is often useful to look for items that stand out from the norm. For example, you might want to know which sales reps sold the most last year, or which departments had the lowest gross margins.

You can do this by setting up *top/bottom rules*, where Excel applies a conditional format to those items that are at the top or bottom of a range of values. For the top or bottom values, you can specify a number, such as the top 5 or 10, or a percentage, such as the bottom 20 percent.

Highlight the Top or Bottom Values in a Range

1 Select the range with which you want to work.

2 Click the **Home** tab.

3 Click **Conditional Formatting** ().

4 Click **Top/Bottom Rules**.

5 Click the type of rule you want to create.

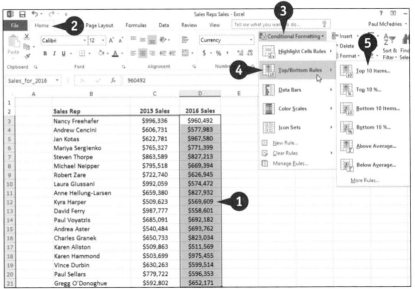

A dialog box appears, whose name depends on the type of rule you clicked in step **5**.

6 Type the value you want to use for the condition.

7 Click this drop-down arrow (), and then click the formatting you want to use.

A To create your own format, click **Custom Format**.

8 Click **OK**.

B Excel applies the formatting to cells that meet the condition you specified.

	A	B	C	D
1				
2		Sales Rep	2015 Sales	2016 Sales
3		Nancy Freehafer	$996,336	$960,492
4		Andrew Cencini	$606,731	$577,983
5		Jan Kotas	$622,781	$967,580
6		Mariya Sergienko	$765,327	$771,399
7		Steven Thorpe	$863,589	$827,213
8		Michael Neipper	$795,518	$669,394
9		Robert Zare	$722,740	$626,945
10		Laura Giussani	$992,059	$574,472
11		Anne Hellung-Larsen	$659,380	$827,932
12		Kyra Harper	$509,623	$569,609
13		David Ferry	$987,777	$558,601
14		Paul Voyatzis	$685,091	$692,182
15		Andrea Aster	$540,484	$693,762
16		Charles Granek	$650,733	$823,034
17		Karen Aliston	$509,863	$511,569
18		Karen Hammond	$503,699	$975,455
19		Vince Durbin	$630,263	$599,514
20		Paul Sellars	$779,722	$596,353
21		Gregg O'Donoghue	$592,802	$652,171

B

TIPS

Can I highlight cells that are above or below the average?

Yes, Excel also enables you to create top/bottom rules based on the average value in the range. First, follow steps **1** to **4** to select the range and display the Top/Bottom Rules menu. Then click either **Above Average** to format those values that exceed the range average, or **Below Average** to format those values that are less than the range average.

How do I remove a top/bottom rule?

If you no longer require a top/bottom rule, you can delete it. Follow steps **1** to **3** to select the range and display the Conditional Formatting drop-down menu. Click **Clear Rules**, and then click **Clear Rules from Selected Cells**. Excel removes the rule from the range.

Analyze Cell Values with Data Bars

In some data analysis scenarios, you might be interested more in the relative values within a range than the absolute values. For example, if you have a table of products that includes a column showing unit sales, how do you compare the relative sales of all the products?

This sort of analysis is often easiest if you visualize the relative values. You can do that by using *data bars*. Data bars are a data visualization feature that applies colored, horizontal bars to each cell in a range of values, and these bars appear "behind" the values in the range.

Analyze Cell Values with Data Bars

1 Select the range with which you want to work.

	A	B	C	D
1	Product Name	Units	$ Total	
2	Northwind Traders Almonds	20	$ 200	
3	Northwind Traders Beer	487	$ 6,818	
4	Northwind Traders Boysenberry Spread	100	$ 2,500	
5	Northwind Traders Cajun Seasoning	40	$ 880	
6	Northwind Traders Chai	40	$ 720	
7	Northwind Traders Chocolate	200	$ 2,550	
8	Northwind Traders Chocolate Biscuits Mix	85	$ 782	
9	Northwind Traders Clam Chowder	290	$ 2,799	
10	Northwind Traders Coffee	650	$ 29,900	
11	Northwind Traders Crab Meat	120	$ 2,208	
12	Northwind Traders Curry Sauce	65	$ 2,600	
13	Northwind Traders Dried Apples	40	$ 2,120	
14	Northwind Traders Dried Pears	40	$ 1,200	
15	Northwind Traders Dried Plums	75	$ 263	
16	Northwind Traders Fruit Cocktail	40	$ 1,560	
17	Northwind Traders Gnocchi	10	$ 380	
18	Northwind Traders Green Tea	275	$ 822	

2 Click the **Home** tab.

3 Click **Conditional Formatting** (⬛).

4 Click **Data Bars**.

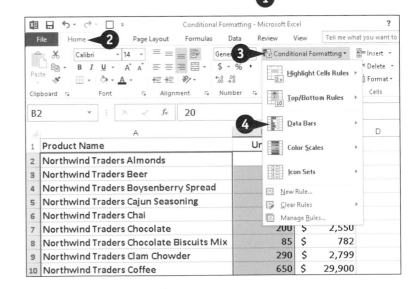

5 Click the fill type of data bars you want to create:

A Gradient Fill data bars begin with a solid color, and then gradually fade to a lighter color.

B Solid Fill data bars are a solid color.

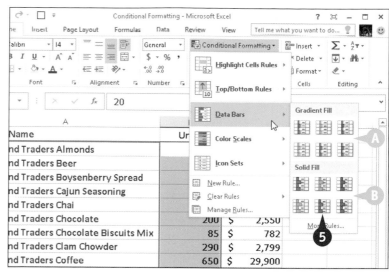

C Excel applies the data bars to each cell in the range.

	A	B	C	D
1	Product Name	Units	$ Total	
2	Northwind Traders Almonds	20	$ 200	
3	Northwind Traders Beer	487	$ 6,818	
4	Northwind Traders Boysenberry Spread	100	$ 2,500	
5	Northwind Traders Cajun Seasoning	40	$ 880	
6	Northwind Traders Chai	40	$ 720	
7	Northwind Traders Chocolate	200	$ 2,550	
8	Northwind Traders Chocolate Biscuits Mix	85	$ 782	
9	Northwind Traders Clam Chowder	290	$ 2,799	
10	Northwind Traders Coffee	650	$ 29,900	
11	Northwind Traders Crab Meat	120	$ 2,208	
12	Northwind Traders Curry Sauce	65	$ 2,600	
13	Northwind Traders Dried Apples	40	$ 2,120	
14	Northwind Traders Dried Pears	40	$ 1,200	
15	Northwind Traders Dried Plums	75	$ 263	
16	Northwind Traders Fruit Cocktail	40	$ 1,560	
17	Northwind Traders Gnocchi	10	$ 380	
18	Northwind Traders Green Tea	275	$ 822	

TIPS

How do data bars work?
The length of the data bar that appears in each cell depends on the value in that cell: The larger the value, the longer the data bar. The cell with the highest value has the longest data bar, the cell with the lowest value has the shortest data bar, and the other cells have data bars with lengths that reflect each cell's value.

How do I delete data bars from a range?
If you no longer require the data bars, you can remove them. Follow steps **1** to **3** to select the range and display the Conditional Formatting drop-down menu, and then click **Manage Rules**. Excel displays the Conditional Formatting Rules Manager dialog box. Click the data bar rule you want to remove, click **Delete Rule**, and then click **OK**.

Analyze Cell Values with Color Scales

When analyzing worksheet data, it is often useful to get some idea about the overall distribution of the values. For example, it might be useful to know whether a range has a lot of low values and just a few high values.

You can analyze your worksheet data by using a conditional format called *color scales*. A color scale compares the relative values of cells in a range by applying shading to each cell, where the shading color is a reflection of the cell's value.

Analyze Cell Values with Color Scales

1 Select the range with which you want to work.

2 Click the **Home** tab.

3 Click **Conditional Formatting** (⊞).

4 Click **Color Scales**.

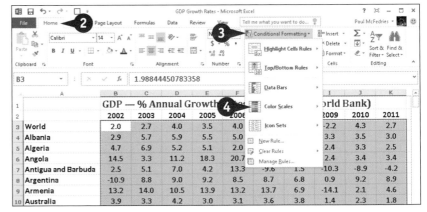

5 Click the color scale that has the color scheme you want to apply.

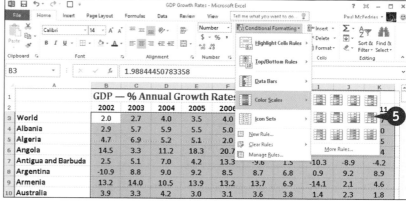

A Excel applies the color scales to each cell in the range.

In what other situations are color scales useful?

Besides showing patterns, color scales can also tell you whether your data includes any *outliers*, values that are much higher or lower than all or most of the others. Similarly, you can also use color scales to make value judgments about your data. For example, high sales and low numbers of product defects are good, whereas low margins and high employee turnover rates are bad.

When should I use a three-color scale versus a two-color scale?

If your goal is to look for outliers or to make value judgments about your data, go with a three-color scale because outliers stand out more, and you can assign your own values to the colors (such as positive, neutral, and negative). Use a two-color scale when you want to look for patterns in the data, as a two-color scale offers less contrast.

Analyze Cell Values with Icon Sets

Whenever you are trying to make sense of a large data set, symbols that have common or well-known associations are often useful for clarifying the data. For example, for most people a check mark means something is good or finished or acceptable, whereas an X means something is bad or unfinished or unacceptable; a green circle is positive, whereas a red circle is negative (think traffic lights).

Excel puts these and many other symbolic associations to good use with the *icon sets* feature. You use icon sets to visualize the relative values of cells in a range.

Analyze Cell Values with Icon Sets

1 Select the range with which you want to work.

2 Click the **Home** tab.

3 Click **Conditional Formatting** (⊞).

4 Click **Icon Sets**.

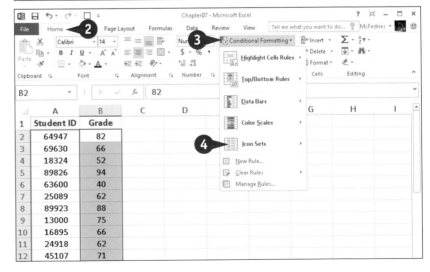

5 Click the type of icon set you want to apply.

The categories include Directional, Shapes, Indicators, and Ratings.

A Excel applies the icons to each cell in the range.

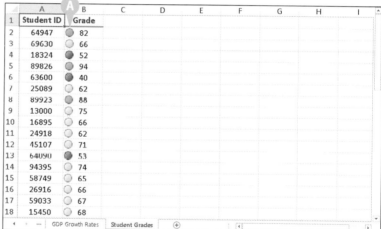

How do icon sets work?

With icon sets, Excel adds a particular icon to each cell in the range, and that icon tells you something about the cell's value relative to the rest of the range. For example, the highest values might be assigned an upward-pointing arrow, the lowest values a downward-pointing arrow, and the values in between a horizontal arrow.

How do I use the different icon set categories?

The Excel icon sets come in four categories: Directional, Shapes, Indicators, and Ratings. Use Directional icon sets for indicating trends and data movement; use Shapes icon sets for pointing out the high (green) and low (red) values; use Indicators to add value judgments; and use Ratings to show where each cell resides in the overall range of data values.

Create a Custom Conditional Formatting Rule

Excel's conditional formatting rules in Excel — highlight cells rules, top/bottom rules, data bars, color scales, and icon sets — offer an easy way to analyze data through visualization.

However, these predefined rules do not suit particular types of data or data analysis. For example, the icon sets assume that higher values are more positive than lower values, but that is not always true; in a database of product defects, lower values are better than higher ones. To get the type of data analysis you prefer, you can create a custom conditional formatting rule and apply it to your range.

Create a Custom Conditional Formatting Rule

1 Select the range you want to work with.

2 Click the **Home** tab.

3 Click **Conditional Formatting** (⊞).

4 Click **New Rule**.

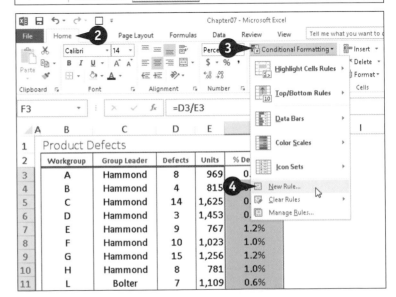

The New Formatting Rule dialog box appears.

5 Click the type of rule you want to create.

6 Edit the rule's style and formatting.

The controls you see depend on the rule type you selected.

Ⓐ With Icon Sets, click **Reverse Icon Order** if you want to reverse the normal icon assignments, as shown here.

7 Click **OK**.

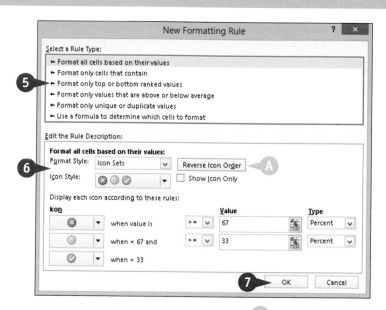

Ⓑ Excel applies the conditional formatting to each cell in the range.

	Workgroup	Group Leader	Defects	Units	% Defective
2	Workgroup	Group Leader	Defects	Units	% Defective
3	A	Hammond	8	969	0.8%
4	B	Hammond	4	815	0.5%
5	C	Hammond	14	1,625	0.9%
6	D	Hammond	3	1,453	0.2%
7	E	Hammond	9	767	1.2%
8	F	Hammond	10	1,023	1.0%
9	G	Hammond	15	1,256	1.2%
10	H	Hammond	8	781	1.0%
11	L	Bolter	7	1,109	0.6%
12	M	Bolter	8	1,021	0.8%
13	N	Bolter	6	812	0.7%
14	O	Bolter	11	977	1.1%
15	P	Bolter	5	1,182	0.4%
16	Q	Bolter	7	961	0.7%
17	R	Bolter	12	689	1.7%
18	T	Bolter	19	1,308	1.5%

Student Grades   Product Defects

TIPS

How do I modify a custom conditional formatting rule?

Follow steps **1** to **3** to select the range and display the Conditional Formatting drop-down menu, and then click **Manage Rules**. Excel displays the Conditional Formatting Rules Manager dialog box. Click the rule you want to modify and then click **Edit Rule**.

How do I remove a custom rule?

Follow steps **1** to **3** to select the range and display the Conditional Formatting drop-down menu, click **Clear Rules**, and then click **Clear Rules from Selected Cells**. If you have multiple custom rules defined for a worksheet and no longer require them, you can remove all of them. Click the **Home** tab, click **Conditional Formatting**, click **Clear Rules**, and then click **Clear Rules from Entire Sheet**.

Consolidate Data from Multiple Worksheets

Ⅰt is common to distribute similar worksheets to multiple departments to capture budget numbers, inventory values, survey data, and so on. Those worksheets must then be combined into a summary report showing company-wide totals. This is called *consolidating* the data.

Rather than doing this manually, Excel can consolidate your data automatically. You can use the Consolidate feature to consolidate the data either by position or by category. In both cases, you specify one or more source ranges (the ranges that contain the data you want to consolidate) and a destination range (the range where the consolidated data will appear).

Consolidate Data from Multiple Worksheets

Consolidate by Position

1 Create a new worksheet that uses the same layout (including row and column headers) as the sheets you want to consolidate.

2 Open the workbooks that contain the worksheets you want to consolidate.

3 Select the upper-left corner of the destination range.

4 Click the **Data** tab.

5 Click **Consolidate** (⬚→⬚).

The Consolidate dialog box appears.

6 Click the **Function** drop-down arrow (▼), and then click the summary function you want to use.

7 Click inside the **Reference** text box.

8 Select one of the ranges you want to consolidate.

9 Click **Add**.

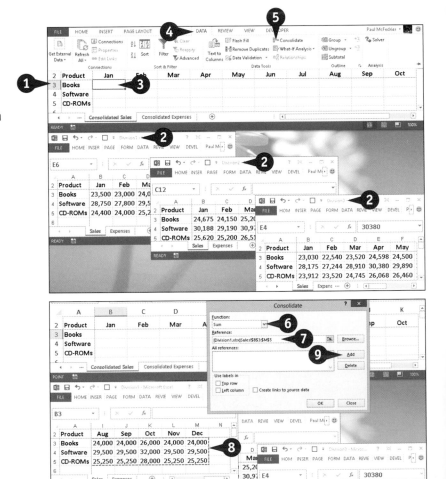

Ⓐ Excel adds the range to the All References list.

⑩ Repeat steps **7** to **9** to add all the consolidation ranges.

⑪ Click **OK**.

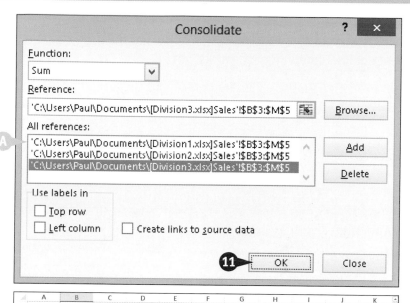

Ⓑ Excel consolidates the data from the source ranges and displays the summary in the destination range.

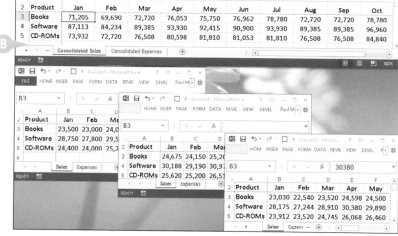

TIP

Is there an easy way to update the consolidation if the source data changes?
If the source data changes, then you probably want to reflect those changes in the consolidation worksheet. Rather than running the entire consolidation over again, a much easier solution is to select the **Create links to source data** check box (☐ changes to ☑) in the Consolidate dialog box. This enables you to update the consolidation worksheet by clicking the **Data** tab and then clicking **Refresh All**.

This also means that Excel creates an outline in the consolidation sheet, and you can use that outline to see the detail from each of the source ranges. See the "Group Related Data" section earlier in the chapter to learn more about outlines in Excel.

continued ▶

259

If the worksheets you want to summarize do not use the same layout, you need to tell Excel to consolidate the data *by category*. This method consolidates the data by looking for common row and column labels in each worksheet.

For example, suppose you are consolidating sales and Division A sells software, books, and videos; Division B sells books and CD-ROMs; and Division C sells books, software, videos, and CD-ROMs. When you consolidate this data, Excel summarizes the software from Divisions A and C, the CD-ROMs from Divisions B and C, and the books from all three.

Consolidate Data from Multiple Worksheets (continued)

Consolidate by Category

1 Create a new worksheet for the consolidation.

2 Open the workbooks that contain the worksheets you want to consolidate.

3 Select the upper-left corner of the destination range.

4 Click the **Data** tab.

5 Click **Consolidate** (⊟→□).

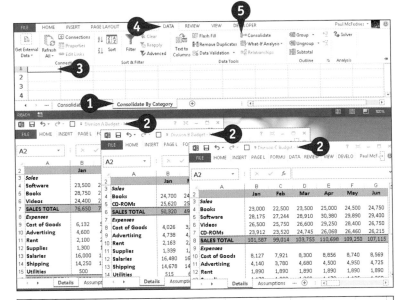

The Consolidate dialog box appears.

6 Click the **Function** drop-down arrow (▼), and then click the summary function you want to use.

7 Click inside the **Reference** text box.

8 Select one of the ranges you want to consolidate.

Note: Be sure to include the row and column labels in the range.

9 Click **Add**.

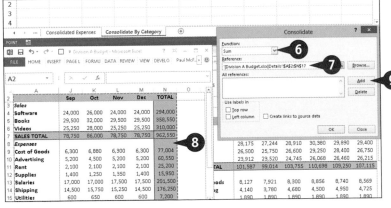

C Excel adds the range to the All references list.

10 Repeat steps **7** to **9** to add all the consolidation ranges.

11 If you have labels in the top row of each range, click **Top Row** (☐ changes to ☑).

12 If you have labels in the left-column row of each range, click **Left Column** (☐ changes to ☑).

13 Click **OK**.

D Excel consolidates the data from the source ranges and displays the summary in the destination range.

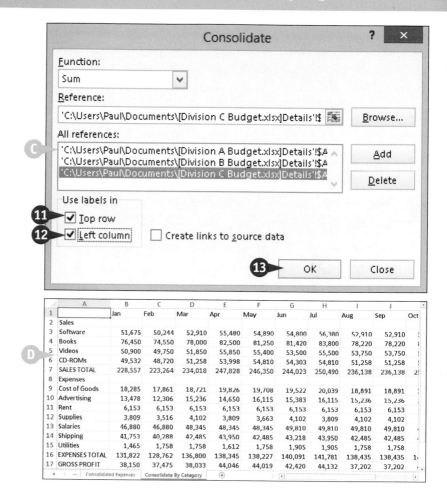

TIP

What happens if the source data layout changes?

If the layout of the source data changes, then you must run the consolidation again.

If you consolidated by position, then before you can rerun the consolidation, you must first adjust the layout of the consolidation worksheet to match the changes to the source data. (You do not need to do this if you consolidated by category.)

No matter which consolidation method you used, before you run the consolidation again, you must delete the existing source ranges. Click the **Data** tab, and then click **Consolidate** (▤→▫) to display the Consolidate dialog box. For each source range, click the range in the **All references** list and then click **Delete**.

Load the Excel Analysis ToolPak

Y ou can get access to a number of powerful statistical analysis tools by loading the Analysis ToolPak add-in. The Analysis ToolPak consists of 19 statistical tools that calculate statistical measures such as correlation, regression, rank and percentile, covariance, and moving averages.

You can also use the analysis tools to generate descriptive statistics (such as median, mode, and standard deviation), random numbers, and histograms.

Load the Excel Analysis ToolPak

1 Click the **File** tab (not shown).

2 Click **Options**.

The Excel Options dialog box appears.

3 Click **Add-Ins**.

4 In the Manage list, click **Excel Add-ins**.

5 Click **Go**.

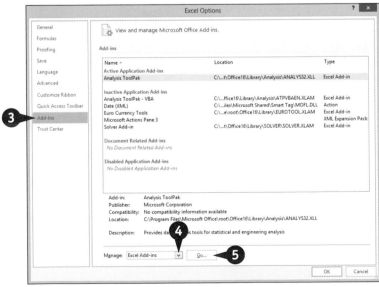

The Add-Ins dialog box appears.

6 Select the **Analysis ToolPak** check box (☐ changes to ☑).

7 Click **OK**.

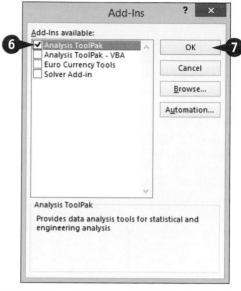

Excel loads the Analysis ToolPak add-in.

8 Click the **Data** tab.

9 Click **Data Analysis** (🖩) to access the Analysis ToolPak tools.

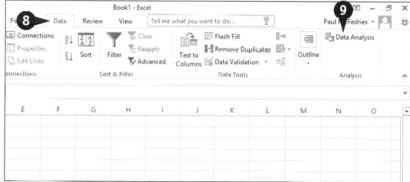

TIP

How do I use the statistical tools?
The specific steps you follow vary from tool to tool, but you can follow these general steps to use any of the Analysis ToolPak's statistical tools:

1 Click the **Data** tab.

2 Click 🖩.

The Data Analysis dialog box appears.

3 Click the tool you want to use.

4 Click **OK**.

Excel displays a dialog box for the tool.

5 Fill in the dialog box (the controls vary from tool to tool).

6 Click **OK**.

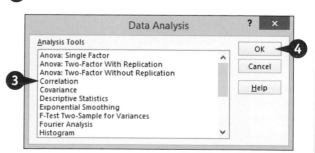

CHAPTER 12

Visualizing Data with Charts

You can take a worksheet full of numbers and display them as a chart. Visualizing your data in this way makes the data easier to understand and analyze. To help you see your data exactly the way you want, Excel offers a wide variety of chart types, and a large number of chart options.

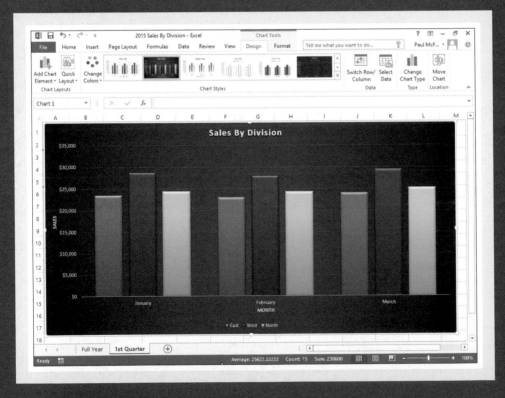

Examine Chart Elements

One of the best ways to analyze your worksheet data — or get your point across to other people — is to display your data visually in a *chart*, which is a graphic representation of spreadsheet data. As the data in the spreadsheet changes, the chart also changes to reflect the new numbers.

You have dozens of different chart formats to choose from, and if none of the built-in Excel formats is just right, you can further customize these charts to suit your needs. To get the most out of charts, you need to familiarize yourself with the basic chart elements.

Ⓐ Category Axis

The axis (usually the X axis) that contains the category groupings.

Ⓑ Chart Title

The title of the chart.

Ⓒ Data Marker

A symbol that represents a specific data value. The symbol used depends on the chart type.

Ⓓ Data Series

A collection of related data values. Normally, the marker for each value in a series has the same pattern.

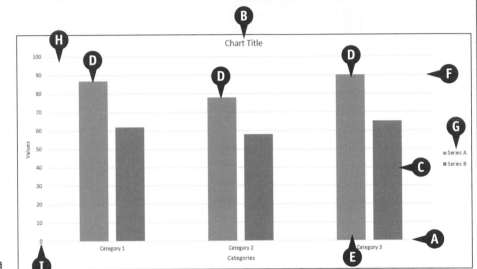

Ⓔ Data Value

A single piece of data, also called a *data point*.

Ⓕ Gridlines

Optional horizontal and vertical extensions of the axis tick marks. These lines make data values easier to read.

Ⓖ Legend

A guide that shows the colors, patterns, and symbols used by the markers for each data series.

Ⓗ Plot Area

The area bounded by the category and value axes. It contains the data points and gridlines.

Ⓘ Value Axis

The axis (usually the Y axis) that contains the data values.

Understanding Chart Types

Excel offers 15 different types of charts, including column charts, bar charts, line charts, and pie charts. The chart type you use depends on the type of data and how you want to present that data visually.

Chart Types

Chart Type	Description
Area chart	Shows the relative contributions over time that each data series makes to the whole picture.
Bar chart	Compares distinct items or shows single items at distinct intervals. A bar chart is laid out with categories along the vertical axis and values along the horizontal axis.
Box & Whisker chart	Visualizes several statistical values for the data in each category, including the average, the range, the minimum, and the maximum.
Column chart	Like a bar chart, compares distinct items or shows single items at distinct intervals. However, a column chart is laid out with categories along the horizontal axis and values along the vertical axis.
Doughnut chart	Like a pie chart, shows the proportion of the whole that is contributed by each value in a data series. The advantage of a doughnut chart is that you can plot multiple data series.
Histogram	Groups the category values into ranges — called *bins* — and shows the frequency with which the data values fall within each bin.
Line chart	Shows how a data series changes over time. The category (X) axis usually represents a progression of even increments (such as days or months), and the series points are plotted on the value (Y) axis.
Pie chart	Shows the proportion of the whole that is contributed by each value in a single data series. The whole is represented as a circle (the "pie"), and each value is displayed as a proportional "slice" of the circle.
Radar chart	Makes comparisons within a data series and between data series relative to a center point. Each category is shown with a value axis extending from the center point.
Stock chart	Designed to plot stock-market prices, such as a stock's daily high, low, and closing values.
Sunburst chart	Displays hierarchical data as a series of concentric circles, with the top level as the innermost circle and each circle divided proportionally according to the data values within that level.
Surface chart	Analyzes two sets of data and determines the optimum combination of the two.
Treemap chart	For hierarchical data, shows a large rectangle for each item in the top level, then divides each rectangle proportionally based on the value of each item in the next level.
Waterfall chart	Shows a running total as category values are added (positive values) or subtracted (negative values).
XY chart	Shows the relationship between numeric values in two different data series. It can also plot a series of data pairs in XY coordinates. (This is also called a *scatter* chart.)

Create a Chart

You can create a chart from your Excel worksheet data with just a few mouse clicks. Excel offers nearly 100 default chart configurations, so there should always be a type that best visualizes your data. If you would prefer to let Excel suggest a chart type based on your data, see the following section, "Create a Recommended Chart."

Regardless of the chart type you choose originally, you can change to a different chart type at any time. See the "Select a Different Chart Type" section later in this chapter.

Create a Chart

1 Select the data that you want to visualize in a chart.

A If your data includes headings, be sure to include those headings in the selection.

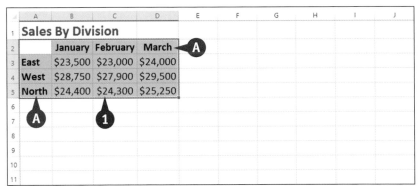

2 Click the **Insert** tab.

3 Click a chart type.

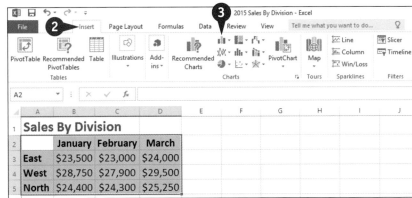

B Excel displays a gallery of configurations for the chart type.

4 Click the chart configuration you want to use.

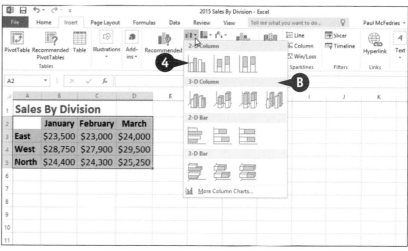

C Excel inserts the chart.

The sections in the rest of this chapter show you how to configure, format, and move the chart.

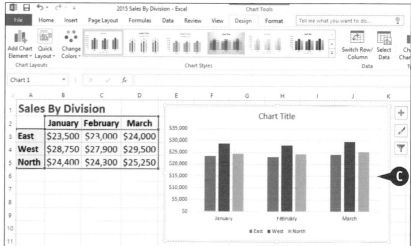

TIP

Is there a way to create a chart on a separate sheet?

Yes. You can use a special workbook sheet called a *chart sheet*. If you have not yet created your chart, select the worksheet data, right-click any worksheet tab, and then click **Insert** to display the Insert dialog box. Click the **General** tab, click **Chart**, and then click **OK**. Excel creates a new chart sheet and inserts the chart.

If you have already created your chart, you can move it to a separate chart sheet. See the first tip in the "Move or Resize a Chart" section later in this chapter.

Create a Recommended Chart

You can make it easier and faster to create a chart by choosing from one of the chart configurations recommended by Excel.

With close to 100 possible chart configurations, the Excel chart tools are certainly comprehensive. However, that can be an overwhelming number of choices if you're not sure which type would best visualize your data. Rather than wasting a great deal of time looking at dozens of different chart configurations, the Recommended Charts command examines your data and then narrows down the possible choices to about ten configurations that would work with your data.

Create a Recommended Chart

1 Select the data that you want to visualize in a chart.

A If your data includes headings, be sure to include those headings in the selection.

2 Click the **Insert** tab.

3 Click **Recommended Charts**.

The Insert Chart dialog box appears with the Recommended Charts tab displayed.

④ Click the chart type you want to use.

Ⓑ A preview of the chart appears here.

⑤ Click **OK**.

Ⓒ Excel inserts the chart.

Is there a faster way to insert a recommended chart?

Yes, you can use the Quick Analysis feature in Excel:

① Select the data that you want to visualize in a chart, including the headings, if any.

② Click the **Quick Analysis** Smart tag (📊).

③ Click **Charts**.

Excel displays the chart types recommended for your data.

④ Click the chart type you want to use.

Excel inserts the chart.

271

Add Chart Titles

You can make your chart easier to understand by adding chart titles, which are labels that appear in specific sections of the chart. By including descriptive titles, you make it easier for other people to see at a glance what your chart is visualizing.

There are three types of chart titles that you can add. The first type is the overall chart title, which usually appears at the top of the chart. You can also add a title for the horizontal axis to describe the chart categories, as well as a title for the vertical axis, which describes the chart values.

Add Chart Titles

1. Click the chart.
2. Click the **Design** tab.
3. Click **Add Chart Element**.
4. Click **Chart Title**.
5. Click **Above Chart**.
   A. Excel adds the title box.
6. Type the title.

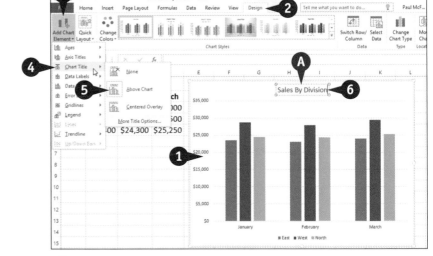

7. Click **Add Chart Element**.
8. Click **Axis Titles**.
9. Click **Primary Horizontal**.
   B. Excel adds the title box.
10. Type the title.
11. Click **Add Chart Element**.
12. Click **Axis Titles**.
13. Click **Primary Vertical**.
    C. Excel adds the title box.
14. Type the title.

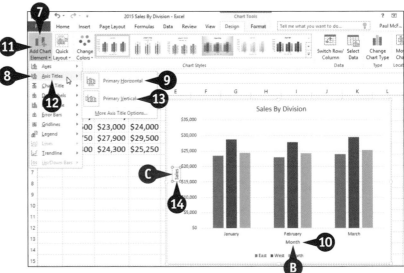

Add Data Labels

You can make your chart easier to read by adding data labels. A *data label* is a small text box that appears in or near a data marker and displays the value of that data point.

Excel offers several position options for the data labels, and these options depend on the chart type. For example, with a column chart you can place the data labels within or above each column, and for a line chart you can place the labels to the left or right, or above or below, the data marker.

Add Data Labels

1. Click the chart.
2. Click the **Design** tab.
3. Click **Add Chart Element**.
4. Click **Data Labels**.
5. Click the position you want to use for the data labels.

Note: Remember that the position options you see depend on the chart type.

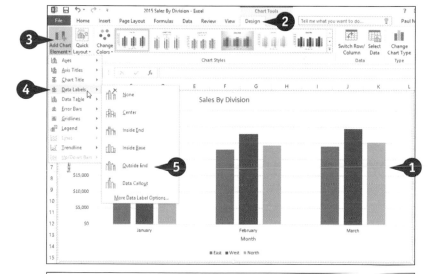

A) Excel adds the labels to the chart.

Position the Chart Legend

You can change the position of the chart *legend*, which identifies the colors associated with each data series in the chart. The legend is a crucial chart element for interpreting and understanding your chart, so it is important that you place it in the best position. For example, you might find the legend easier to read if it appears to the right of the chart. Alternatively, if you want more horizontal space to display your chart, you can move the legend above or below the chart.

Position the Chart Legend

1 Click the chart.

2 Click the **Design** tab.

3 Click **Add Chart Element**.

4 Click **Legend**.

5 Click the position you want to use for the legend.

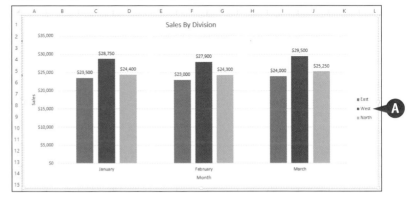

A Excel moves the legend.

Display Chart Gridlines

You can make your chart easier to read and analyze by adding gridlines. Horizontal gridlines extend from the vertical (value) axis, and are useful with area, bubble, and column charts. Vertical gridlines extend from the horizontal (category) axis and are useful with bar and line charts.

Major gridlines are gridlines associated with the *major units* (the values you see displayed on the vertical and horizontal axes), while *minor gridlines* are gridlines associated with the *minor units* (values between each major unit).

Display Chart Gridlines

1. Click the chart.

2. Click the **Design** tab.

3. Click **Add Chart Element**.

4. Click **Gridlines**.

5. Click the horizontal gridline option you prefer.

Ⓐ Excel displays the horizontal gridlines.

6. Click **Add Chart Element**.

7. Click **Gridlines**.

8. Click the vertical gridline option you prefer.

Ⓑ Excel displays the vertical gridlines.

275

Display a Data Table

You can make it easier for yourself and others to interpret your chart by adding a data table. A *data table* is a tabular grid where each row is a data series from the chart, each column is a chart category, and each cell is a chart data point.

Excel gives you the option of displaying the data table with or without *legend keys*, which are markers that identify each series.

Display a Data Table

1 Click the chart.

2 Click the **Design** tab.

3 Click **Add Chart Element**.

4 Click **Data Table**.

5 Click **With Legend Keys**.

A If you prefer not to display the legend keys, click **No Legend Keys**.

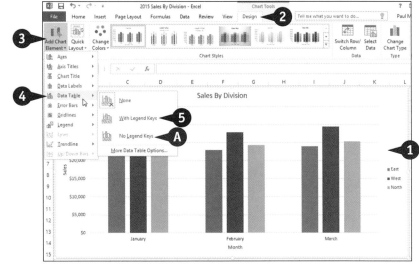

B Excel adds the data table below the chart.

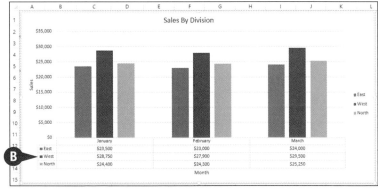

Change the Chart Layout and Style

You can quickly format your chart by applying a different chart layout and chart style. The chart layout includes elements such as the titles, data labels, legend, gridlines, and data table. The Quick Layouts feature in Excel enables you to apply these elements in different combinations with just a few mouse clicks. The chart style represents the colors used by the chart data markers and background.

Change the Chart Layout and Style

1. Click the chart.
2. Click the **Design** tab.
3. Click **Quick Layout**.
4. Click the layout you want to use.
   A. Excel applies the layout.
5. Click the **Chart Styles** ═.

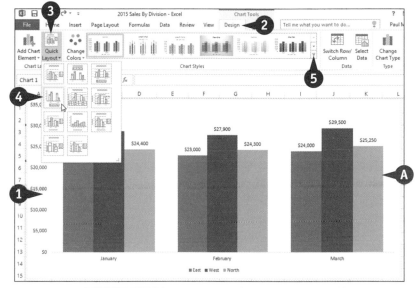

6. Click the chart style you want to use.
   B. Excel applies the style to the chart.

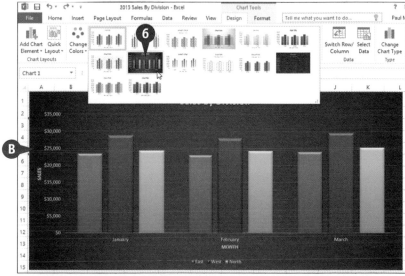

Select a Different Chart Type

If you feel that the current chart type is not showing your data in the best way, you can change the chart type. This enables you to experiment not only with the 11 different chart types offered by Excel, but also with its nearly 100 chart type configurations.

For example, if you are graphing a stock's high, low, and closing prices, a line chart shows you each value, but a stock chart gives you a better sense of the daily price movements. Similarly, if you are using a bar chart to show percentages of some whole, you would more readily visualize the data by switching to a pie chart.

Select a Different Chart Type

1. Click the chart.
2. Click the **Design** tab.
3. Click **Change Chart Type**.

The Change Chart Type dialog box appears.

4. Click the chart type you want to use.

Excel displays the chart type
configurations.

⑤ Click the configuration you want
to use.

⑥ Click **OK**.

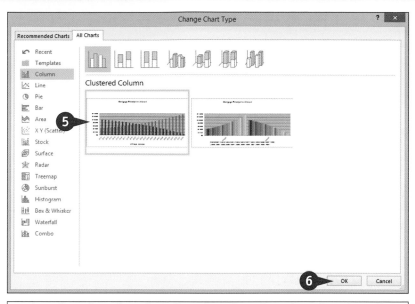

Ⓐ Excel applies the new chart
type.

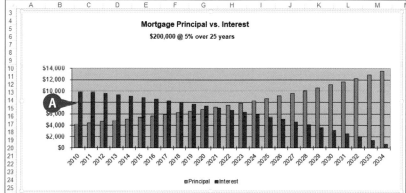

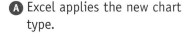

TIP

Can I save the chart type and formatting so that I can reuse it later on a different chart?
Yes. You do this by saving your work as a chart template. Follow the steps in this section and in the
previous few sections of this chapter to set the chart type, titles, labels, legend position, gridlines, layout,
and style. Right-click the chart's plot area or background, click **Save as Template**, type a name for the
template, and then click **Save**. To reuse the template, follow steps **1** to **3**, click **Templates**, click your
template, and then click **OK**.

Change the Chart Source Data

In Excel, a chart's *source data* is the original range used to create the chart. You can keep your chart up to date and accurate by adjusting the chart when its source data changes.

You normally do this when the structure of the source data changes. For example, if the source range adds a row or column, you can adjust the chart to include the new data. However, you do not need to make any adjustments if just the data within the original range changes. In such cases, Excel automatically adjusts the chart to display the new data.

Change the Chart Source Data

1 Click the chart to select it.

A Excel selects the chart's source data.

2 Move the mouse ⊕ over the lower-right corner of the range.

⊕ changes to ↔.

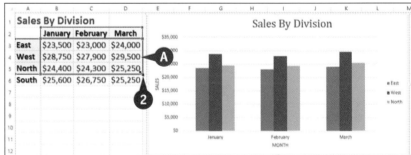

③ Click and drag ↔ until the selection includes all the data you want to include in the chart.

Ⓑ Excel extends the blue outline to show you the new selection.

④ Release the mouse button.

Ⓒ Excel redraws the chart to include the new data.

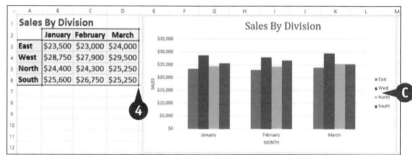

Is there a way to swap the chart series with the chart categories without modifying the source data?

Yes. Excel has a feature that enables you to switch the row and column data, which swaps the series and categories without affecting the source data. First click the chart to select it, and then click the **Design** tab. Click **Switch Row/Column** (⊞). Excel swaps the series and categories. Click ⊞ again to return to the original layout.

Is there a way to remove a series from a chart without deleting the data from the source range?

Yes. You can use the Select Data Source dialog box in Excel to remove individual series. Click the chart to select it, and then click the **Design** tab. Click **Select Data** (⊞) to open the Select Data Source. In the **Legend Entries (Series)** list, click the series you want to get rid of, and then click **Remove**. Click **OK**.

Move or Resize a Chart

You can move a chart to another part of the worksheet. This is useful if the chart is blocking the worksheet data or if you want the chart to appear in a particular part of the worksheet.

You can also resize a chart. For example, if you find that the chart is difficult to read, making the chart bigger often solves the problem. Similarly, if the chart takes up too much space on the worksheet, you can make it smaller.

Move or Resize a Chart

Move a Chart

1 Click the chart.

A Excel displays a border around the chart.

2 Move ⌖ over the chart border. ⌖ changes to ✥.

Note: Do not position the mouse pointer over a corner or over the middle of any side of the border.

3 Click and drag the chart border to the location you want.

4 Release the mouse button.

B Excel moves the chart.

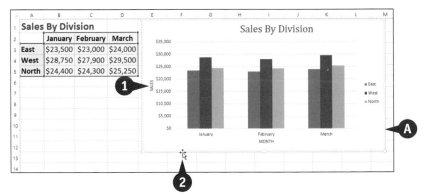

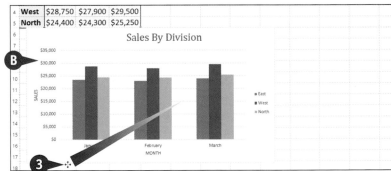

Resize a Chart

1 Click the chart.

C Excel displays a border around the chart.

D The border includes sizing handles on the corners and sides.

2 Move ⌖ over a sizing handle. ⌖ changes to ⟷ (left or right), ⇕ (top or bottom), or ⤢ (corner).

3 Click and drag the handle.

E Excel displays a gray outline of the new chart size.

4 Release the mouse button.

F Excel resizes the chart.

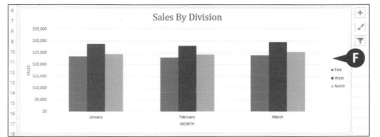

TIPS

Can I move a chart to a separate sheet?
Yes. In the "Create a Chart" section earlier in this chapter, you learned how to create a new chart in a separate sheet. If your chart already exists on a worksheet, you can move it to a new sheet. Click the chart, click the **Design** tab, and then click **Move Chart** to open the Move Chart dialog box. Select the **New sheet** option (◯ changes to ◉). In the **New sheet** text box, type a name for the new sheet, and then click **OK**.

How do I delete a chart?
How you delete a chart depends on whether your chart exists as an object on a worksheet or in its own sheet. If the chart is on a worksheet, click the chart and then press `Delete`. If the chart exists on a separate sheet, right-click the sheet tab, click **Delete Sheet**, and then click **Delete**.

Add a Sparkline to a Cell

If you want a quick visualization of your data without having a chart take up a large amount of worksheet space, you can add a sparkline to a single cell. A *sparkline* is a small chart that visualizes a row or column of data and fits inside a single cell.

Excel offers three types of sparklines: Line (similar to a line chart), Column (similar to a column chart), and Win/Loss (for data that includes positive and negative values).

Add a Sparkline to a Cell

1 Select the row or column of data you want to visualize.

2 Click the **Insert** tab.

3 Click the type of sparkline you want to create.

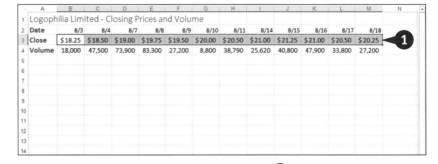

The Create Sparklines dialog box appears.

④ Click inside the **Location Range** box.

⑤ Click the cell where you want the sparkline to appear.

⑥ Click **OK**.

Ⓐ Excel adds the sparkline to the cell.

Ⓑ Excel displays the Sparkline Tools tab.

Ⓒ Use the tools in the Design tab to format your sparkline.

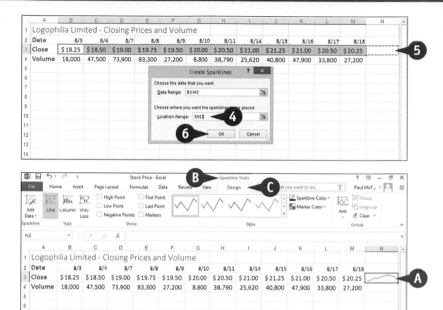

TIP

Can I add a sparkline to multiple rows or columns at once?

Yes. To do this, first select the rows or columns of data that you want to visualize. Follow steps **2** and **3** to open the Create Sparklines dialog box and place the cursor inside the **Location Range** box. Select a single cell for each row or column that you have selected. For example, if you have selected five rows, select five cells. Click **OK**. Excel adds a sparkline for each selected row or column.

CHAPTER 13

Adding Worksheet Graphics

You can enhance the visual appeal and effectiveness of your Excel worksheets by incorporating graphic objects such as shapes, clip art, pictures, or WordArt and SmartArt images. This chapter shows you not only how to insert graphics on your worksheets, but also how to edit and format those graphics.

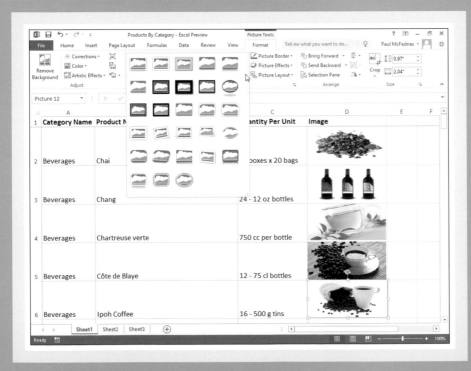

Draw a Shape

Y‌ou can add visual appeal or enhance the readability of your worksheets by adding one or more shapes. The Excel Shapes gallery comes with more than 150 predefined objects called *shapes* (or sometimes *AutoShapes*) that enable you to quickly and easily draw anything from simple geometric figures such as lines, rectangles, and ovals, to more elaborate items such as starbursts, flowchart symbols, and callout boxes. You can add these shapes to a worksheet either to enhance the aesthetics of your data or to help other people read and understand your work.

Draw a Shape

① Display the worksheet on which you want to draw the shape.

② Click the **Insert** tab.

③ Click **Illustrations**.

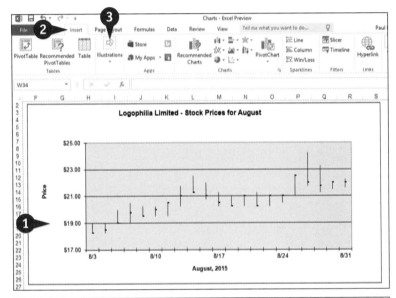

④ Click **Shapes**.

⑤ Click the shape you want to draw.

    ⬈ changes to ✛.

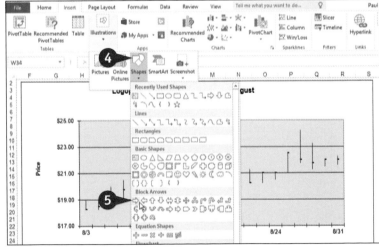

6 Click and drag the mouse ✚ to draw the shape.

7 When the shape is the size you want, release the mouse button.

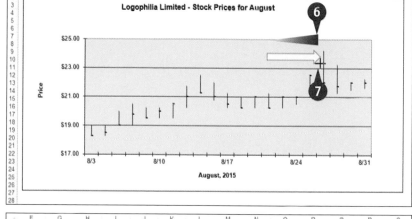

Ⓐ The program draws the shape and adds edit handles around the shape's edges.

Note: If you need to move or size the shape, see the "Move or Resize a Graphic" section later in this chapter.

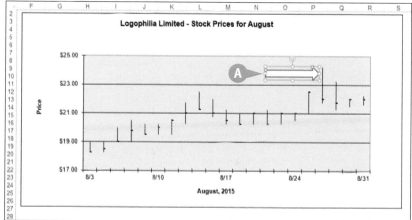

TIPS

Is there an easy way to draw a perfect circle or square?

Yes, Excel offers an easy technique for drawing circles and squares. Hold down the **Shift** key as you click and drag the shape to constrain the shape into a perfect circle or square. When you finish drawing the shape, release the **Shift** key.

Can I add text to a shape?

Yes. You can add text to the interior of any 2-D shape (that is, any shape that is not a line). After you draw the shape, right-click the shape, click **Edit Text**, and then type your text inside the shape. You can use the Home tab's Font controls to format the text. When you finish, click outside of the shape.

Insert a Clip Art Image

You can improve the look of an Excel worksheet by adding a clip art image to the sheet. *Clip art* refers to small images or artwork that you can insert into your documents. Excel 2016 does not come with its own clip art, but it does give you access to online clip art collections that contains thousands of images from various categories, such as business, people, nature, and symbols. By default, these images are licensed under Creative Commons, so you can use them without charge.

Insert a Clip Art Image

1. Display the worksheet on which you want to insert the clip art image.

2. Click the cell where you want the upper-left corner of the image to appear.

3. Click the **Insert** tab.

4. Click **Illustrations**.

5. Click **Online Pictures**.

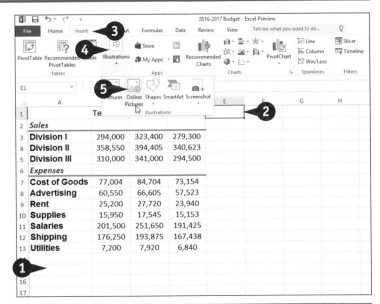

The Insert Pictures window appears.

6. Click **Bing Image Search**.

7. Use the text box to type a word that describes the kind of clip art image you want to insert.

8. Click **Search** ( ).

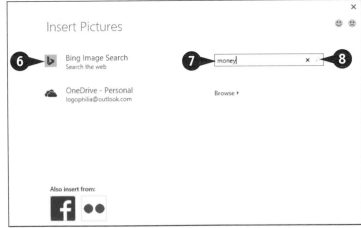

Ⓐ Excel displays a list of clip art images that match your search term.

❾ Click the clip art image you want to use.

Ⓑ The address of the website that offers the image appears here.

❿ Click **Insert**.

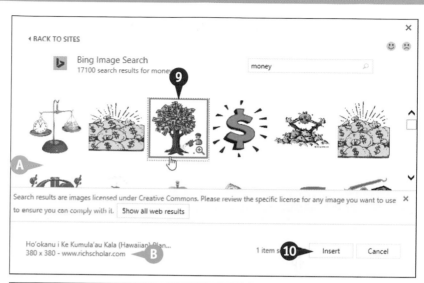

Ⓒ Excel inserts the clip art.

Note: If you need to move or size the clip art, see the "Move or Resize a Graphic" section later in this chapter.

What is a Creative Commons license?
Creative Commons (http://creativecommons.org) is a non-profit organization that enables artists to license their works for other people to use free of charge. There are several different Creative Commons licenses, so you should visit the website that offers the image you select to check the specifics of the license.

Can I insert other online images?
Yes. If you have connected your Facebook or your Flickr account to Windows 8 or later, you can also use the Facebook or Flickr option to choose a photo. If you are using a Microsoft account with Windows 8 or later, you can use the OneDrive option to select an image from your OneDrive.

Insert a Photo

You can enhance the visual appeal and strengthen the message of an Excel worksheet by adding a photo to the file.

Excel can work with the most popular picture formats, including BMP, JPEG, TIFF, PNG, and GIF. This means that you can insert almost any photo that you have stored on your computer. If you would like to insert a photo that is located online instead, see the tips in the previous section, "Insert a Clip Art Image."

Insert a Photo

1 Open the worksheet where you want to insert the photo.

2 Click the cell where you want the upper-left corner of the photo to appear.

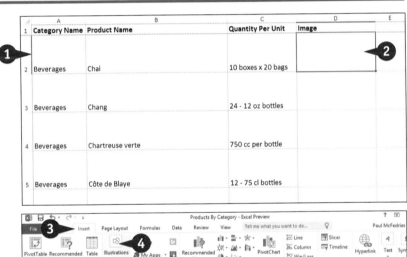

3 Click the **Insert** tab.

4 Click **Illustrations**.

5 Click **Pictures**.

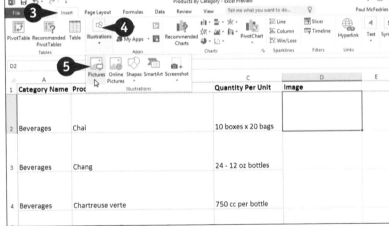

The Insert Picture dialog box appears.

6 Open the folder that contains the photo you want to insert.

7 Click the photo.

8 Click **Insert**.

A Excel inserts the photo into the worksheet.

Note: If you need to move or size the photo, see the "Move or Resize a Graphic" section later in this chapter.

My photo has a distracting background. Can I remove it?

Yes. Excel comes with a Background Removal feature that can eliminate the background in most photos. Click the photo, click the **Format** tab, and then click **Remove Background** (🖼). If part of the foreground is in the removal color, click **Mark Areas to Keep** and then click and drag a line through the part you want to retain. When you are finished, click **Keep Changes**.

Is there a way to reduce the size of a workbook that has a lot of photos?

Yes, you can use the Compress Pictures feature to convert the photos to a lower resolution and so reduce the size of the workbook. Click any image in the workbook, click the **Format** tab, and then click **Compress Pictures** (🖼). Click **Apply only to this picture** (☑ changes to ☐), click a **Target output** (◯ changes to ◉), and then click **OK**.

Insert a WordArt Image

You can add some pizzazz to your Excel workbooks by inserting a WordArt image. A WordArt image is a graphic object that contains text stylized with shadows, outlines, reflections, and other predefined effects.

WordArt images enable you to apply sophisticated and fun effects to text with just a few mouse clicks. However, some of the more elaborate WordArt effects can make text difficult to read, so make sure that whatever WordArt image you use does not detract from your worksheet message.

Insert a WordArt Image

1 Open the worksheet in which you want to insert the WordArt image.

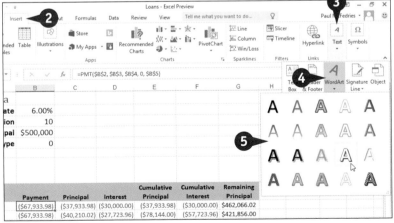

2 Click the **Insert** tab.

3 Click **Text**.

4 Click **WordArt**.

The WordArt gallery appears.

5 Click the WordArt style you want to use.

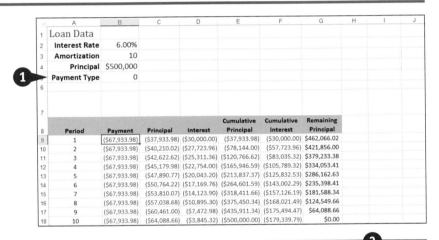

Ⓐ The WordArt image appears in the worksheet.

6 Type the text that you want to appear in the WordArt image.

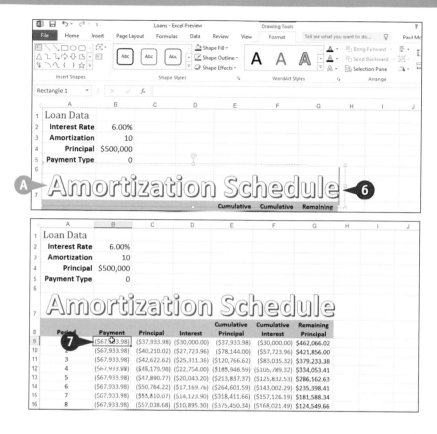

7 Click outside the image to set it.

Note: You will likely have to move the WordArt image into position; see the "Move or Resize a Graphic" section later in this chapter.

Can I change the default WordArt formatting?

Yes. Click the WordArt image to select it, and then use the Home tab's Font controls to adjust the WordArt text font. Click the **Format** tab. In the WordArt Styles group, use the **Text Fill** (Ⓐ), **Text Outline** (Ⓐ), and **Text Effects** (Ⓐ) galleries to format the WordArt image. You can also use the Quick Styles gallery to select a different WordArt style.

Can I make my WordArt text run vertically?

Yes. Click the WordArt image to select it. Click the **Format** tab, and then click the dialog box launcher (🔲) in the **WordArt Styles** group. In the Format Shape task pane, click **Text Options** and then click the **Textbox** icon (🔤). Click the **Text direction** ⯆ and then click **Stacked**. Click **Close**. Excel displays the WordArt text vertically.

Insert a SmartArt Graphic

You can add a SmartArt graphic to a workbook to help present information in a compact, visual format. A SmartArt graphic is a collection of *nodes* — shapes with some text inside — that enables you to convey information visually.

For example, you can use a SmartArt graphic to present a company organization chart, the progression of steps in a workflow, the parts that make up a whole, and much more.

Insert a SmartArt Graphic

1 Open the worksheet in which you want to insert the SmartArt image.

2 Click the **Insert** tab.

3 Click **Illustrations**.

4 Click **SmartArt**.

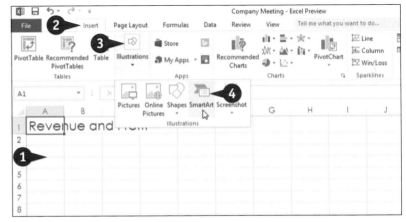

The Choose a SmartArt Graphic dialog box appears.

5 Click a SmartArt category.

6 Click the SmartArt style you want to use.

7 Click **OK**.

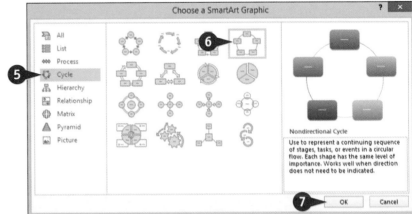

Ⓐ The SmartArt graphic appears in the document.

Ⓑ You use the Text pane to type the text for each node and to add and delete nodes.

❽ Click a node in the Text pane.

❾ Type the text that you want to appear in the node.

Ⓒ The text appears automatically in the associated shape.

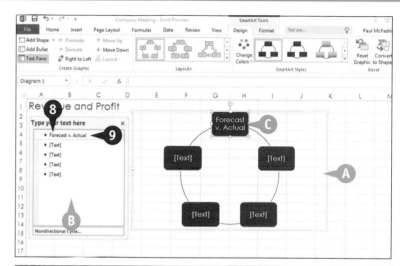

❿ Repeat steps **8** and **9** to fill in the other nodes in the SmartArt graphic.

Ⓓ You can click **Text Pane** (▣) to hide the Text pane.

Note: You will likely have to move the SmartArt graphic into position; see the following section, "Move or Resize a Graphic."

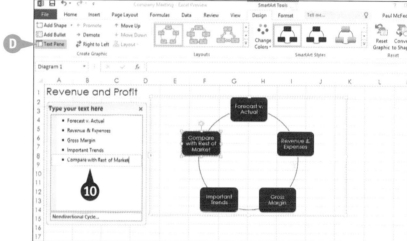

TIPS

How do I add a node to my SmartArt graphic?

To add a node to the SmartArt graphic, first decide where you want that node to appear in the current image. That is, decide which existing node you want the new node to come before or after. Click the existing node, click the **Design** tab, click the **Add Shape** ▼, and then click **Add Shape After**. (If you want the new node to appear before the existing node, click **Add Shape Before**.)

Can I use shapes other than the ones supplied in the default SmartArt graphics?

Yes. Begin by clicking the node you want to change. Click the **Format** tab, and then click the **Change Shape** ▼ to display the Shapes gallery. Click the shape you want to use. Excel updates the SmartArt graphic node with the new shape.

297

Move or Resize a Graphic

To ensure that a graphic is ideally placed within an Excel worksheet, you can move the graphic to a new location or you can resize the graphic in its current location. For example, you might want to move or resize a graphic so that it does not cover existing worksheet text. Similarly, you might want to move or resize a graphic so that it is positioned near a particular worksheet element or fits within an open worksheet area. You can move or resize any graphic, including shapes, clip art, pictures, WordArt images, and SmartArt graphics.

Move or Resize a Graphic

Move a Graphic

❶ Move the mouse pointer over an edge of the graphic you want to move.

The mouse ↖ changes to ✥.

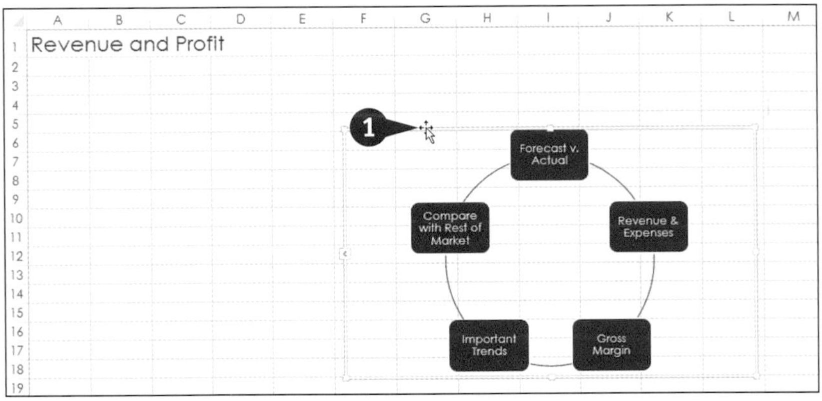

❷ Drag the graphic to the location you prefer.

Ⓐ Excel moves the graphic to the new location.

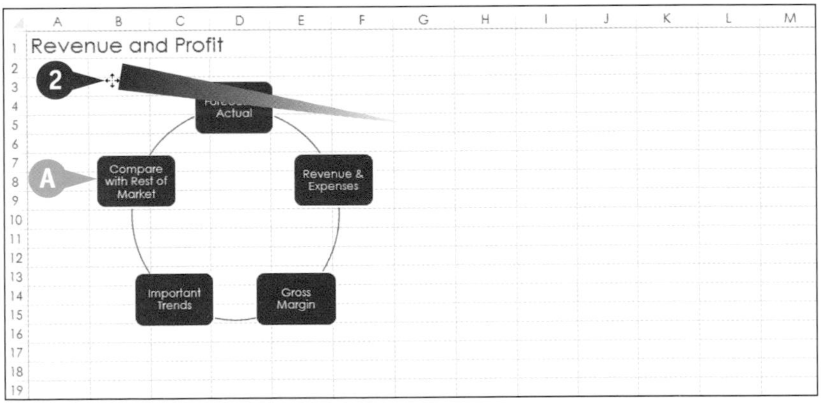

Resize a Graphic

1 Click the graphic.

B Sizing handles appear around the edges.

2 Move the mouse ▷ over a sizing handle.

C Use a left or right handle (▷ changes to ↔) to adjust the width.

D Use a top or bottom handle (▷ changes to ↕) to adjust the height.

E Use a corner handle (▷ changes to ⤢) to adjust the two sides adjacent to the corner.

3 Drag the sizing handle (the mouse pointer changes to ✛).

4 Release the mouse button when the handle is in the position you want.

F Excel resizes the graphic.

5 Repeat steps **2** to **4** to resize other sides of the graphic, as necessary.

TIPS

Can I rotate a graphic?
Yes. Most graphic objects come with a rotate handle. Follow these steps:

1 Move the mouse ▷ over the rotate handle (▷ changes to ↻).

2 Click and drag the rotate handle clockwise or counterclockwise to rotate the graphic.

3 Release the mouse button when the graphic is in the position you want.

Is it possible to resize a graphic in all directions at once to keep the proportions the same?
Yes. You normally resize one side at a time by dragging a side handle, or two sides at a time by dragging a corner handle. To resize all four sides at once, hold down the **Ctrl** key and then click and drag any corner handle.

Crop a Picture

If a picture contains extraneous material near the outside edges of the image, you can often cut out those elements using a process called *cropping*. When you crop a picture, you specify a rectangular area of the image that you want to keep. Excel discards everything outside of the rectangle.

Cropping is a useful feature because it can help viewers focus on the subject of a picture. Cropping is also useful for removing extraneous elements that appear on or near the edges of a photo.

Crop a Picture

1 Click the picture you want to crop.

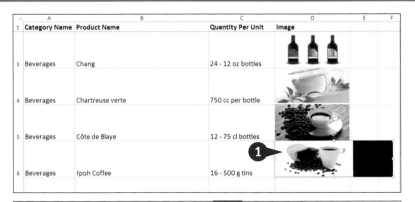

2 Click the **Format** tab.

3 Click the **Crop** button (⬚).

Ⓐ Crop handles appear around the picture.

④ Click and drag a crop handle.

The mouse ✛ changes to ➕.

Ⓑ Click and drag a side handle to crop that side.

Ⓒ Click and drag a corner handle to crop the two sides adjacent to the corner.

⑤ Release the mouse button when the handle is in the position you want.

⑥ Click 🖼.

Excel turns off the Crop feature.

Ⓓ Excel crops the picture.

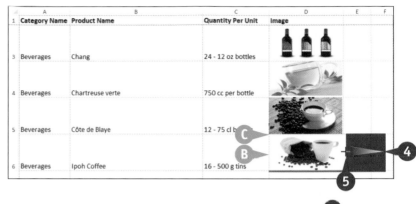

TIPS

If I have a picture with the main element in the middle, is it possible to crop in all directions at once to keep just that middle element?

Yes. You normally crop one side at a time by clicking and dragging a side crop handle, or two sides at a time by clicking and dragging a corner crop handle. To crop all four sides at once, hold down the Ctrl key and then click and drag any corner crop handle.

Can I crop a picture to a particular aspect ratio or shape?

Yes. Excel offers a couple of cropping options. If you know the aspect ratio (the ratio of the width to the height) you want, click the **Crop** ▼, click **Aspect Ratio**, and then click the ratio, such as 3:5 or 4:6. If you prefer to crop to a shape, such as an oval or arrow, click the **Crop** ▼, click **Crop to Shape**, and then click the shape.

Format a Picture

You can enhance your shapes, clip art, photos, WordArt images, and SmartArt graphics by formatting the images. For example, Excel offers more than two dozen picture styles, which are predefined formats that apply various combinations of shadows, reflections, borders, and layouts.

Excel also offers a dozen picture effects, which are preset combinations of special effects such as glows, soft edges, bevels, and 3-D rotations.

Format a Picture

Apply a Picture Style

1. Click the picture you want to format.

2. Click the **Format** tab.

3. Click the **Picture Styles** ▼.

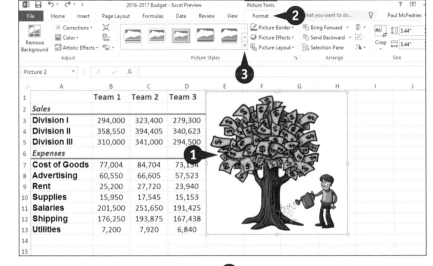

Ⓐ Excel displays the Picture Styles gallery.

4. Click the picture style you want to use.

Ⓑ Excel applies the style to the picture.

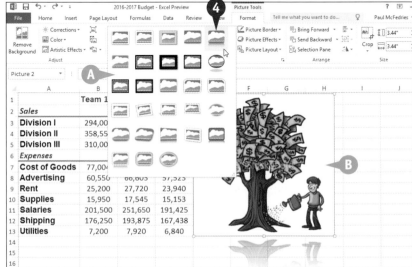

302

Apply a Picture Effect

1 Click the picture you want to format.

2 Click the **Format** tab.

3 Click the **Picture Effects** button (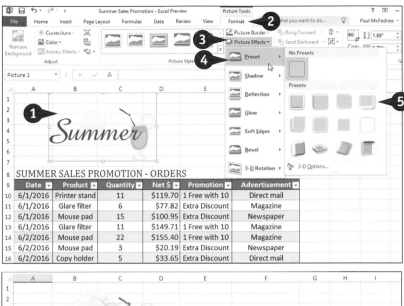).

Note: If the image is a shape, the button is named **Shape Effects**.

4 Click **Preset**.

5 Click the effect you want to apply.

C Excel applies the effect to the picture.

TIPS

I applied a style to a picture, but now I want to change the picture to something else. Do I have to start over?

No. You can simply replace the existing picture with the other picture, and Excel preserves the style so you do not have to repeat your work. Click the existing picture, click the **Format** tab, and then click the **Change Picture** button (🖼). Select the new picture you want to use and then click **Insert**.

If I do not like the formatting that I have applied to a picture, can I return the picture to its original look?

Yes. If you have not performed any other tasks since applying the formatting, click **Undo** (↶) until Excel has removed the formatting. Alternatively, click ⬜, click **Preset**, and then click the icon in the **No Presets** section. To reverse all the changes you have made to a picture since you inserted the image, click the picture, click **Format**, and then click **Reset Picture** (🖼).

CHAPTER 14

Collaborating with Others

If you want to collaborate with other people on a workbook, Excel gives you several ways to do this, including adding comments, sharing a workbook, and even working on a spreadsheet online. You can also control your collaborations by protecting worksheet data and tracking the changes that others make.

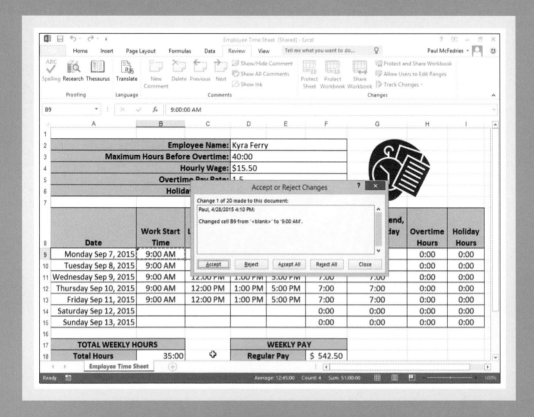

Add a Comment to a Cell

If you have received a workbook from another person, you can provide feedback to that person by adding a comment to a cell in the workbook. A comment is often the best way to provide corrections, questions, critiques, and other feedback because it does not change anything on the actual worksheet.

Each comment is attached to a particular cell and Excel uses a comment indicator to mark which cells have comments. When you view a comment, Excel displays the comment in a balloon.

Add a Comment to a Cell

Add a Comment

1 Click the cell you want to comment on.

2 Click the **Review** tab.

3 Click **New Comment** (🗨).

Note: You can also right-click the cell and then click **Insert Comment**.

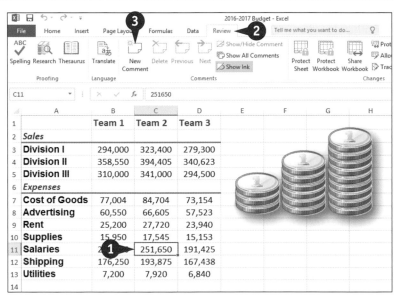

Excel displays a comment balloon.

A Excel precedes the comment with your Excel username.

4 Type your comment.

5 Click outside the comment balloon.

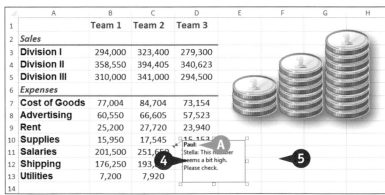

B Excel adds a comment indicator (◥) to the top-right corner of the cell.

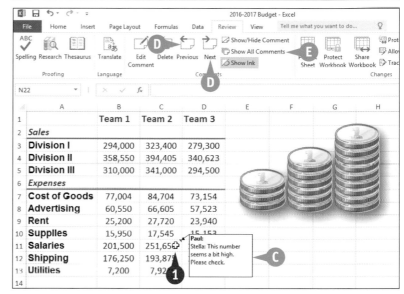

View a Comment

1 Move the mouse ✛ over the cell.

C Excel displays the comment in a balloon.

D In the Review tab, you can also click **Next** (→) and **Previous** (←) to run through the comments.

E In the Review tab, you can also click **Show All Comments** (🗗) to display every comment at once.

Can I edit or remove a comment?

Yes. To edit an existing comment, click the cell that contains the comment, click the **Review** tab, click **Edit Comment** (📝) to open the comment in a balloon, and then edit the balloon text. To remove a comment, click the cell that contains the comment, click the **Review** tab, and then click **Delete Comment** (✖).

How do I change my Excel username?

When collaborating, your username is important because it tells other people who added the comments. If you current username consists of only your first name or your initials, you can change it. Click **File** and then click **Options** to open the Excel Options dialog box. Click the **General** tab and then use the **User name** text box to edit the name. Click **OK**. Note, however, that this does not change your username in any existing comments.

Protect a Worksheet's Data

If you will be distributing a workbook to other people, you can enable the options in Excel for safeguarding worksheet data by activating the sheet's protection feature. You can also configure the worksheet to require a password to unprotect it.

There are two main methods you can use to safeguard worksheet data: You can unlock only those cells that users are allowed to edit and you can configure a range to require a password before it can be edited.

Protect a Worksheet's Data

1 Display the worksheet you want to protect.

2 Click the **Review** tab.

3 Click **Protect Sheet** (🔒).

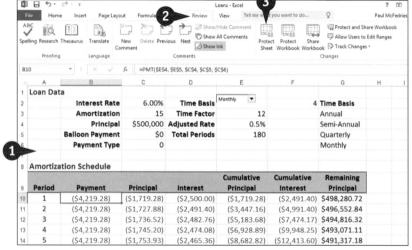

Excel displays the Protect Sheet dialog box.

4 Make sure the **Protect worksheet and contents of locked cells** check box is selected (☑).

5 Use the **Password to unprotect sheet** text box to type a password.

6 Select the check box beside each action that you want to allow unauthorized users to perform (☐ changes to ☑).

7 Click **OK**.

Excel asks you to confirm the password.

8 Type the password.

9 Click **OK**.

If you want to make changes to a worksheet, click the **Review** tab, click **Unprotect Sheet** (🔒), type the unprotect password, and then click **OK**.

TIPS

When I protect a worksheet, no one can edit any of the cells. Is there a way to allow users to edit some of the cells?

Yes. This is useful if you have a data entry area or other range that you want other people to be able to edit but you do not want them to alter any other part of the worksheet. First, unprotect the sheet if it is currently protected. Select the range you want to unlock, click **Home**, click **Format**, and then click **Lock Cell** to turn off that option for the selected range.

When I protect a worksheet, can I configure a range to require a password before a user can edit the range?

Yes. First, unprotect the sheet if it is currently protected. Select the range you want to protect, click the **Review** tab, and then click **Allow Users to Edit Ranges**. In the Allow Users to Edit Ranges dialog box, click **New** to open the New Range dialog box. Type a title for the range, use the **Range** text box to type a password, and then click **OK**. When Excel prompts you to reenter the password, type the password and then click **OK**.

Protect a Workbook's Structure

Y ou can prevent unwanted changes to a workbook by activating protection for the workbook's structure. You can also configure the workbook to require a password to unprotect it.

Protecting a workbook's structure means preventing users from inserting new worksheets, renaming or deleting existing worksheets, moving or copying worksheets, hiding and unhiding worksheets, and more. See the tips to learn which commands Excel disables when you protect a workbook's structure.

Protect a Workbook's Structure

1 Display the workbook you want to protect.

2 Click the **Review** tab.

3 Click **Protect Workbook** (🔲).

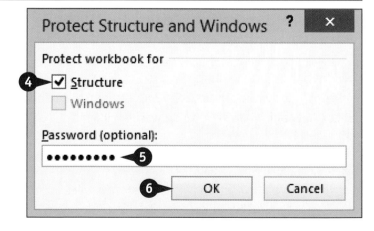

Excel displays the Protect Structure and Windows dialog box.

4 Select the **Structure** check box (☐ changes to ☑).

5 Type a password in the **Password** text box, if required.

6 Click **OK**.

If you specified a password, Excel asks you to confirm it.

7 Type the password.

8 Click **OK**.

Confirm Password

Reenter password to proceed.

Caution: If you lose or forget the password, it cannot be recovered. It is advisable to keep a list of passwords and their corresponding workbook and sheet names in a safe place. (Remember that passwords are case-sensitive.)

Ⓐ Excel disables most worksheet-related commands on the Ribbon.

Ⓑ Excel disables most worksheet-related commands on the worksheet shortcut menu.

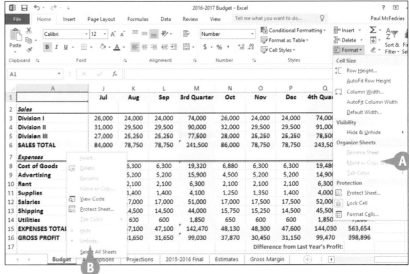

TIPS

What happens when I protect a workbook's structure?
Excel disables most worksheet-related commands, including Insert Sheet, Delete Sheet, Rename Sheet, Move or Copy Sheet, Tab Color, Hide Sheet, and Unhide Sheet. Excel also prevents the Scenario Manager from creating a summary report.

How do I remove workbook structure protection?
If you no longer require your workbook structure to be protected, you can remove the protection by following steps **1** to **3**. If you protected your workbook with a password, type the password and then click **OK**. Excel removes the workbook's structure protection.

Share a Workbook with Other Users

You can allow multiple users to modify a workbook simultaneously by sharing the workbook. Once you have shared a workbook, other users can open the workbook via a network connection and edit the file at the same time. Note that Excel cannot share a workbook that contains a table, so you need to convert any tables to ranges before performing this task. See Chapter 10 for more information.

When you share a workbook, Excel automatically begins tracking the changes made to the file. For more information on this feature, see the following section, "Track Workbook Changes."

Share a Workbook with Other Users

1 Display the workbook you want to share.

2 Click the **Review** tab.

3 Click **Share Workbook** (⊞).

The Share Workbook dialog box appears.

4 Click the **Editing** tab.

5 Select the **Allow changes by more than one user at the same time** check box (☐ changes to ☑).

6 Click **OK**.

Excel tells you that it will now
save the workbook.

7 Click **OK**.

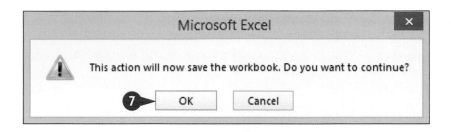

Excel saves the workbook and
activates sharing.

A Excel displays [Shared] in the
title bar.

You and users on your network
can now edit the workbook at
the same time.

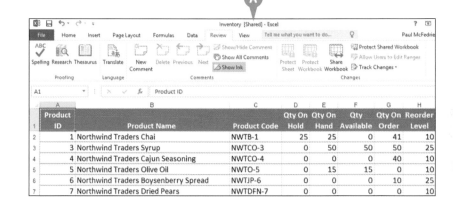

TIP

How do I know if other people currently have the workbook open?

The Editing tab of the Share Workbook dialog box maintains
a list of the users who have the workbook open. To see this
list, follow these steps:

1 Display the shared workbook.

2 Click the **Review** tab.

3 Click [icon].

The Share Workbook dialog box appears.

4 Click the **Editing** tab.

A The **Who has this workbook open now** list displays
the users who are currently editing the file.

5 Click **OK**.

Track Workbook Changes

If you want other people to make changes to a workbook, you can keep track of those changes so you can either accept or reject them (see the following section, "Accept or Reject Workbook Changes"). The Track Changes feature in Excel enables you to do this.

When you turn on Track Changes, Excel monitors the activity of each reviewer and stores that reviewer's cell edits, row and column additions and deletions, range moves, worksheet insertions, and worksheet renames.

Track Workbook Changes

1 Display the workbook you want to track.

2 Click the **Review** tab.

3 Click **Track Changes** (🖹).

4 Click **Highlight Changes**.

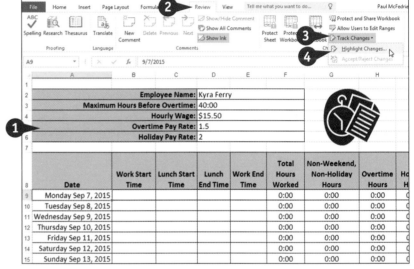

The Highlight Changes dialog box appears.

5 Select the **Track changes while editing** check box (☐ changes to ☑).

Ⓐ Leave the **When** check box selected (☑) and leave **All** selected in the list.

Ⓑ To learn more about the **Who** and **Where** options, see the tips.

Ⓒ Leave the **Highlight changes on screen** check box selected (☑) to view the workbook changes.

6 Click **OK**.

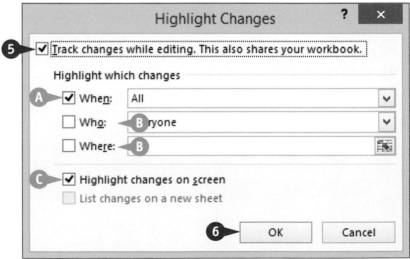

Excel tells you it will now save the workbook.

7 Click **OK**.

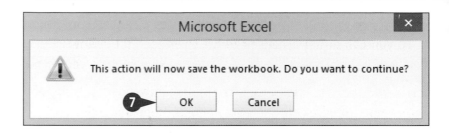

Excel activates the Track Changes feature.

D Excel shares the workbook and indicates this by displaying [Shared] beside the workbook name.

Note: See the previous section, "Share a Workbook with Other Users," to learn more about workbook sharing.

TIPS

Is there a way to avoid having my own changes highlighted?

Yes, you can configure the workbook to show every user's changes but your own. Follow steps **1** to **4** to open the Highlight Changes dialog box. Select the **Who** check box (☐ changes to ☑), click the **Who** ▼, and then click **Everyone but Me**. Click **OK** to put the new setting into effect.

Can I track changes in just part of the worksheet?

Yes, you can modify this task so that Excel only tracks changes in a specific range. Follow steps **1** to **4** to open the Highlight Changes dialog box. Select the **Where** check box (☐ changes to ☑), click inside the **Where** range box, and then select the range you want to track. Click **OK** to put the new setting into effect.

Accept or Reject Workbook Changes

After you turn on the Track Changes features in Excel, as described in the previous section, "Track Workbook Changes," you can accept or reject the changes that other users make to the workbook. As a general rule, you should accept the changes that other users make to a workbook. The exception is when you know a change is incorrect. If you are not sure, it is best to talk to the other user before rejecting a change. If you and another user make changes to the same cell, Excel lets you resolve the conflict by accepting your edit or the other user's edit.

Accept or Reject Workbook Changes

1. Display the workbook you are tracking.

2. Click the **Review** tab.

3. Click **Track Changes** (📝).

4. Click **Accept/Reject Changes**.

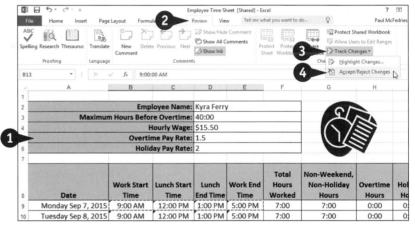

If your workbook has unsaved changes, Excel tells you it will now save the workbook.

5. Click **OK**.

The Select Changes to Accept or Reject dialog box appears.

Ⓐ Leave the **When** check box selected (☑) and leave **Not yet reviewed** selected in the list.

Ⓑ If you only want to review changes made by a particular user, select the **Who** check box (☐ changes to ☑), click the **Who** ▼, and then click the user's name.

6 Click **OK**.

The Accept or Reject Changes dialog box appears.

Ⓒ Excel displays the details of the current change.

7 Click an action for the change.

Ⓓ Click **Accept** to leave the change in the workbook.

Ⓔ Click **Reject** to remove the change from the workbook.

Excel displays the next change.

8 Repeat step **7** to review all the changes.

Ⓕ You can also click **Accept All** or **Reject All** to accept or reject all changes at once.

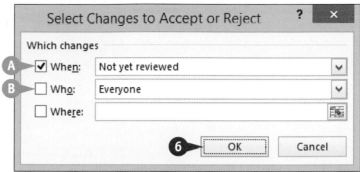

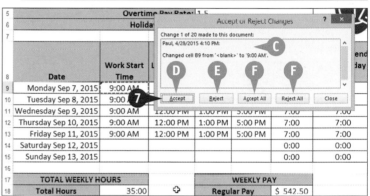

TIPS

What happens if I and another user make changes that affect the same cell?

In this situation, when you save the workbook, Excel displays the Accept or Reject Changes dialog box, which shows the change you made as well as the change the other user made. Click whatever change is the correct one and then click **Accept**. If there are multiple conflicts, you can save time by clicking your change or the other user's change and then clicking either **Accept All** or **Reject All**.

When I complete my review, should I turn off the tracking feature?

Unless you know that other people still require access to the workbook, you should turn off the tracking feature when your review is complete. To do this, click the **Review** tab, click 📝, and then click **Highlight Changes** to open the Highlight Changes dialog box. Select the **Track changes while editing** check box (☑ changes to ☐), and then click **OK**.

Save a Workbook to Your OneDrive

If you are using Windows 8 or later under a Microsoft account, then as part of that account you get a free online storage area called *OneDrive*. You can use Excel to add any of your workbooks to your OneDrive. This is useful if you are going to be away from your computer but still require access to a workbook. Because the OneDrive is accessible anywhere you have web access, you can view and work with your spreadsheet without using your computer.

Save a Workbook to Your OneDrive

1 Open the workbook you want to save to your OneDrive.

2 Click the **File** tab.

3 Click **Save As**.

The Save As tab appears.

4 Double-click **OneDrive**.

A If you see the OneDrive folder you want to use to store the workbook, click it and skip to step **6**.

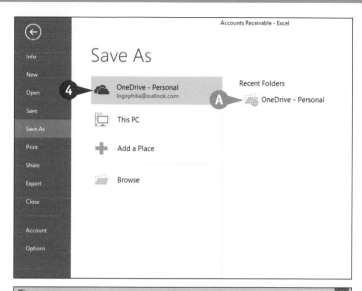

The Save As dialog box appears.

5 Double-click the folder you want to use to store the workbook.

6 Click **Save**.

Excel saves the workbook to your OneDrive.

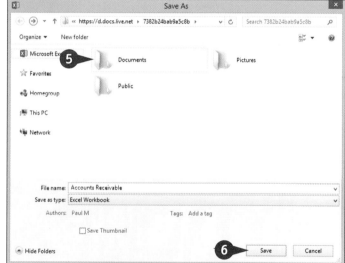

TIP

How do I open a workbook that has been saved to my OneDrive?
Follow these steps:

1 Click the **File** tab.

2 Click **Open**.

3 Double-click **OneDrive**.

The Open dialog box appears.

4 Open the OneDrive folder that contains the workbook.

5 Click the workbook.

6 Click **Open**.

Excel opens the OneDrive workbook.

Send a Workbook as an E-Mail Attachment

If you want to send an Excel workbook to another person, you can attach the workbook to an e-mail message and send it to that person's e-mail address.

A typical e-mail message is fine for short notes but you may have something more complex to communicate, such as budget numbers or a loan amortization. Instead of trying to copy that information to an e-mail message, it would be better to send the recipient a workbook that contains the data. That way, the other person can then open the workbook in Excel after receiving your message.

Send a Workbook as an E-Mail Attachment

1. Open the workbook you want to send.

2. Click the **File** tab.

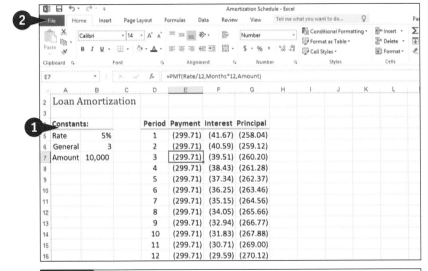

3. Click **Share**.

4. Click **Email**.

   Excel displays the Email commands.

5. Click **Send as Attachment**.

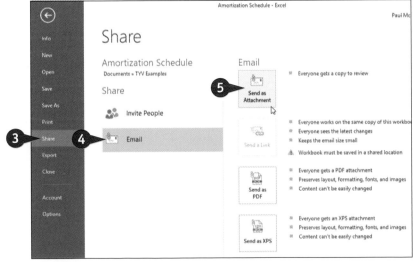

Outlook creates a new e-mail message.

Ⓐ Outlook attaches the workbook to the message.

❻ Type the address of the recipient.

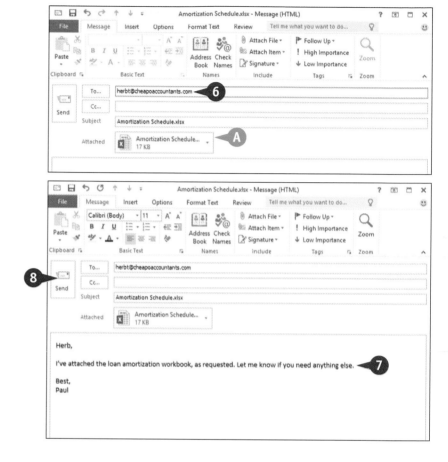

❼ Type your message text.

❽ Click **Send**.

Outlook sends the message.

TIPS

Are there any restrictions related to sending file attachments?

There is no practical limit to the number of workbooks you can attach to a message. However, you should be careful with the total size of the files you send. If you or the recipient has a slow Internet connection, sending or receiving the message can take an extremely long time. Also, many Internet service providers (ISPs) place a limit on the size of a message's attachments, which is usually between 2 and 10MB.

What can I do if the recipient does not have Excel?

If the other person does not use Excel, you can send the workbook in a different format. One possibility would be to save the workbook as a web page (see the following section, "Save Excel Data as a Web Page"). Alternatively, if your recipient can view PDF (Portable Document Format) files, follow steps **1** to **4** to display the Email commands, and then click **Send as PDF**.

Save Excel Data as a Web Page

I f you have an Excel range, worksheet, or workbook that you want to share on the web, you can save that data as a web page that you can then upload to your website.

When you save a document as a web page, you can also specify the title text that appears in the browser's title bar and the keywords that search engines use to index the page. You can also choose whether you want to publish the entire workbook to the web, just a single worksheet, or just a range of cells.

Save Excel Data as a Web Page

1 Open the workbook that contains the data you want to save as a web page.

A If you want to save a worksheet as a web page, click the worksheet tab.

B If you want to save a range as a web page, select the range.

2 Click the **File** tab.

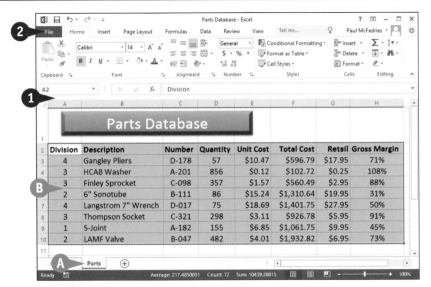

3 Click **Save As**.

4 Click **This PC**.

5 Click **Browse**.

The Save As dialog box appears.

6 Click the **Save as type** ▼ and then click **Web Page**.

7 Select the folder where you want to store the web page file.

8 Click **Change Title**.

The Enter Text dialog box appears.

9 Type the page title in the **Page title** text box.

10 Click **OK**.

11 Click **Tags** and then type one or more keywords, separated by semicolons.

12 Choose which part of the file you want to save as a web page (○ changes to ●):

C Click **Entire Workbook** to save the whole workbook.

D Click **Selection** to save either the current worksheet or the selected cells.

13 Click **Save**.

Excel saves the data as a web page.

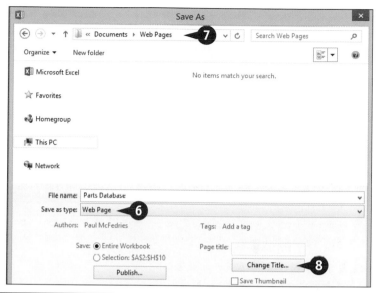

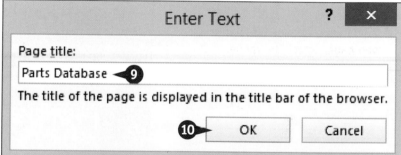

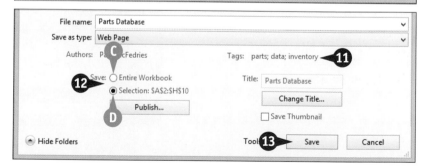

TIP

If I make frequent changes to the workbook, do I have to go through this procedure after every change?
No, you can configure the workbook to automatically save your changes to the web page file. This is called AutoRepublish. To set it up, follow steps **1** to **11** to get the workbook ready for the web and then click **Publish**. In the Publish as Web Page dialog box, click **AutoRepublish every time this workbook is saved** (☐ changes to ☑). Click **Publish**. Excel saves the workbook as a web page and will now update the web page file each time you save the workbook.

Make a Workbook Compatible with Earlier Versions of Excel

You can save an Excel workbook in a special format that makes it compatible with earlier versions of Excel. This enables you to share your workbook with other Excel users.

If you have another computer that uses a version of Excel prior to Excel 2007, or if the people you work with use earlier Excel versions, those programs cannot read documents in the standard format used by Excel 2016, Excel 2013, Excel 2010, and Excel 2007. By saving a workbook using the Excel 97-2003 Workbook file format, you make that file compatible with earlier Excel versions.

Make a Workbook Compatible with Earlier Versions of Excel

1 Open the workbook you want to make compatible.

2 Click **File**.

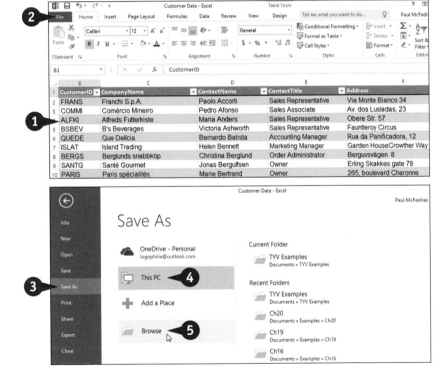

3 Click **Save As**.

4 Click **This PC**.

5 Click **Browse**.

The Save As dialog box appears.

6 Select the folder in which you want to store the new workbook.

7 Click in the **File name** text box and type the name that you want to use for the new workbook.

8 Click the **Save as type** ▼.

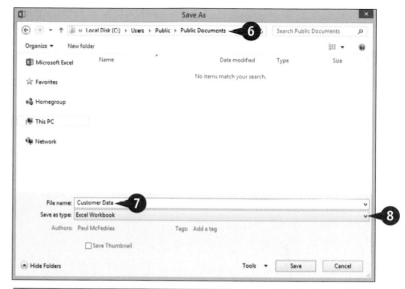

9 Click the **Excel 97-2003 Workbook** file format.

10 Click **Save**.

Excel saves the file using the Excel 97-2003 Workbook format.

TIPS

Can people using Excel 2013, Excel 2010, and Excel 2007 open my Excel 2016 workbooks?

Yes. The default file format used by Excel 2013, Excel 2010, and Excel 2007 is the same as the one used by Excel 2016. If you only work with people who use these Excel versions, then you should stick with the default file format — which is called Excel Workbook — because it offers many benefits in terms of Excel features.

Which versions of Excel are compatible with the Excel 97-2003 Workbook file format?

For Windows, the Excel 97-2003 Workbook file format is compatible with Excel 97, Excel 2000, Excel XP, and Excel 2003. For the Mac, the Excel 97-2003 Workbook file format is compatible with Excel 98, Excel 2001, and Office 2004. In the unlikely event that you need to share a document with someone using either Excel 5.0 or Excel 95, use the Microsoft Excel 5.0/95 Workbook file format instead.

Mark Up a Worksheet with a Digital Pen

Excel comes with a digital ink feature that enables you to give feedback by marking up a worksheet with pen marks and highlights. This is often easier than adding comments or cell text.

To use digital ink on a worksheet, you must have either a tablet PC or a graphics tablet, each of which comes with a pressure-sensitive screen. You can then use a digital pen — or sometimes your finger — to draw directly on the screen, a technique known as *digital inking*.

Mark Up a Worksheet with a Digital Pen

Activate Digital Inking

1. Tap the **Review** tab.

2. Tap **Start Inking** (✐).

   Excel enables digital inking.

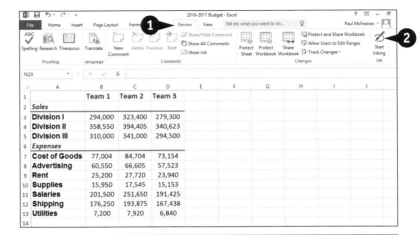

Mark Up with a Pen

1. Tap the **Pens** tab.

2. Tap **Pen** (✐).

3. Use the **Pens** gallery to select a pen color and thickness.

   A. You can also use the **Color** (✐) and **Thickness** (▬) buttons to customize the pen.

4. Use your digital pen (or finger) to write your marks or text on the worksheet.

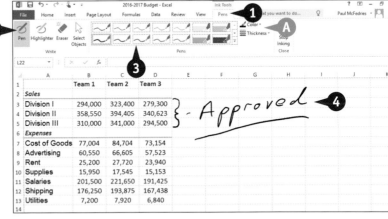

Mark Up with a Highlighter

1 Tap the **Pens** tab.

2 Tap **Highlighter** (✐).

3 Use the **Pens** gallery to select a highlighter color and thickness.

Ⓑ You can also use ✐ and ☰ to customize the highlighter.

4 Use your digital pen (or finger) to highlight the worksheet text.

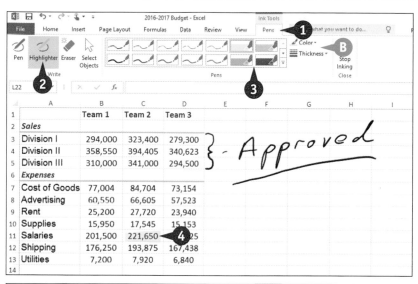

Erase Digital Ink

1 Tap the **Pens** tab.

2 Tap **Eraser** (✐).

3 Use your digital pen (or finger) to tap the ink you want to remove.

Excel erases the ink.

Ⓒ When you no longer need to mark up the worksheet with digital ink, tap **Stop Inking** (☒).

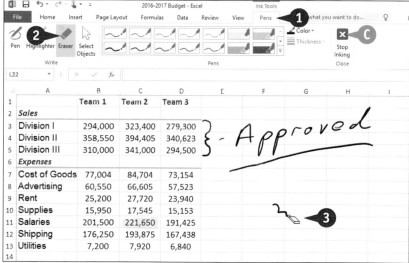

TIP

Is there a way to hide a worksheet's digital ink without deleting that ink?
Yes. This is a good idea if you want to show the worksheet to other people but you do not want them to see the digital ink, either because it contains sensitive information or because it makes the worksheet harder to read. To toggle your digital ink off and on, click the **Review** tab and then click **Show Ink** (✐).

Collaborate on a Workbook Online

If you have a Microsoft account, you can use the OneDrive feature to store an Excel workbook in an online folder (see the "Save a Workbook to Your OneDrive" section earlier in this chapter) and then allow other users to collaborate on that workbook using the Excel Web App.

Collaboration here means that you and the other users can edit the workbook online at the same time. To allow another person to collaborate with you on your online workbook, it is not necessary that the person have a Microsoft account. However, you can make your online workbooks more secure by requiring collaborators to have a Microsoft account.

Collaborate on a Workbook Online

1 Use a Web browser to navigate to https://onedrive.live.com.

Note: If you are not already logged in, you are prompted to log on to your Microsoft account.

Your OneDrive appears.

2 Click the folder that contains the workbooks you want to share.

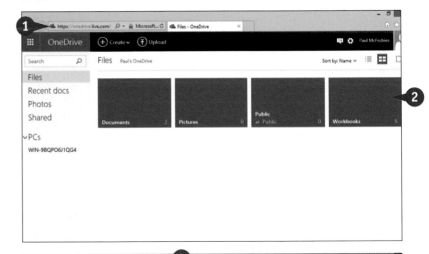

3 Click **Share**.

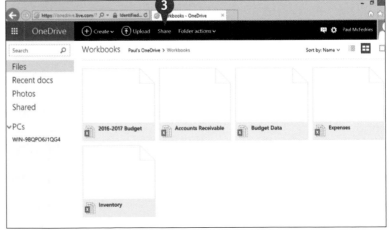

The folder's sharing options appear.

④ Click **Invite people**.

⑤ Type the e-mail address of the person you want to collaborate with.

Note: To add multiple addresses, press `Tab` after each one.

⑥ Type a message to the user.

⑦ Click **Recipients can only view**.

⑧ Select **Recipients can edit**.

⑨ If you want to require users to sign in with a Microsoft account, select **Recipients need to sign in with a Microsoft account**.

⑩ Click **Share**.

OneDrive sends an e-mail message to the user. The user clicks the link in that message, optionally logs on with a Microsoft account, and can then edit a workbook in the shared folder.

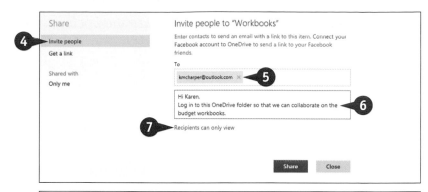

TIP

How do I know when other people are also using a workbook online?

When you open a workbook using the Excel Web App, examine the upper-right corner of the Excel screen. If you see *User* **is also editing**, it means another person (named *User*) is collaborating on the workbook with you. If you see *X* **other people are here**, it means that *X* users are collaborating with you. To see who they are, click the *X* **other people are here** message (Ⓐ), as shown here.

Index